BUILDING WORKPLACE EQUALITY

Ethics, diversity and inclusion

Nelarine Cornelius

CENGAGE
Learning·

Australia • Brazil • Japan • Korea • Mexico • Singapore • Spain • United Kingdom • United States

Building Workplace Equality: Ethics, Diversity and Inclusion

1st Edition

Author: Nelarine Cornelius

For product information and technology assistance, contact **emea.info@cengage.com**.

For permission to use material from this text or product, and for permission queries, email **emea.permissions@cengage.com.**

British Library Cataloguing-in-Publication Data
A catalogue record for this book is available from the British Library.

ISBN: **978-1-86152-585-7**

Cengage Learning EMEA
Cheriton House, North Way, Andover, Hampshire, SP10 5BE United Kingdom

Cengage Learning products are represented in Canada by Nelson Education Ltd.

For your lifelong learning solutions, visit **www.cengage.co.uk**

Purchase your next print book, e-book or e-chapter at **www.cengagebrain.com**

Printed in the UK by Lightning Source
1 2 3 4 5 6 7 8 9 10 – 13 12 11

Contents

Case studies

Preface

Workplace inequality is an area of research and practical interest that is demanding in many ways. The motivation of the academics and practitioners in the team of writers was to try to attempt to answer the question: why does equality action in organisations so often struggle to take hold? We were particularly interested in the perception expressed by those groups that were often the primary target of such action, namely that it had often done little to change the material reality of their daily working lives, and that in spite of the policies and initiatives, their working environments did not *feel* fair.

The failure to create 'felt fairness' was one motivation to write the book. The other was the views expressed, particularly in the academic literature, of unease regarding the rise of diversity management as, it was argued, a less robust and less morally demanding alternative to more mainstream equal opportunities programmes. Not only do we reject such assertions, but we also reject the notion that, in practice, there is a dualism – good workplace equality has at its heart the best practice developed within equal opportunities – whilst we argue that diversity management meaningfully enlarges the equality envelope, and allows issues of difference to be more openly engaged. In any case, given the changing nature of labour markets, with ever-increasing participation of those from traditionally disadvantaged groups, diversity is not an option, it is increasingly the reality.

The main concepts that we build around are capabilities theory, developed by the developmental economist Amartya Sen and the philosopher Martha Nussbaum. The work that they undertook has subsequently been developed further by the UN, and it was the potential of the application of their thinking in a global context, and their fresh ideas about understanding inequality, that first excited us. This was potentially more than a radically new way of thinking about inequalities in the developing world, but, as Sen points out, is of relevance for inequalities in the developed world also.

We have drawn upon academic and practical expertise in the design of and contributions to the book, and have made full use of our critical readers in the UK, USA and Canada. The book is our attempt to put together a multidisciplinary account of workplace inequality that builds centrally on capabilities theory, but that draws also on other important areas such as ethical theory and human and social capital theory, as well as the more familiar ideas of organisational justice, HRM and change management. There is a strong theory base, but our aim is to develop 'employable knowledge', so the relevance of what we have coined 'capabilities equality' is explored in a variety of contexts, including line delivery of HRM, the work of the professions, and international management. It is our intention to introduce the new whilst building and incorporating more familiar theories and practice within the field of workplace equality.

The book should be of interest to academics, practitioners and students in the areas of workplace equality, human resource management, general management, and change management.

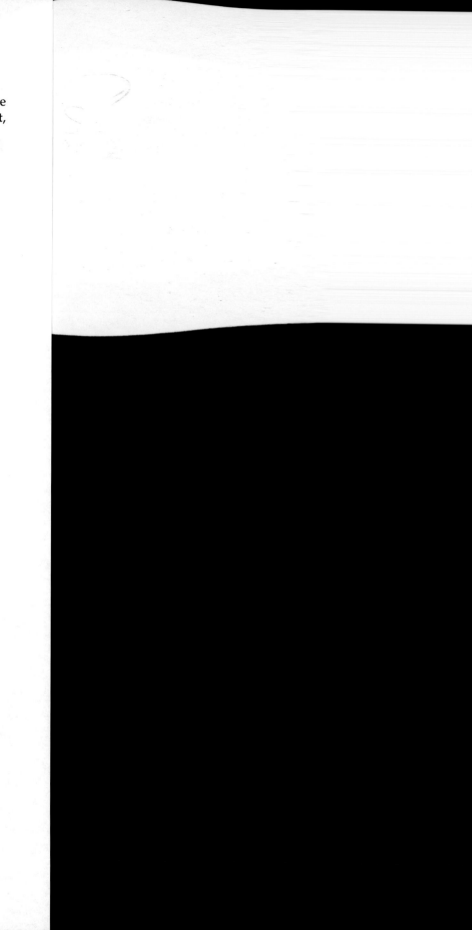

Acknowledgements

In a project of this kind it was important to seek the views of practitioners academics in order to test our thinking. All of those listed have greatly helped shape our ideas, and we gratefully acknowledge these contributions. In particular, we would like to thank: Mike Underhill from BP Amoco; officers and civilian staff at the Kent Constabulary; Judy Clements; Sally MacMahon; governors, officers and staff of HM Prison Service and British Telecom.

Academic colleagues who have also given of their time include: Dr Stephen Smith, Dr Laura Spence and Dr Ruth Simpson of Brunel University; Dr Pauline Gleadle of Cranfield University; Professor Ray Clapp of the University of Hertfordshire; Heba El Sayed of UMIST and Dr Nora Donaldson of the University of London. We were particularly grateful for the opportunity to discuss some of our ideas with Professor Amartya Sen at the University of Cambridge. Feedback on capabilities theory was also provided by Professor Martha Nussbaum, as part of an interview conducted by myself and Nigel Laurie for the journal: *Reason in Practice: Journal of the Philosophy of Management*.

The role of the critical readers (based in the UK, USA and Canada) was a vital one in redirecting our attention at important stages in the writing process, and we are very grateful for the time and effort that they gave.

Many thanks to staff, past and present, at Thomson Learning who were highly supportive throughout: Maggie Smith, Julian Thomas, Jenny Clapham and Anna Faherty.

Last but by no means least, our thanks go to Martha Nussbaum and Amartya Sen, whose ideas provide the conceptual basis for our book.

Every effort has been made to trace all copyright holders, but if any have inadvertently been overlooked the publishers will be pleased to make the necessary arrangements at the first opportunity.

Ade Ajadi is Managing Director of the Equality Foundation Ltd, which is based in Bristol, UK, but operates across Europe. He is also publisher of *Inclusion* magazine, a quarterly publication on Equality and Diversity challenges and solutions. He teaches and consults in all aspects of the subject to organisations operating in many spheres of civil, economic and political life. Ade has undertaken consultancy for a number of organisations in the UK and Europe and has been an adviser to UK governmental departments and agencies on equality issues. He has also given a number of public lectures on equality around the world. He is the originator of the widely used Equal Opportunities Quality Framework (EOQF).

Ade has an MSc in International Business Economics and an LLB in law. He qualified as a Barrister at Law, and practised law for a short period in Nigeria. He is a member of the UK Leadership Forum and a Fellow of the Royal Society of Arts. He currently runs an Executive Coaching programme and trains others in facilitating change in organisations using the EOQF. He is also an avid storyteller and playwright, and his current play *Abyssinia* has received critical acclaim.

Nigel Bassett-Jones

Nigel Bassett-Jones is Senior Lecturer in Human Resource Management at Oxford Brookes University Business School. He teaches across a range of predominantly postgraduate and post-experience programmes at Oxford Brookes, including the MBA, MA in Human Resource Management and the Diploma in Management Studies. He gained his own MBA from Aston University in 1991. He worked in the film and television industries before training as a personnel manager. He has worked in both the public and private sectors and also as a self-employed management consultant. He is a corporate member of the Chartered Institute of Personnel and Development. His research interests lie in the areas of diversity management, creativity and innovation as sources of competitive advantage.

Alan Blackburn

Alan Blackburn is Director of Postgraduate Studies in the Business School at Oxford Brookes University. Alan started his career at Vickers Engineering Group, Newcastle, as a Technician Apprentice before moving into the Personnel Department at Gateshead Metropolitan Borough Council. Here he acted in a consultancy role to departments on various organisational issues. In 1995 he moved to Cranfield Institute of Technology and worked predominantly for the Ministry of Defence. He moved on to Oxford Brookes in 1990 and has managed and played a leading role in the development of postgraduate courses within the Business School. Alan has taught Human Resource Management on the Diploma in Management Studies and MBA programmes and Employee Relations and Employee Reward on the Diploma in Personnel Management Programme. He has undertaken training and consultancy activities for a number of organisations, including Interforward Logistics, Rank Leisure, Oxford Radcliffe Hospital and Unipart. He is presently finalising a PhD in Educational Research entitled 'The knowledge produced by Human Resource Managers through workplace practice'. Alan graduated from Newcastle upon Tyne Polytechnic in Business Studies and was awarded an MA in Industrial Relations by the University of Warwick. He is also a corporate member of the Chartered Institute of Personnel and Development.

Nelarine Cornelius

Nelarine Cornelius is Senior Lecturer in Human Resource Management and Organisational Behaviour in the School of Business and Management at Brunel University, where she is involved in undergraduate, postgraduate and MBA teaching, and supervises PhD students. She is also Senior Honorary Research Fellow, Kings College Hospital Medical School, University of London. She holds a PhD from the University of Manchester and an MBA from the Open University, and is a Chartered Psychologist and Associate Fellow of the British Psychological Society, and Fellow of the Institute of Personnel and Development and the Royal Society of Arts.

She has previously worked in the area of management and organisational change and human resource management at General Motors and in local government, and continues to work as a consultant, most recently for the European-Union-sponsored Scottish Enterprise project on culture and innovation, and a diversity change project for the UK Prison Service. She has undertaken research with Suzanne Gagnon and Larraine Gooch, and has published in *Human Resource Management Journal, Journal of General Management,* and *Business Ethics: a European Review.* She was editor of the book *Human Resource Management: a managerial perspective* (first and second editions published by Thomson), co-edited *Challenging the boundaries: Personal construct psychology perspectives for the new millennium* for EPCA Publications (2000), and is on an editorial panel, headed by Fay Fransella, for *Personal Construct*

Psychology Handbook to be published in 2003 by Wiley. She continues to research in the areas of workplace equality, emotional labour, workplace equality and business applications of personal construct theory.

Suzanne Gagnon

Suzanne Gagnon is a member of the Faculty of Management of McGill University, Montreal, Canada. She teaches Human Resource Management to undergraduates and postgraduates, and within the McGill International Executive Institute. She is currently Acting Area Coordinator for Organizational Behaviour and HRM in McGill's Faculty of Management. She is co-author with Nelarine Cornelius of several articles on organisational ethics and equality; these have been published in journals such as *Business Ethics: A European Review* and *Human Resource Management Journal*. She also conducts research in the area of pay and reward, focusing on the evaluation of strategic reward systems and employee perceptions of payment system reform. Suzanne holds postgraduate degrees in Management (Industrial Relations) from the University of Oxford and in Journalism from Carleton University in Ottawa, Canada, and a BA from the University of British Columbia. She was previously Senior Lecturer in HRM at Oxford Brookes Business School.

Larraine Gooch

Larraine Gooch is a Principal Lecturer in Human Resource Management at Oxford Brookes University Business School. She is the Head of the Management Development and Human Resource Management Unit. She teaches across a wide range of programmes, which involve teaching both personnel specialists and line managers; these programmes include the University Certificate in Management, the Diploma in Management Studies, the Diploma in Personnel Management, the Masters in Human Resource Management and the Masters in Business Administration.

Larraine Gooch gained her MA in Human Resource Management from Thames Valley University in 1993 and became a Fellow of the Institute of Personnel and Development in 1995. She has experience of personnel management in both the public and private sectors, having spent a number of years as a personnel manager in organisations including J. Lyons (now Allied Lyons) and BBC Television. Larraine's research interests are in two main areas: first, diversity issues in the workplace, and second, the role of line managers in managing diverse organisations in partnership with human resource specialists.

Shaun Todd

Shaun Todd is an independent consultant working in the areas of human resource management, training and development, and diversity. He has worked in the field of diversity management for many years. Shaun has worked as an HR consultant in areas of equal opportunities and recruitment for Great Western Trains, UK, and as an HR Manager for Thames Valley Police, UK. In addition to his consultancy work, Shaun has lectured on personnel management professional qualification programmes and has run and lectured on numerous diversity courses. He is a Member of the Chartered Institute of Personnel and Development.

James H. Ward

James H. Ward (BA, MBA) has worked as an internal consultant in a variety of global and pan-European change and HR projects. He is currently pursuing his interests in the area of diversity management as a PhD student at Imperial College Management School, University of London; his research focus is on sexuality in organisations and the construction of sexual identity through organisational discourse.

Clive Wildish

Clive Wildish is Principal Lecturer in International Management in the School of Business and Management, Oxford Brookes University. Clive is Course Manager for the undergraduate degree in Business and International Management and also teaches International Management and Business on Oxford Brookes' MBA, MSc in International Management and MA in Human Resource Management. Clive is a Member of the Chartered Institute of Personnel and Development and of the Institute of Management.

Prior to joining Oxford Brookes in 1991, Clive worked for ten years as Marketing Manager and Project Leader within the academic publishing industry. He has worked with a number of leading publishers in the field, specialising latterly in acquisition studies across the industry. Between 1989 and 1990, Clive completed an MBA at the University of Bradford's Management Centre, specialising in Human Resource Management. Clive's current research interest is globalisation of the publishing and newspaper industries.

Diana Winstanley

Diana Winstanley (BSc, PhD, FCIPD) is a Senior Lecturer, Senior Tutor and Deputy Director of the full-time MBA programme at Imperial College Management School, University of London. She is also a fellow of the

Chartered Institute of Personnel and Development. She lectures in management and personal development, and human resource management, and has written four books and over thirty articles on management development, human resource development and business ethics. Currently she is researching 'working with values' in the charity and voluntary sectors.

Introduction and overview

Practitioners around the world have been exercised by the question: 'How can we reduce workplace inequality?' Over the years, many have attempted to make a difference, with differing degrees of success. I, and a number of my colleagues, have worked in the area of workplace inequality for many years, and have tried to develop an understanding, from both academic and practitioner perspectives, of 'what works', and why.

One of the questions that I have personally asked myself on many occasions is: why do so many workplace interventions fail? There have been many accounts presented in the literature – indeed a number are included in this book – but somehow getting a clear picture regarding the reasons for failure proved difficult. In addition to this, I remained deeply concerned that those for whom many of these workplace policies and interventions were developed – the traditionally disadvantaged – appreciated that some attempt was being made to change things, but felt that things had changed slowly, if at all, where *they* were. There seemed to be a perceptual gap between what organisations believed their policies and procedures had achieved and what the feeling 'on the ground' was.

However, the main impetus for writing this book is the often negative view (more so in Europe than in North America) that there are many shortfalls within diversity management relative to equal opportunities. Crucially, there seem to be an implicit (and at times, explicit) assertion that diversity management was a practice-driven, academically weak and ethically less robust approach than equal opportunities. This is not a view that I share. First, the inherent dualism that underpins such arguments does not appear to fit with my views on what diversity management can add to workplace equality: while equal opportunities concentrates on removing discrimination, diversity management is often more closely associated with focusing on maximising employee potential. Also, there seems to be a wealth of reasons why diversity management was a vital addition to our understanding of workplace inequality: changing demographic profiles, the emphasis on changing organisation culture and the need to celebrate and value difference. Further, the debate in academic spheres seemed out of kilter with practitioner experiences. None of the equality, HRM or line managers that I have spoken to recently saw that they needed to make a choice between *either* equal opportunities *or* diversity management: equal opportunities practice was a central and core component of diversity management in their eyes, and informed their practice also.

An important breakthrough in my understanding in relation to many of these matters, plus other issues, came about purely by chance. A colleague of mine, Suzanne Gagnon, had drawn to my attention a book that had been drawn to hers: *Development as Freedom* by Amartya Sen (1999). I purchased a copy, and took it with me on a trip to Glasgow. I had not anticipated that it would be of central interest to me: I did not think that there would be great potential in a book on developmental economics. During the inevitable flight delay, I started to read it, and a number of the ideas struck me as being not only important, but potentially paradigm challenging.

Sen, in conjunction with his colleague, the philosopher Martha Nussbaum (1995, 1999), had been involved in developing new frameworks for understanding inequality, particularly within the context of developmental economics, but also, as Sen points out, with the potential to be applied to those disadvantaged in developed societies. Their work, which Sen has developed further with colleagues for the United Nations, is concerned with human dignity and freedom. It is important to make clear that this was not a civil libertarian project with rampant individualism at its heart: quite the opposite, as agency and voice are central planks of their thinking.

What Sen and Nussbaum did was to ask some fundamental questions. Sen argues that freedom consists in ensuring people's capabilities, defined as 'to be able to be or do what they have reason to value'. Building on an Aristotelian ethical base, they have developed new understandings of what constitutes quality of life, through the idea of capabilities. The capabilities approach shows that equality must not be looked at in terms of sameness only, or difference only, but that both must form the basis for equality action, through the notion of freedoms. The capabilities framework, which sets out what is necessary for the full expression of freedoms, leads to a set of building blocks that organisations may employ to structure and evaluate their approaches to promoting equality. Key among these are the freedoms required for individual and collective agency to be meaningful in organisations, in order that the equality agenda is broadened and informed bottom-up, not only top-down and 'by proxy'. Because it calls for holistic, integrated, long-term change in organisations, and because it is based on a conviction that such change is not only necessary but possible, it signposts what is required for 'felt fair' equality in organisations.

The challenge we set ourselves in this book was to undertake to try to test the application of these ideas in a developed world, organisational setting. Clearly, there is still much work to be done in terms of getting a full view of the usefulness of capabilities theory for this context. But at this stage, we are sure that there is a great deal more that can be developed from it to enhance our understanding of how to build workplace equality. In our view, these ideas are paradigm challenging; they have already stretched the envelope of our understanding as an exploratory framework and, we believe, have great potential for a new research agenda for understanding workplace inequalities.

The conceptual framework that has helped to shape the text is multidisciplinary. In addition to capabilities theory, we have drawn from fields that include ethics, philosophy, sociology, psychology, personal construct theory, management theory, change management, **human resource management**, critical management accounting, social capital, international and cross-cultural management, organisational theory and analysis, strategic management, organisational learning and management learning.

Structure of the book

The book is organised into three main sections. The first, Foundation theory and concepts, contains three chapters that provide the conceptual framework for the book, and introduces the reader to what we have termed 'capabilities equality'. The second section, The implications of 'capabilities equality' for applicaction, is concerned with testing out the potential usefulness of the application of capabilities equality thinking. This is done in relation to line management, organisations with strong cultures (using organisations dominated by professionals for the purposes of illustration), and the challenges of managing equality and diversity in an international context. The third section, Practitioners and practice, contains accounts of equality practitioners' intervention experiences at the whole organisational, small group and one-to-one levels, and case studies on equality practice in international companies. More outline details relating to the sections is presented in Table 0.1 (pages 5–9). There is a lot of terminology that may be unfamiliar, so a glossary is provided at the end of the book. A number of useful Web addresses are also provided.

This is, by the nature of the enterprise, an ongoing project. There are likely to be errors and omissions, in part as a result of the newness of attempting to use capabilities theory in this context but also as an inevitability in developing any text of this kind, and we accept that there will be ideas that will be usefully revisited in the future.

If we were to answer the question 'why write this book?' it would be in the hope that it will provide new insights into how organisations can create environments in which employees feel included, can achieve their potential, have freedom of opportunity and can have their voices heard.

Internet resources

About Human Resources – Diversity Section http://humanresources.about.com/cs/diversity/
American Institute for Managing Diversity http://www.aimd.org/
Bized HRM Links http://www.bized.ac.uk/fme/3.htm
Diversity Inc http://www.diversityinc.com
Diversophy http://www.diversophy.com/
European Institute for Managing Diversity http://www.iegd.org/
Federation of European Employers http://www.euen.co.uk/
Home Office: Race, Equality and Diversity http://www.homeoffice.gov.uk/new_indexs/index_racial-equality.htm
HR Look http://www.hrlook.com/
HRM Guide – Diversity Section http://www.hrmguide.co.uk/hrm/chap9/ch9-links.html

HRM Guide http://www.hrmguide.net/
HRM Resources on the Internet http://www.nbs.ntu.ac.uk/depts/hrm/ hrm_link.htm
Managing Diversity http://www.diversity.nexus.edu.au/
People Management http://www.peoplemanagement.co.uk/
South African Board for Personnel Practice http://www.sabpp.co.za
South African Department of Labour http://www.labour.gov.za
South African Institute of People Management http://www.ipm.co.za
Workforce http://www.workforce.com/

References

Nussbaum, M (1999) Women and equality: The capabilities approach. *International Labour Review*, **138** (3), 227–245.
Nussbaum, M and Sen, A (eds) (1995) *The Quality of Life*, Oxford University Press, USA.
Sen, A (1999) *Development as Freedom*, Oxford University Press, Oxford.

Further reading

Gagnon, S and Cornelius, N (2000) Re-examining workplace equality: the capabilities approach. *Human Resource Management Journal*, **10** (4), 68–87.
Nussbaum, M and Glover, J (eds) (1995) *Women, Culture and Development: a study of human capabilities*, Oxford University Press, USA.
Sen, A (1992) *Inequality Re-Examined*, Harvard University Press, Cambridge, MA.

Table 0.1   Outline details

CHAPTER TITLE	CHAPTER CONTENT	IMPORTANT CONCEPTS	CAPABILITIES ISSUES
Part I – Foundation theory and concepts			
1. From equal opportunities to managing diversity to capabilities: a new theory of workplace equality?	Moving beyond the dualism of EO versus diversity management, it is suggested that these approaches in practice can be complementary. However, the move to diversity has been in part because of the perceived failure and 'felt fair' of EO initiatives, the limitation of dependence on 'external pressure' and legal compliance (the traditional route). Suggests that the capabilities approach (a) helps to get beyond dualism, (b) promotes dignity and full organisational citizenship, (c) highlights the importance of the organisational, macro and micro environment for allowing equality to take root, and (d) has inclusion, voice and agency as central.	• Beyond EO/DM dualism • Pros and cons of a range of equality approaches highlighted • 'Capabilities equality' (CE) suggested as strong alternative – theory and work organisation application outlined • CE has clear ethical basis (Aristotelian origins), within which human potential, and the potential of organisations to 'become good through doing good', is central and has a clear developmental implication	• Basic, internal and combined capabilities: equality – all seen as important and should be addressed as an ensemble, not one seen as more important than the other • The importance of voice, agency and social climate • Collective voice and employment relations are central • Ends *and* means for achieving equality seen as important • Need to 'measure' what matters, not just what is easy to measure/confirms compliance – for stakeholder groups and organisational domains
2. Evaluating organisational readiness for change	How predisposed are organisations to 'full' equality and diversity management? It is possible to argue that equality and diversity management is a *prerequisite* for effective, sustainable human resource management. Therefore, assessing readiness is particularly important. Can make an assessment through (a) use of strategic HRM archetypes and by (b) an assessment of the psychological contract and trust relationships (where trust is regarded as a form of social capital) that dominate, especially in relation to the archetypes. Suggests also (Herriot's empirical research) that consistency and sensitivity in dealing with fairness, justice and equality are regarded as core to the psychological contract.	• Psychological contract • Strategic archetypes • Trust relationships • Specific types of organisation may be more predisposed, and therefore prepared, for specific types of change i.e. some will be more ready for procedural compliance in 'strict' traditional EO terms, and promotion sameness than for more sophisticated diversity strategies • Addressing and responding naturally to difference • Highlights the importance of informal sources of information for making assessments	• 'Felt fair' equality for employees • Combined capabilities and the importance of assessing the interaction of perceptions of the environment (e.g. strength of law, labour market as opportunity or simply to exploit) with employee aspirations and equality and diversity aims • The importance of 'informal' organisational information as part of the equality and diversity information base

Table 0.1 *Continued*

CHAPTER TITLE	CHAPTER CONTENT	IMPORTANT CONCEPTS	CAPABILITIES ISSUES
3. Multidimensional information and knowledge bases for equality and diversity learning and action	In Chapter 2, the interaction between formal and informal sources of information for informing decision making, re: E&D were considered. This is taken further here, and other important information sources are considered. These are (a) 'traditional' compliance (legal/code of conduct), (b) progression and transgression rates (management information, largely historic or current and may be used to address procedural and legal compliance and formal systems change). Here, consider 'felt fair', capabilities equality demands more than this. Suggest e.g. informal and employee voice important *for significant social and cultural change in particular.* An important source of information for continuous and sustainable change is *organisational learning* – primary source of learning how to do things differently, not just better.	• Information base EO more likely to provide 'traditional' EO accounting (compliance) measures, DM stronger on stakeholder perspectives (including informal) • Measurement of ends, means and environment • HR strategies can provide a powerful basis for 'procedural justice' and compliance • Limitation of measuring what can easily be measured within a narrow range of options, and therefore overlooking important 'soft' HR information which contains stakeholder perspectives and informal sources of opportunities and limitations to change • Importance of informing decision making through organisational learning (paradigm challenging and with an inherent continuous development component) and information sharing (e.g. networks, mentors) • The need to evaluate the learning capability of organisations as key assessment of capacity for change	*The 'right' information base* • The need to 'measure'/evaluate the five instrumental freedoms as a core measure of equality • Multi-stakeholder including 'voice' information important • The need for whole organisational measures of the formal and informal so that combined capabilities can be assessed

Part II – The implications of 'capabilities equality' for application

CHAPTER TITLE	CHAPTER CONTENT	IMPORTANT CONCEPTS	CAPABILITIES ISSUES
4. Managing people – equality, diversity and human resource management issues for line managers	HRM is centrally important as a function within which equality and diversity can be 'delivered'. However, this is not just an 'expert' undertaking, but ideally delivered through line managers with the support of HR where necessary. HRM policy and practice can provide an important vehicle	• HR particularly strong at creating 'legal compliance' and procedural justice • Addressing areas such as harassment, bullying may do much to change the 'department climate and culture' (dilemma, difficult where line manager source of complaint)	• Promotion of five instrumental freedoms, especially through 'formal' channels but in particular, transparency guarantees and protective security (e.g. grievance) • The importance of external environment (law, local labour

Table 0.1 *Continued*

CHAPTER TITLE	CHAPTER CONTENT	IMPORTANT CONCEPTS	CAPABILITIES ISSUES
	for the movement towards creating more diverse cultures. Research suggests that managers have greatest involvement in recruitment, selection and induction, grievance, discipline, training needs. These, plus the setting of equality key results areas and objectives, are therefore likely to provide important 'HR' sources of improvement and change.	• Develop expertise 'locally'. This is where inequality is primarily 'experienced', especially in a 'normal' sense (not the exceptions that the personnel department are often brought in to deal with) • Manager as 'local role model' and demonstrator of local equality leadership	markets, community demographics) in shaping choices • Codes of conduct can highlight 'ethical direction' re: equality, i.e. that organisations can seek to be and act in a virtuous way • Effective employee relations strategies – promote agency and voice (again through formal channels) • Can help to make explicit legal and organisational entitlements (rights) for employees and obligations of managers/the organisation
5. Distinctive organisational characteristics and their influence on equality and diversity action: the illustration of professionalism	Professional groups, especially those in public sector organisations, are in a 'unique' position. They are typically empowered by the State to undertake tasks which may be thought of as 'virtuous', often away from public scrutiny (prison cells, hospitals). They may also be given specific powers (use of reasonable/lethal force; statementing of the mentally ill, etc., supervision of those jailed), i.e. the formal, state denial of 'freedoms'. Therefore, duty of care towards colleagues and clients may also not be open to full public scrutiny. The 'professional ethic' may strongly resist public scrutiny or alleged 'abuses' of duty of care, and provide a powerful basis for institutionalised discrimination and resistance to change. Informal discrimination against colleagues as one ascends the hierarchy, reinforced by the 'virtuous' remit, may be denied and readily	• Organisational culture • Professionalisation versus managerialism • Duty of care • Emotional labour • Autonomy of action versus 'reasonable' public accountable • Professional cultures • Institutionalised discrimination • Reduced transparency of action and the perpetuation of 'antediluvian' practice • The organisational hierarchy is ascended (consultant – interm: dependency and power) • The 'professional project' • Social capital	All five instrumental freedoms (in particular transparency guarantees, social opportunities and protective security) Full versus partial citizenship Combined capabilities (especially social and informal factors) Differential entitlements and resultant inequalities

Table 0.1 *Continued*

CHAPTER TITLE	CHAPTER CONTENT	IMPORTANT CONCEPTS	CAPABILITIES ISSUES
	perpetuated. The difficulties and opportunities for change in such organisations are explored.		
6. Managing equality and diversity in a global context	The international management literature has become increasingly reflective of the importance of cross-cultural and multi-cultural perspectives. We are particularly concerned with the latter. The relationship between the corporate and local national cultural criteria is an important one. Writers such as Hofstede and Trompenaars have identified dimensions that help to differentiate national cultures. However, other dimensions are important, such as goal incompatibilty, the importance of formal and informal information, communication and managerial competence in dealing with such issues are important.	• Corporate versus local national culture • Ethical and cultural clashes • Operating in 'less enlightened' cultural climates which deny rights on basis of e.g. ethnicity or gender • Seeking 'inclusive' versus 'exclusive' corporate cultural characteristics • The importance of effective acculturation and training • The importance of formal and informal communication knowledge • Acceptance of error making and of learning process as by-product of 'culture clash' • Transcendence • International HRM	• Clarity needed, re: organisations' ethical, strategic and operational position, re: capabilities, freedoms and rights (as reflected in organisations' ethics, policies, practices and culture) Need to be clear what organisational position/line manager action is needed to facilitate CE (n.b. use of CE ideas by United Nations suggests has currency across cultures)

Part III – Practitioners and practice

CHAPTER TITLE	CHAPTER CONTENT	IMPORTANT CONCEPTS	CAPABILITIES ISSUES
7. Whole organisation equality and diversity intervention strategies in practice	Highlights the need to understand the parameters from which organisations seek interventions. The bases for interventions which help to facilitate sustainability and **continuous improvement** are considered (building on previous chapters), with continuous improvement regarded as a 'habitual' part of the pursuit of excellence. Equality management considered primarily in terms of the management of intangibles, with healthy human relations as basis for equality management. Considers also different states of readiness (as per Ch.2):	• Impact on relationships with stakeholders • The centrality of accountable leadership • The opportunities and limitations of starting, initiative and strategic organisation • Healthy human relations central to E&D and in turn, to effective HR (and general) management • The advantages and limitations of the external consultant • The importance/limitations of independent external validation	The need to address 'the long agenda' for equality and diversity management The importance of intangibles (including stakeholder rhetoric) as part of information base, including likelihood of securing instrumental freedoms and full citizenship The centrality of the clarity of ends *and* means

Table 0.1 *Continued*

CHAPTER TITLE	CHAPTER CONTENT	IMPORTANT CONCEPTS	CAPABILITIES ISSUES
	(a) the *starting organisation* (emphasis on compliance); (b) *the initiative organisation* (recognition of equality management benefits, HR corporate-led; limited if any stategic perspective) and (c) *the stategic organisation* (clear E&D vision, collective ownership of E&D, individual responsibilities understood and clear).	• The importance/limitations of internal validation • The links between strategy, policy and operations	
Case Studies			
1. Stakeholder perspectives: a personal account of an equality and diversity practitioner's intervention experiences	There is a large literature on the importance of conversations as a source of understanding 'theories in use'. In this case study, a practitioner relates some 'illuminating conversations' where 'getting behind the words' is important for understanding what is not being said, but nonetheless thought or felt, both positive and negative. These conversations are related based on experiences of the practice of E&D awareness and change, and includes senior managers, middle managers, line managers, majority staff, minority staff, candidates, suppliers, community, lobbyists, trade unions.	• Voice • Stakeholder conversations • Interventionist effectiveness • Day to day difficulties	• What helps or hinders in the development of *internal capabilities* • How the informal environment helps or hinders formal and informal development of internal capabilities and thus, combined capabilities
2. Building on a vision: 'inclusive merotocracy' in a major multinational energy company	In this case study, the challenges and difficulties of addressing equality issues 'across borders' is related. The company in the case has designed various processes for 'inclusive meritocracy' as a vehicle for understanding and addressing 'full citizenship' for its employees.	• Inclusion • Inclusive meritocracy • International human resource management • Workforce diversity • Cross-cultural management	• Clarity with regard to the link between capabilities and freedoms in the informal domain from different stakeholder views

Table 0.1 *Continued*

CHAPTER TITLE	CHAPTER CONTENT	IMPORTANT CONCEPTS	CAPABILITIES ISSUES
3. Wearing warm clothes in winter: a pragmatic process approach to promoting cultural diversity in global succession planning	A key issue in this case study is the role of 'traditional' HR concepts practices, such as succession planning and competencies, and how they might potentially help or hinder equality management and specifically, support or undermine a capabilities approach to workplace equality	• Succession planning • Competencies • International HRM policy and practice	• Relationship between competencies and capabilities • Contribution of international HRM policy procedures design in delivering workplace equality • Women and international management
Final Comments	Reflections on areas of conceptual and practical interest that could potentially further develop a 'capabilities equality' approach	• Requisite variety • Climate and environment • Recursion • Measurement and models of HRM • Measurement and social capital • Employee voice • Inclusion • Agency	• Creating an enabling environment • The manager's role in enhancing organisational social capital • Transformational nature of agency • Empowerment from a capabilities perspective

Part I
Foundation theory and concepts

From equal opportunities to managing diversity to capabilities: a new theory of workplace equality? 1

Suzanne Gagnon and Nelarine Cornelius

Chapter overview

The purpose of this chapter is to explain and analyse the two major approaches to workplace equality that have become prominent in the past two to three decades – the equal opportunities approach and the diversity management approach – and to introduce an alternative approach, based on the idea of capabilities. The genesis, promises and premises of both equal opportunities and diversity management are discussed through a review of the literature and research findings from both North America and the United Kingdom. Strengths and shortcomings of each are discussed and analysed. Each approach is found to be wanting, in part because each tends to reflect and give expressions to a concept of equality that may be viewed as partial or limited.

Capabilities theory offers an alternative way of thinking about and pursuing workplace equality, and this approach is outlined and discussed in the second half of the chapter. Capabilities thinking defines equality not in terms primarily of equal rights (although these are subsumed within capabilities thinking) or 'everyone being the same', as in liberal equal opportunities, nor in terms of managing cultural differences among groups or individuals to meet a utilitarian objective of better firm performance as in some diversity management approaches. Rather, the capabilities approach requires equality of overall freedoms of individuals 'to do that which they have reason to value' in the words of eminent development economist Amartya Sen. With philosopher Martha Nussbaum, Sen developed the concept of capability equality for application at the macro-economic level. The approach takes as its starting point a fundamentally different view of what constitutes equality from that underpinning other major ethical theories, and offers a new answer to the question 'equality of what?'. At the organisational level, it presents different requirements for employers interested in pursuing equality for all their members: a holistic, multi-domain, structural and system-wide approach is required and must be developed through the agency of employees, both individually and collectively, and the recognition of this agency through an 'enabling environment'.

Learning objectives

Upon completing this chapter, readers should be able to:

- understand and explain equal opportunities as an approach to pursuing workplace equality;
- understand the differences between liberal and radical equal opportunities;
- define and explain 'managing diversity';
- discuss strengths and weaknesses of both an 'equal opportunities' and a 'managing diversity' approach, and what these imply for what organisations do as part of an 'equality agenda';
- explain what equality means within a capabilities approach and what it contributes to our understanding of why many members of organisations continue to experience inequality;
- define and outline the main elements and requirements for organisations of the capabilities approach.

Key words
managing diversity ● equality in organisations ● ethical theory ●
human resource management ● organisational justice ●
capabilities theory ● Amartya Sen ● Martha Nussbaum

Introduction

Arguably the most fundamental development in approaches to workplace equality in the past 20 years has been the introduction of 'diversity management' as a second major approach in addition to 'equal opportunities'. The first part of this chapter sets out the main tenets of these two dominant ways of thinking about how to promote workplace equality, and considers in particular some of the criticisms directed towards each. The chapter argues that the 'two competing models' view, often presented in the literature and seeing these two approaches as in conflict or opposition to one another, is both unnecessary and misguided. In theoretical terms, both equal opportunities and diversity management have been shown to have shortcomings and, to an extent, these may be minimised by combining the two approaches in practice, something that many progressive organisations seem to do anyway. Indeed, equal opportunities legislation and policy arguably form the essential bedrock for successful diversity management programmes in organisations.

The combining of approaches within organisations suggests that practice may be ahead of theory in the area of workplace equality. Nonetheless, there is ample, highly persuasive evidence that equality continues to elude many organisations. In business terms, a diverse workforce is not just something an organisation ought to have, it is something an organisation has or will have shortly to have in many countries, according to a number of demographic projections (e.g. Johnson and Packer, 1987; Anonymous, 1997(a)(b)(c); Anonymous, 2000). These surveys suggest that for North America and much of Europe, traditional sources of labour are on the decrease, while traditionally disadvantaged groups constitute the fastest-growing labour pool. However, aggregate economy-wide figures, such as promotion rates, unemployment rates and pay differentials, show slow or even negative progress for traditionally disadvantaged employees. Although there is evidence of increasing participation in the labour market of those from traditionally disadvantaged groups, the distribution of members of these groups in the higher organisational levels remains stubbornly low, and lower rates of pay for comparable work persist. Moreover, studies show that despite organisational programmes designed to promote the interests of traditionally disadvantaged groups and ensure against discrimination, employees from these groups often do not feel fairly treated.

In assisting understanding of why perceptions of inequality and unequal treatment persist among organisational members, the capabilities approach provides a more promising approach to workplace equality. Equality of capabilities refers to the equal freedoms that all organisational members must have to pursue and do 'that which they have reason to value'. The theory of capabilities is outlined in the second half of the chapter. Importantly, the approach points to actions that organisations can take to evaluate and improve the ways in which they support equality for all their members. This is a taller order than that required of organisations within either an equal opportunities approach that relies largely on the external force of law, or diversity management which can sometimes be associated with a narrow conception of the **'business case'** for diversity. The chapter identifies a series of 'building blocks' that provide a new template for promoting equality that is both comprehensive and oriented towards action. The argument will be made below that while both equal opportunities and diversity management often fail to deliver permanent change in organisational systems, structures and culture, the capabilities approach offers more promise. It does so for two main reasons: first, because change in these areas is precisely what the capabilities approach requires, whereas the two dominant discourses do not as they have been formulated; and second, because it emphasises the importance of the role of employees, both individually and collectively, in devising and implementing organisational strategies for building equality. Capabilities theory helps make an argument that concepts like equality as 'sameness' or equality as difference are dynamic concepts which, to an extent, should be 'negotiated' within organisations. The operationalisation of both concepts depends crucially on how people view themselves and what they want – it depends on individual and collective agency. This in turn is co-dependent on the existence of an enabling environment or what Sen calls 'instrumental freedoms', at both the workplace and broader legal/political levels.

Box 1.1 Gooch and Cornelius in Cornelius, 2000 (p. 28) 'The diverse UK labour market'

Women

- Since 1975 the number of women in the labour market has increased by 34 per cent to 12.2 million in 1995, the number of men has fallen by 0.5 per cent to 15.6 million.
- Between 1994 and 2001, male employment is likely to see only a slight rise (around 3 per cent) while female employment will increase more quickly (an extra 11 per cent).

Ethnic minorities[1]

- Ethnic minority groups now make up 5.9 per cent of the population of working age (nearly 2 million people) almost half of whom were born in Great Britain.
- The greatest concentration of the ethnic working population is now in the South East (61 per cent); in London almost one-fifth of the economically active population of working age is non-white and 40 per cent of these are black; the next largest concentrations are the West Midlands, the North West and the East Midlands.

Older workforce

By the year 2006 the workforce will be older, with a projected fall of 1.1 million people aged under 35 years in the labour force.

Flexible workforce

- Part-time working is increasing for both men and women: 44 per cent of all women workers are part-time but only 6 per cent of male employees work part-time. Part-time working for men is increasing at more than double the rate for women.
- An increasing number of employees work flexible hours with 10 per cent of men and 15 per cent of women working flexible hours, many of whom work to annualised working hours contacts.

- Between 1994 and 2001 part-time employment is projected to increase by 22 per cent at the same time as full-time employment decreases by 1 per cent.
- An increasing number of employees work in temporary jobs – without a permanent contract: 8 per cent of women and 6 per cent of men.
- A growing number of employees work at home (0.7 million people).

Caring responsibilities

- Two and half million men and three and half million women have caring resposibilities for elderly dependants.
- Thirty-six per cent of working-age women have dependant children under 16 years of age.

Disability[2]

Some 1.2 million disabled people are in employment; disabled people are slightly more likely than non-disabled people to work in a part-time capacity. Unemployment rates among people with disabilities is around two-and-a-half times those for non-disabled people.

Source: Labour Market Trends, February 1997.
IPD Managing Diversity Position Paper (1997a).

1. Definition of ethnic minorities used in Labour Force Survey:

   Black (Black Caribbean, Black African, Black other)
   Indian
   Pakistani/Bangladeshi
   Other (Chinese, other non-mixed, other mixed, Black mixed)

2. Definition of disability: Disability is defined in the Disability Discrimination Act (1996) as physical or mental impairment, which has a substantial and long-term effect on the ability to carry out the duties of a job.

Box 1.2 Diversity issues in the US labour market

The Diversity Training Group, Washington DC, states that:

- More than 19 million skilled people with disabilities in America are unemployed.
- In a short time, only 15 per cent of entrants into the US workforce will be white male.
- In the first decade of the new century, 85 per cent of new workers in America will be women, minorities and immigrants.

- Women in America purchase 82 per cent of all products and services in the United States.

(2001), www.diversitydtg.com

Equal opportunities

In its traditional form, **equal opportunities** has been described as rights-based, **liberal**, rooted in legal compliance, based upon equality through 'sameness' and merit with a focus on non-discrimination, and geared towards increasing the proportion of women and other under-represented groups in senior roles in organisations (Kirton and Green, 2000; Colgan and Ledwith, 1996). **'Radical' equal opportunities** approaches focus on positive action to meet these goals.

Dickens (in Bach and Sisson, 2000) defines equal opportunities initiatives as concerning 'policy and practice designed to tackle the differential distribution of opportunities, resources and rewards (jobs, wages, promotions, employment benefits) among workers, based on their membership of a social group' (2000: 142). Dickens explains that codes of practice and guidance on developing equal opportunities programmes are published by the UK's two equality commissions, the Equal Opportunities Commission (EOC) and the Commission for Racial Equality (CRE). Both commissions call on organisations to introduce an equal opportunities policy. The CRE recommends that the policy state that no job applicant or employee receives less favourable treatment on racial grounds, or is placed at a disadvantage by requirements or conditions that have a disproportionately adverse effect on his or her racial group and which cannot be shown to be justifiable on other than racial grounds. EOC guidance calls for a policy that ensures that no direct or indirect discrimination operates to the detriment of women or married people in any area of employment, including access to employment (Dickens, 2000: 143).

Kirton and Greene (2000) argue that as an approach to promoting equality in the workplace, equal opportunities is not in fact easily defined. EO is difficult to theorise, they suggest, because a wide variety of meanings have been attached to it. They distinguish the liberal EO tradition that centres on equality of opportunity from the radical perspective that centres on equality of outcome. Each of these approaches is set out next.

Table 1.1 Participation of women and men in European labour markets

Economically Active Population by Sex: 1999
'000

	Total ('000)	% Total Population	Males ('000)	% Total EAP	Females ('000)	% Total EAP
EU						
Austria	3,882	47.5	2,197	56.6	1,685	43.4
Belgium	4,288	42.2	2,461	57.4	1,827	42.6
Denmark	2,872	54.4	1,533	53.4	1,338	46.6
Finland	2,614	50.6	1,393	53.3	1,221	46.7
France	26,844	45.6	14,630	54.5	12,214	45.5
Germany	39,894	48.5	22,619	56.7	17,275	43.3
Greece	4,197	39.5	2,563	61.1	1,634	38.9
Ireland	1,681	45.4	1,024	60.9	657	39.1
Italy	21,950	38.3	13,548	61.7	8,402	38.3
Luxembourg						
Netherlands	7,909	50.3	4,532	57.3	3,377	42.7
Portugal	5,325	53.9	2,909	54.6	2,416	45.4
Spain	16,324	41.2	9,851	60.3	6,473	39.7
Sweden	4,309	48.5	2,255	52.3	2,053	47.6
United Kingdom	31,773	54.1	17,634	55.5	14,139	44.5
EFTA						
Iceland						
Norway	2,358	53.1	1,264	53.6	1,094	46.4
Switzerland	4,083	55.6	2,356	57.7	1,728	42.3
Eastern Europe						
Albania						
Belarus	4,760	46.3	2,213	46.5	2,546	53.5
Bulgaria	3,721	44.9	1,759	47.3	1,962	52.7
Croatia	2,079	46.4	1,141	54.9	938	45.1
Czech Republic	5,356	52.2	2,957	55.2	2,400	44.8
Estonia	702	49.7	365	52.0	337	48.0
Hungary	4,085	40.5	2,263	55.4	1,822	44.6
Latvia	1,172	49.1	620	52.9	552	47.1
Lithuania	1,851	50.3	959	51.8	892	48.2
Macedonia						
Moldova						
Poland	17,690	45.7	9,623	54.4	8,067	45.6
Romania	11,371	50.8	6,174	54.3	5,197	45.7
Russia	65,620	44.6	35,022	53.4	30,598	46.6
Slovakia	2,533	47.1	1,388	54.8	1,145	45.2
Slovenia	989	49.7	531	53.7	458	46.3
Ukraine	25,130	49.6	12,263	48.8	12,866	51.2
Other Europe						
Cyprus						
Gibraltar						
Malta						
Turkey	23,843	36.4	16,881	70.8	6,962	29.2

Source: National statistical offices/Eurostat/ILO/Euromonitor
Notes: EAP = economically active population
Other notes: see end of section

Table 1.1: *Continued*
Labour force by age group (men and women). 1000s

	15–64			15–24			25–49			50–64			
	1988	1993	1998	1988	1993	1998	1988	1993	1998	1988	1993	1998	
EU–15	:	:	:	:	:	:	:	:	:	:	:	:	EU–15
EUR–11	:	:	:	:	:	:	:	:	:	:	:	:	EUR–11
B	3,857	4,052	4,238	545	449	410	2,747	3,054	3,179	565	549	649	B
DK	2,811	2,823	2,793	595	499	460	1,721	1,773	1,697	494	552	636	DK
D	28,544	38,794	39,046	5,348	5,260	4,366	17,068	24,606	25,815	6,138	8,928	8,865	D
EL	3,834	3,952	4,331	513	535	567	2,355	2,519	2,831	966	898	933	EL
E	14,455	15,122	16,126	3,243	2,799	2,568	8,073	9,401	10,399	3,139	2,922	3,159	E
F	23,773	25,570	25,457	3,538	2,884	2,467	16,016	17,781	18,499	4,219	3,905	4,491	F
IRL	1,284	1,335	:	313	278	:	764	842	:	207	214	:	IRL
I	23,325	22,318	22,629	4,221	3,436	3,057	14,559	14,724	15,585	4,545	4,158	3,987	I
L	154	168	175	29	23	17	102	120	132	23	25	25	L
NL	6,454	7,025	7,687	1,355	1,291	1,247	4,212	4,786	5,160	887	948	1,281	NL
A	:	:	3,802	:	:	539	:	:	2,654	:	:	608	A
P	4,527	4,532	4,734	983	763	756	2,556	2,842	3,000	988	927	977	P
FIN	:	:	2,495	:	:	311	:	:	1,647	:	:	536	FIN
S	:	:	4,271	:	:	425	:	:	2,641	:	:	1,205	S
UK	27,777	27,973	28,205	6,256	4,982	4,368	16,125	17,563	17,838	5,397	5,428	5,998	UK
IS	:	:	:	:	:	:	:	:	:	:	:	:	IS
NO	:	:	:	:	:	:	:	:	:	:	:	:	NO
EAA	:	:	:	:	:	:	:	:	:	:	:	:	EAA
CH	:	:	:	:	:	:	:	:	:	:	:	:	CH

Further reading: Labour force survey, results 1998. Eurostat.   D: only West Germany in 1988.

Labour force by age group, men 1000s

	15–64			15–24			25–49			50–64			
	1988	1993	1998	1988	1993	1998	1988	1993	1998	1988	1993	1998	
EU–15	:	:	:	:	:	:	:	:	:	:	:	:	EU–15
EUR–11	:	:	:	:	:	:	:	:	:	:	:	:	EUR–11
B	2,364	2,383	2,446	280	236	228	1,659	1,760	1,788	425	387	430	B
DK	1,510	1,492	1,487	313	255	225	913	933	898	284	305	364	DK
D	17,214	22,308	22,072	2,789	2,769	2,357	10,377	13,993	14,437	4,048	5,545	5,279	D
EL	2,415	2,481	2,613	272	290	304	1,487	1,562	1,675	656	629	633	EL
E	9,525	9,594	9,807	1,778	1,565	1,423	5,398	5,913	6,176	2,349	2,115	2,208	E
F	13,403	13,498	13,807	1,807	1,482	1,297	9,122	9,782	10,009	2,474	2,234	2,501	F
IRL	861	841	:	174	151	:	525	530	:	162	159	:	IRL
I	14,873	14,108	13,916	2,262	1,922	1,738	9,247	9,173	9,418	3,364	3,012	2,761	I
L	100	107	108	15	12	9	68	76	82	18	18	17	L
NL	3,984	4,161	4,423	687	657	644	2,662	2,855	2,949	634	648	830	NL
A	:	:	2,134	:	:	281	:	:	1,474	:	:	379	A
P	2,594	2,494	2,598	546	417	409	1,433	1,517	1,617	614	560	572	P
FIN	:	:	1,304	:	:	161	:	:	868	:	:	275	FIN
S	:	:	2,263	:	:	229	:	:	1,402	:	:	632	S
UK	15,976	15,733	15,694	3,426	2,715	2,375	9,251	9,849	9,886	3,298	3,169	3,434	UK
IS	:	:	:	:	:	:	:	:	:	:	:	:	IS
NO	:	:	:	:	:	:	:	:	:	:	:	:	NO
EAA	:	:	:	:	:	:	:	:	:	:	:	:	EAA
CH	:	:	:	:	:	:	:	:	:	:	:	:	CH

Further reading: Labour force survey, results 1998. Eurostat.   D: only West Germany in 1988.

Table 1.2   Participation levels of women in management in the UK

The use of the category 'Managers and administrators' in the following tables relates to the Standard Occupational Classification group 1.

Table 1: Number of managers in the UK Winter 1999/2000

	All in employment (millions)	Percentage self-employed (per cent)
All occupations	27.69	11.5
Managers and administrators	4.46	17.4

Source: Labour Force Survey Quarterly Supplement, May 2000.

Table 2: Number of managers in the UK 1994–1999

	1994	1995	1996	1997	1998	1999
Managers and administrators	4,002,000	4,095,000	4,088,000	4,208,000	4,306,000	4,459,000

Source: Labour Force Survey Quarterly Supplement, May 2000.

Table 3: Number of female and male managers in the UK Winter 1999/2000

	Women	Men	Total
Managers and administrators	1,471,000	2,988,000	4,459,000

Source: Labour Force Survey Quarterly Supplement, May 2000.

Table 4: Managerial responsibilty of men and women in Great Britain Winter 1999/2000

	Managers	Foremen and supervisors	Not managers, foremen or supervisors	Base: all employees of working age
Men	23%	12%	65%	12,337,000
Women	14%	11%	75%	10,719,000

Source: Labour Market Trends, June 2000.

Table 5: Percentage of managers who are women at different responsibility levels in the UK 1974–1999

	2001	2000	1999	1998	1997	1996	1995	1994
Director	9.9	9.6	6.1	3.6	4.5	3.3	3.0	2.8
Function head	15.8	15.0	11.0	10.7	8.3	6.5	5.8	6.1
Department head	25.5	19.0	16.9	16.2	14.0	12.2	9.7	8.7
Section leader	28.9	26.5	24.9	21.9	18.2	14.4	14.2	12.0
All managers	24.1	22.1	19.9	18.0	15.2	12.3	10.7	9.5

Source: National Management Salary Survey, Institute of Management/Remuneration Economics, April 2001 (a survey of 19,836 individuals employed by 421 companies).

Box 1.3 Minority Performance in work organisations: the situation in the UK for minority ethnic communities

The emphasis of many (initiatives) has been on improving the opportunities to access in the organisation, i.e. recruitment initiatives. Increasingly, though, it is being recognised that improving representation is only one step on the way to acknowledging diversity and creating fairer working practices. Organisations need also to address the experience of minority ethnic groups after they have been recruited, and tackle potential 'treatment' discrimination once they have been employed.

The implications for organisations is that they should be concerned not only with appropriate representation of ethnic minority staff within the workplace, but also need to consider whether their procedures and practices inadvertently contribute to discrimination in the workplace. At the corporate level, unequal practices are manifested by a number of indicators:

● The increasing management/supervisory gap between minority ethnic employees and their white counterparts. The recent TUC analysis of the

Labour Force Survey (LFS) data (TUC, 2000) indicated that the gap between widened from 4.6 per cent in 1992 to 5.7 per cent in 1999.

● The almost total absence of minority ethnic representation at senior management level in some of Britain's largest corporations (Runnymede Trust, 2000).

● The disproportionately high numbers of minority ethnic employees experiencing disciplinary action in a number of local authorities (Rick *et al.*, 2001).

● Of particular concern is that these trends are occurring against the background of rising skill levels among minority ethnic employees, with the statistics showing that they are more likely to hold higher level qualifications than their counterparts (TUC, 2000)

Source: Tackey, Tamkin and Sheppard (2001) The problem of minority performance in organisations, Institute for Employment Studies. Reproduced with permission.

'Liberal' equal opportunities

Kirton and Greene explain that equality of opportunity aims to achieve what Webb (1997) calls a 'metaphorical level playing field' for all, based on the political ideals of liberal democracy whereby all individuals have rights to universally applicable standards of justice and citizenship. Liff and Wajcman (1996) argue that this model depends on an idea of equality as 'sameness': individuals should have access to and be assessed within the workplace as individuals, regardless of social group. The approach thus requires people to deny or minimise differences arising from social group membership and compete on the ground of individual merit (Liff and Wajcman, 1996).

Developing a line of reasoning presented by Jewson and Mason (1986), Kirton and Greene show that this fits with Anglo-American free market philosophy, whereby 'policies based on the neutral individual are seen as the most efficient means of achieving a fair distribution of resources in the workplace' (2000: 101). According to this view, free market competition is the best guarantee of justice, Kirton and Greene write, and any discrimination is not an inherent feature of this, but rather a distortion of the rational labour market. Thus efforts to correct this distortion are designed to remove obstacles to free market, meritocratic competition. These have sometimes included relatively progressive actions or 'positive action', such as childcare facilities at work. However, in general terms they have tended to be limited to procedural

---

Box 1.4 Anti-discrimination legislation in the UK

It is the liberal equal opportunities tradition that forms the foundation for anti-discrimination legislation. In the UK, this legislation comprises: the Sex Discrimination Act (1975), the Race Relations Act (1976 and 1994), the Equal Pay Act (1970 and 1983), the Disability Discrimination Act (1995), the Equal Rights Act (1996), and the Employment Relations Act (1996), which contains some 'family friendly' provisions such as parental leave plus enhanced employee protections.

From the EU, important legislative measures are the Equal Treatment Directive and the EU Code of Practice on Harassment. This *original* legislation encourages employers to formalise fair and meritocratic methods of access to jobs, training and promotion.

Box 1.5(a) Mapping the legal framework for facilitation of equality, diversity and inclusion in different countries (liberal democracies)

In practical terms:

- What are the most important contributions that the law makes to facilitate equality, diversity and inclusion in work organisations?
- What are the limits of the 'protections' that the law provides?
  (If employee *seeks* redress for injustices, is it typically 'David versus Goliath', given that it is often the individual versus the organisation?)
- How might law contribute to organisational change?

e.g. United Kingdom

1. Anti-discrimination laws

- Contractual (Employment Rights Act, 1996; Equal Pay Act)
- 'Group-based rights' (Sex Discrimination Act (1975), Race Relations Act, Disability Discrimination Act, 1995 Race Relations (Amendment) Act; Fair Employment Acts, 1976, 1989, 1998 (Northern Ireland) – forbids employment discrimination on religious grounds)

2. Work–life balance

- Broad-based benefit but minimise potential impact of differential home commitments (parents, women, carers, etc.) e.g. Employment Rights Act, 1996

3. Universal rights – personal liberties, e.g. Human Rights Act, 1999

4. Public employees (including those who provide special, statutory services)

- special requirements, re: employment of public employees (and also organisations are expected in law to be 'good employers')
- public authorities also more likely to deliver 'special services' and address specific needs that may allow positive action (e.g. recruitment of native Bengali speakers as carers for children: special training for women where can demonstrate under-representation) where otherwise Race Relations and Sex Discrimination Acts respectively would otherwise normally be contravened.

PLUS

- European Union, including European Court of Justice (Supra-governmental policy and laws though national laws take priority, e.g. Equal Treatment Directive, 1976; EU Code of Practice on Harassment)
- UN (Supra-governmental policy development that may influence both UN members, international law and national law).

Box 1.5(b) Employment Rights Act, 1996 – List and rights and protections

EMPLOYMENT PARTICULARS
Right to statements of employment particulars
Right to itemised pay statement.

PROTECTION OF WAGES
Deductions by employer: right not to suffer unauthorised deductions.

GUARANTEE PAYMENTS

SUNDAY WORKING FOR SHOP AND BETTING WORKERS
Protected shop workers and betting workers
Opting-out of Sunday work
Contractual requirements relating to Sunday work.

PROTECTION FROM SUFFERING DETRIMENT IN EMPLOYMENT
Rights not to suffer detriment
Health and safety cases
Sunday working for shop and betting workers
Employee representatives.

TIME OFF WORK
Public duties: Right to time off for public duties
Right to time off to look for work or arrange training
Right to time off for antenatal care
Right to time off for employee representatives
Right to remuneration on suspension on medical grounds
Suspension on maternity grounds; right to offer of alternative work; right to remuneration

MATERNITY RIGHTS
General right to maternity leave
Contractual rights to maternity leave
Right to return to work
Contractual rights to return.

TERMINATION OF EMPLOYMENT
Minimum period of notice
Rights of employer and employee to minimum notice
Rights of employee in period of notice
Right to written statement of reasons for dismissal.

UNFAIR DISMISSAL

RIGHT NOT TO BE UNFAIRLY DISMISSED

FAIRNESS
General
Pregnancy and childbirth
Health and safety cases
Shop workers and betting workers who refuse Sunday work
Trustees of occupational pension schemes
Employee representatives.

PARTICULAR TYPES OF EMPLOYMENT
Crown employment
Armed forces
National security
Parliamentary staff
House of Lords staff
House of Commons staff.

Excluded classes of employment
    Employment outside Great Britain
    Fixed-term contracts
    Short-term employment
    Mariners
    Police officers.

Offshore employment
    Power to extend employment legislation to offshore employment.

CONTINUOUS EMPLOYMENT
Period of continuous employment
Weeks counting in computing period
Intervals in employment
Special provisions for redundancy payments
Employment abroad, etc
Industrial disputes
Reinstatement after military service
Change of employer
Reinstatement or re-engagement of dismissed employee.

Source: UK Government website: www.legislation.hmso.gov/uk/acts/

safeguards such as efforts to develop non-biased hiring processes, perhaps including EO training for employees involved in these processes.

'Radical' equal opportunities

In contrast to the liberal tradition, the radical EO perspective aims to achieve equal *outcomes* or fair distribution of rewards rather than equal opportunities through fair procedures – Webb's level playing field. Liberal and radical approaches pursue equality through different types of **organisational justice: procedural** or **distributive**. The North American organisational justice litera-ture has focused on testing the perceived importance of these two types of jus-tice in relation to different organisational practices, for example compensation systems. Procedural justice refers to fairness of decision-making *processes* as perceived by those affected by the decisions; distributive justice refers to the fairness of outcomes or the distribution of rewards and resources, and seeks to explain how individuals react to an unfair distribution (Greenberg, 1987).

Kirton and Greene (2000) point out that the radical perspective accounts for the reality that discrimination in outcomes is identifiable at group rather than individual level. The underpinning idea is that equality, irrespective of social group, should be reflected in the distribution of rewards in the workplace; the absence of fair distribution is evidence of unfair discrimination (Kirton and Greene, 2000). Equality through individual merit alone is not adequate because ideas about ability and talent are not neutral: they 'contain and con-ceal a series of value judgments and stereotypes' (2000: 103).

The radical perspective thus begins to move towards an idea of equality through difference rather than sameness. Equality does not come purely through people's essential 'sameness' but is also important in view of people's differences, in particular those differences that draw from a person's member-ship in particular social groups that have been traditional recipients of discrim-ination on the part of dominant groups. Radical EO proposes using 'positive discrimination' to achieve equality. This refers to the deliberate manipulation of employment practices to achieve fairer outcomes for those from disadvantaged groups, for example through hiring and promotion quotas.

Thus the radical approach attempts to get beyond some of the limitations of the 'sameness' approach to equality. Those espousing a more radical agenda have noted that the effects of liberal equal opportunities can be characterised by the weak adherence in practice to EO legislation, and the continuing evi-

Table 1.3 'Liberal' versus 'Radical' equal opportunities

'Liberal' equal opportunities	*'Radical' equal opportunities*
● Advancement for all should be on individual 'merit' ● Similar treatment for all ● Focus on procedures, 'level playing field' ● Equality of opportunity ● Procedural justice	● Positive discrimination is needed to redress past imbalances ● Recognises different conceptions of merit and ability ● Equality of outcome ● Distributive justice

dence of discrimination in employment practices. Some of these arguments are based on the weakness of a 'legal compliance' approach in general. Dickens (2000) and Kirton and Greene (2000) cite several arguments that have been made in this regard:

- There are accounts of legislation and its prescriptions being ignored in practice (e.g. Cockburn, 1989; Collinson, Knights and Collinson, 1990).
- Some explanations focus on lack of political will underlying the legislation.
- Other accounts stress the lack of power or institutional influence of the personnel managers responsible for implementing EO policy (e.g. Hackett, 1988).
- Some point to lack of support from senior management for EO initiatives (e.g. Colgan and Ledwith, 1996). Some have cited limited resources of national bodies like the EOC and CRE (Webb, 1997).
- Some have pointed to the considerable differences in 'espoused' models and 'operational models', for example in recruitment and selection (Jenkins, 1986).

Another line of criticism of 'liberal' equal opportunities focuses more directly on the underpinning model of equality that it utilises. For example, Jewson and Mason (1986) argue that the liberal view that fair procedures lead to fair outcomes is misguided. As Kirton and Greene point out, critics such as Cockburn, Webb, and Jewson and Mason have shown that a model of 'procedural formalisation' 'promises more than it can deliver and is no guarantee of fairness' (2000, p. 106). This is because: procedures can be evaded; over-bureaucratisation of processes is out of step with the commonly stated need for greater workplace flexibility; and many aspects of work life cannot be formalised anyway since behaviour is often governed by informal norms and codes of conduct (Kirton and Greene, 2000).

On the other hand, radical EO approaches have also been criticised, sometimes by the same thinkers. Cockburn (1989) shows that interventions aiming to deliberately enhance the position of workers from particular groups can be negatively viewed as special treatment; the women employees in her study of the high street retailer said they disliked favouritism, in part because of the 'backlash' they expected. More significantly and profoundly, the women did not see such interventions as changing the *nature* of the organisation, which was required for real progress to happen.

Equal opportunities approaches, be they liberal or radical, have been criticised for failing to advance the interests of disadvantaged groups of employees, and failing to challenge the status quo. Only a minority of workers from disadvantaged groups who most easily meet the dominant norm have been assisted by these policies (Kirton and Greene, 2000). The conceptualisation of equality around 'sameness' clearly appears to be limited in its ability to deliver equality to all.

Perhaps not surprisingly then, conceptualisations of workplace equality have moved broadly from thinking about equality as sameness, prevalent in the later 1970s and 80s, to thinking about equality in terms of 'difference', in recognition of the heterogeneous nature of organisations. Managing diversity is based on a conception of equality that recognises differences, rather than diluting them, in Liff's words (1996). Diversity management as a distinctive approach to workplace equality reflects this shift.

Diversity management

Diversity management as it is most frequently theorised is distinct from equal opportunities, although in theory and in practice both are intended to pursue and promote equality in the workplace. As seen in the previous section, equal opportunities in Britain and North America draws its force from a legal framework that outlaws discrimination against women and racial minorities and to a lesser extent at present, people with disabilities.

In contrast, diversity management depends more heavily on organisational commitment. It most frequently refers to a set of initiatives or interventions that are internally driven and proactive. For those organisations that have embraced diversity management, a central aim is to manage equality within the context of differing employee expectations, cultural traditions, religious requirements, and so on. To this end, respect for this aspect of employee identity is explicitly acknowledged and diversity of cultural heritage is viewed as positive and enriching for organisational culture. Diversity management (DM) looks at 'difference' across a range of categories and, in common with equal opportunities, these include race, ethnicity, sexual orientation, age and disability, in addition to these cultural aspects.

Clearly, some employees will be members of more than one social group, and *employee-centred* generation of group categories is crucial within DM initiatives. It could be argued that choice about which range of groups an employee belongs to is more pressing within DM than within an equal opportunities approach. It is often stated that a benefit of DM is that a better representation of the community within an organisation increases its knowledge base for sectors of the community-at-large, whose wants and desires would traditionally be overlooked from a commercial point of view, so that there is a potential commercial benefit to the company.

In general terms, diversity management as an approach to workplace equality draws its distinctiveness largely from its focus on equality through 'difference' rather than 'sameness'. Like equal opportunities both liberal and radical, however, this approach has been criticised on both practical and theoretical grounds. In part these criticisms can be viewed as stemming from the lack of a widely accepted definition or interpretation of diversity management. The section that follows sets out some of the debates around defining diversity management, and discusses the main criticisms that have been put forward in the literature. These criticisms are shown to result from a narrow conception of diversity management, and one that has been questioned by both researchers and practitioners in the field. Nonetheless, both strengths and weaknesses of diversity management as an approach to promoting workplace equality arise from considering these issues, and are drawn out below.

Diversity management focuses on the idea of valuing difference ('equality through difference'), on non-dominant or under-represented social groups, and on respecting diversity at an individual level (e.g. Gentile, 1994; Cornelius, Gooch and Todd, 2000(a)(b); Thomas Jr., 1993, 1996). In the UK, diversity management has sometimes been presented as a 'new' approach brought in from the USA, with a particular self-interest appeal to organisations operating in a context where minority groups are important customers, and in a country where these groups constitute the fastest-growing segment of the population.

Diversity management is distinguished by some as based upon a desire to 'take equality further' by increasing the focus on ethnicity and race in addition to gender, and through recognizing the distinctive contribution that members of minority groups can make to the organisation. In Greenslade's words, DM seeks to create a climate whereby those involved want to:

(a) move beyond the achievement of statistical goals,
(b) accept and value the differences between individuals and groups, and
(c) recognise the benefits that diversity can bring to an organisation.

(1992, as cited in Cornelius, 2000)

So while equal opportunities concentrates on removing discrimination, diversity management is often viewed as focusing on maximizing employee potential.

There have been a number of drivers for diversity management, including the limited success of more traditional equal opportunities initiatives (Cockburn, 1989; Liff and Cameron, 1997; Thomas Jr., 1996). In the West in particular, the demographic profile of communities and in turn, organisations, has changed and continues to change, with those from traditionally disadvantaged groups increasingly present and active in the labour market (Anonymous, 1997(a)(b)(c); Johnson and Packer, 1987). Thus, with increases in labour market diversity, workforce diversity is increasingly the norm. Not surprisingly, there are rising demands and expectations, particularly on the part of the traditionally disadvantaged, that organisations operate in a manner that reflects such changes (Gentile, 1994; Thomas Jr., 1996). Internationally, managing across borders has sharpened the increase in practice and theory development in the field of cross-cultural awareness and management (Moon and Woolliams, 1999; Trompenaars and Hampden-Turner, 1998).

The literature on diversity management includes an eclectic and not always complementary range of interpretations and practice. Definitions of diversity management vary considerably. For example, some have suggested that there are different approaches to diversity management in the USA and UK, with the former more concerned with gender, race and sexuality, and the latter with 'culture' and the culturally diverse workforce (Trapp, 1994). However, in general a similar range of interpretations of what is meant by **managing diversity** has arisen in both countries. Within multinational and global organisations, important aspects of diversity management are cross-cultural interactions and communication (Riccucci, 1997) as this is seen as important for enhancing business transactions across borders. On both sides of the Atlantic the importance of the potential of 'diversity knowledge' to customer service and increasing market share – the business case – has taken the management of equality and difference beyond its more traditional, largely legally, morally and politically defined boundaries.

So for example, Kandola and Fullerton (1994) have researched and advocated 'management of the mosaic' through approaches taking a strategic orientation. They argue that demographic shifts make it imperative to move the focus of attention from equality of opportunity for traditionally disadvantaged groups to the business imperative of attracting and retaining a workforce attracted from a diverse pool of labour. Further, they argue that it is important to have, first, a demonstrably strategic approach to managing diversity, and second, an approach that pays sufficient attention to the prevailing organisational and managerial cultures, as those that do not are likely to fail.

Inherent in some of these definitions is a view that diversity is 'about' groups as well as individuals. Diversity management does not, by definition, undermine recognition of the differential power positions of dominant and non-dominant groups in organisations and society more generally. Rather, for many it attempts to push the pursuit of equality further to give a positive value to difference. Thus diversity management can indeed be viewed as directed towards constructing a 'mosaic' within the organisation, in contrast to the melting-pot analogy that may be applicable if equality interventions are limited to externally imposed or reactive measures. Liff and Dickens' (1998) reference to the 'Procrustian' approach to workplace equality is relevant here: as opposed to such an approach, the promotion and achievement of equality must fundamentally question the fitting of individuals or non-dominant groups into a template based upon the 'norm' of the white male and geared to 'allowing' others to share in their benefits.

Table 1.4 The main tenets of equal opportunities and diversity management as they have been commonly presented in the literature

Equal opportunities	Managing diversity
• Workplace programmes derive from legal framework outlawing discrimination	• Depends upon organisational initiative; internally driven, proactive
• Compliance, e.g. with recruitment targets	• Business case arguments part of rationale
• Melting-pot result? 'equality through sameness', based on merit	• Taking equality further through contribution of ethnic minorities
• Aims to increase proportion of under-represented groups in senior roles	• Moving beyond statistics: valuing differences, recognising benefits diversity can bring (Greenslade, 1995)
• Main focus has tended to be gender	• Maximising employee potential
• 'Liberal' approach	• About groups as well as individuals
• May include positive action to redress past discrimination ('Radical approach')	• Mosaic result, equality through difference

Diversity management: lessons from the American literature

It would be fair to say that, until recently, diversity management has been more readily embraced in the United States than in the UK and Europe. Indeed, the majority of the literature written about it originates from the USA, and this literature is in general more positive in tone. This said, the American experience has not been unproblematic, and in spite of widespread support, problems have been highlighted.

Beyond 'noble rhetoric': the view from employees

For example, many case study accounts relate how diversity programmes, typically driven by HRM departments, have sprung up within corporate America (see Flynn, 1995; Mueller, 1996; Hopkins, Sterkell-Powell and Hopkins, 1994; Ellis and Sonnenfeld, 1994). Often, the detail and reality of such programmes are difficult to discern from these accounts, as they are often anecdotal and reflect the 'noble rhetoric' (Fineman, Gabriel and Sims, 2000) of American corporate communications. In particular, these accounts have been written against a background of a backlash against affirmative action programmes in some sectors and indeed, the repealing of affirmative action laws in some American states. For the critical observer, the accounts thus beg two questions: to what extent is the nature and impact of diversity management programmes really understood from these case examples; and, is diversity management 'equal opportunities without legal teeth'?

Other writers point to the limited application of diversity management in practice. For example, Ellis and Sonnenfeld (1994) and Trapp (1994) emphasise the danger of diversity management becoming solely concerned with the entry level to the organisation (although in the United States, monitoring may only legally take place amongst existing, not potential employees and is therefore a retrospective act). Ellis and Sonnefeld (1994) reviewed three corporate diversity programmes. The initiatives they reviewed differed in their design and implementation, but could be put into the following categories:

- multicultural workshops;
- multicultural 'core groups' that met on a monthly basis to confront stereotypes and personal biases;
- female and minority support groups and networks, as well as advisory councils that report directly to upper management;
- managerial reward systems that were based partially on managers' ability to train and promote women and minorities who demonstrate exceptional talent and potential;
- mentoring programmes that paired women and minorities with senior managers;
- a range of corporate communications announcing the appreciation of

corporate pluralism and top-level commitment to creating an environment where members of diverse groups can thrive. (1994: 84)

The results of their workforce surveys suggested that such programmes *did* positively affect workplace attitudes. However, factors such as the roles of top leadership, participant mix, instructor quality and corporate culture were important variables that greatly influenced whether the impact of the programmes would be positive or negative.

Nonetheless, many of the comments offered by questionnaire respondents in Ellis and Sonnefeld's research reflected the hopes, fears and disappointments of employees. Roughly speaking, employees responded according to what they considered would be the likely gains and losses of the diversity programme, and whether they felt that diversity was a 'fair' mechanism. For example, some women and those from ethnic minorities in particular felt that much of what was asserted in such programmes was mere rhetoric. 'Glass ceilings' appeared to be firmly in place. Basic grade and senior white male managers feared that qualifications were all that mattered and that such programmes would lead to segregation. There seemed to be a gap, therefore, between the kinds of changes that could be effected by senior managers, and those that employees further down the line, in particular from traditionally disadvantaged groups, felt were needed to change the material reality of where *they* were, in their section or department. However, it is worth considering whether such change is characteristic of diversity management initiatives exclusively: our earlier account of equal opportunities and its failings resonates strongly with these findings.

Organisational dynamics and 'social traps'

Any discussion of diversity management programmes should include analysis of 'unspoken concerns and agendas' that can distort the potential of those programmes. Barry and Bateman (1996) have argued that management initiatives influence diversity-related outcomes in work organisations because they create 'social traps'. Social traps are situations where decision problems involve conflicts between individual and near-term outcomes on one hand, and collective or long-term consequences on the other.

Barry and Bateman's social trap model for diversity management suggests that there are sources of difficulty at the individual, group and organisational levels. The authors outline potential solutions to specific social trap attributes. These they place under the headings of:

- training and development;
- work design;
- staffing;
- compensation;
- informational solutions;

- group structure solutions (including increasing group identity);
- trap structure solutions (management of timing of actions).

Some of these solutions centre around operational, core personnel activities, such as training and development, work design, staffing and compensation policies, and improved employee communications. Other interventions are geared more towards enhancing employee voice and identity for the traditionally disadvantaged, through, for example, networking. In addition, thought had to be given to the exact timing of introducing such changes, and to their implementation. So, for example, the timing of the introduction of diversity-centred activities was done in a way that was not politically naïve.

Thus, Barry and Bateman's work highlights the difficulty of managing official and unofficial social structures, and of getting to grips with the organisational cultural web and social interactions therein. More generally, their work provides persuasive arguments that employment management and general organisational systems and structures should be utilised proactively as levers for diversity change.

Structural and systemic embedding of diversity management

Others who have considered diversity management take a similar position. Such authors tend to criticise the individualism promoted as important in Kandola and Fullerton's outline of effective diversity management (Kandola and Fullerton, 1994). For example, Rosen and Lovelace (1994) suggest that the success of diversity management depends on:

- a shared responsibility between policy makers and employees at all levels;
- employees' perceptions of organisational (person-environment) fit and their degree of comfort with this;
- the degree of effectiveness with which those from traditionally disadvantaged groups are assimilated into organisational life and culture;
- the degree of structural **exclusion** that is built into the work organisation's systems, structures and practice.

Problems which these authors suggest are commonly encountered by those who are the primary targets of diversity programmes include:

- a desire for better work–family balance is regarded as a lack of commitment;
- 'organisational game playing' which may compromise personal values;
- a failure to build an inclusive corporate culture (modelling from the top is poor).

Many of these observations suggest the need for a far more *root and branch* approach to the management of diversity than that often proposed in the prescriptive literature. Such an approach should build upon and greatly extend the more traditional equal opportunities mechanisms for addressing inequalities and difference. For example, Vince and Booth (1996) suggest that:

- there is a need to move away from a culture of opposition to (in)equalities towards learning from and about 'equalities', and indeed from traditional training and development models towards models of organisational learning;
- organisations should move away from an individualised perspective on equality towards one that includes social power relations;
- equality should be embedded into organisational design; in particular they highlight the potential of networked organisations.

Systemic changes in human resource management are important for the success of organisational equality programmes, particularly given that: (a) HRM is often an effective internal driver for organisational and cultural change; and (b) the impact of diversity management is often directly or indirectly influenced by HRM policy, strategy and change. The role and potential in promoting workplace equality of such systems as staff appraisal, remuneration and reward, and training and development are clear.

Diversity management, the European experience: a cool reception?

In Europe, diversity management has experienced a difficult and slow birth, despite a sizable pre-existing literature on cross-cultural management. In the UK, some observers have raised concerns about the efficacy and legitimacy of diversity management as an approach to pursuing equality and ending discrimination in organisations. Specifically, some have suggested that diversity management may be a 'soft option' for those who would rather not embrace political, social justice, and discrimination and fairness issues championed by more traditional equal opportunities processes (e.g. Lorbiecki and Jack, 1999; Kaler, 2001; Webb, 1997). Some have expressed concern that aspirations of diversity management approaches, such as the business case or improving performance, and addressing diversity of need, are normative and utilitarian, and individualistic, respectively (Lorbiecki and Jack, 1999).

The contention that diversity management is built upon weaker moral foundations than those of equal opportunities (Lorbiecki and Jack, 1999; Webb, 1997) can be supported by apparently powerful ethical arguments, drawn from classical ethical theory. Because diversity management models often make reference to the 'business case' as a justification for action, DM is seen as limited to utilitarian conceptions of the moral good. Social justice, employee rights and fairness are secondary to organisational outcomes such as improved performance and competitive advantage. Making a business case argument offends notions of 'right in principle' Kantian theory which requires that people be treated as ends in themselves.

In contrast, others have argued that many businesses base 'effectiveness' upon more than financial considerations, so that social justice reasons can *coincide* with the business case (Liff and Dickens, 2000). Once social justice and efficiency arguments are counter-posed, it is argued, the logical consequence would be that an intervention cannot be both ethical and acting in the interests of business. There is evidence that organisations do not necessarily experience social justice and business case arguments in a polarised way: surveys indicate that managers see no contradiction between simultaneously pursuing business case and social justice arguments for equality initiatives. For example, the Department of Employment (Anonymous, 1994) found that 88 per cent of 75 organisations surveyed said they pursued racial equality to demonstrate a commitment to social justice, and 87 per cent of the same respondents said it was to make better use of human resources (Liff and Dickens, 2000). Supporting evidence comes from the more recent EOR study which found that while the most popular reason for adopting an equal opportunities policy was complying with the law (87 per cent), 84 per cent also cited social justice, and 77 per cent the business case (*IRS Employment Trends 691*, November 1999).

Elsewhere, Dickens distinguishes broadly two categories of reasons why organisations pursue equal opportunities. The first is organisational self-interest, which includes improving organisational effectiveness. The second is legal compliance. She argues that initiatives to promote greater equality, presumably including those that might be labelled diversity management initiatives, can arise from a sense of social justice or moral responsibility, e.g. the case of John Moores of Littlewoods. Although often posed as alternatives, business rationales for equality action may go hand in hand with social justice and/or compliance considerations, argues Dickens. In practice, she adds, social justice or altruistic considerations probably have 'the most purchase' when operating in combination with organisational self-interest or compliance factors (2000: p. 144).

Equal opportunities 'versus' diversity management?

The literature on workplace equality theory as outlined in this chapter may be viewed as being riddled with a series of dichotomies. A summary of these dichotomies includes:

- liberal versus radical approaches;
- equality of opportunity versus equality of outcome;
- procedural justice versus distributive justice;
- equality through 'sameness' versus equality through difference;
- equality for social justice reasons versus equality for 'competitive advantage' or business case reasons;
- equal opportunities versus diversity management.

As seen above, some commentators have pitted equal opportunities and diversity management in opposition to one another. However, in practice it is doubtful that equal opportunities and diversity management are widely viewed as an either-or proposition. For example, a recent survey of 140 organisations employing over 1.6 million people in the UK found that 'for the majority of employers, equal opportunities and managing diversity are complementary rather than distinct concepts' (*IRS Review 691*, November 1999). In the American context, influential writers on the subject state that diversity management must be built upon a legal foundation of affirmative action legislation. Thomas Jr. writing in Gentile (1994), for example, argues that 'affirming diversity' is the next step to achieving equality in the workplace, following the essential and 'stupendous achievements' of affirmative action (1994: 27–29).

At the conceptual level, persisting with either-or propositions arguably serves to compromise equality and justice, according to Liff and Dickens (2000): the 'equality through sameness or difference' debate points to the 'false choices' that result from attempts to counterpose equality versus merit, they argue. Liff (1999) argues elsewhere, however, that in practice, it may be precisely the tensions between 'equal treatment' and diversity or difference approaches that can lead to greater achievements in organisations. Dickens has recently called for a 'three-pronged approach' to pursuing equality in organisations (2000). This would combine robust legal regulation with social regulation through committed trade unions on one hand, and strong organisational commitment on the other.

Cockburn's 'long agenda' for workplace equality

Cockburn's seminal work analysing the pursuit of equality in organisations recognises that such a pursuit is a dynamic exercise and looks for commitment over the long term at the organisational level (1989). In an important sense, Cockburn's work indicates that the debate about the relative value of EO versus DM approaches may well miss the point. She argues persuasively that legal compliance approaches are insufficient on their own because they do not necessitate commitment from the organisation to transform itself. This would require, in contrast, that disadvantaged groups have access to power beyond a 'numbers game', and that a powerful check on managerial priorities in the form of collective action, most probably through trades unions (who as organisations also need to transform themselves), can bring the equality agenda forward.

Cockburn's work thus brings a different but important perspective that helps to qualify and illuminate some of the concerns raised by others in the field. She confronted the issue of disillusionment among activists concerning the lack of progress resulting from equal opportunities policies in organisations, and called for an approach centred on progressive change. Her proposals are partially founded on what she saw as the limitations of both the liberal and radical agendas for addressing issues of inequality and managing difference. For example, she argues that the liberal agenda tends to play down or not acknowledge historic disadvantage and therefore does not compensate for it (and by implication, does not therefore genuinely reduce or eliminate inequalities). In contrast, the radical agenda often seeks to right old wrongs by means that may be felt to be wrong, such as affirmative action or positive discrimination, even by those whom such actions are designed to help.

Cockburn suggests that the radical–liberal dichotomy could be supplanted with the notions of short- and long-term agendas. Specifically, short-term agendas would be more concerned with addressing biases while long-term agendas are geared to transformation – 'a project of transformation'. In other words, Cockburn calls for an approach to equality that goes beyond some calculation of whether the traditionally disadvantaged are winning or losing and focuses instead on questioning *how the organisation is developing*. This supports other later thinkers calling for systemic and structural change in support of equality, some of whom have come from the diversity management 'school' within the UK.

More recently, scholars have used similar lines of argument to those of Cockburn when considering 'traditional' equal opportunities, questioning its ability to deliver long-term, sustainable, cultural change. Further, it has been suggested that individualism and a failure to address wider organisational dynamics that mediate discrimination and disadvantage characterise a number of equal opportunities approaches.

For example, argues Dickens (2000), much equal opportunities prescription 'rests on an inadequate conceptualization of the problem; assumes unitary interests where divergent interests exist; pays inadequate attention to the resistance equal opportunities generates; and simplifies the reasons for it' (in Bach and Sisson, 2000: 163). What equal opportunities initiatives have tended to pursue, she continues, 'focuses on helping individuals from disadvantaged groups get in and get on within existing organisations, with no real challenge being mounted to the nature, structure and values of the organisations themselves'. 'Valuing diversity' as an alternative approach may provide promising methods of opening the way for:

> different formal and informal organisational culture and structures, reflective of diverse contributions, need and attributes; at its most radical, valuing diversity calls for an holistic, positive approach which recognises and values social group differences and which challenges the nature of organisations as currently constructed. (2000: 162)

That is, as long as valuing rather than dissolving differences, and not moving away from redressing historical disadvantages towards a focus on 'all individuals as individuals', is the result. Dickens concludes that much practice falls short of the requirement for real culture-change approaches to promoting equality. This assertion of the importance of challenging and changing the dominant culture within which equality action is sought is echoed in the work of Liff and Cameron (1997) on women and equality.

Given evident problems or lack of progress associated with a legal compliance approach to organisational equality, one might argue that Cockburn's 'project of transformation' is increasingly articulated in the diversity literature calling for organisational will to change. This *will* may come from strong trades unions that provide a countervailing pressure to management's potentially narrow conception of organisational interests, which would be most consistent, perhaps, with Cockburn's vision. Or the will may come from the vision of a broader base of leaders or change agents within an organisation, some of whom may be trades union leaders, some of whom may be employees more generally, and some of whom may be managers, even top managers. A focus on the need for a *dynamic* model such as Cockburn's, directed towards systemic and structural change, reveals the shortcomings of both known equal opportunities models, whether liberal or radical, and restricted conceptions of diversity management based on a narrow construing of organisational interests around an economic or financial model of the 'business case'.

In summary, organisational approaches to equality that result solely from external pressures, approaches that are limited to complying with the law and thus tend to be focused on procedures or 'artefacts' such as labelling oneself an 'equal opportunities employer', and approaches that do not bring real change in organisations are unlikely to result in true equality in the workplace. This provides, perhaps, at least a partial explanation of aggregate statistics that continue to show comparatively high unemployment rates and rates of promotion for members of ethnic minority groups. The sustained pay gap between white and ethnic minority employees, and between men and women, also attests in part to the limited progress of equality initiatives to date.

The current state of workplace equality: the view from the top and the view on the ground

Real problems persist in practice in achieving workplace equality, fairness and non-discrimination. For example, according to a recent survey of FTSE 100 companies sponsored by the Runnymede Trust, ethnic minority groups remain seriously under-represented at senior management level in private sector organisations in the UK (Sanglin-Grant and Schneider, 2000). Black African-Caribbean workers experience even greater under-representation than ethnic groups generally. Yet nearly all companies participating in the survey reported that their recruitment, retention and employee development policies do not discriminate against ethnic minorities. Importantly, however, the study also collected responses from ethnic minority employees themselves. Here there was a 'yawning gap' between companies' beliefs about their equality policies and how individuals perceived their employers' treatment of them. We will return to this study later when we explore how the role of measurement may contribute to this gap.

While these figures indicate slow progress towards equality, more disturbing is the fact that nearly all companies participating in the survey reported that their recruitment, retention and employee development policies do not discriminate against ethnic minorities. Why then have 'equal outcomes' been so elusive? This evidence clearly suggests that current approaches to workplace equality continue to be out of step with the grievances of members of traditionally disadvantaged groups who do not believe that their interests are being protected and promoted in organisations.

Introduction to the capabilities approach

Our discussion above of the major approaches or 'dominant discourses' of workplace equality points strongly towards the need for a more multi-domain, system-wide and structural approach. Organisations must transform themselves, as Cockburn persuasively demonstrated more than a decade ago, for all employees to believe that they are treated fairly and equally valued in their workplaces, regardless of their social group membership. But what is needed in order to achieve such a transformation? Where it focuses on organisational change and embedding equality into organisational strategies and structures, recent thinking in diversity management points to some possible solutions. Such approaches do not obviate the need for a robust legal framework, the 'floor' of rights so important to the equal opportunities approach. We have argued that diversity management must be EO-centred, with the legal framework providing the 'bedrock' of diversity management strategies.

Strengthening legal provisions, therefore, may be part of the answer, and new legislation in the UK around employee rights, plus European directives on human rights, now incorporated into UK law, will extend individuals' and groups' legal protections against discriminatory behaviour by employers. But there is danger in advocating an approach based solely on legal change, as some in the EO field continue to do, given ample and persuasive argument and evidence that organisational equality programmes based on legal compliance are narrow, limited and unsatisfactory for organisational members. More 'radical' EO approaches may produce more positive results or 'outcomes' but these have tended to be limited to 'hard' measures such as numbers of those hired from disadvantaged groups.

Thus diversity management as an approach to workplace equality offers real promise, not least because it attempts to put the equality agenda into a more positive light, through 'valuing difference' rather than viewing it as a problem. Nonetheless, diversity management lacks a clear, robust theoretical underpinning. As shown above, it is viewed by some as lacking a theoretical foundation of the type that grounds equal opportunities as an approach to organisational equality. Some have argued that diversity management is strictly utilitarian in nature, geared towards improving an organisation's performance or effectiveness, and that this renders it inferior to the rights-based, 'end-in-itself' ethical foundation of EO.

Precisely because it provides this strong ethical foundation to the conception of respecting and valuing diversity and difference as part of what is required for equality to exist, the theory of **capabilities** presents a promising alternative way of addressing the challenges of building equality in organisations. The capabilities approach shows that equality must not be looked at in terms of sameness only, or difference only, but that both must form the basis for equality action, through the notion of freedoms. The capabilities framework, which sets out what is necessary for the full expression of free-doms, leads to a set of building blocks that organisations may employ to structure and evaluate their approaches to promoting equality. Key among these are the freedoms required for individual and collective agency to be meaningful in organisations, in order that the equality agenda is broadened and informed bottom-up, not only top-down and 'by proxy'. Because it calls for holistic, integrated, long-term change in organisations, and because it is based on a conviction that such change is not only necessary but possible, it signposts what is required for 'felt fair' equality in organisations.

Capabilities: a new way of thinking about, and pursuing, workplace equality

What is capabilities theory?

Applied to organisations, the **capabilities approach** starts from the proposi-tion that because organisations are social entities, they can and do engage in social change. Capabilities theory was developed by Amartya Sen and Martha Nussbaum in the field of development economics. Sen is known as the econo-mist who constructed the Human Development Index (HDI) used by the United Nations. The index is used to evaluate and rate the degree of 'quality of life' achieved by citizens within different countries at the macro-economic level. The index departed from conventional measures of economic growth or well-being in assuming a multifaceted 'quality of life' position. While con-ventional approaches measure income, economic growth, or human capital formation, the HDI views human development in terms of 'the process of widening people's choices and the level of their achieved well-being . . . three essential elements of human life are measured: longevity (life expectancy at birth), knowledge (e.g. literacy), and living standards (e.g. command over resources needed for a decent living)' (World Resources Institute website, 2001, www.igc.org/wri). The most recent United Nations Development Program (UNDP) Annual Report describes the index as having helped to 'redefine development away from solely economic indicators, and towards a balanced concern for equity, sustainability, productivity and empowerment' (2001).

Giving expression to this view of what constitutes development (e.g. widening people's freedoms and choices), Sen and American ethicist Martha Nussbaum had conceived of *the capabilities approach* to understanding human development. This approach is set out in detail in Sen's 1999 book, *Development as Freedom*, and in his earlier work, notably *Inequality Re-Examined* (1992).

Sen's use of the term 'capabilities' refers to individuals' freedoms to achieve what they have reason to value. Drawing from Sen's book, *Inequality Re-Examined* (1992), the basic question to ask when evaluating social arrangements using this approach is: what is the person's capability to achieve 'functionings' that he or she has reason to value? Does the person have the freedom to do so?

The focus on functionings, Sen argues, differs from more traditional approaches to equality, involving concentration on such variables as income, wealth or happiness, and is closely related to the fact of human diversity (1992: 6). Sen writes:

> Human beings are thoroughly diverse, . . . the assessment of the claims of human equality has to come to terms with the existence of pervasive human diversity. The powerful rhetoric of 'equality of man' often tends to deflect attention from these differences. Even though such rhetoric is typically taken to be part and parcel of egalitarianism, the effect of ignoring the interpersonal variations can, in fact, be deeply inegalitarian, in hiding the fact that equal consideration for all may demand very unequal treatment in favour of the disadvantaged. The demands of substantive equality can be particularly exacting and complex when there is a good deal of antecedent inequality to counter . . . Sometimes human diversities are left out of account on the 'low ground' of the need for simplification . . . But the net result of this can also be to ignore centrally important features of demands of equality. (1992: 1)

The capability perspective differs from various concepts of 'equality of opportunities' which have been championed, as Sen states, for a long time. 'In a very basic sense, a person's capability to achieve does indeed stand for the opportunity to pursue his or her objectives', states Sen (1992: 7). But he points out that the concept of equality of opportunities is often used in the policy literature in more restrictive ways, 'defined in terms of the equal availability of some *particular means*, or with reference to equal applicability (or equal non-applicability) of some *specific barriers or constraints*' (Sen, 1992: 7). Thus characterised, equality of opportunity, according to Sen, does not amount to anything like equality of *overall* freedoms. This is so, in Sen's words, because of '(1) the fundamental diversity of human beings, and (2) the existence and importance of various means (such as income or wealth) that do not fall within the purview of standardly defined "equality of opportunities"' (1992: 7). In terms of the position outlined and defended in Sen's work, a more adequate way of considering 'real' equality of opportunities must be through *equality of capabilities*.

In the macro-economic and public policy sphere, Sen's work is widely seen as offering a 'paradigm-altering' foundation for understanding and pursuing economic development in both rich and poor countries through the pursuit of greater liberties or freedoms for all citizens. Applying this thinking to the organisational level, the lessons in part are on the level of metaphor. However, there are also more concrete contributions of capabilities thinking to how we understand the meaning of equality and inequality in the workplace. In line with Sen and Nussbaum's thinking, human development in organisations can also be viewed in terms of widening people's choices, of enhancing their freedom. Freedom is both the end and the means of development, Sen argues in *Development as Freedom* (1999). This is the core of his thesis. If organisations are to pursue equality of their members, they must pursue equal freedoms for all organisational members.

Taking Sen's thinking further, one might argue that freedom is both the ends and the means of equality. Sen argues that freedom consists in ensuring people's capabilities, defined as their 'ability to pursue what they have reason to value'. If an organisation is going to work to achieve equality of all of its members, it needs to ensure people's capabilities, and to ensure that this is done equally for all organisational members. Organisations can achieve this by focusing on Sen's five instrumental freedoms, presented in detail later in the chapter. It is these freedoms that together constitute the 'enabling environment' necessary for capabilities to be expressed. However, building this environment is not something external to organisational members: individuals and groups within the organisation at every level have a role in making this happen. The requirement for individual and collective action and involvement can be understood in looking at Sen's concept of agency, discussed in detail later in the chapter.

Overall, the application of capabilities theory to the workplace can be viewed as providing a holistic, integrated framework for evaluating organisational approaches to promoting equality for all their members.

An 'alternative ethical framework'

Returning to our discussion of ethical theory and the ways in which the literature on equality in organisations has appealed to ethical theory, Sen offers an 'alternative ethical framework' in the capabilities approach. At the macroeconomic level, capabilities theory provides an evaluative tool that is stronger than those provided by other widely used ethical theories such as a purely rights-based approach and utilitarianism, for the analysis of equality, freedom and the resulting quality of life (Sen, 1999). In order to move beyond the 'either-or' thinking of juxtaposing rights-based ethical theory and utilitarianism, Sen has developed his capabilities approach grounded in the ethics of Aristotle. Here, human potential, virtue and the capacity to become good through doing good are central. To the extent that the workplace equality literature has appealed to ethical theory to evaluate the equal opportunities and diversity management approaches, there is a strong parallel with the 'either-or' focus that Sen wishes to set aside. Writers about workplace equality have contrasted the grounded-in-law EO approach as the Kantian, 'right-in-principle' position, with the utilitarian position characterising the DM approach which is based upon organisational will and is thus assumed to narrowly define 'what is good for the company' in terms of increasing profits or efficiency (Lorbiecki and Jack, 1999; Kaler, 2001).

Sen writes that: 'The Aristotelian connections (to capabilities theory) are obvious enough: Aristotle's focus on "flourishing" and "capacity" clearly relate to the quality of life and to substantive freedoms, as have been discussed by Martha Nussbaum' (1999: 24); and further, that:

> The concept of 'functionings', which has distinctly Aristotelian roots, reflects the various things a person may value doing or being. The valued

functionings may vary from elementary ones, such as being adequately nourished and being free from avoidable disease, to very complex activities or personal states, such being able to take part in the life of a community and having self-respect. (1999: 75)

Sen states that in developing his theory of capabilities, he is also indebted to the major 20th-century political philosopher John Rawls and his 'justice as fairness' position (Sen, 1992: xi). The leading idea within Rawlsian theory is

the hope for social institutions that do not confer morally arbitrary advantages on some persons at the expense of others . . . This condemns as unjust not only racial, sexual and religious discrimination, but also many forms of social and economic inequality; the view is a strongly egalitarian form of liberalism, based on the idea that all persons are in an 'original position' of equality. (Honderich, 1995)

Whereas Rawls' focus is on what Sen calls the *means* of freedom (primary goods in Rawls' terms), Sen's focus is on the extents of freedom (Sen, 1992: xi).

There are additional implications from this belief in the universal capacity to 'know' good and 'become' good, concerning social identity. In a recent paper to the British Academy in which he critiques the idea of social identity, Sen (2000) asserts that: 'Our identification with others in one group or another can have a strong influence on our thoughts and feelings, and through them, on our deeds as well' (2000: 1).

As part of his critique, Sen argues that in all societies, our social identity may be linked to several groups in one or other way: that we possess a plural identity, and that a person may invoke a specific identity in particular contexts (e.g. at work or at home). Sen makes it clear that it would be absurd to suggest that *any* identity whatever can be chosen, but the issue is: where there is choice, does an individual have the substantial freedom over what priority to give the various identities that he or she may simultaneously have?

Further, Sen considers the notion of transcendence – 'beyond identity' – to be important: 'we need to consider the claims of other people who do not share our own identities' (2000: 10) '. . . to entertain sympathy without actually inserting one's own self into the lives of others' (2000: 11). Put simply, Sen argues that the values and actions of moral and political inclusion 'transcend the domain of identity' (2000: 13).

The implications of these distinctions for work organisations are substantial. In our view, they suggest the need to think about identity not only in terms of 'making good' historic injustices, but also according to the definitions of the array of identities that an individual may have. In other words, an employee-centred, self-definitional approach is likely to enhance our understanding of the interplay between equality and difference. Further, it becomes the duty of organisations seeking to embrace capabilities equality to be clear about the formal and informal structures that may impede moral and political inclusion and in turn, compromise the freedom of opportunity – the freedom to exercise the full capabilities set.

The following section looks at each of the fundamental elements of the capabilities approach, and sets out their applicability and implications for the pursuit of more 'equal' workplaces.

The importance of freedoms

Freedoms of individuals are the basic building blocks of development, states Sen. Therefore the expansion of freedoms of persons 'to lead the kind of lives they value, and have reason to value', is key. These freedoms can be enhanced by public policy, but equally, on the other side, the direction of public policy can be influenced by the effective use of participatory freedoms by the public. This two-way relationship is central to Sen's analysis. So substantive individual freedoms are taken to be critical. The success of a society is to be evaluated, in this view, primarily by the substantive freedoms that the members of that society enjoy. This view differs from the more traditional normative approaches, which focus on variables such as utility ('the greatest good for the greatest number'), procedural liberty (equal rights) or real income. The theory sees justice in terms of individual freedoms and its social correlates: the social policies, processes and mechanisms that allow individuals to lead the lives they would choose to lead, and that allow them the opportunity to influence and shape the decisions and choices that in turn shape their lives. Freedoms, Sen argues, provide an alternative and fuller foundation for individual and social justice (and see Box 1.6).

In other words, freedom is a principal determinant of individual initiative and social effectiveness. Greater freedom enhances the ability of people to help themselves, and also to influence the world, and these matters are central to the process of development. The concern related to what we may call 'agency', the agency aspect of the individual, goes to his definition of **agency** (1999: 20–21), which addresses not only poverty and inequality, but also the

---

Box 1.6 Amartya Sen on 'Freedoms and a freedom-centred perspective'

. . . a freedom-centred perspective has a generic similarity to the common concern with 'quality of life', which too concerns the way human life goes (perhaps even the choices one has) and not just the resources or incomes that a person commands (1999: 24). . . . Development (can be seen as) a process of expanding the real freedoms that people enjoy. In this approach, the expansion of freedom is the primary end and the principle means of development. They can be called respectively the 'constitutive role' and the 'instrumental role' in development. The constitutive role of freedom relates to the importance of substantive freedom in enriching human life. The substantive freedoms include elementary capabilities like starvation, undernourishment, escapable mortality and premature morbidity (1999: 36). . . . The instrumental role of freedom concerns the way different kinds of rights, opportunities and entitlements contribute to the expansion of human freedom in general, and thus to promoting development (1999: 37). . . . (Instrumental freedoms) contribute directly or indirectly, to the overall freedom people have to live the way that they would like to live (1999: 38).

Excerpts from Sen (1999) *Development as Freedom*

economic, structural and societal roots of *social exclusion*. Therefore the presence of agency allows individuals and groups to have a say in defining and addressing the inequalities that they do or may face, and moreover, this influence is both a right and an expectation within a society. A lack of agency, and thus the power for individuals or groups to inform the society's policies and agendas for addressing inequalities, limits individual and collective voice, and makes it more likely that the needs of such groups are systematically neglected and ignored so that in turn, these groups too are neglected and ignored. Further, at its most extreme, there may be such an overwhelming absence of agency that the needs and views of such groups are seen by the majority (explicitly or implicitly) as of so little importance that the groups exist and suffer on the margins of the society.

Capability deprivation, injustice and inequality

In Sen's theory, the expansion of freedom is viewed as both the primary end and the principal means of development (1999, p. 36). These are respectively the 'constitutive role' and the 'instrumental role' of freedom. The constitutive role of freedom refers to the importance of substantive freedom in enriching human life. The substantive freedoms include elementary capabilities like being able to avoid deprivations such as starvation, being literate and numerate, but also enjoying political participation and uncensored speech, etc. In this constitutive perspective, development involves expansion of these and other basic freedoms. Development is the process of expanding human freedoms.

This is distinct from the instrumental argument that these freedoms and rights may also be effective in *contributing* to economic progress. This instrumental connection is important as well, but the significance of the instrumental role of political freedom as a *means* to development does not in any way reduce the evaluative importance of freedom as an *end* of development. The effectiveness of freedom as an instrument lies in the fact that different kinds of freedom interrelate with one another, and freedom of one type may greatly help in advancing freedom of other types.

So, in any organisation interested in pursuing equality, it could be argued that the first stage is the recognition that inequalities and prejudice exist in relation to disadvantages based on, say, ethnicity, gender, disability and sexuality. However, if capabilities equality were to be pursued, the organisation would have to choose to eliminate these inequalities and prejudices *through the enhancement of employees' freedoms*, the workplace (meso and micro) equivalent to the societal (macro) development that Sen describes: in other words, an *organisational* form of development to enhance people's freedoms.

Equality of what?

The capabilities approach helps to answer the question often implied in the workplace equality literature: 'equality of what?' Should organisations pursue equality of opportunity, equality of outcomes, both? This theory contends that they should pursue equality of capabilities. And what does this mean specifically? The authors in this field, sensitive to the potential to 'impose' culturally biased, absolutist or 'colonial' definitions of particular capabilities, have defined capabilities in terms of the freedoms they *afford* individuals, rather than in terms of what they are (Nussbaum, 1999). So what does this mean? The dilemma here can be illustrated by an attempt to compare the situation of a poor black man in the USA with that of his equivalent in a poor country in the developing world. Both are clearly disadvantaged, albeit that the man in the USA is richer in absolute economic terms, literate, well fed, and adequately housed. For both men, it is their freedom to lead the lives that they would wish to lead that is the issue, and their inclusion or exclusion within their host societies.

Sen (1999) argues that capability equality is a primary feature of well-being (physical, economic, social and self-actualising). **Capability equality** concerns how a person can 'function', what a person can and wishes to do or be. From an ethical viewpoint, 'basic' capabilities can be associated with Aristotelian 'potentialities'. Put simply, we might regard capabilities as the gifts and talents that individuals possess in concert with factors such as education, training, legislation, policies and practices that allow these gifts and talents to be exercised: it is the *ensemble* that allows the gifts and talents to flourish and therefore, individuals and groups to have the potential to function fully within a society.

Sen argues that freedom consists in the expansion of the capabilities of persons to lead the kind of lives they value and have reason to value. He also makes the distinction between realised functioning (what a person actually does) and the capability set she has (her real opportunities). The two give different kinds of information: 'the former about the things a person does and the latter about the things a person is substantially free to do'.

The concept of capabilities is not an easy one, but there is a useful typology that helps us to get to the guts of the idea, developed by Martha Nussbaum (1999). Nussbaum's views on capabilities have been shaped through the avenue of her interest in women's development (Nussbaum and Glover, 1995; Nussbaum and Sen, 1995; Nussbaum, 1999). Like Sen, she agrees that societies limit the likelihood of full development and freedoms for all, if women are not permitted full and equal expression of capabilities and freedoms. She proposes three fundamental types of capabilities (Nussbaum, 1999):

- *Basic capabilities*: These refer to the innate abilities, the 'equipment' that individuals possess, that forms the basis for developing more advanced capabilities. Put another way, these are the innate gifts, talents and predispositions that people possess but may not have the opportunity to express or develop (e.g. an aptitude for working with numbers, a talent for writing, an aptitude for working with others).
- *Internal capabilities*: These are 'internal' or personal states of readiness to act or function. These may be secured through, for example, literacy, numeracy, education or training. In other words, individuals may have

developed levels of competence that potentially enable them to undertake a variety of roles, jobs or decisions.

- *Combined capabilities*: These can be defined as internal capabilities operating in combination with suitable external conditions, for example, laws within the society or structures within a public institution or work organisation. This can be referred to as the socio-political environment required to enable the person to function fully as he or she would wish to do. The ways in which it is possible to conceptualise environment, in a manner that allows us to clarify what organisations can shape or create to enhance this vital aspect of combined capabilities, will be addressed more fully on page 46 in discussing Sen's notion of instrumental freedoms.

Nussbaum writes further about combined capabilities in a critical definitional passage:

> To secure a capability in a person it is not sufficient to produce good internal states of readiness to act. It is necessary to prepare the material and institutional environment so that people are actually able to function . . . Capability is thus a demanding notion. In its focus on the environment of choice, it is highly attentive to the goal of functioning (but) . . . it does not push people into functioning: once the stage is fully set, the choice is theirs. (1999: 240)

Individual and collective agency

The notion of agency can thus be viewed as being of central importance within the capabilities approach. Sen uses the term agency in what he calls its 'older and grander' sense:

> an agent is someone who acts and brings about change, and whose achievements can be judged in terms of her own values and objectives, whether or not we assess them in terms of some external criteria as well. (1999: 18)

Capabilities theory is particularly concerned with the agency role of the individual as a member of society and as a participant in economic, social and political actions. This position on individual and collective agency implies the importance of the mechanism of social commitment at the individual, organisational and public policy levels in order for agency to become a reality.

Crucially, this agency cannot simply be taken for granted. Rather, it can only flourish if all three types of capabilities are present, if an enabling environment – combined capabilities – is present. This is illustrated in Nussbaum's example of the profound difference between fasting and starving. She writes: 'The person with plenty of food may always choose to fast, but there is a great difference between fasting and starving, and it is this difference that we wish to capture' (1999: 233). Or, another example:

> A person who has opportunities for play can always choose a workaholic

life; again, there is great difference between that chosen life and a life con-strained by insufficient maximum-hour protections and/or the 'double-day' that makes women unable to play in many parts of the world. (1999: 233)

Sen's discussion of the importance of women's 'well-being' as essential for agency to be exercised is illustrative here. Ensuring better treatment for women is essential, he argues, as a 'corrective' to discriminatory conditions, but a focus on 'rights aimed at the free agency of women' is also to be wel-comed in the overall desire to promote freedom and capability-equality. Thus ensuring well-being or a floor of protections for groups who have been the recipients of discrimination must come first, but once this is ascertained, members of these groups can collectively or individually become 'dynamic promoters of social transformations' that can alter their lives and the lives of others. This agency, according to Sen, is essential for the full achievement of freedom.

Instrumental freedoms: shaping the environment

The importance of the institutional environment, including the legal frame-work and policies and structures within an organisation, is highlighted in the notion of combined capabilities. Sen's concept of **instrumental freedoms** pro-vides another way of understanding what this enabling environment must contain (1999). These freedoms should be subject to systematic evaluation, Sen argues, and the effectiveness of any intervention should be assessed against the freedoms that it affords. Universal in nature and sensitive to cross-cultural concerns, Sen's five instrumental freedoms have great resonance and potential application for work organisations. They are:

- *Political freedoms*, e.g. civil rights, determining who should govern, free-dom of political expression and association, dialogue and critique, voting rights and participatory selection of legislators and executives; in work organisations these include freedom to join trades unions, other 'choice' and 'voice' mechanisms, access to decision-making power, or to what Nussbaum (1999) calls agenda-shaping; in short, agency expressed through political action.
- *Economic facilities*: opportunities to utilise economic resources; in organi-sations, these include fair wages and equal pay.
- *Social opportunities*: key examples of social opportunities are education and health care; parallels at workplace level are an organisation's duty of care, access to training, advancement, and to similar treatment in these areas.
- *Transparency guarantees*: these are concerned with the freedom to deal with one another under guarantees of disclosure and lucidity, as a basis for cre-ating demonstrable openness and trust; in work organisations, this is very important for 'felt fairness' – the 'rules of the game', e.g. how to progress

in the organisation, need to be commonly known and require transparency of action.

- *Protective security*: this concerns how social safety needs are addressed, in order that those in financial difficulty do not become marginalised from the society as a whole with their life chances systematically and dramatically reduced; at the organisational level, an organisation may choose to support its employees above what is provided through e.g. unemployment benefits, national minimum wage.

Sen regards fragmentation and concentration of effort on securing one freedom over another as undermining the necessary ensemble of instrumental freedoms. So for example, in a work context, having the opportunity of access to advancement (social opportunities) is compromised if the method of promotion is largely hidden and opaque to those from traditionally disadvantaged groups (as transparency guarantees are thus violated).

Explaining the relationship between agency, both collective and individual, and instrumental freedoms, Sen states that the freedom of agency that individuals have is inescapably qualified and constrained by the social, political and economic opportunities that are available to them. 'There is a deep complementarity between individual agency and social arrangements', he writes (1999: xii). He argues for an integrated analysis of economic, social and political activities, and says that institutions can be evaluated 'in terms of their contribution to enhancing and guaranteeing the substantive freedoms of individuals, seen as active agents of change rather than as passive recipients of dispensed benefits' (1999: xiii).

Implications of the capabilities approach for theorizing workplace equality

In our view, the work of Nussbaum and Sen creates the potential for a rich and deep understanding of workplace equality. The emphasis on agency and voice highlights the importance of the employee perspective, and the need not only for organisational equality initiatives to be fair, but also to be 'felt fair' by those targeted by the associated policies, initiatives and strategies.

Applying capabilities thinking, equality would clearly require that both procedural and distributive justice be present for '**felt fairness**' to be present (Figure 1.1). A high degree of distributive equality would need to be achieved for those who had not received this, for example groups of women who had been underpaid relative to men doing work of equal value. This is akin to the 'equal outcomes' of organisational equality literature. At the same time, the procedures used to determine outcomes would need to be viewed as fair, a defining characteristic of the enabling environment. Research has found that people view procedural justice as including notions such as a degree of control in the decision-making process, clearly part of Sen's instrumental freedoms.

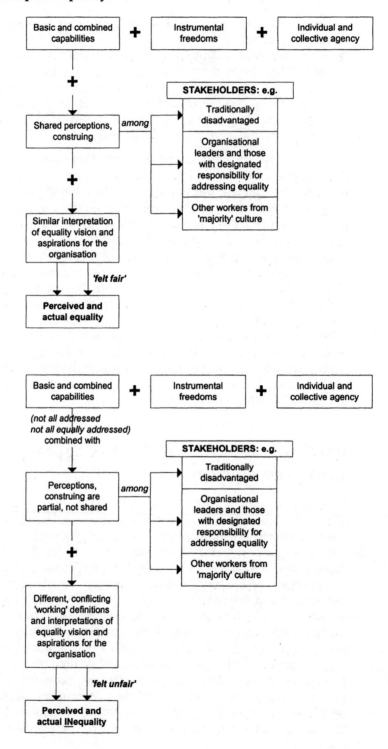

Figure 1.1 Schema outlining key aspects of capabilities equality

Again we see here the potential of capabilities theory to draw together the conceptual dichotomies that tend to characterise organisational equality literature. As a conception of equality based on human freedom and choice, the capabilities approach views freedom as both the ends and means of equality: outcomes *and* opportunities are important, agency *and* enabling environment are essential.

What are the implications of the capabilities approach for building a framework for workplace equality? Let us take a familiar example. A city-based organisation wishes to promote equality and fairness towards those from traditionally disadvantaged groups and recruit more from these groups into its organisation. It has 'multicultural' and inclusive imagery in its advertising, is a positive-action employer, and has developed EO fair recruitment and selection. But, new and existing staff either become, or remain, disenchanted with the 'seriousness' of the organisation towards these issues. There are many possible reasons, but applying the capabilities concept, the focus becomes:

- 'feels fair';
- 'feels unfair' – do I have 'agency'?
- what is the organisation really doing for me and for my aspirations?

Recently, an example appearing in the media which highlights these concerns is that of Coca-Cola (Cooper, 2000: 17). An organisation regarded by many as an exemplary equal opportunities employer, it recently was issued with a lawsuit by 1,500 of its African-American employees who claimed company-

---

Box 1.7 Bursting the bubble

In April 1999 four Coca-Cola workers brought a lawsuit against the company for racial discrimination, their lawyers applied for the suit to be given 'class' status, which would extend the action to cover 1,500 employees across the US. This will be decided later this year.

In December, the claimants' lawyers asked for four more names to be added to the suit on grounds that Douglas Ivester and his senior managers knew about 'company-wide discrimination against African-Americans' since 1995.

In a 1995 memo to Ivester, Carl Ware had stated that black employees felt they were seen as incapable of succeeding in certain fields and felt 'humiliated, ignored, overlooked or unacknowledged'.

Ware made eight recommendations, including that US managers' compensation be tied to diversity targets and that more ethnic minority staff be promoted to the position of executive assistant, a springboard for more senior

jobs. But the problems were not to be so easily solved.

In a 1997 letter to Ivester, Ingrid Saunders Jones, vice-president of corporate external affairs and a black American, complained that she had suffered from 'invisibility driven by chauvinism, power and, sometimes, pure and absolute disrespect'.

And a 1997 audit by the US Department of Labor found that Coke's managers were unclear about the firm's affirmative action programmes, and diversity goals were not part of performance reviews. The company had also failed to survey its staff to find gaps in recruitment and promotion procedures. Coke remedied these failures and the case was dropped.

It was not until last year that the firm established a diversity advisory council of the kind that already existed in other Fortune 1,000 companies.

Note: This table was reproduced with permission from People Management, June 2000.

wide discrimination and who felt 'humiliated, ignored, overlooked or unac-knowledged' by their employer. Crucially, a relatively sophisticated equality programme, to which setting diversity targets for managers and promoting more ethnic minority staff into senior jobs is central, does not appear to have substantially solved the difficulties.

The Coca-Cola example is an important one for a number of reasons, but not specifically because it is Coca-Cola. The company is no worse, indeed, is likely to be better, than many organisations in dealing with equality issues. One main interest in the context of this chapter is that it is African Americans who demographically are unlikely to reach real critical mass (e.g. near major-ity status) in work organisations in the USA or, indeed, in Europe, who have voiced their grievance. Secondly, the failure of equality initiatives at compa-nies like Coca-Cola can be viewed as a failure to achieve 'felt fair' equality. This is so despite a 'best practice' equality programme, and despite the fact that African Americans are one of the specific ethnic minority groups that has been targeted in US employment law and work organisations for nearly 50 years. But clearly Nussbaum's 'combined capabilities' are nonetheless not present.

Table 1.5 sets out the capabilities approach in contrast to the approaches to organisational equality that are discussed earlier in this chapter. We believe that a discussion of capabilities theory helps to draw out comparisons with the two 'dominant discourses' in organisational equality, EO and DM, and show where it can overcome some of their shortcomings.

How would a capabilities approach to workplace equality differ?

For a capabilities-based approach to workplace equality, the principle would be: 'What is a person actually able to do and to be?'

A capabilities approach would be centrally concerned with the things a per-son is substantially free to do, the real choices that they have. Methods would centre on facilitation of 'internal readiness' combined with creating a political and social climate to enable full use of one's capability set. For example, development of potential is important, but creating the environment in which that potential can be freely used, and enabling all members the opportunity to shape the official and unofficial rules of the game fully, what we might call full agency, are core organisational responsibilities if equality is to be advanced.

Sen's arguments about agency can perhaps be explained with the term 'full citizenship'. Second-class citizenship, where only a subset of capabilities or of freedoms, operates, where there is little or no real agency, is the basis for lim-ited and partial citizenship. This sows the seeds of an organisation that is not addressing inclusion, which thus may be seen as another important measure of addressing capabilities-based equality.

Further, the material reality of employees' frustrations of lack of real equal-ity and real opportunities, as highlighted by the Coca-Cola case, is at the heart of shaping a full understanding of what are the sources of inequality. In other

Table 1.5 Comparison of types of equality initiative From Kirton and Greene (2000: 102), based upon Miller 1996: 205, 506; modified for Gagnon and Cornelius, 2000: our additions are in bold

Approach	Principle	Strategy	Method	Type of equality
Liberal	Fair equal opportunity	Level playing field	Policy statement, equality-proof recruitment and selection procedures	Equality of opportunity
	Positive action	Assistance to disadvantaged social groups	Monitoring, pre-entry training, in-service training, special courses, elevate EO within management	Equality of opportunity
	Strong positive action	Give positive preference to certain groups	Family-friendly policies, improve access for disabled, make harassment a disciplinary offence	Moving towards equality of outcome
Radical	Positive discrimination	Proportional equal representation	Preferential selection, quotas	Equality of outcome
Managing diversity	Maximise individual potential	Use diversity to add value	Vision statement, organisation audit, business-related objectives, communication and accountability, change culture	Equality means profit aligned with organisational objectives*
Capabilities	**Human-dignity-centred equality: being able to be or do what one has reason to value**	**Establishment of (a) the five instrumental freedoms based upon (b) combined capabilities and (c) agency**	**Multi-method, domain, stakeholder interventions, through line-informed policy**	**Equality of choice and outcomes resulting from the 'free' exercise of freedoms**

* Note: The current authors view this definition as a narrow and unclear characterisation of diversity management.

words, employees' perceptions, feelings and construing provide vital information and measures (see Cornelius and Gagnon, 1999).

In order to more fully make the distinction between a capabilities-based equality and more familiar forms, the following propositions are suggested.

Proposition 1: Measurement is determined by method is determined by principle

The underlying equality principles determine the methods employed and in turn, the measurements that are regarded as fair and appropriate – 'principle determines method, and method determines measurement'.

How might one assess or measure equality initiatives? Consider where the emphasis would lie, on the basis of the Kirton and Greene table (based on Miller, 1996).

- For fair equal opportunities – the table states that the focus is on policies and fair recruitment and selection procedures.
- For positive action, the focus is on monitoring, 'special' training and management awareness.
- For strong positive action, the focus is on constraint-lifting policies and human resourcing policies for countering 'negative', discriminatory behaviour.
- For radical equal opportunities, the focus is on preferential selection and quotas.
- For managing diversity, the focus is on top and line management vision, measures and accountability, culture change and communication.

None of these focus specifically and explicitly either on what individuals or groups are free to do, or on what the organisation is doing to enable this freedom to become a reality. Nussbaum's combined capabilities concept would demand that attention be paid to (a) how the organisation was enabling internal capabilities, and (b) how the organisation was creating the conditions in which the internal capabilities could be fully and freely employed, in other words, combined capabilities. Further, what will feel fair and feel right is what materially affords personal dignity and freedom of choice.

Moreover, this may suggest that there is insufficient attention addressed to empowerment through agency, in order to facilitate agenda-shaping by traditionally disadvantaged groups. Even a more industrial relations-based pluralistic approach, which Miller does not outline in the table, which may afford more voice than some of the other approaches, may still underplay agency, and indeed, unions are as susceptible to inequality of opportunity as any other organisation. From this emerges our second proposition.

Proposition 2: Agency is central to 'felt fair' equality

Within capabilities-based equality, individual and collective voice and agency for the traditionally disadvantaged *is* central to shaping organisational equality action – it cannot be engaged with remotely, predominately top-down or 'by proxy'. Thus, again, within this framework, organisations and support institutions are duty-bound to create the mechanisms within which agency can be fully exercised. A contemporary account of the wants of the traditionally disadvantaged is imperative also, as there are limits to what the law and policy can deliver. First, this is because the law is often out of step or lags behind the material reality of people's lives: it gives largely historical accounts of inequality (Annas in Sen and Nussbaum, 1995) rather than contemporary and forward-looking accounts, as it is easier to see where equality and inequality have travelled than where they currently are. Second, such approaches are subject to what Nussbaum (1999) refers to generically (and in a gender-neutral way) as 'paternalism', largely developed within the mindset of those who are the powerful in a society or an organisation, rarely the traditionally disadvantaged.

Conclusions

Capabilities theory is about freedom for all; it is about the development, growth and actualisation of human beings through freedom. Through the concept of instrumental freedoms, it calls for a level playing field, as does traditional equal opportunities theory. However, the nature of this field is much more fundamental and profound than the procedural, rule-bound field – the 'artefacts of equality' – suggested by EO. Capabilities thinking does not negate other approaches to workplace equality; indeed, some of the instrumental freedoms are very much dependent on public policy and legislative measures rather than lying in the domain of the organisation. Emphases on legal protections against discrimination, or on diversity management approaches calling for systemic change, are in no way diluted by the capabilities approach. Indeed, the instrumental freedoms as a framework for an enabling environment encompasses much of this thinking. Yet in stressing each of these freedoms, and in calling for their common presence – one is of little real value without the others – capabilities theory assists in a fuller engagement with what is required in organisations if felt-fair equality is to be achieved.

There are several ways in which 'capabilities thinking' can deepen our understanding of workplace equality. These are outlined below.

1. Given its foundation in ethical theory, in particular in Sen's paradigm-altering ethical framework, the capabilities approach gets beyond dichotomous accounts of equality management by placing freedoms centre-stage as both the ends and the means of equality. The way that this approach is conceptualised returns to first principles, bringing a broader base than its antecedents; and therefore a broader and holistic theory providing the basis for a holistic application. It is a theory of justice, freedom and dignity. Looking at studies such as the Runnymede Trust survey, these are the central issues: do people feel they are being treated with dignity and trust?

2. Capabilities theory does not place into competition the rights of the individuals and the rights and needs of groups, particularly those that are traditionally disadvantaged. Both are to be sought, and are construed as of equal importance.

3. It does not place 'the system' above or below 'the individual' or 'the law and policy'. The position on combined capabilities makes it clear that it is not right to 'prioritise' a particular class of capability: capabilities and freedoms have to be addressed as an ensemble and are indivisible. In this sense, the approach demands a holistic and meta-systemic approach.

4. The Aristotelian basis to the theory, in an organisational context, affords

an ethical positioning for the importance of training and development as an important means by which individuals and their organisations can in practice become more virtuous. Overall, capabilities theory offers a position that is inherently developmental, more hopeful, and less fatalistic.

5. In so doing, however, the theory puts the onus on organisations as social entities to develop the whole; equality and freedom are not just about imposition of the law, but centre in the notion of development; in the possibility that organisations and people can change – a very important notion. This implies that the organisation is duty-bound to become more fully human.

6. Accountability is big in the capabilities approach, as witnessed in the arguments about information base. The interest in process (means) as well as ends, and the informal nature of much that perpetuates disadvantage, again suggests a need for measuring what matters, which goes well beyond, for example, density and hard measures of fairness.

7. Instrumental freedoms provide a basis for the development of individual and collective rights. Thus the capabilities approach to equality could potentially sit better than 'traditional' equality practice by extending the rights base (EO rather narrowly proscribes this, relatively speaking).

8. The importance of voice and agency suggests that (a) there should be mechanisms for individual voices to be heard but that also (b) collective voice must inform the equality agenda. This places employment relations in a central position, and suggests that trades unions and other employee groups need proactive strategies for facilitating the voices of those with least industrial muscle.

Text-based questions

1. What are the differences between equal opportunities and diversity management as approaches to equality of employees in organisations? How might these differences be reflected in practice in a workplace?

2. What have been some of the criticisms levelled at diversity management and how can these be answered?

3. What does it mean to say that thinking about organisational equality has been 'riddled with dichotomies'? What are some of these dichotomies?

4. What are the main arguments within Cockburn's 'long agenda' for workplace equality?

5. How does the capabilities approach differ from current ways of thinking about equality in organisations? What are its main components?

6. How does equality of capabilities differ from equality of opportunity?

7. What steps could an organisation take to promote and reflect the equality of capabilities of its members?

Library and assignment-based questions

1. Study the Annual Reports of a selection of FTSE 100 or Fortune 500 companies. What do these reports say about promoting equality of employees? Is there an indication of an Equal Opportunities or Diversity Management approach, or both? How are these described in the reports?
2. Analyse critically these companies' statements of equality and diversity of employees. How specific are they? How 'multi-domain' are they? To what extent do they show involvement of employees in the formulation and implementation of equality initiatives or strategies?
3. Study the Statistics Canada and US Census websites. What do they say about the reality of labour force diversity in North America?

Internet resources

Canadian Race Relations Foundation http://www.crr.ca/rt/

Chartered Institute of Personnel and Development, UK – this is the lead body on personnel issues in the UK – their People Management website has a number of case examples: www.peoplemanagement.co.uk

CocaCola http://www.coca-cola.com/

Commission for Racial Equality UK http://www.cre.gov.uk/

Department of Education and Employment UK http://www.dfes.gov.uk/

Equal Opportunities Commission UK http://www.eoc.org.uk/

European Union http://www.europa.eu.int/

Family Village: Global Community Diversity Resource, USA: http://familyvillage.wisc.edu/index.htmlx

HR Internet guide – a good source of a range of general information on HRM: www.hr-guide.com

Human Resources Development Canada: http://www.hrdc-drhc.gc.ca/common/acts.shtml

In Celebration of Diversity, USA: http://www.leveragingdiversity.com/

Littlewoods plc http://www.littlewoods.co.uk/corporate/index.htm

National Organisation on Disability, USA: http://www.nod.org

Ontario Equal Opportunities, Canada: http://www.equalopportunity.on.ca/

SeniorNet, USA: http://www.seniornet.org

Statistics Canada: http://www.statcan.ca/

The African-American Mosaic: A Library of Congress Resource Guide for the Study of Black History and Culture: http://lcweb.loc.gov/exhibits/african/afam001.html

The Diversity Training Group, Washington DC: www.diversitydtg.com

The Institute for Employment Studies, UK: www.employment-studies.co.uk

The Runnymede Trust http://www.runnymedetrust.org/

United Nations http://www.un.org/

University of Maryland Diversity Database: http://www.inform.umd.edu/EdRes/topic/diversity

US Census Bureau: http://www.census.gov

US Department of the Interior, Workforce Diversity website: http://www.doi.gov/diversity

Further reading

Cockburn, C (1989) Equal Opportunities: the long and short agenda. *Industrial Relations Journal*, Autumn, 213–225.

Dickens, L (1999) Beyond the business case: a three-pronged approach to equality management. *Human Resource Management Journal*, **9** (1), 9–19.

Dickens, L (2000) 'Still Wasting Resources? Equality in Employment' in S. Bach. and K. Sisson (eds) *Personnel Management: A Comprehensive Guide to Theory and Practice*, 3rd edn, Blackwell, Oxford.

Gagnon, S and Cornelius, N (2000) Re-examining workplace equality: the capabilities approach. *Human Resource Management Journal*, **10** (4), 68–87.

Kirton, G and Greene, AM (2000) *The Dynamics of Managing Diversity*, Butterworth Heinemann, Oxford.

Nussbaum, M (1999) Women and equality: The capabilities approach. *International Labour Review*, **138** (3), 227–245.

Sen, A (1992) *Inequality Re-Examined*, Harvard University Press, Cambridge, MA.

Sen, A (1999) *Development as Freedom*, Oxford University Press, Oxford.

Sen, A (2000) *Beyond Identity*, British Academy, London, http://www.britac. ac.uk/pubs/

Thomas, DA and Ely, RJ (1996) Making differences matter: a new paradigm for managing diversity. *Harvard Business Review*, September-October, 79–90.

References

Annas, J (1995) Women and the quality of life: Two Norms or One? in M Nussbaum and A Sen (eds) *The Quality of Life*, Oxford University Press, USA, 279–296.

Anonymous (1994) *Flexibility at Work in Europe*, Chartered Institute of Personnel and Development, London.

Anonymous (1997a) *Employment in Europe – 1997*, European Commission, Brussels.

Anonymous (1997b) *Labour Force Survey*, Department of Employment, HMSO, London.

Anonymous (1997c) *Labour Market Trends*, HMSO, London.

Anonymous (1999) *IRS Employment Trends*, IRS Review 691.

Anonymous (2001) *Monitoring for equality*, IRS, London, January, 4–13.

Anonymous (2000) People in the labour market, Eurostat Yearbook 2000, London.

Anonymous (2001) European Marketing data and statistics.

Barry, B and Bateman, TS (1996) A social trap analysis of the management of diversity, *Academy of Management Review*, **21** (3), 757–790.

Colgan, F and Ledwith, S (1996) in *Women in organisations: challenging gender politics*, Macmillan Business, London.

Cockburn, C (1989) Equal opportunities: the long and short agenda. *Industrial Relations Journal*, Autumn, 213–225.

Collinson, D, Knights, D and Collinson, M (1990) *Managing to Discriminate*, Routledge, London.

Cooper, C (2000) Coca-Cola loses its perfect harmony. *People Management*, 22 June, 16–17.

Cornelius, N (2000) *Human Resource Management: a managerial perspective*, International Thomson Publishing, London.

Cornelius, N and Gagnon, S (1999) From ethics 'by proxy' to ethics in action: new approaches to understanding HRM and ethics. *Business Ethics: A European Review*, **8** (4), 225–235.

Cornelius, N and Gooch, L (2001) Recruitment, selection and induction in a diverse and competitive environment, in N Cornelius (ed.) *Human Resource Management: a Managerial Perspective*, Thomson Learning, London.

Cornelius, N, Gooch, L and Todd, S (2000a) Managers leading diversity for business excellence. *Journal of General Management*, **25** (3), 67–79.

Cornelius, N, Gooch, L and Todd, S (2000b) Managing difference fairly: an integrated 'partnership' approach, in E Ogbonna and M Moon (eds) *Equality and diversity in employment*, Macmillan, London.

Dickens, L (2000) Still Wasting Resources? Equality in Employment, in S Bach and K Sisson (eds) *Personnel Management: A Comprehensive Guide to Theory and Practice*, 3rd edn, Blackwell, Oxford.

Ellis, C and Sonnenfeld, JA (1994) Diverse approaches to managing diversity. *Human Resource Management Journal*, **33** (1), 79–109.

Fineman, S, Gabriel, Y and Sims, D (2000) *Organising and Organisations*, Sage, London.

Flynn, G (1995) Do you have the right approach to diversity? *Personnel Journal*, October, 68–75.

Gentile, MC (ed.) (1994) *Differences that work: organisational excellence through diversity*, Harvard Business Review Books, Cambridge, USA.

Gagnon, S and Cornelius, N (2000) Re-examining workplace equality: the capabilities approach. *Human Resource Management Journal*, **10** (4), 68–87.

Greenberg, J (1987) A taxonomy of organisational justice theories. *Academy of Management Review*, **12**, 9–22.

Hackett, G (1988) 'Who'd be an Equal Opportunities manager? *Personnel Management*, April, 48–55, as cited in Dickens, L (2000) 'Still Wasting Resources? Equality in Employment' in S Bach and K Sisson (eds) *Personnel Management: Comprehensive Guide to Theory and Practice*, 3rd edn, Blackwell, Oxford.

Honderich, Ted (ed.) (1995) *Oxford Companion to Philosophy*, Oxford University Press, Oxford, 745.

Hopkins, WE, Sterkel-Powell, K and Hopkins, SA (1994) Training priorities for a diverse workforce. *Public Personnel Management*, **23** (3), 429–435.

Jenkins, R (1986) *Racism and recruitment: managers, organisations and equal opportunity in the labour market*, Cambridge University Press, Cambridge, as cited in Dickens, L (2000) 'Still Wasting Resources? Equality in Employment' in S Bach and K Sisson (eds) *Personnel Management: A Comprehensive Guide to Theory and Practice*, 3rd edn, Blackwell, Oxford.

Jewson, N and Mason, D (1986) 'The theory and practice of equal opportunities policies: liberal and radical approaches. *Sociological Review*, **2** (30), 307–334.

Johnson, WB and Packer, AH (1987) *Workforce 2000 and Workers for the 21st century*, The Hudson Institute, Indianapolis, USA.

Kaler, J (2001) Diversity, equality, morality, in M Moon and E Ogbonna (eds) *Equality, diversity and disadvantage in employment*, Palgrave (Macmillan), Basingstoke.

Kandola, B and Fullerton, J (1994) *Managing the mosaic: diversity in action*, Institute of Personnel and Development Books, London.

Kirton, G and Greene, AM (2000) *The Dynamics of Managing Diversity*, Butterworth Heinemann, Oxford.

Liff, S (1996) Two routes to managing diversity: individual differences of social group characteristics. *Employee Relations*, **19** (1), 11–26.

Liff, S (1999) Diversity and equal opportunities: room for a constructive compromise? *Human Resource Management Journal*, **9** (1), 65–75.

Liff, S and Wajcman, J (1996) 'Sameness' and 'difference' revisited: which way forward for equal opportunity initiatives? *Journal of Management Studies*, **33** (1), 79–95.

Liff, S and Cameron, I (1997) Changing Equality Cultures to Move Beyond Women's Problems. *Gender, Work and Organisation,* **4** (l) (Jan), 35–48.

Liff, S and Dickens, L (2000) Ethics and equality: reconciling false dilemmas, in D Winstanley and J Woodall (eds) *Ethical Issues in Contemporary Human Resource Management,* Macmillan Business, London.

Lorbiecki, A and Jack, G (1999) Critical turns in the evolution of diversity management. *Proceedings of the British Academy of Management Annual Conference 'Managing Diversity',* Manchester.

Miller, D (1996) Equality management – towards a materialist approach. *Gender, Work and Organisation,* **3** (4), 202–214.

Moon, M and Woolliams (1999) Developing insights into cross-cultural business ethics through an interactive computer model. Proceedings of the fourth Annual Conference of the UK Association of the European Business Ethics Network 'Business Ethics for the New Millennium', Christ Church College, Oxford.

Mueller, NL (1996) Wisconsin Power and Light's model diversity programme. *Training and Development,* March, 57–60.

Nussbaum, M (1999) Women and equality: The capabilities approach. *International Labour Review,* **138** (3), 227–245.

Nussbaum, M and Sen, A (eds) (1995) *The Quality of Life,* Oxford University Press, USA.

Nussbaum, M and Glover, J (eds) (1995) *Women, Culture and Development: a study of human capabilities,* Oxford University Press, USA.

Riccucci, NM (1997) Cultural diversity programs to prepare for work force 2000: what's gone wrong? *Public Personnel Management* **26** (1), Spring, 35–41.

Rosen, B and Lovelace, K (1994) Fitting square pegs into round holes. *Human Resource Magazine,* January, 86–93.

Sanglin-Grant, S and Schneider, R (2000) *Moving On Up? Racial equality and the corporate agenda.* Runnymede Trust, London.

Sen, A (1992) *Inequality Re-Examined,* Harvard University Press, Cambridge, MA.

Sen, A (1999) *Development as Freedom,* Oxford University Press, Oxford.

Sen, A (2000) *Beyond Identity,* British Academy, London.

Tackey, ND, Tamkin, P and Sheppard, E (2001) *The Problem of Minority Performance in Organisations,* Institute for Employment Studies, Eastbourne.

Thomas, Jr RR (1996) *Redefining diversity,* Amacom, New York.

Thomas, Jr RR (1993) From Affirmative Action to Affirming Diversity, in M Gentile (ed.) *Differences at Work,* Harvard Business Books, Cambridge, MA.

Trapp, R (1994) The uses of diversity. *Human Resources,* Autumn, 10–16.

Trompenaars, F and Hampden-Turner, C (1998) *Understanding Cultural Diversity in Business,* Irwin.

Vince, R and Booth, C (1996) *Equalities and Organisational Design,* Local Government Management Board Research Report, London.

Webb, J (1997) The politics of equal opportunities. *Gender, Work and Organisation,* **4** (3), 159–169.

Evaluating organisational readiness for change

2

Nigel Bassett-Jones

Chapter overview

This chapter aims to establish the 'business case' for the capabilities approach. In order to do this, it opens with an exploration of the literatures relating to the psychological contract and trust. The objective is to show that the psychological contract determines the nature of trust in organisations and that the climate of trust has culture-shaping implications. An exploration of conceptions of organisational justice follows. This discussion distinguishes between distributive and procedural justice and draws attention to the need for human resource policies and practices that recognise equality as a central tenet of effective management.

Organisations develop different approaches to Human Resource Management. These are shaped by the business models organisations adopt and the competitive strategies they deploy. Some approaches are more conducive to supporting and promoting combined capabilities than others; nevertheless, a business case can be made in each case. The practitioner and the effective manager, however, need to understand the 'soft issues' that shape culture in each context, in order to recognise the challenges ahead and the most suitable position from which to address them.

Learning objectives

As a result of studying this chapter you should be able to:

- determine the relationship between trust and the psychological contract;
- evaluate the links between trust, the psychological contract and conceptions of organisational justice;
- explain why the nature of trust has culture-shaping implications;
- ascertain why different approaches to the Strategic Human Resource Management (SHRM) results in different patterns of trust and alternative forms of psychological contract;
- reconcile the business case for equality of opportunity and diversity management having regard for the 'capabilities approach,' different business models and alternative approaches to SHRM.

Key words
psychological contract ● trust ● labour market contexts ●
organisational justice

Introduction

The centrality of equality to effective human resource management

In Chapter 1 three issues were identified as key ideas that were central to the development of this book. Firstly, the proposition that ethical and business case approaches to equality and diversity management are irreconcilable was rejected. Secondly, it was asserted that equality of opportunity in its broadest sense is an essential precondition for effective equality and diversity management. Finally, it was argued that for the management of change to be effective, equality of opportunity and management of diversity must be firmly rooted in an organisation-wide, strategic position, if far-reaching and sustainable equality is to become an organisational reality.

There is a need to take one step back before deciding on any approach to managing equality and diversity in the workplace. Otherwise, there is a danger that inappropriate priorities will be established. The discussions in Chapter 1 concerning the ethical underpinnings of different approaches to equality and diversity highlighted the range of perspectives that can be adopted. Much of this discussion was broadly academic and incorporated ethical interpretations and deconstruction of action. In fact, much equality and diversity policy and practice is just that – best practice, with perhaps a sense of moral purpose. Too often, there is no clearly articulated ethical position upon which organisational equality/diversity strategies and practices can be founded. We would argue that unless an organisation *is* able to articulate clearly the *ethical* basis upon which its approach to managing equality and diversity is grounded, there is a strong possibility that inconsistencies in strategy, policy development and practice will result. As we will show later, this can have implications for competitiveness in both product/service offers and also in labour market contexts.

In this chapter we will argue that equality and diversity management is potentially a vital source of competitive advantage in a modern economy. Before this potential can be realised, however, the implementation of effective strategies for the promotion of equality, in its broadest sense, represents an essential precondition.

Furthermore, we intend to argue that rather than being an adjunct to the effective management of human resources, equality management is central, in fact a *key* precondition, to effective human resource management.

Towards a structured evaluation of organisational readiness to address equality and diversity

The importance of 'core personnel' policy and practice

There are a number of themes that are core to this line of argument. First, we suggest that the evaluation of equal opportunities/diversity management needs to have a conceptually robust people management 'core' that informs practice. To this end, we propose that a review of human resource management/**personnel management** policy and practice is not only essential, but needs to be addressed at different levels. Indeed, in the following chapter, a more detailed account of evaluating 'core' personnel policy and practice is undertaken that underlines the importance of the line delivery of 'core' personnel practices for effective equality and diversity management.

Culture, climate and strategic human resource management

Commentators have noted the importance of **organisational climate** and culture in determining why equality and diversity do, or do not, take root (Bevan and Hayday, 1994; Patterson and West et al., 1997; Torrington and Hall, 1998). We will argue that **strategic human resource management** (SHRM) and HRM are key levers for culture and attitudinal change.

We argue that some of the key attributes that can be used to assess SHRM, namely the **psychological contract, trust,** conceptions of **organisational justice** and the labour market 'contexts' from which an organisation primarily seeks its employees, help us understand the character of organisations better. We believe that an appreciation of different organisational approaches to SHRM will help us to develop insights into organisations' readiness and 'predisposition' to respond to the challenges of managing equality and diversity. By understanding these aspects of the organisational landscape, practitioners can identify the most appropriate starting point from which to pursue equality and diversity issues.

Our approach implies that different types of intervention will be needed. They must be tailored to the character of an organisation. In other words, not only will the degree of preparedness for new or improved approaches to dealing with equality and diversity be different, but an understanding of fundamental and often hidden 'soft structural' differences is the key to managing effective change.

The potential for pursuing a 'capabilities approach'

One of the main implications of the arguments outlined in Chapter 1 is that the capabilities approach is a more 'employee centred' account of employee management. If the obligations of the employer are grounded in a clear ethical basis, made more transparent, and reinforced through 'freedoms' that create entitlements and transparency guarantees and that demand agency and voice, then the capabilities approach is more likely to create a demonstrably equitable and enabling environment.

It would, however, be both rash and imprudent to suggest that all organisations are likely to provide the ideal seedbed for capabilities-centred equality management. We begin, therefore, by posing thee key questions.

1. Do certain approaches to SHRM predispose organisations to embrace particular kinds of policies and strategies for managing equality?
2. Are some approaches more likely to provide a context within which capabilities equality is likely to take root and grow?
3. Drawing upon our current level of understanding of the psychological contract, trust, organisational justice and the labour market approach, can a capabilities perspective be used to evaluate different approaches to HRM?

The nature and role of the psychological contract

Rousseau and Shalk (2000) suggest that psychological contracts are subjective individual and cultural phenomena representing the belief systems of individual workers and employers regarding their mutual obligations. They suggest that the primary requirements for establishing a psychological contract are:

*   some degree of personal freedom to enter into a voluntary commitment;
*   some degree of social stability that is sufficient to support a joint agreement about the future that will enable each party to honour its commitment.

The literatures dealing with the psychological contract adopt one of three perspectives. A *universalist* approach argues that there is a group of general principles that when fully understood will result in generalisable best practice. This can be contrasted with the *contingency perspective*, which argues that the problems that organisations face will vary. Indeed Rousseau and Shalk (2000) suggest that the nature of the psychological contract is subject to influences at three levels, societal, government and the firm. A society's history, cultural values and norms in part shape, and are shaped by, legislative frameworks. Firms interact with the other two levels. Their policies and strategies are moulded and framed by their standing as domestic, multinational or global operations. Thus, a range of contingencies exists that renders any search for universal principles counter-productive. Finally, there is the *particularist approach*. This perspective, unlike the contingency view, sees the environment in which an organisation operates as so complex as to be unique. In other words, the range of contingencies is so large that organisations need to be studied in isolation, if the implications of all the variables are to be understood.

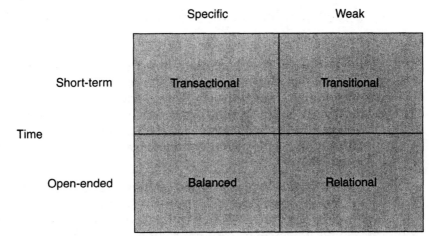

Figure 2.1 Typology of psychological contracts. *Source:* Rousseau, DM and Wade-Benzoni, KA (1994) Linking strategy and human resource practices. How employee and customer contracts are created. *Human Resource Management* (1994) **33**, 463–89. Copyright © 1994 John Wiley & Sons, Inc. Reproduced by permission of John Wiley & Sons, Inc.

In a bid to manage the emerging complexity, Rousseau and Wade-Benzoni (1994) developed a typology of psychological contracts. They argued that HRM practices shape the nature of the psychological contract that develops between employers and the employed and that it is as a result of experiencing HR practices that employees come to recognise and understand the terms and conditions of their employment. They posit that such practices operate on two dimensions: a time dimension that can be either short or long term, and a specificity dimension that determines the extent to which performance is specified and incorporated as a condition of employment. This resulted in the categorisation of four major types of psychological contract: the *relational*, the *transactional*, the *balanced* and the *transitional*.

The relational is open ended and non-specific. This means that employers seek high levels of commitment in return for substantial investments in training, development, employment stability and progression. The balanced contract also tends to be long term; however, it is more focused and prescriptive in defining performance requirements. The transactional contract, in contrast, is short term and tends to focus on specific performance standards in return for financial rewards. The transitional contract identifies what is effectively a breakdown in the psychological contract. It is normally associated with a period of transition from one type of contract to another. In this context, there is no assurance of employment continuity or any substantial specificity in respect of the standard of performance required.

Psychological contract as a key to organisational analysis

Interest in the psychological contract developed as research evidence accumulated that there is a link between employee motivation, commitment and organisational performance. Views, however, vary. Guest (1998) posits that the psychological contract presents us with an analytical nightmare that stands on a par with constructs such as flexibility, job satisfaction and commitment in evading precise 'operationalisations'. Sparrow (1998) in contrast, asserts that

> the psychological contract stands alongside other organisation-wide frames of analysis and constructs such as culture, climate and competencies. They are tools that in times of high uncertainty, help practitioners and researchers capture complex phenomena, discriminate between organisations and serve as a basis for predicting individual behaviour.

Sparrow (1996, 1998) has identified a range of contractual stances amongst employees, including the 'frustratedly mobile', 'still ambitious', 'passively flexible', 'guidance seekers', 'don't push me too fast', 'just pay me more' and 'buy-me-outers'. All could exist within a single department of an organisation. The variety is further compounded by changes in career anchors over the working life cycle. Sparrow poses the question, 'are then the consequences of this renewed diversity in psychological contracts manageable through HRM policies and practices?'. Citing the work of Herriot, Manning and Kidd (1997) who examined the perceived obligations of a matched set of 184 managers and 184 employees, he concludes that they are. Success, he asserts, relies on managing the content items of the contract. We endorse this position.

Psychological contract and employer and employee expectations

In the context of the United Kingdom, Herriot *et al.* (1997) found that employers had six and employees twelve constructs, which together captured the most common perceptions of mutual obligation.

Employers expected employees to:

1. work contracted hours;
2. do a quality piece of work;
3. deal honestly with clients;
4. be loyal and guard the organisation's reputation;
5. treat property carefully;
6. be flexible and go beyond the job description.

Employees expected employers to:

1. ensure fairness in selection, appraisal and promotion and redundancy procedures;

2. provide justice, fairness and consistency in the application of rules and disciplinary procedures;
3. provide equitable pay in relation to market values across the organisation;
4. be fair in the allocation of benefits;
5. provide adequate induction and training;
6. allow time off to meet personal and family needs;
7. consult and communicate on matters that affect them;
8. interfere minimally with employees in terms of how they do the job;
9. act in a personally supportive way to employees;
10. recognise and reward special contribution or long service;
11. provide a safe and congenial work environment;
12. provide what security they can.

A refined working definition of the psychological contract

Having regard for these perspectives, in the context of this chapter, we define the psychological contract as a set of perceptions and beliefs about the nature of the employment relationship. These constitute a set of interlocking responsibilities perceived by each of the parties as constituting a 'fair deal'. From the perspective of an individual manager and employee, the contract can exist at two levels. At the meta level, HR subsystems provide a framework of 'hygiene', rather than 'motivating' factors, that define the limits of discretion managers have in their dealings with individual members of staff. These subsystems can have a negative impact on employee behaviour in respect of **voice**, motivation and exit. They also determine the extent to which the employment relationship is perceived to be 'arm's length' or 'obligational' in nature. There is, however, another level at which the contract operates. It is defined by the nature of the relationship between individual managers and their staff. This relationship provides the foundation for *cognition- or affect-based trust* (see Table 2.1). To a large degree, it also determines the extent to which an employee experiences a *positive* motivational dimension in the psychological contract.

As Sparrow (1998) suggests, employers can improve the level and quality of trust by attending to the basic and transactional constituents of the psychological contract. It is to the issue of trust that we turn next.

The nature and role of different types of trust in shaping the psychological contract

Conceptualisations of trust

Organisations do not have perceptions: people do. So, when an employer/employee–managerial consensus is built around 'the deal', an organisational view can be said to operate. The nature of the specific employment relationship and each party's perception of its own obligations, as Guest (1998) has suggested, is influenced by the degree to which each party perceives the 'deal' to be fair and by the extent to which there is confidence that the other party will deliver.

Trust, therefore, is generally perceived to reflect the degree to which one party feels that it can rely upon the other to deliver. Fukayama (1995) likened trust to oil that lubricates a modern economy by reducing transaction costs. It is an output that is created as a result of a sustained period during which the parties to a psychological contract each perceive that the other has discharged its obligations. This has led some writers (Ghoshal and Bartlett, 1998; Thompson, 1998) to assert that *trust is a form of social capital that can be viewed as a firm specific strategic asset*. The psychological contract, therefore, is seen as the vehicle through which the trust relationship is created and upon which employee commitment can be developed.

The literatures on trust can be distinguished by the extent to which they stress an inter-organisational, intra-organisational or interpersonal bias. Whatever approach is adopted, writers present their ideas in terms of a continuum. They may compare *short-term legalistic instrumentalism* with *longer-term symbiosis* or they may adopt a more *psychological perspective*. The efforts of different writers in the field are summarised in Table 2.1.

These different conceptions of trust are of value when considering the nature and role of the psychological contract in the context of different HR subsystems.

The relationship between types of trust and types of psychological contract

Cognition and affect-based trust will be relevant in the context of employee appraisal and development. It is more likely that an employee will go the extra mile for a manager who is liked and trusted, and conversely, a manager who likes and trusts an employee is more likely to encourage his or her development. The *relational* versus *transactional contract* might help us to understand different approaches to recruitment and selection.

A relational psychological contract will be fostered amongst employees recruited to work in the operational core of a business, whilst a transactional psychological contract will pertain when recruiting temporary staff or employees who will work on the periphery of the organisation.

Employee relations is concerned primarily with individual and collective compliance. Employee discipline and the resolution of individual and collective grievance tend to be its primary focus. In consequence, transactional approaches that emphasise and compare short-term instrumental strategies with relational approaches that stress loyalty, security and trust tend to dominate. Crucially, the preoccupation with compliance within the field ensures that in this context the nature of the psychological contract has a culture-shap-

Low ——————————————————————————————————————→ High

		Low		High
Inter-organisational	Lewis and Weigart (1985)[i] Gulatti (1995)[ii]	*Deterence-based trust* Utilitarian and instrumental based on a belief that the other party fears loss of reputation or future business		*Knowledge-based trust* Founded on experience of previous dealings
	Sako (1992)	*Arms-length-contract relationship* Discrete economic transactions founded upon specific agreements		*Obligation-contract relationship* Predicted on a strong psychological contract of mutual reciprocation built up over time
	Barney and Hansen(1994)[iii]	*Weak* exists where there are limited possibilities for opportunism or moral hazard	*Semi-strong* created through mechanisms of governance and regulation	*Strong* emerges in situations where there are real vulnerabilities
	Williamson (1993)[iv]	*Calculative* based on an assessment of risk	*Institutional* social and organisational contexts in which psychological contracts become embedded	*Personal* only justified in exceptional situations
	Lewis and Weigart (1985)	*Cognition-based trust* Founded on perceptions and beliefs about colleague and peer reliability		*Affect/Emotion-based trust* Founded upon a reciprocal interpersonal liking, care and concern
Intra-organisational/ interpersonal	Rousseau and Wade-Benzoni (1994)	*Transactional* Short-term, instrumental change		*Relational* Long-term, complex, high trust

[i] Lewis, JD and Weigart, A, Trust as a social reality. *Social Forces, 63,* 1985
[ii] Ibid
[iii] Ibid
[iv] Williamson, OE, Calculativeness, trust and economic organisation. *Journal of Law and Economics 36,* April 1993

ing role. *Conceptions of the psychological contract, therefore, are* fundamental *in shaping organisational approaches and policies in relation to equality of opportunity and the management of diversity.* Before we can explore these, however, we must first consider the implications of conceptions of organisational justice in sustaining or changing the nature of the psychological contract. This will provide us with a secure foundation upon which we can proceed to examine the central role of strategic human resource management (SHRM) in delivering 'felt fair' equality upon which effective diversity management must be founded.

Conceptions of organisational justice

Dualistic (utilitarian/Kantian) illustrations of differences in employer/employee perceptions

Greenberg (1990) was the first to articulate the idea that a conception of organisational justice could be embedded in a descriptive rather than the prescriptive tradition of moral philosophy. He used the term to categorise theories of social and interpersonal fairness as they were applied in the context of organisational behaviour.

Historically, employer orientations to principles of equality have tended to be influenced by business case arguments that are rooted in utilitarianism. It is largely as a consequence of this that exponents of equality of opportunity have viewed business case arguments with suspicion. One of the problems with the utilitarian position is that it never really offered any principles of justice that extended beyond the basic idea that everyone's happiness or preferences, depending on the form of utilitarianism, counted equally. Employees, the literatures suggest, are strongly drawn to conceptions of organisational justice.

The nature and role of distributive justice

Briefly, the literatures dealing with conceptions of organisational justice can be divided into three strands. The oldest relates to distributive justice, and is founded on the ideas developed by the moral philosopher John Rawls. The other two are dimensions of procedural justice that we will consider later.

Rawls (1971) challenged the principle of maximising utility through his notion of distributive justice. He postulated that individuals founding an imaginary new society would not seek to maximise overall utility if they were required to choose principles of justice from behind a 'veil of ignorance' that prevented them from knowing what their own position in society would be. Instead, they would opt for the maximum amount of liberty compatible with the like liberty for others. They would also seek to maximise the welfare of those at the lower levels of society.

In the organisational context these ideas translate into a view that if individuals do not know what position they might ultimately hold, they will want equality of access to opportunity and the same degree of liberty to pursue their career and/or lifestyle aspirations as everyone else.

Rawls' speculation cannot be tested in the real world; however, his propositions have been tested in the laboratory (Lossowski, Tyszka and Okrasa, 1991; Frohlich, Oppenheimer and Eavy, 1987). Using Polish undergraduates to undertake an experimental task, Lossowski *et al.* required the students to agree, as a group, on a rule for payment, under which some individuals could be paid more than others. Most groups were able to agree on a payment framework. Thereafter, individuals were assigned to their payment condition by lot. Whereas Rawls had posited that individuals would seek to maximise minimum income, the subjects selected a distribution principle that maximised the average income whilst also maintaining a base level for all, thereby retaining a minimum income for those who would be worst off. Frolich *et al.*, using American and Canadian subjects, achieved similar results. The implication of these findings suggest that Rawls' conception of distributive justice is a valid proposition in an organisational context. When individuals are unable to determine what outcomes they will enjoy, they will engineer a framework that *will ensure their own well-being, as well as everyone else's.*

Cooper and Robertson (2001), drawing upon an extensive review of the literatures, have suggested that when making allocation decisions in respect of economic resources, groups either adopt a rule of equity that is designed to ensure *equality*, or pursue an instrumental orientation and reward on principles of *equity*. The former represents a normative position that is designed to maintain harmony, whilst the latter is a utilitarian position that aims to stimulate performance. Their choice in selecting allocation rules appears to be a function of cultural characteristics. Citing Greenberg and Cohen (1982), Kabanoff (1991), Skita and Tetlock (1992) and James (1993), they suggest that people in North American organisations are predisposed to choose reward systems that are based upon principles of equity that are founded upon merit, whereas the Chinese (Greenberg, 1982) are predisposed to seek group harmony and, therefore, choose equality criteria when making reward allocations.

Conceptions of procedural justice

Whilst distributive justice has, as its primary concern, the 'ends' of social exchange, procedural justice focuses on the 'means' by which the ends are achieved (Cooper and Robertson, 2001). They go on to suggest that the study of procedural justice in the organisational context has been a growing source of interest to students of organisational behaviour because high correlations with desirable organisational outcomes have been identified. Studies have shown that procedures that are perceived as fair have made individuals more tolerant in accepting disciplinary action (Ball, Trevino and Simms, 1994), smoking bans (Greenberg, 1994) and pay systems (Miceli, 1993; Miceli and Lane, 1991). Citing Lind (1995), Tyler and Dawes (1993) and Tyler and Lind (1992), they assert that people are accepting of organisational decisions when they perceive that they have been derived from a procedurally just process, even though they may not be benificiaries of the process. They also foundthat employees are more inclined to cooperate with those exercising authority in the implementation of the decisions even when they did not stand to gain.

Greenberg (1990) established that people are more inclined to steal from their employer when they perceived themselves to be the victims of a pay-cut derived from unfair processes. More importantly, Tyler and Lind (1992) found that employee experiences of procedural fairness shaped employee perceptions of the organisation and of the employment relationship. This influenced loyalty to the organisation as well as levels of employee motivation and commitment.

Levanthal (1976, 1980) and Levanthal, Karuza and Fry (1980) have identified six criteria through which procedures come to be perceived as fair. They suggest that consistency, freedom from bias, accuracy, provision for adjustment to correct errors, representation of relevant interests and consistency with prevailing ethical standards provide the foundations for effective procedural justice.

In evaluating fairness, people appear to be sensitive to two factors. Greenberg (1993) identified what he called structural and social determinants. Structural determinants relate to factors in the environmental context in which interactions occur and to the extent to which reward allocations are determined by formal organisational processes. Social determinants focus on the quality of interpersonal treatment that people experience when dealing with those in authority. Bies and Moag (1986) have defined this process as **interactional justice**.

Because of the difficulty in distinguishing between the effects of formal procedures and the nature of interpersonal interactions arising in the context of those procedures, some writers, including Konovsky and Cropanzano (1991) and Clemmer (1993), have suggested that it is counter-productive to separate

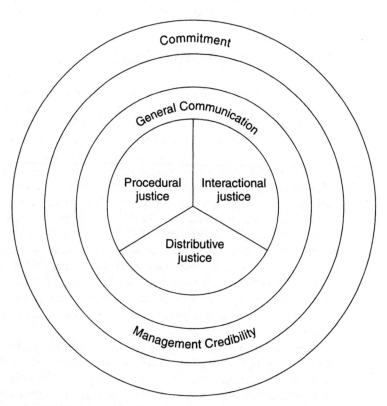

Figure 2.2   A model of organisational justice. *Source:* Thornhill and Saunders, 2000

them. The result is that some researchers now regard interactional justice as a social dimension of procedural fairness. Their attention has been drawn instead to another distinction, that of social sensitivity and accessibility. The former focuses on how conceptions of fairness are influenced by the way in which people perceive that they have been treated. In a study of a coal mine dispute, conducted by Shapiro and Brett (1993), adjudicators who demonstrated high degrees of knowledge, impartiality and a sensitivity to the feelings of the aggrieved and to their concerns were perceived to have been fair in resolving the grievance. Leugh, Chiu and Au (1993) attained similar results in a study of a Hong Kong strike. These findings support the view that perceptions of fairness are influenced by the way in which those who have been tasked with exercising judgement do so in a socially sensitive way. It also appears that there is evidence of cross-cultural consistency. A second variable, however, must also be present, namely that the appellants must have access to information about the outcomes to be determined that are deemed to be relevant (Daley and Geyer, 1994, 1995; Konovsky and Folger, 1991; Schaubroeck, May and Brown, 1994).

Whilst some writers have rejected the concept of interactional justice, because of the problems associated with separating structural and social determinants, others, such as Thornhill and Saunders (2000), have preserved the distinction. In so doing, they have drawn the different conceptions of organisational justice into a framework that helps us to understand how employee motivation and commitment are influenced by different conceptions of organisational justice. Their framework is shown in Figure 2.2.

Why do procedures matter?

Cooper and Robertson (2001) pose the question, why do procedures matter? In seeking an answer, they draw a distinction between the *instrumental model*, which states that individuals value procedural justice for instrumental reasons, and the *relational model*. The latter posits that individuals join groups for instrumental reasons; however, their purpose may not be to seek material gain. Social status, self-esteem and a need to belong can also be powerful motivators in providing individuals with a sense of personal worth. Drawing on the work of Tyler (1989, 1990), they suggest that individuals have three relational preoccupations. These concern neutrality, trust and standing, because these factors influence an individual's sense of dignity and worth. A neutral arbiter is someone who is free of bias. Trust exists to the extent that people believe that an arbiter will act in a fair and unbiased manner, whilst standing is conveyed by the respect shown towards an appellant by those tasked with making a decision. Studies have shown that perceptions of procedural fairness are enhanced when the neutrality, trust and standing dimensions of the relational model have been observed (Tyler and Lind, 1992; Tyler, 1990; Lind *et al.*, 1993). According to Cooper and Robertson (2001), procedures matter because perceptions of procedural fairness are developed as a result of both instrumental considerations associated with the magnitude of the economic consequences and voice in the process, and by relational considerations associated with perceptions of neutrality, trust and standing. Citing research conducted by Brockner, Tyle and Cooper-Schneider (1992) they suggest that there is a clear relationship between employee commitment and procedural justice and that where there are violations, those demonstrating a historically high level of commitment tend to be the ones that are most offended by any perceived violation. When employee commitment is low, however, the effects on commitment arising from perceptions of poor procedural justice tend to be lower.

The implications of distributive and procedural justice in the employment context

According to Greenberg (1990), inconsistencies in distributive and procedural justice produce different consequences. Distributive justice is linked with outcome satisfaction, whilst procedural justice influences how people perceive the system itself. Confidence in organisational systems has been found to be a central factor in ensuring employee trust in management and willingness to remain loyal to organisations (Lind, 1995; Tyler and Degoey, 1995). These results hold good even when, for example, pay decisions go against employees (Schaubroeck *et al.*, 1994; McFarlin and Sweeney, 1992). This has prompted researchers to suggest the existence of a two-factor model (Tyler, 1990; Tyler and Lind, 1992). Others have suggested that the relationship between the two forms of justice interact and may vary over time (see Lowe and Vadanovich, 1995). In evaluating the effect of the interaction, Brockner and Siegel (1995) argue that rather than procedures interacting with outcomes, the acceptance of outcomes is significantly influenced by levels of trust and that it is the perception of the fairness of procedures that influences the levels of trust.

An evaluation of the research on organisational justice and its links with HRM

What value is there in studying organisational justice? Greenberg (1993, 1996), argues that an understanding of the principles that underlie perceptions of organisational justice should inform *all aspects* of strategic HRM. He also asserts that context-specific studies are vital in aiding our understanding of organisational behaviour. An understanding of how fairness is perceived in different contexts is vital in facilitating and finessing our understanding of the concept. By drawing together results from different contexts, we are able to evaluate the extent to which specific principles can be generalised. A wide range of studies primarily, but not exclusively, conducted in the USA, have highlighted that perceptions of organisational justice can be influential in determining the success and effectiveness of a range of HR activities. These include recruitment and selection, layoffs, informal conflict resolution and employee theft, as well as the successful implementation of new strategic business initiatives.

Recruitment and selection

Selection fairness has long been the subject of scrutiny. Perceived injustice, research suggests, results in negative organisational outcomes that include a reluctance to accept job offers, poor work attitudes and lower job performance (Gilliland, 1993; Singer, 1992, 1993). The tools deployed in the selection process, such as personality tests (Ambrose and Rosse, 1993; Rosse, Miller and Stecher, 1994; Rynes and Connerley 1993), aptitude tests (Kluger and Rothstein, 1993; Rosse, Miller and Stecher, 1994), interviews (Rynnes and Connerley, 1993; Singer, 1992, 1993; Latham and Finnegan, 1993), assessment centres (Gilliland, 1993; Singer, 1993) and the taking up of references (Rynes and Connerley, 1993), have each been the subject of scrutiny. Employee concerns in respect of perceptions of procedural fairness have emerged in every case.

Layoffs

Studies have looked at both the victims and the survivors. Victim studies have highlighted that their perception of the fairness of the selection process was a strong predictor of how the company was perceived and the extent to which victims would call for legislative protection (Brockner, 1994; Brockner and Greenberg, 1990).

Survivor studies also highlight concerns for procedural justice. Brockner and Greenberg (1990) found that when the causes of the layoff were fully explained, along with the reasons for selection, survivors felt less guilt and perceived the organisation more positively.

Conflict resolution

An important management function involves resolving conflict between employees. The success of the process and the willingness of the protagonists to accept a manager's judgement has been found to correlate with their perceptions of the manager's even-handedness in dealing with the situation and the amount of voice that the manager permitted (Cropanzano, Aguinis, Schminke and Denham, 1996; Elangovan, 1995). Similar results were found in a Turkish study undertaken by Kozan and Itler (1994). Unfortunately, whilst employees value impartiality, transparency and voice, studies have found that many managers tend to favour autocratic solutions to conflict situations (Karambayya, Brett and Lytle, 1992).

Employee theft

In several empirical studies, Greenberg (1990, 1997) and Greenberg and Scott (1996) showed that when employees experience inequitable treatment, in line with Adams' (1995) prediction, they will often seek to re-establish equity through theft, thereby redressing their grievances.

New strategic business initiatives

Earlier, we suggested that employee acceptance of managerial authority is influenced by the extent to which employees recognise the existence of due process and perceive the process to be fair. Several studies have suggested that when organisations implement strategies for change, employee willingness to accept change is influenced positively, to the extent that the process is executed having regard for procedural justice. Positive perceptions have been found to result in higher levels of trust, commitment and outcome satisfaction (Kim and Maubourne, 1991, 1993; Korsgard, Schweiger and Sapienza, 1995).

Drawing the links between the psychological contract, trust and organisational justice together

As we have shown, studies across the spectrum of HR activity draw attention to the need to recognise the significance that organisational justice plays in shaping employee attitudes to their managers and to their employing organisations. An understanding of organisational justice also helps to explain employee preoccupations with justice and fairness articulated in Herriot's list of employee expectations in respect of the psychological contract and the different types of trust that develop. Managerial behaviours that infringe the principles of distributive and procedural justice, and ignore the tenets of due process, transparency and voice, have significant consequences. Once entrained, these consequences have to be managed. They create dynamics that shape future organisational outcomes.

Our aim in this section has been to demonstrate the fragile nature of the psychological contract and the critical role that perceptions of organisational justice play in either reinforcing or changing the nature of trust in organisations upon which the psychological contract is founded. We have also argued that HRM subsystems create the essential hygiene factors that influence employee voice, motivation and exit. Internal alignment between HR subsystems is important in delivering consistent reinforcing messages concerning the status of the psychological contract. HR practice, however, is delivered through line managers. Their behaviours to a large extent shape employee perceptions of organisational justice. We have seen that conceptions of distributive justice play an important role in shaping employee expectations in respect of both equality and equity and that the emphasis can vary according to cultural context. Conceptions of procedural justice, in contrast, appear to manifest less cultural variability and play a fundamental role in the delivery of 'felt fair' outcomes.

Now that we have reviewed the linkages between trust, the psychological contract, organisational justice and HRM, we are in a position to address the three questions outlined in the introduction to this chapter.

The central role of strategic human resource management (SHRM)

Strategic human resource management, trust, the psychological contract and 'felt-fair' equality

Both SHRM and business objectives have a controversial connotation in an equality context, as discussed in the Introduction and in the previous chapter: indeed, any use of the language of management in this context will be controversial. It is important, therefore, to be clear about how and in what context we are using each term.

The main thrust of the argument that we will develop in this section will be that effective strategic human resource management (SHRM) must be founded upon internal consistency and fit between human resource (HR) subsystems on the one hand and the alignment between SHRM and 'business objectives' on the other. We propose that *the primary role of SHRM* is to *create* and *sustain an appropriate, 'felt fair' psychological contract* between the employer and the employed. If the former is to optimise its 'return' on its human capital base, 'felt fair' considerations amongst all the parties must be a key point of reference for the creation of any effective psychological contract. This implies that HR subsystems operating in the areas of recruitment, selection, development, reward and separation all contribute to the creation of such a contract and, as a collectivity, represent HRM in action. The policies and philosophies that determine their shape and focus constitute the field of study that we define as SHRM. Put another way, we believe that *equality needs to reside at the core of SHRM policy and practice*, in order for both not only genuinely to operate effectively but, more crucially, to ensure their sustainability and impact. By drawing upon our current level of understanding of the psychological contract, trust, organisational justice and the labour market approach, we propose to explore whether the capabilities perspective can be used to evaluate different approaches to HRM. It is our contention that certain approaches to SHRM predispose organisations to embrace particular kinds of policies and strategies for managing equality and that some approaches are more likely to provide a context within which capabilities equality can take root.

We begin with the suggestion that an essential precondition in creating a business case for equality of opportunity and diversity management is to establish a clear nexus between SHRM and business performance. Once again, the use of the term performance is a controversial one in this context, so further elaboration will help to contextualise its specific use here.

SHRM and its links to organisational effectiveness?

Is there a link between organisational performance and strategic human resource management? Scholars working in the field have been preoccupied with this question ever since the assumptions underpinning the strategic marketing and strategic conflict views of strategy began to be challenged. Teece, Pisano and Shuen (1997) have traced the emergence of the resource-based view and the way in which the focus has shifted in favour of the dynamic capabilities perspective. This transition has at its core the recognition that in the information economy it is the human resource and the way it is deployed that provides the distinctive capabilities that form the basis of a defining competitive advantage (Prahalad and Hamel, 1990; Hamel and Prahalad, 1994). One of the key strands of the literatures on dynamic capability has examined the contribution of HRM to competitiveness. Research has tended to concentrate in two areas. Initially, attention focused on the effect of HR subsystems on 'hard' measures: aspects of business performance that included employee motivation and productivity, labour turnover, wastage rates, quality standards and so forth. More recently, attention has shifted to overall organisational performance (Arthur, 1994; Macduffie, 1995; Huselid, 1995).

In a comprehensive review of the literatures, Bamberger and Meshoulam (2000) concluded that there was substantial evidence to support the proposition that consistency and internal fit between HR subsystems has a positive impact on employee motivation and, therefore, does result in improvements in a range of internal indicators. They argue:

> firstly HR strategy is likely to shape the human capital base of the firm by means of policies and practices having to do with recruitment and selection, as well as training and development. Second, HR strategy is likely to influence the degree to which the firm is able to exploit this human capital base in terms of employee motivation to stay with the firm and perform; this by means of policies and practices having to do with career development and advancement, compensation, and commitment-building benefits (e.g., employee assistance). Third, HR strategy can have an impact on firm performance by influencing the degree to which talented and motivated employees are provided with the job related opportunities and discretion to contribute.

They also found compelling links in the literatures between SHRM and business performance. Unfortunately, the wide diversity of methodology and a lack of consensus within the research community as to what constitutes an appropriate set of measures have, they suggest, given rise to complications.

The result is that there is a range of views on the matter that tend to cluster around *universalistic, contingency* or *configurational* explanations. These different approaches have made the overall picture very complex.

Citing Osterman (1995), Pfeffer (1994) and Terpestra and Rozell (1993) (p. 175), they assert that *universalists* perceive *the effects of high performance HR work practices as additive. Contingency theorists* in contrast, argue that to have a significant positive impact on firm performance, *HR practice must be aligned with the organisation's overall business strategy* (Jackson and Schuller, 1995; Baird and Meshoulam, 1988). *Configurational theorists* (Doty, Glick and Huber, 1993; Meyer, Tsui and Hinings, 1993) explain the link by emphasising *the importance of internal coherence between individual HR practices.* By adopting a position of equafinality, they assert that combinations of HR practice will be more powerful in generating improvements to the bottom line than the sum effect of individual work practices.

In summary, therefore, whilst different opinions remain, the existence of a clear link between SHRM and business performance is no longer a source of major contention, and as a result the position of dynamic capability as a significant strand of strategic thought is now becoming established.

Ways of categorising strategic human resource management

Various attempts have been made to develop typologies that categorise different approaches to HR strategy formulation. Huselid and Becker (1997) have suggested that HR practices cluster around two core HR strategies, **cost reduction mass production** versus high commitment flexible production. Lepak and Snell (1999), in a study of 153 firms operating in 97 industries, developed a more comprehensive framework consisting of four different types of strategy. Their approach not only distinguished between a process and output orientation but also the degree to which an organisation relies upon either an internal or external labour market.

Archetypes of strategic human resource management

Drawing on this earlier work, Bamberger and Meshoulam (2000) have produced a model that offers four distinctive approaches to HR strategy formulation (see Figure 2.3). On the vertical axis, strategies are distinguished by the extent to which organisations are primarily focused either on outputs that are difficult to define and specify, or on processes that can be measured, such as customer satisfaction and quality. The horizontal axis is used to identify the extent to which HR strategy relies upon either an internal or external labour market for skills and expertise.

The resulting 2 × 2 matrix provides four theoretically alternative forms of HR strategy: *'commitment'*, characterised by a reliance on the internal labour market and an output orientation; *'free agent'*, distinguished by its reliance on the external labour market and an output orientation; *'paternalism'*, which focuses on processes, whilst developing and exploiting an internal labour market; and the *'secondary strategy'*, which has a process emphasis and an external labour market orientation.

Hybrid strategies are also identified. They are founded upon more than one approach. The most obvious is the core–periphery model (Atkinson, 1984). Firms using this approach adopt either a commitment or a paternalist strategy

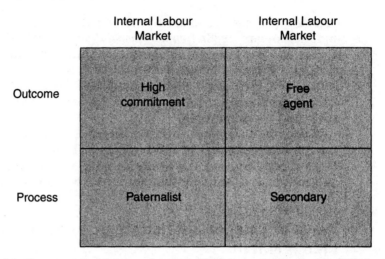

Figure 2.3   Four strategic archetypes of strategic HRM. *Source:* Bamberger, P and Meshoulam, I (2000) *Human Resource Strategy: Formulation, Implementation, and Impact.* Reprinted by permission of Sage Publications, Inc.

when dealing with core personnel, whilst applying a secondary strategy to the periphery.

The four approaches represent what Bamberger and Meshoulam call four ideal types. They are described as a set of *archetypes*. In using this terminology, they are careful to draw a distinction between a *taxonomy*, the definitional characteristics of which are mutually exclusive, and archetypes. The latter are less rigid in terms of boundary definition. This more flexible device allows for many permutations within a broad general framework and facilitates sense-making in dealing with the many contingencies present.

Characteristics of the 'commitment' SHRM archetype

The commitment strategy is widely associated with HRM bundles of practice often referred to in the USA as high performance work systems and in the UK as high commitment strategies. Their origins lie in the American response to Japanese process innovation. Japanese approaches to quality management forced competitors to focus on internal processes that resulted in high quality output. In order to survive, Western firms had to consider how best to develop the workforce. The idea that it was necessary to instil a commitment to continuous improvement and a willingness to go beyond contract became widely accepted. Previously, highly demarcated Taylorised work processes had to give way to multi-skilled working and to team approaches to problem solving and reward, based upon merit. This resulted in a stronger recognition of the need to create and sustain an internal labour market. Empowerment resulted in lower transaction costs. Reductions in the level of supervision meant that managers had to 'trust' employees to take charge of complex operations. Management became increasingly concerned with output rather than the supervision of process. High commitment organisations sought to achieve this by promoting a 'relational' contract founded on 'strong' trust.

Characteristics of the 'free agent' SHRM archetype

The free agent approach is typically associated with activities that require high levels of process skill, often on an intermittent basis. High skills and low levels of supervision result in low transaction costs. Organisations with a free agent orientation seek to control costs by buying in the skills when needed. They use either self-employed contractors or employees working on short-term contracts, often at premium rates. This means that barriers must be created to prevent the migration of core competence from the organisation to the environment. Firms adopting this approach rely upon a transactional psychological contract that is founded on 'weak' trust.

Characteristics of the 'secondary ' SHRM archetype

The secondary strategy also reflects a strong reliance on an external labour market. Typically, the skills level is low and easy to acquire. Competition amongst the unskilled and semi-skilled for such employment tends to be high. Wages are low, along with job security. Employers focus their effort on controlling processes. This is accomplished through close supervision. Transaction costs, therefore, are high, trust is weak and a transactional or transitional psychological contract can be perceived to operate. Typical areas of employment include clothing manufacturing and various parts of the service sector, including hotels and catering.

Characteristics of the 'paternalistic' SHRM archetype

Paternalism is usually associated with bureaucratic organisations where status and hierarchy are emphasised. The bureaucratic structure, as Mintzberg and Quinn (1992) have shown, whilst inflexible, does ensure consistency of output. This is achieved by adherence to rules and complex procedures. Clearly, knowledge of the rules takes time to acquire. This results in a need to create an internal labour market. Loyalty and length of service are rewarded. Employees exchange job security for loyalty and compliance to the rules. The psychological contract tends to be balanced and obligational.

Characteristics of 'hybrid' SHRM archetypes

There is potential for many hybrids. Reference to the Atkinson core–periphery model, which mixes high commitment at the core with secondary approaches at the periphery, has already been made. Paternalistic organisations that utilise free agents as part of a cost reduction strategy in non-core areas are another example. High commitment organisations behave similarly when confronted with challenging tasks that sit outside their base of expertise. In short, no approach to SHRM is likely to exist in a completely pure form.

However, there is invariably a *dominant tendency* that characterises an organisation's approach to the management of its core activities. The philosophy that is adopted will have *culture-shaping implications* which, as we have seen, result in the emergence of a *particular form* of psychological contract.

Equality and diversity in relation to strategic human resource management archetypes

We are now in a position to utilise the framework of strategic archetypes to explore the possibilities of making a case for the deployment of equality of opportunity within each category of SHRM.

We have taken as our starting point the finding that the literatures suggest that if SHRM is to make a contribution to business and organisational performance, then internal consistency and external alignment of such a strategy with business objectives represent an important precondition. Systems that are internally inconsistent, or conflict, have not been found to result in improvements in levels of trust, commitment or performance (Thompson, 1992; Cannell and Wood, 1992; Marsden and Richardson, 1994).

The choice of strategy defines the nature of the psychological contract. This in turn determines the nature of trust and the cultural constraints that operate. Drawing upon the configurational and universalistic positions, we assert that the conscious incorporation of equality of opportunity across all areas of SHRM is not only ethically responsible, it also makes sound business sense; however, the state of organisational preparedness will vary according to the strategy that is adopted.

Strategic human resource management, the psychological contract, equality and diversity

Differing perceptions of the psychological contract and their ethical implications

We begin with the proposition that regardless of an employer's approach to SHRM, there is an expectation of compliance to the employer's expectations in respect of the six areas identified by Herriot, Manning and Kidd (1997) in return for the wages paid. Success in delivering the desired outcome, however, is contingent upon employee perceptions that the employer is making a reasonable effort to meet their expectations in respect of their twelve areas of concern. This is reflected strongly in the prevailing psychological contract.

Equity theory posits that individuals respond to an inequitable employment relationship in terms of job dissatisfaction, non-compliance or exit. The implication, borne out by the research of Herriot *et al.*, is *that employees are deeply influenced by* an employer's *consistency and sensitivity* in dealing with issues of fairness, justice and equality. Crucially, the more locally any breach is experienced, the more acutely it is likely to be felt by the injured party. When a management acts in a way that is perceived to be unfair, inconsistent or unjust, then an adjustment is likely to occur in respect of the injured party's level of commitment to meeting the employer's seven expectations. If the injustice is perceived to be systemic then an entire group will adjust its conception to the prevailing psychological contract and its behaviour and expectations will change accordingly.

Dualistic (utilitarian/Kantian) illustration of differences in employer/employee perceptions

Drawing upon our current level of understanding of the psychological contract, trust, organisational justice and the labour market approach, can a capabilities perspective be used to evaluate different approaches to HRM?

When considering the four strategic HRM archetypes proposed by Bamberger and Meshoulam, it is clear that the case for embracing a policy of equality of opportunity might *in practice* be justified on utilitarian grounds, or upon principles of organisational justice and sometimes both. For example, both apply in the case of high commitment SHRM.

Equality of opportunity and the commitment SHRM archetype

As we have already observed, organisations that embrace a commitment strategy develop an internal labour market orientation (ILO) as part of a strategy for minimising transaction costs and promoting functional flexibility and incremental innovation.

The creation and development of high levels of core competence can only be accomplished through employment stability and team working that facilitates the accretion of knowledge and the empowerment of those in possession of that knowledge. Trust is a central consideration. In concentrating upon managing outputs, management must trust employees to manage processes effectively.

Walton (1985) described the new commitment approach thus:

> Individual responsibilities are expected to change as conditions change, and teams, not individuals, often are the organisational units accountable for performance. With management hierarchies relatively flat and differences in status minimised, control and lateral coordination depend on shared goals, and expertise rather than formal position.   (1985: 15)

Box 2.1

On 21 February 2001 the *Daily Telegraph* reported that Johnnie Cochran, one of America's top lawyers, had filed a suit against Microsoft, the world's largest software company. It alleged that the company had discriminated when evaluating and promoting blacks. The suit was filed in Seattle on behalf of Landruff Trent. It would be brought alongside that of Monique Donaldson, a former Mircrosoft employee who had also claimed discrimination.

It was also reported that seven other current and former employees were suing the company for nearly $5 billion on grounds of discrimination. During the previous week, Carl Taylor Lopez, a Seattle lawyer, had filed a separate suit on behalf of Ronald Douglas, a former Microsoft employee. Douglas claimed he was given fewer stock options and paid less than white employees in comparable positions.

The company, which at the time of the report employed 27,000 people, claimed that promoting diversity in the workplace was an industry-wide problem and that Microsoft was actively addressing the problem by providing diversity training for its managers and operating a 'zero tolerance policy' in respect of discrimination in the workplace.

(Adapted from: 'The level of minorities in the tech industry is lower than in other industries.' 21 February 2001, *Daily Telegraph.*)

Employees working in teams must also learn to trust one another. They have to learn to recognise individual strengths and limitations and to play to strengths, whilst tolerating one another's limitations. *A climate of trust can only be sustained if individuals feel that they are being treated fairly.* We have seen that when individuals feel that they have been the victims of discrimination, there will be an erosion of both motivation and commitment. A decline in commitment will impair the capacity of other members of the team to perform. This may give rise to resentment and sanctions. A vicious cycle of declining team working and effectiveness can result. In consequence, organisations that embrace a high commitment strategy cannot sustain their vision if they fail to embrace policies of equality of opportunity and of treatment that ignore Sen's capabilities and instrumental freedoms approach.

Equality of opportunity and the 'paternalist' SHRM archetype

Organisations that display a paternalistic approach to SHRM develop an (ILO) orientation because of *the need to marshal and husband process knowledge.* Over time, employees acquire high levels of expertise in respect of procedures and precedents. This knowledge can be difficult to replicate or replace. Unlike high commitment organisations that tend to compete through creativity and innovation, organisations that adopt the paternalist approach are preoccupied with *consistency* in their processes. Perkins (1988) suggests that:

> In these circumstances, organisations and their management may, consciously or unconsciously, settle for a re-scoped form of job and organisational attachment, which managerial discretion may encourage, at least in a bounded and time limited form . . .

Firms such as Marks & Spencer in the UK and Anglo Dutch firms such as Unilever, offer instrumental (in the past perhaps, paternalistic) extrinsic rewards in exchange for people's commitment to follow the instructions of management, in support of organisational objectives. Such extrinsic offerings may include continuous professional development opportunities, as well as more intrinsic gains for individuals such as acquiring the cachet of past employment with such a *'brand named firm'* as a platform for future career progress within the organisation's internal labour market or elsewhere. (1988: 17)

Organisations that seek to create a balanced contract recognise the **bounded** nature of the **commitment** they can command. *If they are strongly bureaucratic in their approach then there is likely to be a predisposition to be suspicious of the need for change.* Importantly, outdated practices in relation to discrimination, eschewed elsewhere, may continue to flourish until they are challenged. The consequences, when this happens, can have a profound impact. In these circumstances, managers are forced to address the need for change and managers and employees struggle to accept criticism of both their organisation and the way in which they have previously worked.

A 'capabilities' view of the equality challenges confronting organisations with a 'paternalistic' orientation to SHRM

The reluctant acceptance by the Metropolitan Police Commissioner of the charge of 'institutionalised racism', arising from the Macpherson enquiry, represents an important example of an organisation that has been forced to recognise that the attitudes and practices within the organisation are no longer acceptable to wider society.

The Metropolitan Police were found to have bungled their investigation of the tragic murder of the black teenager Stephen Lawrence. The stinging criticism that followed the acquittal of a group of suspected racists, widely believed to have committed the crime, is believed to have reduced police morale to an all-time low. As a result, attempts to maintain staffing levels and also to recruit more personnel from ethnic minorities have run into serious difficulties.

At the level of individual policemen, officers from minority ethnic communities such as Girpal Virdi have articulated a sense of injustice and outrage at what they perceive to be unfair discriminatory practices and an absence of instrumental freedoms. Amongst female officers, the settlements agreed with former officers, such as Sarah Locker and Belinda Sinclair, point to a service that is dipping into the public purse in an attempt to suppress details of how it has treated certain officers.

In-text exercise

Set out in Box 2.2 is a summary of the Belinda Sinclair case. The case was originally reported in *People Management News*, 14 September 2000, p. 14, by Paul Donovan. Read it carefully and then undertake a critical evaluation of the managerial behaviours that created the impetus for the case to reach a tribunal.

Box 2.2

The Metropolitan Police employs 9,000 officers. It has been very active in trying to improve an image that was badly tarnished as a result of the Stephen Lawrence enquiry. Despite these efforts, the organisation is facing a significant number of claims. Amongst them are the cases of Belinda Sinclair, Sarah Locker and Gordon Warren.

The Sinclair case

Sinclair, a former sergeant who is reputed to have received an out of court settlement of £200,000, is one of 29 other similar cases, including Sarah Locker who had claimed racial discrimination and settled for £500,000. As a result, the competence of the Met in managing its people is coming under close scrutiny.

Whilst the Sinclair case involved allegations of sex discrimination, other management failures and malpractices emerged as a result of documents released for the hearing. During an appraisal that had begun with her being told that she was 'mediocre to the point of anonymity' her line manager had gone on to suggest she could 'project a dominant image on occasion, which can be perceived as intimidating to others'. People Management allege that 'the comment was made without any supporting evidence and that it had documentation to support the allegation.' It was also suggested that two months after the appraisal, the line manager had made changes to the report, claiming that the matter had been clarified, a position that was rigorously denied by Sinclair.

The relations deteriorated further after Sinclair, who was suffering from pleurisy, went off sick for a month. Despite the fact that the Met requires line managers to check up on staff regularly when they are ill, in order to document absence, her line manager contacted her only once whilst she was ill.

Sinclair lodged a grievance in July 1998, alleging that her manager had failed to supervise her absence. Other managerial shortcomings were also identified. Amongst them was the allegation that her appraisal had not been conducted in accordance with service guidelines.

At a meeting with her line managers held to discuss the grievance claim on 7 August 1998, involving Chief Superintendent Derek Cook, her line manager and Sinclair, Cook refused to accept any complaint against his management team. Six days later, he wrote to an occupational health adviser about Sinclair's mental health. On 24 November 1998, Sinclair was called to another meeting with Ann Beasley, area business manager and head of personnel for South-West London. Beasley was Cook's boss.

Four days prior to the meeting, a memo signed by Cook had been produced stating that on 3 June 1998, Sinclair had threatened to kill her line manager. Sinclair denied the comment, asserting that if such a threat had been made and taken seriously, it would have been recorded as a criminal offence. No action had been taken.

Beasley undertook go back to Sinclair's line manager and Cook, and ensure that the unsupported comment on the original appraisal would be removed, leaving the box markings in place. She would also take up an earlier comment made by Cook suggesting that Sinclair was 'very confident for a woman'. According to Sinclair, after the meeting little had happened, resulting in additional pressure when she tried to do her job.

As a result of this inaction, Sinclair proceeded to take her case to an employment tribunal, believing it to be the only route through which she could seek any recompense. 'All I actually wanted to do was get on with my own job, but this was being made impossible,' she told People Management.

The Warren case

In 1982, Gordon Warren was a police constable at Sutton in Surrey. Warren claims that whilst the rest of his shift were at an illegal drinks party organised in the station by his commanding officer, he continued to patrol.

At his annual appraisal, he was accused of having poor judgment and sent for a mental health check. The examination showed no problem. In 1985, a Met doctor declared that he was paranoid and unfit for duty. The doctor was over-ruled by two medical referees. The following year the same doctor declared Warren to be suffering from a personality disorder with paranoid tendencies. Warren said, 'I was then kicked out of the force'.

Warren was awarded £12,000 in 1988, after the High Court declared that the medical certificate was unlawful on the grounds that it had 'the appearance of bias'. Later the same year, the Court of Appeal upheld the High Court decision. Warren was awarded a further £3,500. Eventually, the case went to the House of Lords and was upheld.

The Met has held four investigations into Warren's complaints since 1990; offers of compensation ranging from £50,000 to £95,000 have been made. In 1995 Sir Paul Condon admitted that 'there was no truth in the allegations of mental illness or personality disorder with paranoid tendencies'. A full apology was made. Warren and his local MP, Tom Brake, have sought £150,000 in compensation for his 18 years of suffering. Despite a full apology and a certificate of exemplary service, he was still waiting at the time of the Sinclair settlement.

On 10 April 2001, Met deputy commissioner Ian Blair gave Warren 28 days to accept an offer of £85,000 in compensation. On 8 May, he sent a letter withdrawing the offer.

'From the date of this letter onwards, no correspondence about this matter will be entered into, nor any communication accepted by this service. For the avoidance of any doubt, any letters received will not be acknowledged and telephone calls will be promptly terminated', he wrote.

The Liberal Democrat MP for Carshalton and Wallington, who represents both Warren and Sinclair, suggests the Met is in denial about its problems.

Home Office figures suggest further evidence of difficulties with people management in the force. According to People Management, statistics reveal that £516,274 was paid to settle 29 employment tribunal cases out of court last year. Hampshire Police was ranked the next highest in the table, with £176,500 paid out for three cases.

Sinclair believes that her own case, together with those of Warren and Locker, are the tip of an iceberg of intimidation operating within the police service. Since her settlement, she claims to have been contacted by a number of officers with similar stories. Sinclair asserts that settling cases out of court is not a sign of a compensation culture, rather it reveals a police service that is trying to suppress details of how it has treated certain officers.

(Adapted from: 'Tribunal cases indicate a major problem for Met management' in *People Management News*, 14 September 2001, p. 14)

The cases of fire fighters Raj Patel and David Jackson, the only serving ethnic minority community officers in the Cumbria Fire Service, who both suffered years of racial harassment, serve to highlight the pervasiveness of overt discriminatory practices in paternalistic, machine-bureaucratic organisations in the UK.

When discriminatory practices are ignored or condoned within hierarchical, high-power-distance cultural contexts, then from time to time, these attitudes produce behaviours that are thrust into public view, where they are widely and robustly condemned. The beating of Rodney King by the Chicago police is an obvious American example.

'Felt fair' considerations, as we have already seen, sit at the heart of the Coca-Cola case evaluated in Chapter 1. The plaintiffs were in effect asserting that whilst they possess both basic and internal capability, they were prevented from exercising combined capabilities because the firm failed to monitor access to the full range of instrumental freedoms for all its staff adequately. African American employees believed that they were being denied equal access to social opportunities, because transparency guarantees had not been implemented effectively. This resulted in a perception that the principles of both distributive and procedural justice had not been met. In consequence, the plaintiffs argued that they were being subjected to discrimination in economic facility. This is an experience that is likely to resonate amongst many women and members of ethnic minorities employed in paternalistic bureaucratic public service organisations in both Britain and the USA. This may have the effect of depressing the effectiveness of overall recruitment efforts, as in the case of the Metropolitan police cited earlier; it might also reduce the calibre of prospective recruits presenting themselves for selection, especially amongst those already under-represented. Evidence of under-representation will in turn erode the perceived legitimacy and authority of such agencies within those communities that perceive themselves to be the butt of discrimination. The Watts riots in the USA in 1965, the riots in a number of English cities in the 1980s and more recently the riots in Bradford in July 2001, and the reported tensions in the prison service both in the UK and the USA are all symptomatic of the type of vicious cycle described above.

A 'capabilities' view of the equality challenges confronting organisations embracing the free agent SHRM archetype

The importance of equality of opportunity in the context of an *internal* labour market is not difficult to discern. A sense of 'felt' injustice at the very least results in tension and the withdrawal of an individual's goodwill. At its worst it can generate open conflict that can result in loss of individual and organisational effectiveness and create further real and demonstrative injustices.

Upon what basis can an argument in support of capabilities equality be advanced, in the context of organisations that are committed to exploiting the opportunities and advantages afforded by the *external* labour market? Does the appeal to principles of organisational justice still apply?

Perkins (1998) has suggested that *organisations that rely upon the external labour market do so as a device for securing and sustaining managerial control. Labour in this context is a commodity that is procured when needed and disposed of when it ceases to offer utility.* Rousseau and Wade-Benzoni, (1994) described the psychological contract that typically operates in this context as transactional. The relationship is often short term and instrumental on both sides. As a result, it tends to be characterised by weak trust and mutual suspicion.

Organisations with a free agent approach seek to secure the best skills available in the marketplace at the going rate, without seeking or giving commitment. The contractor will strive to moderate demands for performance or pursue some degree of commitment, whilst striving to maximise reward.

However, the labour market becomes more employer or contractor 'powerful' in the context of the economic cycle. In view of this, it is not in an employer's interest to develop a reputation for discriminatory or unfair practice.

Contractors with skills possess a degree of market power. In a tight labour market, individuals alienated by a past experience will elect to work for a competitor, or exact a premium to work for an organisation that is perceived to deny combined capabilities.

Discriminatory experiences whilst under contract give rise to felt injustice and can, as we have seen, through Greenberg's theft studies, result in retaliation that may take many forms. One of the economic advantages of the free agent strategy is that transaction costs can be kept low because the contractor's skill requires low levels of supervision. The absence of supervision, however, can leave the organisation vulnerable to theft, sabotage or a breakdown in the customer relationship arising from a contractor's actions. Reports of computer fraud and the planting of computer viruses in company computer systems are typical of the more lurid examples that get reported in the press. The implications, therefore, are clear. Whilst the relationship may not be long term, it is not in the employer's interests to engage in discriminatory practices that give rise to 'felt' injustice. To do so invites poor performance and higher overheads in the short term. It also risks the development of a bad reputation within the contractor community in the long term. This could make it difficult to secure the best skills during periods of market expansion or indeed, when there are many alternative homes for specific, high demand skills and knowledge. A bad reputation in these circumstances will place an organisation at a competitive disadvantage. Fear of the millennium time-bomb and the IT skills shortage that developed in the run-up to the year 2000 exemplifies the potential for such problems to develop.

A 'capabilities' view of the equality challenges confronting organisations that adopt the 'secondary' SHRM archetype

Like the free agent, the secondary approach is also dependent upon the external labour market. It is characterised by a short-term transactional or transitional approach to the psychological contract. *The secondary approach aims to maximise managerial control by recruiting low levels of skill and imposing either Taylorised work methods or high levels of supervision.* The relationship is characterised by mutual suspicion. Any appeal to policies and practices of equality, as in the case of the free agent approach, tends to be founded upon a utilitarian position. The lack of market power on the part of individual employees promotes what Goldthorpe (1968) described as a *solidaristic culture.* There is an impetus to organise in order to counter managerial power.

An organisation can either seek to suppress trades union representation or accept it. If the employer opts for the former, two alternatives present themselves. A climate of managerial intimidation and fear may be fostered as a device for keeping trades unions at bay. Alternatively, the employer can seek to remove the need for third-party involvement by offering superior conditions. Employers that opt for the former incur costs. These costs can only be sustained as long as all the competitors behave similarly. If some competitors sustain better working relationships, their labour turnover and the transaction costs associated with supervision and control are likely to decline. This will result in the margins of those organisations with poor labour relations coming under pressure.

The costs of collusion in the interest of a quiet life

Even in organisations where trades unions are recognised, however, situations can arise where both sides collude in supporting discriminatory practices in a bid to sustain the status quo. Over the years, there have been a number of examples of this kind of behaviour. The Ford plant at Dagenham represents a contemporary British example. Minority ethnic employees at Dagenham complained that discriminatory practices blocked their progression to supervisory roles and sought redress in the courts. An account of the company's difficulties, entitled 'Ford halted by 'racism' strike', appeared in the *Guardian* on Wednesday 6 October 1999; a summary is provided in Box 2.3.

Box 2.3 Ford halted by racism strike

Ford's Dagenham factory, the largest in the UK, was hit by a strike yesterday involving 1300 employees who were protesting at alleged systematic racism. The stoppage was given covert backing by union leaders, production of Fiestas and Mazda 121s was halted and the night shift was expected to support the action.

This is the latest unofficial action in a plant where 45% of the workforce is non-white. Workers were said to be wearing stickers on their overalls demanding the sacking of an allegedly racist manager and 'justice and respect'.

The Dagenham plant was known some 15 years ago to be a recruiting ground for the British National Party and other racist bodies, though union sources say they have no evidence of such activities.

Yesterday's action is the latest incident to hit the plant. For the past six months, union leaders have failed to persuade local managers to hold a joint inquiry into the implications for Dagenham of the report of the Stephen Lawrence inquiry into institutional racism.

According to one insider, the last straw came last week when an AEEU shop steward, Jaswir Tega, who was working near the production line, was shouted at and pushed by a white foreman dangerously close to the conveyor belt. Local managers had refused to heed demands for the foreman to be suspended and a full inquiry to be held. Instead, he was kept away from the shop floor and returns today.

Shop stewards led the walk-out in the paint, trim and assembly areas of the plant after losing confidence in the ability of local managers to resolve what they called the endemic problem of racism. They accused local managers of turning a blind eye to repeated incidences of racist abuse and bullying, and at worst of complicity, and demanded an urgent inquiry by the Commission for Racial Equality. Insiders said: 'There's a hell of a lot of racist attitudes and actions within Dagenham. It's like a tinder box and takes little to light the fuse.'

Ford is insisting it operates a policy of 'zero tolerance' towards racism and is unaware of the reason for the action.

Bill Morris, general secretary of the Transport and General Workers' Union, reiterated his call for talks with Jac Nasser, Ford president. Two weeks ago at an east London tribunal Ford admitted racial discrimination, harassment and victimisation towards Sukhjit Parma, an engine plant worker, who had suffered a four-year campaign of racist abuse, culminating in threats to his life. Bill Morris described the Parma incident as the worst case of racist intimidation his union had experienced.

'Unless people outside the plant get a grip on the situation and put structures in place that the staff have confidence in, there'll be more of these wildcat walk-outs', union sources said.

(Adapted from David Gow, 'Ford halted by 'racism' strike, www.guardianunlimited.co.uk, 6 October 1999.)

In the short term, Machiavellian arguments around 'expediency' may well be perpetrated. In the long term, the argument is less convincing because breaches in distributive and interactional justice are likely to erode managerial authority, especially when it is founded upon high power distance.

A strategy of 'divide and rule' can only work in the absence of effective moral leadership amongst the workforce. An articulate leader can justifiably assume the moral high ground by identifying and attacking policies and strategies that deny combined capabilities. By appealing to conceptions of distributive justice within the workforce, feelings of resentment and discontent can be generated. In such circumstances, the nature of the high-power-distance relationship will make it difficult for the employer to communicate messages that are perceived as credible by those who 'feel' disadvantaged. Thus, when confrontation does come, it will be especially bitter and acrimonious. The resulting costs incurred by both sides will be significant and, if not resolved, will result in the erosion of competitive advantage.

Collusion also legitimises discriminatory practices, as seen earlier in the case of the Metropolitan Police. Over time, persistent failures on the part of management to address discrimination in the workplace results in the escalation of such behaviour, leading eventually to institutionalised bullying and intimidation. Whilst this type of behaviour can serve to bolster in-group solidarity, it is only sustainable as long as victims are widely dispersed across the organisation and elect to remain mute or leave quietly, when the pressures become too much to bear. Any change arising from shifting demographic trends or tight labour market conditions will sooner or later result in those being denied their instrumental freedoms finding voice and demanding organisational justice. Typically, an individual will refuse to go quietly. He or she then becomes a *cause célèbre* around which those who have shared the experience will gather. Within the 'in group' divisions will appear. Most individuals within the 'in group' will respond to the pressure to conform. A few will become more circumspect in response to appeals for distributive and procedural justice. The complexity of the management challenge will multiply. If management elects to concede, it will lose face and incur costs. If it refuses to recognise the need for change, it may be able to postpone the necessity to face up to the nature of a changing world, but it will also reinforce the prevailing culture, leading to greater oppression in the short term. In the long term, institutionalised injustice, in whatever form, will prompt those who perceive themselves to be the unfairly treated to seek redress in the courts. The costs incurred by employers losing a series of cases are likely to be small by comparison with the costs arising from loss of reputation and the need to promote cultural change. In Box 2.4 there is a summary of the knock-on effects of the Belinda Sinclair case originally reported by Paul Donnovan.

How can the costs be measured?

Ford, Coca-Cola, Microsoft, the Metropolitan Police, the Cumbria Fire Service and many other organisations are now beginning to discover the magnitude

Box 2.4

Bullying in Manchester and Lincolnshire Police
Two former Manchester police constables, Dave Wilson and Denise Haworth, who were retired on ill-health pensions, claimed that mismanagement within the service is responsible for much of its staff turnover. The two read about the case of Metropolitan Police officer Belinda Sinclair in *People Management News*, 14 September

2000. They claim they had been bullied by an inspector and two sergeants whilst working as part of 'D relief' at the Crescent police station in Salford, Greater Manchester.

In another case, an employment tribunal ruled that Detective Inspector Dena Fleming had been victimised by her former employer, Lincolnshire Police.

of the task that confronts them. Each has lost cases taken to tribunal or before the courts. Each has made a public commitment to bring about change. Large sums have been invested in training and development and in reviewing HR policies and practices. New machinery has been established for the purpose of monitoring progress and achievement. Despite these efforts, cases continue to emerge. In the face of all this managerial effort and the commitment of significant levels of resource, progress is invariably inordinately slow. This prompts the question, why?

The case for diversity-centred equality management

Earlier it was postulated that a psychological contract exists at two levels.

At the *meta level*, the contract is given expression through the policies and practices manifested by HR subsystems. Are the recruitment and selection, training and development, reward, appraisal and progression subsystems in alignment? Do they meet employee expectations in respect of fairness and justice?

When employers seek to meet transparency guarantees by publishing statistics that reflect labour force characteristics along with statements of policy intent, their efforts are designed to bring HR subsystems into alignment. Employees expect to see changes over time. If progress is perceived to be slow, then continued discrimination against minorities is suspected, if progress is fast then those who form the majority suspect reverse discrimination. Prima facie, employers appear to be caught between Scylla and Charybdis.

At the *micro level*, in the same way that employees operating at the customer interface become the face of the company in the customer's eyes, so individual line managers come to represent the organisation in the minds of individual employees. When Sergeant Sinclair was appraised as intimidating others and entered into grievance over her appraisal and subsequent treatment during a period of sick leave, senior managers are reported to have closed ranks behind her line manager. This response might be instinctive in a strongly hierarchical organisational context. The question is, was it an appropriate response? The HR subsystems of Microsoft, Coca-Cola and the Metropolitan Police may have flaws, but few would deny that serious attempts had been made to bring the subsystems into alignment in terms of the development of equality and anti-discrimination policies prior to the recent court cases.

Sergeant Sinclair's grievance was not against either the organisation or its policies. *It was against the behaviour of individual managers acting as agents of the organisation within a specific context.* From her perspective, their behaviour did not deliver fairness in assessment or provide justice, fairness or consistency in the application of rules. The result of their behaviour would depress both her long-term pay trajectory and quality of life, not to mention inducing unnecessary stress and damaged apperception.

Another example is the case of Harling v CL Plastics Ltd. Harling, who was a dyslexic, resigned as a result of suffering 18 months of both verbal and physical abuse. He was discouraged from complaining to senior managers. Nevertheless, he did so. Unfortunately, his grievance was not taken seriously. This induced depression and emotional stress. He complained of *disability discrimination*. When his case was heard, the tribunal found in his favour on grounds that included the period of abuse, the fact that management had ignored the situation and the demeanour of three witnesses.

Here again, we see evidence of a management that lacked the skills to manage diversity and rather than face the challenge, was prepared to contest the case and collude in sustaining the status quo. Any such decision is likely to send a powerful signal to employees that discriminatory behaviour is acceptable. This will increase the probability of further cases arising in the future, resulting in further damage to reputation together with the associated costs.

Conclusions

In this chapter, we have attempted to convey the importance of undertaking a systematic evaluation of less visible, but nonetheless vitally important characteristics of organisations. We have reviewed some of the literatures on trust, the psychological contract and conceptions of organisational justice with a view to making a business case for the adoption of policies of equality. The aim has been to develop a deeper understanding of a number of fundamental dynamics, and to get a better feel for the climate and culture of organisations. We have not attempted to consider these elements in isolation. We have argued, instead, that they are a consequence of organisational approaches to SHRM.

We have asserted that these approaches are shaped by the business models and competitive strategies that organisations choose to adopt and that organisations are predisposed to embrace particular ethical orientations when formulating policies and strategies for managing equality. We have seen that organisations that promote an internal labour market and adopt a high commitment approach to SHRM are more likely to provide a context within which capabilities equality can take root and grow. Their business orientation is likely to make them highly sensitive to issues of organisational justice.

Paternalist organisations with an internal labour market orientation, in contrast, share a similar need to be responsive to demands for distributive and procedural justice. Unfortunately, they provide grounds for less optimism.

There is both an ethical and social imperative that they should be seen as exemplars of good practice in promoting capabilities equality. This imperative arises not only because of their mission and role in society, but also because many are funded from taxation to which all are required to subscribe. Unfortunately, their machine and professional bureaucratic characteristics result in high power distance and organisational norms that demand conformity and loyalty. These characteristics, combined with a cultural myopia in recognising discrimination that may be embedded in HR systems and practices, make these organisations vulnerable to denial and highly resistant to change.

Utilitarian arguments tend to drive the business case when we consider organisations with an external labour market orientation. Organisations that deploy a free agent strategy must be mindful of their vulnerability to contractor hostility arising from felt injustice. Organisations with a secondary approach place themselves at a competitive disadvantage if their labour relations deteriorate to the point where industrial disputes rage around issues of felt inequity. Whilst employers may not be moved by calls for distributive and procedural justice, their long-term interests are not best served by ignoring such issues.

We are not suggesting that these are the only 'implicit' soft factors that merit consideration, but we do believe that they provide a useful and powerful basis for evaluation and comparison.

By developing a deeper understanding of these aspects of the organisational landscape, those with responsibility for managing and coordinating equality and diversity issues are placed in a stronger position to start looking at other aspects of 'people management' strategy and practice.

Most controversially, we are suggesting that certain organisational environments are unlikely to provide fertile ground for many types of equality and diversity intervention, without fundamental cultural and systemic root and branch change. Determining the initial conditions that need to exist in order create a climate that will support change, therefore, requires a clear, uncluttered view of the factors that are likely to kill specific types of initiative, strategy or practice choice. Chapter 3 examines some of the key issues from the line management perspective.

Text-based questions

1. Why does the psychological contract together with conceptions of trust and organisational justice help us to understand the character of organisations better?
2. Why will an ability to categorise different manifestations of the psychological contract help us to understand how and why conceptions of a 'fair deal' vary in different employment contexts?
3. What are the three conceptions of justice in an organisational context and in what ways does each influence employee commitment to the organisation?
4. What contribution do universalist, contingency and configurational explanations play in enhancing our understanding of SHRM?

5. Outline the business case for promoting and supporting combined capabilities that might be applied to each of the four Bamberger and Meshoulam archetypes.

Library and assignment-based questions

Use an electronic search facility to identify at least one newspaper or law report on a case of:

- Sex discrimination;
- Racial discrimination;
- Disability discrimination (not discussed in this chapter).

Read the report carefully and then:

1. Identify the labour market context in which the organisation is likely to be operating and then locate the type of HR strategy that the organisation is probably deploying (using the Bamberger and Meshoulam typology).
2. Evaluate the nature of the psychological contract each organisation is aspiring to sustain (using the Rousseau and Wade-Benzoni framework).
3. Examine the case from the plaintiff's perspective and isolate those factors that you believe may have given rise to breaches of organisational justice.
4. Categorise each possible breach in terms of distributive, procedural or interactional justice. (You may find it useful to use the Thornhill and Saunders', model.)
5. Categorise the likely direct and indirect costs that the organisation is likely to incur in the event of its losing the case. Assume the organisation will make a public commitment to improve its future performance.
6. Evaluate the organisation's state of readiness to implement change and the ethical basis upon which any change strategy should be founded.
7. Write a short report explaining and justifying your analysis.
8. Read Box 2.3: Ford halted by racism strike, on p. 88.
   Questions:
   (a) If you were the senior manager responsible for promoting good employee relations, what action would you take to address employee concerns?
   (b) If you were the line manager responsible for the paint shop, how would you handle the situation arising as a result of the foreman returning to work in the paint shop?
   (c) Does it make good business sense for an employer to collude in sustaining historic behaviours and obstruct combined capabilities?

Internet resources

Coca-Cola http://www.coca-cola.com/
Cumbria Fire Service http://www.cumbriafire.fire-uk.org/
Marks & Spencer http://www2.marksandspencer.com/thecompany/
Metropolitan Police http://www.met.police.uk/
Unilever http://www.unilever.com/

Further reading

Maier, M (1997) We have to make a MANagement Decision: *Challenger* and Dysfunctions of Corporate Masculinity, Chapter 10, in *Managing the Organisational Melting Pot: Dilemmas in Work Place Diversity.*
An excellent and detailed account of the organisational pathology that gave rise to the *Challenger* disaster

Caproni, P and Finley, J (1997) When Organisations Do Harm: Two Cautionary Tales, in *Managing the Organisational Melting Pot: Dilemmas in Work Place Diversity.*
A review and analysis of the cultural climate in two American organisations found to have displayed institutionalised sexism and racism. The first case evaluates the Tailhook incident and the second, the beating of Rodney King.

References

Ambrose, ML and Rosse, JG (1993) Relational justice and personality testing: Sometimes nice guys do last. Unpublished manuscript. University of Colorado, Boulder, CO.

Arthur, J (1994) Effects of human resource systems on manufacturing performance and turnover. *Academy of Management Journal*, **37**, 670–687.

Atkinson, J (1984) Manpower strategies for flexible organizations. *Personnel Management*, **16** (8), 18–31.

Baird, L and Meshoulam, I (1988) Managing two fits of strategic human resource management. *Academy of Management Review*, **13** (1), 116–128.

Ball, G, Trevino, A and Simms, HP, Jr (1994) Just and unjust punishment: Influences on subordinate performance and citizenship. *Academy of Management Journal*, **37**, 299–322.

Bamberger, P and Meshoulam, I (2000) *Human Resource Strategy: Formulation, Implementation, and Impact*, Sage, Thousand Oaks, CA.

Barney, JB and Hansen, MH (1994) Trustworthiness as a source of competitive advantage. *Strategic Management Journal*, 15, 175–90.

Bevan, S and Hayday, S (1994) Towing the line: Helping Managers to Manage People. *IMS Report 254.*

Bies, RJ and Moag, JS (1986) Interactional Justice: Communication criteria of fairness, in RJ Lewicki, BH Sheppard and M Bazerman (eds), *Research on Negotiation in Organisations*, Vol. 1 (pp 43–55), JAI Press, Greenwich, CT.

Brockner, J and Greenberg, J (1990) The impact of layoffs on survivors: An organisational justice perspective, in JS Carrol (ed.) *Applied Social Psychology and Organisational Settings*, pp. 45–75, Erlbaum, Hillsdale, NJ.

Brockner, J and Siegel, P (1995) Understanding the interaction between procedural and distributive justice, in RM Kramer and TR Tyler (eds) *Trust in Organisations*, Sage, Newbury Park, CA.

Brockner, J (1994) Perceived fairness and survivors' reactions to layoffs, how downsizing organisations can do well by doing good. *Social Justice Research*, **7**, 345–363.

Brockner, J, Tyler, TR and Cooper-Schneider, R (1992) The influence of prior commitment to an institution on reactions to perceived unfairness: The higher they are, the harder they fall. *Administrative Science Quarterly*, 37, 241–261.

Cannell, M and Wood, S (1992) *Incentive Pay*, IPM, London.

Clemmer, EC (1993) An investigation into the relationship of fairness and customer satisfaction with services, in R Cropanzano (ed.) *Justice in the workplace: Approaching Fairness in Human Resource Management*, pp. 193–207, Erlbaum, Hillsdale, NJ.

Cooper, C and Robinson, J (eds) (2001) *Organisational Psychology and Development*, Wiley, Chichester.

Cropanzano, R and Greenberg, J (2001) Progress in Organisational Justice: Tunneling through the Maze, in C Cooper and I Robertson (eds) *Organisational Psychology and Development*, pp. 243–298, Wiley, Chichester.

Cropanzano, R, Aguinis, H, Schminke, ME and Denham, DL (August 1996) Disputant reactions to managerial conflict intervention strategies: A comparison among Argentina, the Dominican Republic, Mexico and the United States, in JG Rosse (chair) *Justice and Fairness in Organisations*, Symposium conducted at the 1996 meeting of the Academy of Management, Cincinnati, OH.

Daley, JP and Geyer, PD (1994) The role of fairness in implementing large-scale change: Employee evaluations of process and outcome in seven facility relocations. *Journal of Organisational Behavior*, **15**, 623–638.

Daley, JP and Geyer, PD (1995) Procedural fairness and organizational commitment under conditions of growth and decline. *Social Justice Research*, **8**, 137–151.

Doty, DH, Glick, WH and Huber, GP (1993) Fit, equifinality and organizational effectiveness: A test of two configurational theories. *Academy of Management Journal*, **36**, 1196–1250.

Elangovan, AR (1995) Managerial third-party dispute intervention: A perspective model of strategy selection. *Academy of Management Review*, **20**, 800–830.

Frohlich, N, Oppenheimer JA and Eavy, CL (1987) Laboratory results on Rawls's distributive justice. *British Journal of Political Science*, **17**, 1–21.

Fukayama, F (1995) *Trust*, Hamish Hamilton, London.

Ghoshal, S and Bartlett, C (1998) *The Individualised Corporation*, Heinemann, London.

Gilliland, SW (1993) The perceived fairness of selection systems: An organizational justice perspective. *Academy of Management Review*, **18**, 694–734.

Goldthorpe, JH,, Lockwood, D, Beckhofer, F and Platt, J (1968) *The Affluent Worker: Industrial Attitudes and Behaviour*, Cambridge University Press, Cambridge.

Greenberg, J (1982) Approaching equity and avoiding inequity in groups and organizations, in J Greenberg and RL Cohen (eds) *Equity and Justice in Social Behavior* (pp. 389–435), Academic Press, New York.

Greenberg, J (1990) Organizational justice: Yesterday, today, and tomorrow. *Journal of Management*, **16**, 399–432.

Greenberg, J (1993) The intellectual adolescence of organisational justice: you've come a long way, maybe. *Social Justice Research*, **6**, 135–147.

Greenberg, J (1993) The social side of fairness: Interpersonal and informational classes of organizational justice, in R Cropanzano (ed.) *Justice in the Workplace: Approaching Fairness in Human Resource Management*, pp. 79–103, Erlbaum, Hillsdale, NJ.

Greenberg, J (1994) Using socially fair treatment to promote acceptance of a work site smoking ban. *Journal of Applied Psychology*, **79**, 288–297.

Greenberg, J (1996) *The Quest for Justice on the Job: Essays and Experiments*, Sage, Thousand Oaks, CA.

Greenberg, J and Scott, KS (1996) Why do employees bite the hands that feed them? Employee theft as a social exchange process, in BM Staw and JL Cummings (eds) *Research in Oraganisational Behaviour* (pp. 111–166), JAT Press, Greenwich, CT.

Greenberg, J (1997) The STEAL motive: managing the social determinants of employee theft, in R Glacalone and J Greenberg (eds) *Antisocial Behaviour in the Workplace*, pp. 85–108, Sage, Thousand Oaks, CA.

Guest, DE (1998) The role of the psychological contract, in SJ Perkins and St John Sandringham (eds.) *Trust Motivation and Commitment: A Reader*, Strategic Remuneration Research Centre, Faringdon, Oxford.

Hamel, G and Prahalad, CK (1994) *Competing for the Future*, HBS Press, Boston, MA.

Herriot, P, Manning, WEG and Kidd, JM (1997) The content of the psychological contract. *British Journal of Management*, **8** (2), 151–162.

Huselid, MA (1995) The impact of human resource management practices on turnover, productivity and corporate financial performance. *Academy of Management Journal*, **38**, 635–672.

Huselid, MA and Becker, B (1997, August) The impact of high performance work systems implementation effectiveness and alignment with strategy on shareholder wealth. Paper presented to the annual meeting of the Academy of Management, Boston.

Jackson, SE and Schuler, RS (1995) The need for understanding human resources management in the context of organisations and their environment. *Annual Review of Psychology*, **46**, 237–264.

James, K (1993) The social context of organisational justice: Cultural, intergroup, and structural effects on justice behaviours and perceptions, in R Cropanzano (ed.) *Justice in the Workplace: Approaching Fairness in Human Resource Management*, pp. 79–103, Erlbaum, Hillsdale, NJ.

Kabanoff, B (1991) Equity, equality, power and conflict. *Academy of Management Review*, **16**, 416–441.

Karambayya, R, Brett, JM and Lytle, A (1992) Effects of formal authority and experience on third-party-roles, outcomes, and perceptions of fairness. *Academy of Management Journal*, **35**, 426–438.

Kim, W and Maubourne, C (1991) Implementing global strategies: The role of procedural justice. *Strategic Management Journal*, **12**, 125–143.

Kim, W and Maubourne, C (1993) Procedural justice, attitudes, and subsidiary top management compliance with multinationals' corporate strategic decisions. *Academy of Management Journal*, **36**, 502–526.

Kluger, A and Rothstein, HR (1993) The influence of selection test type on applicant reactions to employment testing. *Journal of Business and Psychology*, **8**, 3–25.

Konovsky, MA and Cropanzano, R (1991) The perceived fairness of employee drug testing as a predictor of employee attitudes and job performance. *Journal of Applied Psychology*, **76**, 698–707.

Konovsky, MA and Folger, R (1991, August) The effects of procedural and distributive justice on organizational citizenship behaviour. Paper presented at the annual meeting of the Academy of Management, Miami Beach, FL.

Korsgard, MA, Schweiger, D and Sapienza, HJ (1995) Building commitment, attachment and trust in strategic decision-making teams: The role of procedural justice. *Academy of Management Journal*, **38**, 60–84.

Kozan, MK and Iltler, SS (1994) Third party roles played by Turkish managers in subordinates' conflicts. *Journal of Organizational Behavior*, **15**, 453–466.

Latham, GP and Finnegan, BJ (1993) Perceived practicality of unstructured patterned, and situational interviews, in H Schuler, JL Farr and M Smith (eds) *Personnel Selection and Assessment: Individual and Organizational Perspectives*, pp. 41–55, Erlbaum, Hillsdale, NJ.

Lepak, DP and Snell, SA (1999) The Strategic Management of Human Capital: Determinants and implications of different relationships. *Academy of Management Review*, **24** (1), 1–18.

Leugh, K, Chiu, W-H and Au, Y-F (1993) Sympathy and support for industrial actions: A justice analysis. *Journal of Applied Psychology*, **78**, 781–787.

Levanthal, GS (1976) Fairness in social relationships, in JW Thibaut, J, T, Spence and RC Carson (eds) *Contemporary Topics in Social Psychology*, pp. 211–240, General Learning Press, Morristown, NJ.

Levanthal, GS (1980) What Should be Done with Equity Theory? in GK Gergen, MS Greenberg and RH Wills (eds) *Social Exchange: Advances in Theory and Research*, pp. 27–55, Plenum, New York.

Levanthal, GS, Karuza, J and Fry, WR (1980) Beyond fairness: A theory of allocation preferences, in G Milkula (ed.) *Justice and Social Interaction*, pp. 167–218, Springer-Verlag, New York.

Lind, EA, Kulik, CA, Ambrose, M *et al.* (1993) Individual and corporate dispute resolution: Using procedural fairness as a decision heuristic. *Administrative Science Quarterly*, **38**, 224–251.

Lind, EA (1995) Justice and authority relations in organisations, in R Cropanzano and MK Kacmar (eds) *Organisational Politics, Justice and Support: Managing the Social Climate of the Workplace*, pp. 83–96, Quorum Books, Westport, CT.

Lissowski, G, Tyszka, T and Okrasa, W (1991) Principles of distributive justice: Experiments in Poland and America. *Journal of Conflict Resolution*, **35**, 98–119.

Lowe, RH and Vadanovich, SH (1995) A field study of distributive and procedural justice as predictors of satisfaction and organisational commitment. *Journal of Business and Psychology*, **10**, 99–114.

Macduffie, JP (1995) Human resource bundles and manufacturing performance: Organizational logic and flexible production systems in the world auto industry. *Industrial and Labor Relations Review*, **48**, 197–221.

Marsden, D and Richardson, R (1994) Performing for pay? The effects of merit pay on motivation in public service. *British Journal of Industrial Relations*, **32**, 2.

McFarlin, DB and Sweeney, PD (1992) Distributive and procedural justice as predictors of satisfaction with personal and organisational outcomes. *Academy of Management Journal*, **35**, 626–637.

Meyer, AD, Tsui, AS and Hinings, CB (1993) Configurational approaches to organizational analysis. *Academy of Management Journal*, **36**, 1175–1195.

Miceli, MP (1993) Justice and pay system satisfaction, in R Cropanzano (ed.) *Justice in the workplace: Approaching Fairness in Human Resource Management*, pp. 257–283, Erlbaum, Hillsdale, NJ.

Miceli, MP and Lane, MC (1991) Antecedents of pay satisfaction: A review and extension, in KM Rowlands and G Ferris (eds) *Research in Personnel and Human Resources Management*, **9**, 235–309, JAI Press, Greenwich, CT.

Mintzberg, H and Quinn, JM (1992) *The Strategy Process: Concepts and Contexts*, Prentice Hall International, Englewood Cliffs, NJ.

Osterman, P (1995) Work/family programs and the employment relationship. *Administrative Science Quarterly*, **40**, 681–700.

Patterson, M, West, M, Lawthom, R *et al.* (1997) Impact of People Management Practices on Business Performance. *Issues in People Management:* CIPD, London.

Prahalad, S and Hamel, G (1990) The Core Competence of the Corporation. *Harvard Business Review*, May–June.

Perkins, S (1988) Trust Motivation and Commitment: manacles of mantra? in SJ Perkins and St John Sandringham (eds) *Trust Motivation and Commitment: A Reader*, Strategic Remuneration Research Centre, Faringdon: Oxford.

Pfeffer, J (1994) *Competitive Advantage through People: Unleashing the power of the workforce*, Harvard Business School Press, Boston, MA.

Rawls, J (1971) *A Theory of Justice*, Harvard University Press, Cambridge, MA.

Rosse, JG, Miller, JL and Stecher, MD (1994) A field study of job applicants' reactions to personality and cognitive ability testing. *Journal of Applied Psychology*, **79**, 987–992.

Rousseau, DM and Shalk, R (2000) *Psychological Contracts in Employment: Cross National Perspectives*, Sage, Thousand Oaks, CA.

Rousseau, DM and Wade-Benzoni, KA (1994) Linking strategy and human resource practices. How employee and customer contracts are created. *Human Resource Management*, **33**, 463–489.

Rynes, SL and Connerley, ML (1993) Applicant reactions to alternative selection procedures. *Journal of Business and Psychology*, **7**, 261–277.

Schaubroeck, J, May, DR and Brown, FW (1994) Procedural justice explanations and employee reactions to economic hardship: A field experiment. *Journal of Applied Psychology*, **79**, 455–460.

Sako, M (1992) *Prices, Quality and Trust: Inter-Firm Relations in Britain and Japan*, Cambridge University Press, Cambridge.

Shapiro, DL and Brett, JM (1993) Comparing three processes underlying judgements of procedural justice: A field study of mediation and arbitration. *Journal of Personality and Social Psychology*, **65**, 1167–1177.

Singer, MS (1992) Procedural justice in managerial selection: Identification of fairness determinants and associations of fairness perceptions. *Social Justice Research*, **5**, 49–70.

Singer, MS (1993) *Fairness in Personal Selection*, Avebury, Aldershot, New Zealand.

Skitka, LJ and Tetlock, PE (1992) Allocating scarce resources: A contingency model of distributive justice. *Journal of Experimental Psychology*, **28**, 491–522.

Sparrow, PR (1996) Transitions in the psychological contract in UK banking. *Human Resource Management Journal*, **6** (4) 479–500.

Sparrow, PR (1998) Can the psychological contract be managed? *Trust Motivation and Commitment: A Reader*, Strategic Remuneration Research Centre, Faringdon: Oxford.

Teece, D, Pisarno, G and Shuen, A (1997, August) Dynamic Capabilities and Strategic Management. *Strategic Management Journal*, **16** (7).

Terpestra, DE and Rozell, EJ (1993) The relationship of staffing practices to organizational level measures of performance. *Personnel Psychology*, **46**, 27–48.

Thompson, M (1992) *Pay and Performance: The Employer Experience*, Report 218, Institute of Manpower Studies, Brighton.

Thompson, M (1998) Trust and reward, *Trust Motivation and Commitment: A Reader*, Strategic Remuneration Research Centre, Faringdon: Oxford.

Thornhill, A and Saunders MNK (2000) Organisational Justice and Strategic Change: The development and Exploration of a Conceptual Framework. Paper presented at the British Academy of Management Annual Conference, Edinburgh.

Torrington, D and Hall, L (1998) Letting go or holding on: The Devolution of Operational Personnel Activities. *HRM Journal*, **8** (1).

Tyler, TR (1989) The psychology of procedural justice: A test of the group value model. *Journal of Personality and Social Psychology*, **57**, 830–838.

Tyler, TR (1990) *Why people obey the law: Procedural Justice, Legitimacy and Compliance*, Yale University Press, New Haven, CT.

Tyler, TR and Dawes, RM (1993) Fairness in groups: Comparing self interst and social identity perspectives, in BA Mellers and J Baron (eds) *Applied Social Psychology and Organizational Settings*, pp. 77–98, Erlbaum, Hillside, NJ.

Tyler, TR and Degoey, P (1995) Collective restraint in social dilemmas: Procedural justice and social identificiation effects on support for authorities. *Journal of Personality and Social Psychology*, **69**, 482–497.

Tyler, TR and Lind, EA (1992) A relational model of authority in groups, in MP Zanna (ed.) *Advances in Experimental Social Psychology*, Vol. 25, pp. 115–191, Academic Press, San Diego, CA.

Walton, RE (1985) From control to commitment in the workplace. Harvard Business Review, **63**, 2, March–April, 76–84.

Multidimensional information and knowledge bases for equality and diversity learning and action

3

Nelarine Cornelius

Chapter overview

Many researchers and practitioners will be familiar with formal monitoring in relation to equality and diversity issues. Indeed, many organisations have gone beyond the basics of monitoring, and generated more complex and powerful formal information systems.

Further, an organisation's formal information and knowledge base not only says a lot about how equality and diversity is perceived, but also the organisation's culture. For example, what is regarded as legitimate or unacceptable measures, given the dominant culture and values? Equally important is how this information is used, whether it is merely collected, or is an undervalued and underutilised resource. We can think about the information base as reflecting the type of equality or diversity information that organisations are *willing*, not just able, to generate.

There are other important mechanisms besides the collection of formal information and knowledge, in particular in learning processes for equality and diversity that can also usefully be used in order to enhance and develop a broader and deeper information and knowledge base for understanding of workplace equality and diversity. We are going to consider the ways in which learning in organisations is a critical means for the development and, importantly, embedding of sustainable developmental means for equality and diversity understanding. Finally, we will consider the implications of capabilities equality for what ought to be paid attention to, re: information, knowledge and learning base. It is suggested that one broad implication is that the equality and diversity information, knowledge and learning envelope needs to be enlarged and deepened, better embedded, and more reflective of 'felt fair' equality. As a basis for challenging the current dominant approaches, we have drawn in particular from the areas of critical management accounting and social capital theory.

Learning objectives

After studying this chapter you should understand:

- the importance of knowledge and information base in defining and shaping equality understanding and action;
- the importance of the 'ethics, values and aspirations landscape' as a critical part of the social fabric of an organisation that can help or impede equality and diversity action;
- learning processes as key mechanisms for acquiring knowledge about an organisation's equality and diversity past, present and possible futures, providing a powerful vehicle for improvement and change;
- the role that information provides in unearthing explicit and tacit knowledge about the social mechanisms that help or impede equality and diversity action;
- the potential enlargement of formal and informal equality and diversity information, knowledge and learning through the application of ideas from critical management accounting and social capital theory.

Key words
information base • learning processes • organisational learning • situated learning • situated knowledge • social capital • social accounting

Introduction

Over the years, the development and use of formal equality and diversity information has been written about extensively by both practitioners and academics. There is a wide range of such approaches, some of which appear simple, at times naïve prescriptions, while others assert themselves to be more sophisticated.

There has been real progress in many organisations as a result of many of the more robust information-gathering initiatives. The support for employees and those acting in their interests that good information provides can be crucial. However, although the collection of such information has and can provide a spur to action, there is clearly no guarantee that it will create widespread motivation or will to change. Importantly, one reason is that many organisations struggle to convert the raw data into useful information.

In other words, what is created are *data generating and gathering hubs*, largely resident in personnel or specialist equality units, that may disseminate personnel statistical and generalist best practice information, but are unlikely to be able to create what is seen as localised, line-relevant knowledge.

So, the collection of certain types of equality information, such as *standardised monitoring information*, if not used well, often fails to connect the auditing process of the equality monitoring to the day-to-day experiences of inequality. Such monitoring can signal best practice compliance for the organisation, but does insufficient for how employees feel. Moreover, 'evidence-based' equality change is too often pursued differentially, with greater scrutiny and transparency in the 'lower status' parts of an organisation, whilst those in more powerful positions who espouse the benefits continue to operate within a set of opaque and elitist rules that perpetuate historical advantages enjoyed by them. The more negative aspects of how high status groups in organisations address equality and diversity issues are dealt with later in this chapter in the section on 'defensive reasoning' and also in Chapter 5.

It should be pointed out that what we will be suggesting is not simply about gathering more and more information for the sake of it, or a plea to create information and knowledge systems that are so complicated that making use of them requires a level of expertise that many organisations would not be able to develop and use. What we are suggesting is that an equality and diversity information and knowledge base very much shapes how equality and diversity issues are understood by an organisation in the first place, and thus what kinds of action are then likely to be seen as reasonable and consequently taken. Therefore, we shall argue that there is a need to include, but also extend well beyond, traditional areas of data collection.

The previous chapters contain a number of ideas that provide an important backdrop to our understanding of managing equality, diversity and inclusion in work organisations. Important ideas that it is worth highlighting and in particular, from a capabilities perspective are outlined in Table 3.1. For each of these ideas, there is a question about information, knowledge and learning, or some combination of these, that can be posed. This list is by no means exhaustive: it is merely indicative of the fuller 'data picture' that emerges from a more holistic and multidimensional account of equality and diversity, which we believe the **capabilities approach** in particular can deliver.

Table 3.1 Outline of the proposals made within the 'foundation theory' chapters of this book and some information, knowledge and learning implications

Proposals made within this book	The 'information, knowledge and learning' implication
The rejection of the traditional 'dualism' of equality that, broadly, places equal opportunities in opposition to diversity management. Not only do we see the approaches as complementary concepts, but also complementary practice	How can we best capture information that informs 'complementary' practice?
The importance of ethics in understanding the underlying philosophy of particular approaches to understanding approaches to addressing inequality, with 'traditional' equal opportunities more closely associated with Kantian, distributive justice thinking and 'traditional' diversity management attributed as utilitarian	What is the ethical landscape of an organisation/section? What are the ethical 'theories in use'? What does this landscape most closely resemble in terms of 'established' ideas on ethics? Are these likely to be commensurate with a 'capabilities'? approach?
The potential application of the capabilities approach, which highlights the importance of voice, agency, working environment, instrumental freedoms (including transparency), information base in enabling or limiting equality	What information/knowledge is regularly called upon to capture and inform understanding of internal, basic and combined capabilities, employee voice and freedom of opportunity? If none, how could such information and knowledge be built up? How can new knowledge development be facilitated through learning processes?

Continued overleaf

Table 3.1 *Continued*

Proposals made within this book	*The 'information, knowledge and learning' implication*
The importance of 'felt fair' equality, as a way of moving beyond 'acting fair' equality	How 'authentic' and present is the voice of employees in an organisation's equality and diversity information and knowledge base (formally and informally?)
The need to develop the concept of inclusion	What does inclusion mean (a) in general, (b) in a specific organisation? How can we evaluate the degree of inclusion that an organisation's members experience and feel?
The importance of evaluation of the psychological contract and model of trust 'in practice' as indicators of the approach to more informal issues for specific archetypes of strategic HRM and, more broadly, the socio-psychological landscape	What evidence (formal or informal) can we identify to locate the type and character of the psychological contract?
The importance of mapping the difference between historical and contemporary sources of inequality and discrimination, with the latter less visible even to the expert eye	Does the main source of equality and diversity information and knowledge used by an organisation (a) look forward, (b) look backward, (c) is concerned with the here and now or (d) some combination of these?
The importance of line delivery of operational HRM/core personnel for delivery of equality and diversity (given that much personnel practice is 'gate-keeping' in nature – e.g. recruitment, selection, appraisal monitoring) and therefore addresses less well the continuous and local aspects of inequality	What is the evidence that personnel/HRM policy and practice helps procedural justice, where, for whom, and at what level in the organisation? How can it be ensured that equality and diversity knowledge is most widely disseminated, embedded and informing local views and action 'in the line'?
The importance of line delivery of equality and diversity for embedding these into the core functional activities in a way that is locally meaningful	What are the measures and indicators that are particularly useful for line managers and their team members?
The potential of strategic and operational HRM to help transform organisational equality action	How might we best link macro-, meso- and macro-level knowledge and learning?
The potential for political, social and labour economic (competition) issues or 'social traps' to remain as the hidden agenda undermining the addressing of equality and diversity issues	How well does an organisation understand/is able to learn about the real rules of the game?
To raise the issue of the need to challenge areas of 'invisibility' and opaqueness that cloak the *realpolitik* of institutional inequalities that often lie within the remit of the most powerful	How does an organisation map and consider stakeholders, in particular, their power and political clout? What other structures (social, economic, physical, etc.) help or hinder equality and diversity learning and action?
Equality, diversity and inclusion management as a core line management competence	How should/could an organisation measure equality and diversity management as a management core competence, and enable managers to learn how to manage equality formally and informally?

Generating formal data, information and knowledge for equality and diversity action

The danger of prescription

What kind of information and knowledge base is likely to be most useful? There is no simple answer. We know from Chapter 2 that factors such as the type of psychological contract and the strategic HRM aspirations and intent can influence equality and diversity choices and action. Therefore, organisations are likely to emphasise aspects of their HRM systems that are most likely to gain attention given the attributes of the approach to people management that predominates. In turn, there will be differences in what is seen as the 'right' approach to dealing with equality and diversity issues.

Moreover, it was also suggested that specific approaches are less likely to deliver 'capabilities equality' than others. So, by implication, if equality and diversity issues addressed historically have been highly selective and narrowly focused, then the information and knowledge base is likely to be similarly so. Therefore, if more sophisticated approaches to equality and diversity management such as capabilities equality are to be undertaken, then aspects of the information and knowledge base will need to shift also to match the manner in which strategy, policy and practice are addressed.

It is clear that any discussion about the fine detail of what constitutes a 'good' information and knowledge base cannot be a prescriptive one (although it will be argued that there are areas attention must be paid to), and needs to be shaped by the specific needs of organisations. However, it would be fair to say that a richer, more holistic, and well-designed knowledge and **information base**, in a suitably receptive environment, is more likely to yield a broader and deeper understanding of equality and diversity choices and actions. Certainly, generating such a base requires not only will, but good investigative (and at times, forensic) skills, able to get 'below the surface' and yield formal and informal data to guide informed, measured and reflective practice.

Further, the thinking that we suggest needs to be employed is metasystemic, as it needs to be understood that changes in one part of the organisation are likely to impact on other parts. For the development of such an equality and diversity information and knowledge base, particular importance is also placed on human resourcing (monitoring) statistics, which if collected regularly and used well, can provide useful high-level indicators of the impact of equality and diversity change.

How do information, knowledge and learning processes interact with equality and diversity action? In Chapter 1, it was proposed that the underlying equality principles determine the methods and actions employed and in turn, the measurements that are regarded as fair and appropriate – 'principle determines method, and method determines measurement'. We will now look first at what kinds of measures are commonly used for the formal assessment of equality and diversity action.

Common formal measures of workforce equality and diversity

If one were to take a straw poll of the core formal 'measures' of equality as commonly used, it is likely that the list would contain measures which were broadly monitoring, density and resource allocation, including pay and conditions. A number of these are outlined in more detail in Chapter 4, but other writers such as Kirton and Green (2000) have attempted to summarise what is commonly done (see Table 3.2). It could be argued that a characteristic of

Table 3.2   Comparison of types of equality initiative. From Kirton and Greene (2000: 102), based upon Miller 1996: 205, 506; modified for Gagnon and Cornelius, 2000: our additions are in bold

Approach	Principle	Strategy	Method	Type of equality
Liberal	Fair equal opportunity	Level playing field	Policy statement, equality-proof recruitment and selection procedures	Equality of opportunity
	Positive action	Assistance to disadvantaged social groups	Monitoring, pre-entry training, in-service training, special courses, elevate EO within management	Equality of opportunity
	Strong positive action	Give positive preference to certain groups	Family-friendly policies, improve access for disabled, make harassment a disciplinary offence	Moving towards equality of outcome
Radical	Positive discrimination	Proportional equal representation	Preferential selection, quotas	Equality of outcome
Managing diversity	Maximise individual potential	Use diversity to add value	Vision statement, organisation audit, business-related objectives, communication and accountability, change culture	Equality means profit aligned with organisational objectives*
Capabilities	**Human-dignity-centred equality: being able to be or do what one has reason to value**	**Establishment of (a) the five instrumental freedoms based upon (b) combined capabilities and (c) agency**	**Multi-method, domain, stakeholder interventions, through line-informed policy**	**Equality of choice and outcomes resulting from the 'free' exercise of freedoms**

* Note: The current authors view this definition as a narrow and unclear characterisation of diversity management.

many of these approaches is that they often provide a 'snapshot' of the status quo, though they can also be used as the basis for periodic review of the impact of measures introduced to address workplace inequality, and importantly, comparisons within and between organisations.

Typically these are the most usual *primary formal measures* of inequality, and stem from broadly *labour economics* and *labour relations* traditions (e.g. Anonymous, 2001). These measures usually centre around comparing the fortunes of the majority group against those of traditionally disadvantaged groups. In the UK, the IRS (2001) report on their study, 'Monitoring for equality', based on 75 organisations from the private and public sectors. They found that the main employee characteristics that were subject to equality monitoring by employers were gender and ethnic origin, with disability and age also growing in importance. They assert that :

> The principle behind monitoring is to check that there is equality of opportunity for all groups in the workforce, particularly for groups that face discrimination in society as a whole, and to take steps to correct policy or procedures if there appears to be inequality. Its use can also enable provision to be made for particular needs, for example to help identify whether or not any special equipment should be used to assist staff with disabilities.
>
> Monitoring enables an employer to check whether or not the characteristics of the workforce as a whole match those of the relevant population (whether there is under representation).   (IRS, January 2001: 4)

Broadly, the following are often monitored in organisations:

- numbers from a particular group recruited to an organisation and/or sector;
- numbers in post at different levels in the hierarchy (non-senior) of an organisation and/or sector;
- job segregation in relation to a 'traditional disadvantage' (usually better assessed for gender than for other sources of traditional disadvantage);
- progression rates;
- number holding senior positions;
- differences in income levels;
- differences in contractual terms and conditions.

Secondary formal measures are used less commonly and collected less systematically and routinely, possibly as they are regarded as more sensitive (and often negative) information about an organisation, but also possibly because there is less inter-organisational or sector comparative data. Examples include legal and quasi-legal measures of 'transgressions' and climate- and attitude-based survey assessment. These stem from *institutional and organisational psychology-centred HRM traditions* respectively. Examples of these include:

- number of equality-related grievances;
- number of equality-related harassment cases;

Box 3.1 Summary of IRS 2001 review of monitoring for equality

Summary

Monitoring is essential in medium-sized and large organisations if practitioners are to check that equal opportunities policies and procedures are working effectively, and to identify direct or indirect discrimination, according to an IRS survey of 75 employers.

Characteristics monitored: Among the IRS panel, which was questioned during autumn 2000, the most commonly monitored workforce characteristics are gender, ethnic origin, disability and age. Around three-quarters of our respondents – 59 employers – undertake some form of monitoring on one or more of these characteristics.

Organisation size: Respondents who undertake equal opportunities monitoring range in size from 37 employees, at the Metropolitan Police Authority, to 93,000 at US-owned retailer Asda Stores. Those that do not make use of monitoring, however, tend to be smaller employers.

Categories used: Categorising employees by straightforward characteristics, such as gender and age, is a fairly clear-cut operation in the overwhelming majority of cases. By contrast, more complex and less-easily defined personal characteristics, such as ethnic origin and disability, can cause employers significant problems when they are trying to categorise workers for monitoring purposes.

Official statistics: Many employers choose to make use of the categories describing ethnic origin and different types of disability that are used in official statistics, such as the population census and the Labour Force Survey, because this makes their workforce profile more readily comparable with government data for national, regional and local populations.

Key findings: Most of our analysis is based on detailed questioning of the 59 employers in our panel that make use of some form of equality monitoring. Findings include:

- *the main **reason for monitoring** is to check the effectiveness of equal opportunities policies and procedures* – 55 employers cite this as one reason for monitoring. In a similar vein, 39 say they monitor to ensure the best person is appointed to any position, and 26 use monitoring to help avoid or reduce the costs associated with employment tribunals (as a result, for example, of sex or race discrimination claims);

- *the main **practical use made of monitoring data** is to check the effectiveness of equal opportunities policies and procedures* – this reflects the reason monitoring is introduced, and hence is reported to be the case by a large majority of our respondents (50 of the 59 that make use of monitoring). The next most common use to which monitoring data are put is to prepare reports, which typically go to boards or other senior managers;

- *more than half of our sample monitor the take-up of **equal opportunities initiatives*** – in addition to personal characteristics such as gender, monitoring can be used to measure the use of policies and procedures relating to issues such as parental leave, bullying and harassment, and childcare provision;

- *the most common **technique for equal opportunities monitoring** among the IRS panel is self-classification by job applicants, who are asked to complete a monitoring form with a job application* – this approach is used by 49 organisations in our sample. Next most common is self-monitoring by new recruits, who are asked to complete a monitoring form upon appointment (used by 23 employers). However, workforce audits are also popular: this method is used by 21 respondents;

- *rather surprisingly, just 12 employers report that they have made changes to their monitoring procedures as a result of the **Data Protection Act 1998*** – however, a further 11 IRS panel members say that they are planning changes because of this legislation; and

- *in general, a picture of considerable **change** emerges from our survey* – 36 panel members out of 59 that undertake equal opportunities monitoring have made changes to their policies or practices on monitoring, on issues unrelated to the Data Protection Act, within the past five years. A further 27 employers report that they plan to make changes.

Box 3.2 Marks & Spencer monitoring results, June 2000

Ethnicity, gender and age company statistics

The key points are summarised below. Information is retrieved from the June payroll reports, compared historically with data gathered in January in previous years.

Ethnicity

● Ethnic minority representation is slightly lower. This could be due to numbers being inflated in January with temporary seasonal staff; however, as a business we still have a higher than average representation:

	JUN 00	JAN 00	JAN 99	JAN 96
Total company	8.9%	10.5%	9.5%	8%
Stores, distribution centres, service centres	8.9%	11%	9.5%	7.9%
Head office	8.8%	9%	8.4%	8.4%

(91 census – 5.5%)

● In total there are proportionality more men than women from ethnic minorities:

	JUN 00		JAN 00		JAN 99	
	MALE	FEMALE	MALE	FEMALE	MALE	FEMALE
Total company	22.1%	5.3%	15%	9%	13.7%	8.3%
Stores, distribution centres, service centres	23.7%	5%	16%	9%	14%	8.3%
Head office	7.6%	9.5%	10%	8%	7.1%	9.1%

● Ethnic minority representation in senior management remains relatively the same:

	JUN 00	JAN 00	JAN 99
Total company – band 5+	2.2%	2%	2%
Stores, distribution centres, service centres – band 5+	0.4%	1%	0%
Head office – band 5+	2.7%	2%	2%

Management trainees from ethnic minority groups have increased by 0.5% to 7.5%
Store administered management from ethnic minority groups has increased by 0.2% to 2.2%

Gender

● Female/male proportionality remains unchanged (proportion that is female set out below):

	JUN 00	JAN 00	JAN 99
Total company	78.6%	79%	79%
Stores, distribution centres, service centres	79.5%	80%	80%
Head office	64.2%	64%	63%

● The proportion of females represented in senior management has grown, but has reduced in head office:

	JUN 00	JAN 00	JAN 99
Total company – band 5+	46.8%	44%	40%
Stores, distribution centres, service centres – band 5+	40.2%	40%	37%
Head office – band 5+	48.8%	57%	54%

Working time

● The proportion of managers working less than maximum hours reduced after growing last year:

	JUN 00	JAN 00	JAN 99
Total company	8.2%	11%	9%
Stores, distribution centres, service centres	12%	14%	10%
Head office	6.2%	10%	9%

Age						

● In total our workforce is becoming older, however figures could have been inflated in January owing to the volume of temporary seasonal staff:

	JUN 00		JAN 00		JAN 99	
	–45	+45	–45	+45	–45	+45
Total company	66.3%	33.7%	71%	29%	66%	34%
Stores, distribution centres, service centres	65.2%	34.8%	70%	30%	64%	36%
Head office	82.6%	17.4%	84%	16%	81%	19%

Note: Band 5+ signifies the level of senior management.
Source: Marks & Spencer

- number of equality-related disciplinary cases;
- number of equality-related industrial tribunals;
- equality-related employment legislation;
- human rights legislation (of late);
- equality-focused climate surveys;
- equality-focused attitude surveys;
- key informant interviews.

All of these formal measures have played a vital role in bringing out of the shadows aspects of inequality that could easily have remained out of sight. Crucially, they provide organisations with important management information necessary to evidence the need for action, and in turn, provide a benchmark against which progress can be assessed: what you cannot measure will be harder to manage.

Organisations will have a number of policies and activities in place that help to create a more supportive environment as a more proactive, positive action approach, largely though not exclusively in response to gender issues. The range available can also be used as a benchmark of the seriousness of the organisation towards creating a more enabling environment. These might include:

- 'family friendly' policies;
- women-only training sessions;
- mentoring schemes;
- support networks.

All 'environmental' activities are important, but they tend to be measured in terms of their presence or absence, rather than in terms of their effectiveness and impact.

Further, as HRM is often the lead function in relation to these issues, the policy and practice that is developed for equality and diversity reflects the core personnel activities that relate to these measures and in which HRM takes the most active role, typically more vigorously around recruitment and selection policy and procedures (i.e. *entry level assessment*), as it appears in practice to be regarded as the main vehicle for redressing the balance and facilitating procedural justice.

However, in spite of the advancements made through the use of these formal measures, a number of propositions can be made (see also Cornelius and Gagnon, 2002).

1. The dominant approach to measuring equality and inequality systematically centres on the fairness of outcomes, particularly through the use of labour-market-informed density and distribution measures. Such approaches (a) largely neglect the issue of the measurement of fairness of processes, and equally, (b) systematic and robust measures need to be developed for the latter. This is a narrow reflection of the breadth and complexity of the manifestation of inequality in the workplace.

2. Most of (1) centres on presence and pay differentials, undervaluing in turn the importance of evaluation of 'felt fair' equality for employees, by highlighting 'acting fair' for 'auditing' purposes. Increasing the prominence of 'felt fair' equality is likely to be best built around factors such as agency, inclusion and agenda shaping, and to this end, more robust measures of these are necessary for progress beyond these areas.

3. Within the critical HRM academic literature, the formal measurements which are most commonly construed as 'legitimate' reflect specifically a Rawlsian–Kantian approach (discussed more fully later in this chapter), tend to be outcome-oriented (e.g. pay and density) and are often seen as prime measures. Confusingly, the most commonly used formal measures within the diversity literature, which is often placed in opposition ethically to equal opportunities as it is categorised as a utilitarian approach, often use the same measures that dominate the Rawlsian–Kantian traditions.

4. Organisational and management action is shaped by the measurements used to evaluate those actions. These in turn are often the most transparent and lend themselves readily to inter-organisational comparison, but are not necessarily of primary importance for addressing the underlying causality of inequality within a specific organisation.

We would further highlight the following:

5. The most commonly used formal measure is primarily the collection of organisation-wide monitoring information, which is often only collated and circulated annually. This is likely to be very removed from the material reality of the formal and informal social processes and management and colleague actions that are the engine-room of the day-to-day dynamics of inequality.

6. The range of measures is likely to be indicative of attitudes and, in turn, values and cultural responses to dealing with inequality. For example, if a narrow, 'management information system' range is the extent of what Sen (1999) would call the 'information base', this may become an organisational signal/symbol of remoteness from the cut and thrust of the real difficulties and hardships of inequality at the coalface, for example issues of workplace inclusion (Gagnon and Cornelius, 2000).

Measurement and perceptual gaps: the 'act fair'–'felt unfair' divide

In Chapter 1 research undertaken for the Runnymede Trust in the UK was mentioned briefly, and it is worth revisiting this research in more detail and from the point of view of the information and knowledge base and *perceptual gaps*, specifically between those with responsibility for equality and diversity issues and those at whom equality and diversity action is targeted.

In the UK, the Runnymede Trust commissioned a report on racial equality and the corporate agenda based around a study of FTSE 100 companies (Sanglin-Grant and Schneider, 2000), which had three aims:

- to assess the numbers of ethnic minority professional and managerial staff in FTSE companies in the UK;
- to identify the type of best practice, policies and systems in place to actively promote equality or opportunity for ethnic minority employees;
- to describe opportunities and barriers that ethnic minority professionals and managers experience as they progress through organizations.

The key findings in the report were:

1. There was a lack of ethnic minority staff in senior positions (*a hard or density measure* in our terms).
2. Ethnic minority professionals and managers feel excluded by subtle non-overt discrimination.
3. Race is still not firmly on the business agenda.
4. Leadership on equality issues was present in only a few companies.
5. 'When there's a will there's a way': determination was as important for progress as the mechanisms in place.

Focusing on point 2 in particular, all of the responding companies believed that their policies and procedures for progression did not discriminate, but this view was not shared by ethnic minority employees themselves. All those involved in the focus groups and one-to-one discussions reported occasions when they had felt excluded by colleagues or not supported by their managers, and many had felt it necessary to move companies to get on. This was deemed easier than confronting the issues. One of those interviewed remarked that: 'I worried how it would affect my references, would I be seen as some sort of troublemaker. But it means that I didn't get it off my chest, which I regret.'

The employees were anxious not to attract special favours (and have concerns about targets in this regard) but they did expect companies to have policies in place and to address the behavioural issues.

The report's authors concluded that:

1. There is a *mismatch* between the perceptions of companies and their ethnic minority employees; responding companies had considerable faith in their policies, responding almost uniformly that:

    (a) promotions in our organisations are entirely based on merit;

(b) ethnic minority staff are readily accepted and respected in our organisation;

(c) policies and procedures we have for recruitment do not discriminate against ethnic minority groups;

(d) there is a real commitment from the top to improve the company's performance on race equality issues;

(e) further, the report says that the certainty of the responses (around 95% for 1(a) to 1(c), 75% for 1(d)) is particularly startling *given the few organisations who actually take any steps to get feedback from ethnic minority employees.*

2. There was *strong agreement*, however, between companies and their ethnic minority employees on the barriers to progress; the main ones were (ranked first four out of 13 possibilities):

- lack of awareness of problems;
- perception that it is not an issue for business;
- lack of time;
- lack of line management support.

Thus organisations *believed* that they were doing a good job of addressing inequality, while ethnic minority employees *felt* otherwise. Importantly, the evidence brought forward to support the organisations' view consisted of their 'equality statistics', majoratively falling into the primary formal density measures category presented earlier in this chapter. Crucially, these formal measures did not appear to tap into how employees felt about equality and, in turn, about what in the organisation 'felt unfair' to them.

This 'act fair'–'felt unfair' gap is likely to be more than just an artefact of public relations stances and rhetoric on the part of organisations, or of self-centredness and excessively unrealistic aims on the part of employees. Such a perceptual gap is as likely to exist in the most proactive equality-oriented companies as it is in the equality-insensitive ones (though not necessarily to the same degree).

To reiterate, measurement must play a vital role in enhancing our understanding of difficulties encountered and progress made in relation to change and equality and diversity. However, a number of the areas that we have highlighted as important sources of information and knowledge – in particular, feelings, tacit knowledge, formal and informal power and status – are not as readily amenable to the formal equality data collection methods that are most commonly used. There is, we believe, a need to enhance the measurement, or at least the evaluation, of intangibles to complement these.

Importantly, it could be argued that much of this kind of information is targeted primarily for use centrally, by HQ, core personnel or senior management. So there is a danger that although equality and diversity information is gathered, equality knowledge resides within a small section of the organisation, such as the board or the personnel department, though intranet or electronic-HRM (e-HRM) systems increasingly provide an opportunity for such information to be shared organisation-wide (see Harris and Cornelius, 2002).

Exploring the measurement of inequality through an ethical lens

Capabilities' equality and information base

How might one consider the issue of the measurement of inequality from the perspective of ethical theory? Sen, Nussbaum and their colleagues have considered this question as part of their work for the United Nations. For example, Sen has argued that the dominant ethical discourses influential in the field of developmental economics are lacking in their evaluative strength if freedoms, equality and justice are not taken to be important. This is because the 'information base' on which they draw is flawed or deficient in each case. For example, the Rawlsian perspective draws its information in the main from the measurement of primary goods (i.e. income), in large part because a better measure of distributive justice has not been identified or widely adopted. Thus this information base is limited in that it allows a focus on the fairness of outcomes only, neglecting the fairness of processes. Within libertarianism, a 'purist' rights-based approach, the information base or evaluative measures used ignore consequences altogether and posit that the presence of freedom, justice and equality can be determined by evaluating whether individuals have equal rights, equal opportunities or equality before the law. Utilitarianism, on the other hand, does take a keen interest in results, but belies a 'distributional indifference' of goods in that 'happiness' in the aggregate is its primary concern, to the neglect of rights, freedoms and other non-utility concerns (Sen, 1999). Thus each of these major ethical theories can be viewed as depending for their evaluative strength on a flawed information base.

Using capabilities theory to develop new measures of equality at work

Nussbaum, like Sen, is critical of traditional measures used within the 'dominant discourses' of equality within development economics. She argues that the two conventional criteria or measures, namely preference satisfaction on one hand and resource allocation on the other, are deficient for the measurement of equality and thus quality of life (Nussbaum, 1999). A focus on resource allocation, for example through GNP per capita, leaves out many important measures at the macroeconomic level, e.g. educational opportunities, life expectancy, health care, land rights, political liberties, employment opportunities. A focus on preference satisfaction brings another set of difficulties because preferences, Nussbaum argues, are not exogenous, made independently of economic and social conditions. Preferences are at least partly socially shaped; they are not fixed in the nature of things but are constructed by social traditions of privilege and subordination. Thus a pure preference-based approach typically will reinforce inequalities, especially those inequalities that are entrenched enough to have crept into people's very desires.

Nussbaum argues that these deficiencies are transcended by a capabilities approach, which takes human dignity as its starting point, involving the idea of equal worth. This entails a different set of criteria or measures, much more complex and multi-layered than those used within the traditional paradigms. Rather than asking 'how satisfied is this woman?' or 'how much in the way of resources is she able to command?', a capabilities approach asks 'what is she actually able to do and to be?'. Its measurement or evaluation thus demands a dramatically different information base.

Sen and Nussbaum argue that a much more satisfactory information base is possible when evaluating or measuring the degree of equality within a society than those in conventional use. Nussbaum sets out a variety of measures in this regard and Sen has developed the UN Human Development Index which is an attempt to get beyond one-dimensional measurement. In both cases these theorists have been concerned to see their ideas enacted or put into practice. Persuading policy makers of new measures has been a central part of this wish to see theory affect practice. To a degree, this is a distinguishing factor in comparison with the authors or proponents of traditional ethical theories.

The capabilities approach as applied to development economics suggests that through the use of a wider information base, through information broadening, it is possible to have consistent, coherent criteria for social and economic assessment. Sen writes in *Development as Freedom* (1999):

> On the evaluative side, the approach used here concentrates on a factual base that differentiates it from more traditional practical ethics and economic policy analysis, such as the 'economic' concentration on the primacy of income and wealth (rather than on the characteristics of human lives and substantive freedoms); the 'utilitarian' focus on mental satisfaction (rather than on creative discontent and constructive dissatisfaction), the 'libertarian' preoccupation with procedures for liberty (with deliberate neglect of *consequences* (our italics) that derive from those procedures) and so on. *The over-arching case (is) for a different factual base, which focuses on substantive freedoms that people have reason to enjoy....* (our italics) (1999: 19)

There is an important comparison that can be made here with dominant approaches to measuring workplace equality. Both equal opportunities and diversity management have rested upon a relatively narrow range of formal measures or criteria in assessing progress towards objectives. These have tended to be limited to density measures, numbers of members of targeted groups in senior positions or at certain income levels, and to a lesser extent, progression rates. Transgression measures have also been used to assess progress (or its absence), for example the tracking of grievance and disciplinary matters related to discrimination or harassment.

Further, strict legal compliance and use of 'hard', accounting-type measures only to assess equality in an organisation have obvious limits (although legal provisions are none the less essential, and can also play an important role in agenda-setting, e.g. through well-publicised cases involving high levels of compensation). But a focus on hard measures (density measures) can be criticised and found deficient just as the Rawlsian use of primary goods or income as key criteria of equality is found deficient by Sen, and resource allocation measures within economic approaches to equality generally are found deficient by Nussbaum.

Applying the capabilities approach to measuring workplace inequality

In Chapter 1 we highlighted that different approaches to workplace equality are likely to have a different formal measurement emphasis. To recall,

- for positive action, the focus is on monitoring, 'special' training and management awareness;
- for strong positive action, the focus is on constraint-lifting policies and human resourcing policies for countering 'negative', discriminatory behaviour;
- for radical equal opportunities, the focus is on preferential selection and quotas;
- for managing diversity, the focus is on top and line management vision, measures and accountability, culture change and communication.

We pointed out also that none of these focus specifically and explicitly either on what individuals or groups are free to do, or on what the organisation is doing to enable this freedom to become a reality. A combined capabilities concept would demand that attention be paid to (a) how the organisation was enabling internal capabilities, and (b) how the organisation was creating the conditions in which the internal capabilities could be fully and freely employed, in other words, combined capabilities. Further, what will feel fair and feel right to members of traditionally disadvantaged groups is what materially affords personal dignity and freedom of choice.

Is the measurement 'gap' inherent to law and policy?

A contemporary account of the wants of the traditionally disadvantaged is also imperative, as there are limits to what the law and policy can deliver. First, this is because the law is often out of step or lags behind the material reality of people's lives: it gives largely historical accounts of inequality (Annas in Nussbaum and Sen, 1995), rather than contemporary and forward-looking accounts, as it is easier to see where inequality has travelled than where it currently is. Second, such approaches are subject to what Nussbaum (1999) refers to generically (and in a gender-neutral way) as 'paternalistic': largely developed within the mindset of those who are the powerful in a society or an organisation, rarely the traditionally disadvantaged.

Diversity of measures to capture diversity of issues: 'information and measurement' lessons from other academic traditions and practices

Ideas from critical management accounting

The emphasis within the primary formal measures used for addressing workplace equality and diversity management centre around one particular kind of measurement, that of **density**: the numbers of particular groups of employees present at different levels or within different parts of an organisation. So, although this may include gender, ethnicity, disability, sexual orientation and so on, they are all fundamentally the *same* kind of measure.

In order to understand more clearly the impact of particular kinds of measure, we have drawn, first, from the field of critical management accounting. In an accounting context, we could argue that the parallel for using the same kind of measure would be to measure only profit (albeit different kinds of profit) – clearly crucially important to any commercial enterprise, but revealing very little about *why* a company is making or losing money, or how it could improve its overall performance. No management accountant worth his or her salt would under any circumstances expect an organisation to depend on a single measure and, in turn, to use this to assess the health of an organisation. First, the information it generates would be limited, and second, it is too obviously prone to manipulation and distortion, so that performance becomes merely compliance and meeting set targets, and efforts to 'prove' how the size of the single measure has been maximised. So for example, within the field of critical management accounting, where finding the 'right' measures is the bread and butter of the work undertaken in research and practice, and where there are relatively sophisticated models of measuring performance, some such as economic value add (EVA), which until recently have been widely used, are increasingly being viewed less favourably as they are considered to be, in essence, a sophisticated but *single* measure, and some writers have argued strongly for more sophisticated and holistic approaches to measurement (e.g. Otley, 1999).

In critical management accounting, there is an increasing interest in how measures influence the behaviour and outlook of people. An important area of concern would be how well the enterprise is managed, and how effectively resources and processes are being utilised for overall organisational effectiveness and health. The move within this field is towards *more holistic, balanced measurement*. For example, in France, there has been the development of an approach called the *tableau de bord* (*the dashboard*, e.g. Lebas, 1993) – an array of measures that is tailored for individual organisations. The underpinning logic is important to understand: the unique characteristics of an organisation that may contribute to performance; individuals and groups in different organisations are likely to have different factors that contribute to success or failure.

Whose voice? Increasing employee voice in accounting practice

The dashboard analogy is useful in one sense but limited in another. Its usefulness is that it is easy to understand that a high reading on the fuel gauge is clearly an insufficient guide for establishing whether a car is working well or not. Understanding how specific interrelations add value to or inhibit performance is vital for improving overall performance and building internal expertise that can be self-managed, not driven by visiting management accountants and auditors when they do their annual rounds. The limitation is that the imagery could be seen as inherently about the view of the person in control, a top-down account, with the view simply being generated from the top and for the interests of the top.

Critical accounting authors such as Robert Simons (1995) have questioned the limitations of the centralist approach to management accounting. Simons makes the distinction between different kinds of control.

- *Diagnostic control.* These are the kinds of controls that generate measures and indices of performance that are particularly amenable to external scrutiny.
- *Interactive control.* Such control enables line managers to interact with staff in order to understand better the dynamics of how the business is being managed locally.
- *Collegial control.* This is the kind of control that takes place primarily in an interpersonal manner – this is social control that also allows tacit and expert management knowledge to build locally and in the line, rather than residing solely with accountancy professionals, and requires social 'measures' of performance.

Macintosh argues that for employee accounting, where employee performance is assessed, the emphasis very much errs towards the kinds of controls that are amenable to external scrutiny. He has suggested that many of the approaches to employee accounting, which purport to capture employee contribution and empowerment, are managerialist and have tight senior command and control interests within them: they are often reflective of pseudo-empowerment and pseudo-participation, and are essentially feudal in nature (1994: 247). Core to Macintosh's radical thinking is the difficulty of loosening the reins of power in the centre, and the rhetoric of democratisation of management accounting processes that are underpinned by the reality of centralist, mock federalist action (1994: 248), and the liberation of authentic employee voice. Macintosh argues that:

> The privileging of shareholders over other stakeholders is merely a 'cover story' to the hide the reality that maximising shareholders' wealth is a narrow, parochial, exploitative and self-serving discourse of an elite group (1994: 253) . . . The (management accounting discourse) constructs the role of managers as scorekeeping, attention directing, problem solving, and decision-making in the interests of organisational efficiency and goal congruence in order to maximise shareholders' wealth. This discourse is . . .

exploitative since (although) these managers have reasonable chances to rise to the level of upper executives. (The) reality is that for the most part, the manager's job is one of surveillance, watching, controlling, and evaluating the performance of the rest of the employees . . . In short, the manager's job is to see that the employees deliver the required profits. (1994: 254)

Clearly, Macintosh's ideas reflect the post-modernist, neo-Marxist position that he develops within his research and to this extent, is a particular and not necessarily widely shared point of view. However, his ideas do suggest that the measurement of performance locally may be primarily to benefit those at the top but with little regard for employee concerns, and we can readily find parallels within the context of equality and diversity management. Many of us will have had experience of monitoring statistics gathered to demonstrate that the executive team is 'taking equality issues seriously', and for external appreciation (for example, by the government or other companies) rather than as a basis for internal evaluation and change. The challenge, then, is to establish measures that place employee voice more explicitly within them.

Evaluation of tangible and intangible contributions to performance

The importance of different kinds of measure, depending upon the degree of tangibility and intangibility of what is to be measured, and that allow an evaluation that can guide action, is understood well within this literature.

Macintosh (1994) has extended thinking in relation to more complex understanding of management accounting and control by also making distinctions between what can reasonably be 'measured' and what is less easily measured, but none the less needs to be evaluated. He argues that there are factors within management systems that are clear and unambiguous and readily amenable to instrumental tests. However:

(An) assessment situation occurs when both the ends and the means are non-rational, and uncertainty reaches its maximum and assessment takes on a new dimension. . . . Efficiency and instrumental tests are unsatisfactory, so organisations must retreat to (a) more appropriate means of assessment, the social test. (For such tests) assessment leaves the realm of economics and enters the domain of social opinions, beliefs and values . . . . Coping with the need to satisfy simultaneously many different elements is not (an) easy task but the problem becomes all the more difficult when there is a dependency on various groups. Here the organisation must adjust the relative weighting of the multiple and different criteria . . . That accountants should gather, store and report information about social opinions and beliefs remains a novel and perhaps uncomfortable idea. The idea, however, is increasing in importance in the accounting domain. Socially and environmentally concerned groups of ethically-based mutual investment funds purchase securities of only those firms with a strong record in these areas. (1994: 129–132 and 143)

Clearly, we are not suggesting that critical management accounting is a viable or desirable approach to addressing equality and diversity measurement, especially given the persistent predominance of bureaucratic efficiency and instrumental measures as a means of management control.

What we are saying is that what critical management accounting highlights – the weakness of single point measures, the 'dashboard' and tailoring of measurement, the realisation that different kinds of measures are needed depending upon the degree of intangibility, the importance of social tests and measures, more interactive forms of control, and indeed, the inappropriateness of formal measurement for certain kinds of social actions – are analogies that can be put to good use within the equality and diversity context.

Social capital and contributions to more 'holistic' measurement and learning

The term 'capital' has been applied in a variety of ways as a means of understanding more fully the contribution that individuals and groups make. In a review of the use of social capital ideas in a range of contexts, Baron, Field and Schuller (2000) refer to social capital as 'broadly, social networks, the reciprocities that arise from them, and the value of these for achieving mutual goals' (2000: 1). It is an idea that is cross-disciplinary. Ideas that dominate within their edited review include trust, networks, inclusion, belongingness and the challenge of meaningful measurement. The challenge of measurement relates firstly to the range of understandings that have been used to define social capital over the years, but also there is the challenge of developing valid measures. Importantly, they also ask the question: 'Is social capital itself a characteristic of a flourishing society or a means of achieving it?' (2000: 29) and there is also real concern that it could be abused in a normative manner, that it could be misused in an oppressive, normative fashion. A key concern of those with an interest in social capital is its erosion from various social contexts. However, Baron *et al.* argue that in spite of the academic, methodological and practitioner difficulties, social capital matters for a variety of reasons. Specifically:

1. It shifts the focus of analysis from the behaviour of individual agents to a pattern of relationships between agents, social units and institutions.
2. Its development out of research of a diverse kind acts as a link between micro-, meso- and macro levels of analysis.
3. It is inherently multidisciplinary and interdisciplinary.
4. It reasserts issues of value at the heart of social science discourse, as terms such as trust, sharing and community are central to it.
5. The approach to inquiry which has drawn attention to crucial aspects of social relations that impinge on economic and political life, and that are neither easily nor convincingly incorporated into an explanatory model based on the rational pursuit of individual self-interest (after Edwards and Foley, 1998, cited in *Baron et al.*, 2000), is essentially a *pluralistic* idea.

So models of social capital have the potential to bring together a range of perspectives that, on the face of it, fit well with a capabilities equality position. Importantly, Sen's (1999) argument, outlined in Chapter 1, that within capabilities equality, freedoms provide the ends and means of equality, it might be argued also that *social capital is a different but consonant kind of ends* and *means of a flourishing social system.*

Different kinds of 'people capital': the work of Nan Lin

Perhaps one of the most respected accounts of social capital is that offered by the sociologist Nan Lin (2001), who has worked in the field for over twenty years.

Lin outlines the manner in which 'people as capital' has been conceptualised over the years. He makes the distinction between these different accounts of 'people capital'.

- In Marxist terms, the classic theory of capital is what emerges from the social relations between capitalists and workers in the processes of commodity production and consumption. It is part of the surplus value (both revenue and capital or increments of valued resources) that is 'pocketed' by capitalists. Importantly, Lin points out that 'capital is intrinsically a social notion. Capital entails processes of social activity. The production processes . . . involve social processes . . . The exchange process, by definition, is also social' (2001: 7). 'Within this model of capital, workers involved in the process of production do not generate or accumulate capital for the labourers . . . investment and profit reside with the capitalists' (2001: 8).
- **Human capital**. This idea was developed in particular by Theodore Schultz (1961). Human capital is the value added to employees through the acquisition of knowledge, skills and other kinds of know-how: *the added valued is embedded in employees themselves*, and adds to the value of their labour.
- **Cultural capital**. Bordieu (1990) argues that the acquisition of the dominant culture of skills and knowledge is transmitted to students who reproduce the values of the dominant culture. In other words, training and education might be seen as human capital by some, but as *cultural capital* by others. Bordieu's work highlights the maintenance of status and power through the use of cultural capital, which is in contrast to Schultz's more hopeful account of the inherent and more potentially universal potential for workers to acquire personal value. However, both human and cultural capital theories are *neo-capital theories*, within which workers are capable of gaining and keeping some of the surplus value of their own labour. It is the investment of personal resources for the production of profit.
- **Social capital**. Lin argues that the premise behind social capital is that of investment in social relations with expected returns in the 'marketplace' where the market may be economic, political, labour or community (2001:

19). Lin argues that the individual perspective at the heart of neo-capital theories can be expanded with the notion of social capital, or capital captured through social relations. He states that 'In this approach, capital is seen as a social asset by virtue of the actors' connections and access to resources in the network or group of which they are members' (2001: 19).

Lin's laudably clear definition of social capital belies the complexity of what it is in practice. Importantly, the implications for information, knowledge and learning for equality and diversity action are substantial. The theory suggests that social networks may be key to individual achievement and social inclusion, and that important mechanisms for enhancing or diminishing these reside within social stratification, networks and mobility. Importantly, Lin puts forward the argument, supported by empirical research, *that differential access to social capital shapes social inequalities*, citing in particular his study of inequality in social capital in China, within the context of labour market opportunities and access to different categories of jobs. His analysis is detailed, but some of the headline findings underpinning his calculations on access to general social capital (positions accessed, status and seniority in the labour market and in organisations) and political social capital (as per general, but within organisations) suggest that women consistently have less access to general and political social capital, and had a deficit in social, human and institutional capital, i.e., that there was *capital inequality*. Lin also suggests that:

- *Capital deficit* is the extent to which different social groups, for reasons of investment or opportunities, have come to possess a different quality or quantity of capital.
- *Return deficit* is the extent to which a given quality or quantity of capital generates differential returns for different social groups, due to different mobilisation strategies or institutional responses.

Lin argues strongly that:

> differential access to social capital deserves much greater research attention. It (is) suggested that social groups (gender, race) have different access to social capital because of advantaged or disadvantaged structural positions and social networks. For the disadvantaged to gain a better status, strategic behaviours required them to access resources beyond their usual social circles, find ties outside their own neighbourhood or those who are employed, or find ties across ethnic boundaries ... (Inequality in social capital) helps to isolate the cultural and institutional nature of such inequalities for a given society (our italics) and demonstrate the strategic significance of (specific strategies for these disadvantaged) within such institutional contexts. (2001: 122–123)

A full account of Lin's work is beyond the scope of this chapter, but importantly, he has developed his thinking over the years within strongly cross-cultural (in the USA) and multicultural contexts, originating in his work on social networks in the USA, Central America, Haiti and East Asia.

What is the importance of the ideas of social capital to equality and diversity action? Sen (1999) has argued strongly for the importance of the information base, and in Chapter 1 we have suggested that the quality of the information base will influence greatly its potential for use as a mechanism for enhancing accountability. Further, we have suggested that:

> The interest in process (means) as well as ends, and the informal nature of much that perpetuates disadvantage, again suggests a need for measuring what matters, which goes well beyond, e.g., density and hard measures of fairness. (p. 54)

Ideas on social capital from the field of management

More specifically within the area of management research, some scholars have started to incorporate social capital thinking into new ways of thinking about important aspects of strategic management. For example, Nahapiet and Ghoshal (1998) have suggested that there is a perceptible shift in theories from market failure towards organisational advantage, the latter achieved through capabilities (in the strategic management sense) of creating and sharing knowledge. Nahapiet and Ghoshal suggest the following:

1. Social capital facilitates the creation of new intellectual capital.
2. Organisations, as institutional settings, are conducive to the development of high levels of social capital.
3. It is because of their density of social capital that firms, within certain limits, have an advantage over markets in creating and sharing intellectual capital.

The use of the term intellectual capital is interesting, as it signals an interest within the business world of the added value of the intangible knowledge. However, their focus on structure focused very heavily on what is shared – for example, shared codes and language, shared narratives, which might limit the scope from social structures that enhance the value of difference, in other words, that need to be enlarged in order to avoid becoming Bordieu's elitist cultural capital. Further, it could be argued that this is a limited view of value add, and that human capital, a much broader and richer view of value add, as described by Schultz, and the more cross-cultural views on social capital developed by Lin, builds more strongly and explicitly a wider set of 'diversity friendly' attributes of human and social capital.

What additionally might we measure?

The social capital literature suggests that there is a strong belief that the 'right', or appropriate, *ensemble of measures* can greatly assist our understanding of the organisational structures that perpetuate inequality, from the macro- through to micro- levels, and importantly, where there are deficiencies, that there are ways in which they can be enriched, but crucially, that they always have the potential to have their social capital *eroded* also.

An effective system of measurement and evaluation of equality must be multidimensional, formal and informal, multi-domain and multi-stakeholder in orientation and contain a balance of long- and short-term criteria. What does the information tell us about the concept of equality behind the decisions made? Largely, this will be determined by the range, breadth and depth of sources the database draws upon, which might include:

- The character, number, distribution and effectiveness of the strategies, policies, procedures and other actions, the equality processes, and the outcomes of equality processes, such as advancement and movement towards and achievement of freedom of choice of career options for the traditionally disadvantaged when compared with the choices available to the majority of advantaged organizational members.

- The methodology and methods of evaluation of equality and diversity action, including review. The methodology and methods should be understood through the intellectual, behavioural and affective spheres ('head, hands and heart'). Because freedom and equality are acted out in the social and psychological domains, this broad approach is important. Climate and dissatisfaction surveys, and focus groups, are examples of methods that in combination with other 'harder' data, such as progression rates, may help to capture this range of information. However, other processes of information generation and capture, such as those most commonly associated with organisational learning, are likely to be equally informative, and can operate on a day-to-day, rather than just a period basis.

- An overall assessment of 'hard' and 'soft' strategic and change management equality inputs (including meta-systemic knowledge and the degree and nature of the movement created). These strategic measures are an indication of the organisation's commitment to equality and of the degree of integration into general strategic and human resource management policy and practice.

- The degree of 'voice' and agency of the traditionally disadvantaged, and its role in shaping the decisions informing the equality agenda, e.g. via trade union action or other representative means.

- The number of channels for expressing dissatisfaction, their frequency of use, the nature of the concerns unearthed and the courses of action typically undertaken, e.g. via HRM policies and systems such as grievance procedures, or dedicated equality systems to highlight and tackle discrimination such as racial or sexual harassment procedures.

- The degree of attention or neglect of 'duty of care': in a more sociological vein, narrowly defined identities for traditionally disadvantaged groups may result in them being viewed as of lesser value than the dominant group. Of lesser value, these 'other' identities may be so narrowly scoped and elaborated in a negative way that hostility, physical or psychological, is readily justified by the dominant group. In an organisational context, we can think of this in two ways. First, in the context of stereotyping, in which the traditionally disadvantaged will be viewed with reference to deviations from the stereotype, be they positive or negative deviations. The second concerns duty of care, which is enshrined in UK health and safety law, such that all organisations are legally bound to provide a safe system of work, both physically and psychologically. However, if identities are narrowly scoped, it may be that duty of care is not exercised uniformly, and is regarded as an entitlement of the dominant group, while for the traditionally disadvantaged, it may be construed as within the gift of the dominant group.

- A clearer understanding of organisational structures that help to develop social capital, including awareness of the differential and disadvantaged access to it that different groups may have. In other words, they should attempt to assess the amount of social capital, even just in broad terns, that different groups have.

There is a major implication for practitioners and line managers with responsibility for equality issues: *if the information base needs to be broadened, then the skills and competency base that practitioners and line managers bring to bear upon such issues will need to be substantially broadened also.*

It is suggested, therefore, that additional mechanisms are needed for more widespread equality and diversity knowledge acquisition and dissemination, particularly *locally*, within specific functions, departments and teams, for it to be more widely distributed. Moreover, for such information and knowledge acquisition to become continuous, sustainable and self-manageable, *it can be argued that the focus needs to be on the development of process skills for knowledge generation and capture, that embeds at the level of the workgroup.* Such mechanisms should consistently enable stakeholders, in particular managers and their teams, to be able not only to capture readily formal and informal sources of equality and diversity information that resides in formal and informal systems and structures, but also provide the basis for a *continuous acquisition* of equality and diversity knowledge and, importantly, individual and social learning that more closely reflects and 'feels real' in their local context.

Knowledge, learning and equality and diversity information

Within the context of workplace equality and diversity, knowledge and learning are often represented as mechanisms for change, and would be discussed in the context of training and development, and in particular, information transfer. So, for example, training and development might be used for 'expert–novice' (often on-off) *transfer* of information, for example equality and the law, or attempts to raise awareness of equality and diversity issues (learning and development issues are addressed more fully in Part 3).

However, in this chapter, knowledge and learning are considered in terms of their potential to act as enabling mechanisms that allow learning in relation to equality and diversity to be more firmly situated within the context and locality within which equality and diversity action takes place, and therefore for experts and expertise to develop more naturally, locally, and in a more widespread manner.

Given these suggestions, in the next section of this chapter, we will consider one of the most important mechanisms for capturing equality and diversity knowledge – that of *learning*, which also provides a critical lever for equality and diversity action. Importantly, capabilities equality would demand that attention be paid to all capabilities levels, basic internal and combined. Much of what is most commonly captured in the development of an equality and diversity formal information and knowledge base is readily accessible 'above the surface' data. This is where understanding *informal learning processes* can be particularly powerful, as a vehicle for developing 'below the surface' knowledge.

Different ways of understanding learning processes

Different models of **learning processes** have emerged from different social science traditions. In order to highlight the kinds of processes to which attention needs to be paid, from equality and diversity perspectives, three in particular are highlighted:

● from the *managerial and organisational psychology* tradition in particular, **organisational learning**;
● from the *organisational sociology* tradition in particular, **situated learning**;
● from the *personal construct psychology* tradition in particular, *learning, emotion and transition*.

Learning and knowledge in organisations: the 'organisational learning' viewpoint

There are numerous detailed accounts of the definition of organisational learning, which is more concerned with analysis and the development of an understanding of learning processes and, increasingly, how it is distinct from the 'learning organisation' concept which, though useful conceptually, is more action-oriented and rooted in the development of 'idealised', more normative and strategic approaches (Easterby-Smith, 1997). Much of the original organisational learning literature has its roots in the organisational development ideas (of social-science-informed change management) of the 1950s through to the 1970s (see Cummings and Huse, 1980; Marguiles and Raia, 1978). Key words and phrases that have been used to define organisational learning include the process of improving learning through better knowledge and understanding (Fiol and Lyles, 1985); and Practitioners and Practice as a process of detecting and correcting error (Argyris and Schon, 1978; Argyris, 1994).

The Argyris and Schon account of organisational learning is probably one of the most widely known and celebrated and, in particular, their distinction between single and double loop learning. For single loop learning, the underlying assumptions and values of the learning are not questioned, while in double loop learning there is a questioning of and possible change in the criteria, procedures and values underpinning what is learned. Furthermore, it is argued that there is a third, additional layer of learning (Argyris and Schon, 1978, cited in Snell and Chak, 1998) known as triple loop learning. This is most closely associated with inventing new processes for generating mental models (Table 3.3). However, in order to best evaluate the potential for organisational learning, one needs to evaluate the status of social learning and its mechanisms within organisations, and it is to this that we now turn our attention.

Social processes, social learning and equality and diversity action

The importance of social process and social understanding in determining the effectiveness of learning in organisations has been discussed and reviewed by others (e.g. Gherardi, Nicolini and Odella 1998; Snell and Chak, 1998; Argyris, 1994; Marguiles and Raia, 1978), and a detailed account goes beyond the scope of this chapter.

However, the view common among the authors cited is that if *social under-*

Table 3.3   Single, double and triple loop learning

Type of learning knowledge	Indicative question	Kind of action that learning of this kind is able to deliver
Single loop learning	Where are we now and how do we do things around here? &/or	Doing things *better* within our current dominant view and understanding, knowledge and rules (*paradigm*). Existing dominant 'world view' or mental model is maintained (*paradigm-consistent thinking*). *Incremental changes* are the most likely outcome.
Double loop learning	What could/should we be doing to challenge things as they are? Where could/should we be? &/or	Doing things *differently* by challenging current dominant view/mental model. *Paradigm-challenging thinking*: new key attributes of the world view/mental model creating critical alterations to the dominant paradigm. *Step change* is the most likely outcome.
Triple loop learning	How can we make more radical departures from the way we could/should do things around here? How can we create more 'root and branch' changes to thinking, feeling and doing?	Doing things differently by creating a new paradigm through the creation of new mental models. *Radical change* is the most likely outcome.

standing and social learning processes are neglected, the likelihood of organisational learning occurring is compromised. Gherardi, Nicolini and Odella (1998) emphasise the importance of understanding learning in the workplace as a social as well as a cognitive activity. Pedler, Boydell and Burgoyne (1989; 1991) define the learning organisation as 'an organisation that facilitates the learning of all of its members and continuously transforms itself' and cite as important characteristics a list that includes the following:

- the 'learning approach' to strategy;
- participative policy making;
- informating;
- internal exchange;
- enabling structures;
- boundary workers as environmental scanners;
- inter-company learning;
- learning climate.

One outcome is that such an intervention may not have an impact at the organisation-wide or group/community level at all, but may resonate for some members of the organisation, creating deep learning as the 'message' is construed primarily as *personally* meaningful. So for example, Snell and Chak (1998) suggest that learning empowerment is important, which, it could be argued, could provide one enabling mechanism for employee participation and voice. Another might be, for some groups within the organisation, the opportunity to create what the psychologist George Kelly referred to as 'the laboratory' (1991, Vol. 1, p. 118): the opportunity to try out new ideas is in place. Though they may be, laboratories need not be formal classroom settings, but could be, and often are, informal ones. Importantly, laboratories may be functional or dysfunctional, and it could be argued that one role of organisations is to create the environment within which the 'right' laboratories can, in turn, be created.

Learning, culture and climate

It has been suggested that structure, culture and climate provide an important context for knowledge exchange and openness, and risk taking is characteristic (Liff and Cameron, 1997; Trapp, 1994; Thomas Jr., 1996). These ideas mirror the views of some of those in the field of diversity management on what is likely to promote it. Thomas and Ely (1996) have argued that the preconditions necessary for making the paradigm shift towards a 'learning and effectiveness' vision of diversity include many that are grounded in culture, and he suggests that organisational culture must:

- create an expectation of high standards of performance from everyone;
- stimulate personal development;
- encourage openness;
- make workers feel valued.

They also highlight the importance of a well-articulated and widely understood mission, making explicit the links with strategy, and others have discussed the importance of the links to the organisation's value chain (Cornelius *et al.*, 1999).

Management and organisational structures that facilitate equality and diversity action and learning

In his book, *Managing Diversity in Organisations* (1995), the political scientist Robert Golembiewski argues strongly for the structural embeddedness of diversity. He argues that *bureaucracy* is a difficult structure within which to locate diversity action, because of its primary concern with consistency and reduction of deviation from this: it generates high prescription cultures which are inflexible and within which work is highly gendered and gender segregated.

Golembiewski asserts that to manage diversity successfully, it is important to address *management infrastructure*, in particular, structures of work, policies and procedures that embed and build diversity.

In the *post-bureacractic structure*, he argues, there is a quite different management infrastructure and a more low-prescription culture. In contrast to traditional bureaucracies, within post-bureacractic structures there is an emphasis on related (rather than discrete) activities; authority and responsibility are both vertical and horizontal (rather than broadly vertical); the span of control can be very wide or narrow, given the ease of measuring holistic performance (rather than measurement of discrete performance); and the primacy is on holistic performance relative to a good or service, for which team members

---

Box 3.3 A post-bureaucratic structural model

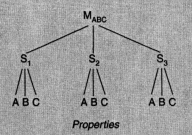

Properties

Basic departmentation puts *related activities* together in an S-unit – flows of work, discrete subassemblies, products, strategic operating areas or units, and so on.

Integration of related activities helps minimize errors of omission and also encourages cross-training, job enrichment, as well as in-process setups and inspection.

Authority and responsibility are both vertical and horizontal in each S-unit – following the chain of command

and also building around personal as well as group loyalties and commitment integrating the several contributions to an immediate flow of work. Hence control is pervasively both 'up' the chain of command and 'across' it in each S-unit, due to shared social and psychological membership.

The span of control can be very wide, or narrow, given the ease of measuring holistic performance.

The primacy is on holistic performance relative to a good or service for which all S-unit members share responsibility, which reduces transfer costs and moderates jurisdictional issues as it locates them within each S-unit rather than between two or more S-units.

Source: Golembiewski, RT (1995) *Managing Diversity in Organizations.* Reproduced by permission of University of Alabama Press.

Box 3.4 High prescription and low prescription cultures

High-prescription culture	Major dimensions	Low-prescription culture
Do both at the top, once, do them right, and be consistent: 'tight' systems that are centralized	Policy-making and implementation mix	Within policy and mission constraints, implementation can proceed in many styles and at various paces: 'tight/loose' systems can permit broad delegation
Narrow	View of 'right' or 'good' behaviours or styles	Broad, except for core values like quality
Quick to express evaluations, especially negative and punitive ones	Orientation to judgemental behaviour	Evaluations follow attempts to encourage expression of the full range of ideas as well as exploration of their sense and connotations
Risk-aversive	Orientation to risk	Calculated risks are accepted and even encouraged, as necessary for learning and innovation
Intolerance of and focus on, even to the detriment of positive contributions	Reaction to mistakes	Equal or greater status of positive contributions and even a view of mistakes as unexpected learning opportunities
Tends to be degenerative	System of interaction	Tends to be regenerative
Must be based on comparisons of different activities	Measurement of performance	Can be based on comparisons of similar activities
Loyalty, which may be reinforced by coercion or conformity	Basic identification	Commitment to shared goals and missions, which imply local empowerment and a narrower sense of 'management prerogatives'
On parts: e.g. roles and jurisdictions	Basic focus	On wholes, e.g. flows of work, customers

From Cox (1993), esp. pp. 169–70, and extended from that source.
Source: Golembiewski, RT (1995) *Managing Diversity in Organizations.* Reproduced by permission of University of Alabama Press.

share responsibility. All of these post-bureaucratic characteristics, Golembiewski argues, are more amenable to workforce diversity.

Golembiewski suggests that one important alternative structure is the *affirming infrastructure*. Such a structure contains a number of flexibilities, including working hours, place of work, and manner of execution of work, and can accommodate better work–life balance.

Romme (1996) has suggested that organisational learning can be effectively facilitated through a *circular organisation*, in which learning processes in teams (circles) are combined with the administrative hierarchy. The circle structure is used for policy making, while implementation remains within the domain of supervisors and managers. Romme suggests that within such a structure, feedback rather than power is the key organising principle. Similarly, Easterby-Smith (1990) argues that more flexibility in structure is important, and suggests that this can be achieved through job rotation, planned experience, and transient project groupings.

Further, Di Bella, Nevis and Gould (1996) have argued that important dimensions for developing organisational learning capability include:

- the location of sources of knowledge;
- a product and process focus;
- clarity about documentation and dissemination modes;
- a learning focus;
- value chain focus and skill development.

Moreover, they argue that this flourishes best in a *pluralistic environment*. This view on plurality is reinforced by others such as Easterby-Smith (1990), who suggests that too much homogeneity reduces the potential for novel ideas and viewpoints to emerge. From a diversity management perspective, Garvin (1993) argues that organisational leadership must understand that a diverse workforce will embody different perspectives and approaches to work and must truly value variety of opinion and insight, and that learning opportunities and challenges arise from the expression of different perspectives.

What hinders organisational learning? The resistance to new knowledge acquisition

Rhetoric and reality of difficulties – defensive reasoning

From an equality and diversity management position, one wishes to shift the organisational paradigm towards an enriched vision. However, it would be unrealistic to assume that even if the knowledge were there, all organisational members would have the will to acquire it.

Argyris (1994) argues that everyone develops a theory of action: 'a set of rules that individuals use to design and implement their own behaviour as well as to understand the behaviour of others.' He further adds that 'one of the paradoxes of human behaviour . . . is although we operate within a master program *people don't even realise they are using them*' (our italics). These theories in action, argues Argyris, rest on the same set of governing values, most commonly observed in influential and high status groups:

- to remain in unilateral control';
- to maximise 'winning' and minimise 'losing';
- to suppress negative feelings; and
- to be as 'rational' as possible, by which people mean defining clear objectives and evaluating their behaviour in terms of whether or not they have achieved them.

Argyris' statement that 'the purpose of these values is to avoid embarrassment or threat, feeling vulnerable or incompetent' suggests that this 'master program' is fundamentally defensive and furthermore, encourages individuals to 'keep private the premises, inferences, and conclusions that shape their behaviour and (to) avoid testing them in a truly independent, objective fashion'.

Argyris' work suggests that in practice, some resistance may be construed as a type of 'coping behaviour' and anxiety management, wired into the individual and collective subconscious of the majority group and particularly those in the more powerful and influential organisational groups. Although political manoeuvring, espoused fear of the loss of power and status or spoiling tactics may be the symptoms that manifest themselves, the underlying cause of a reluctance to move towards diversity may significantly come about as a result of defensive reasoning: a reflection not only of how people feel and learn but importantly, their 'master programs' and how fundamentally they think.

Furthermore, Argyris argues that such defensive routines are often 'self-sealing loops', as they are 'undiscussable, proliferate in an underground manner; the social pollution is hard to identify until something blows up. If the defensive routines then surface, it is difficult for those with the stewardship to do much about them. They have been skilful going along with, not questioning or confronting the routines.'

Therefore, censorship and mis-communication flourish, with real thoughts and feelings not communicated, rather than open conversations taking place. This echoes the work of writers on gender studies, who refer to the invisibility of the norms and mores of dominant male groups relative to the more ascribed and 'marked' attributes designated to the disadvantaged.

This defensive reasoning position is a powerful one, and has strong support in related fields of psychology, for example, social trap theory (Barry and Bateman, 1996) and validation and narrowing of the range of convenience of meanings of personal constructs (Kelly, 1991 – discussed later in this chapter). In Kellyan terms, the outcome would be constriction and inflexibility of re-construal, whilst for Argyris, 'defensive' master programs short-circuit double and triple loop learning.

Social traps for equality and diversity in the organisational landscape: the importance of social structure for social learning

Barry and Bateman (1996) discuss the importance of dilemmas in undermining movement towards engagement with the potential benefits of equality and diversity management. They have developed the idea of social trap theory and social trap analysis as a way of understanding how management initiatives influence diversity-related outcomes within work organisations. These were introduced briefly in Chapter 1, in the context of understanding how management initiatives can create decision problems involving conflicts between individual, near-term outcomes on the one hand, and collective, long-term consequences on the other. The difficulty of managing official and unofficial social structures lies at the heart of their work and their impact on decision making pertaining to equality and diversity issues. In this chapter we revisit their work but from a different perspective, namely that of how social traps, through undermining decision making, in turn undermine equality and diversity social learning

Barry and Bateman outline how specific interventions, for example relating to employee and organisational development, work design, staffing and compensation policies, soon become vulnerable to equality and diversity traps, as the existence of publicly available goods or services, once provided, cannot in theory be withheld from some members of the organisation. In the context of organisational equality and diversity, the goods might include assignments, promotions, resources, development opportunities, and so on, which potentially benefit all organisational members and the organisation as a whole. However, in practice, they accrue to some organisational members and not to others: individual gains are placed above the collective good.

Another example would be the manager who fails to pursue allegations of a valued subordinate who has made a racist remark as he or she fears that the confrontation will be unpleasant, and the manager simply hopes that the undesirable behaviour will not recur. This is an example of the *counter-trap or social fence*: the manager's short-term personal interest in avoiding a difficult confrontation precludes action that will create long-term benefits. Further, at the group level, managers and their subordinates may be required through developmental activities or changes to HRM policy and practice to be exposed to and then to create an equality and diversity climate of acculturation, but the failure to proactively manage inter-group conflict and inter-group issues such as gender bias or ethnocentrism undermines this. At the individual level, the broader, more negative aspects of the diversity climate merely reinforce prejudice and bias and make it difficult to identify with those outside that individual's 'core' group membership (e.g. white male, African Caribbean, and so on).

Social traps impact upon two important aspects of the equality and diversity social learning context. First, there is the *equality and diversity climate*, which may be made more hostile to engaging with equality and diversity learning as social traps emerge, and second, the **social capital** – trust relationships, belongingness, and so on – may be systematically eroded.

These authors suggest that organisations need to consider models of equality and diversity management that help to redress equality and diversity traps and counter-traps. Core to their recommendations is the need to counteract some of the negative attributes of traps. For example:

- The attribute of exclusivity (for example, access to resource allocation decisions may be held by a relatively small number of people) is tempered with the *dispersal of control around the organisation.*
- The attribute of cognisance (e.g. low cross-cultural sensitivity or abuse of cross-cultural knowledge on the part of those more powerful in the organisation) is tempered with the sharing more explicitly and tangibly of outcome awareness.
- The attribute of a constituency (a feeling of belonging to one group and the desire to exclude others from it) is tempered through *social proximity.*
- The attribute of temporality (individual short-term gain versus collective long-term outcomes) is tempered through building *outcome immediacy* into aspects of the initiatives.

Organisational memory and learning

Organisational memory, which can be considered in terms of 'sedimentation' of construing (Thorman, 1990), was somewhat fragile. This was in part because of the practice of moving to new internal posts frequently amongst 'governor grades' and headquarters and personnel staff in particular, reflected in transient responsibilities and initiatives, with their ideas started but often not seen through beyond the policy document. For many interviewees, this reduced the likelihood of seeing things through (and for myself, I believe double and triple loop *organisational learning* is likely to be difficult to establish also).

Situated knowledge and learning, practical and multi-voiced thinking

Equality expertise

The crux of the matter is what 'traditional' information bases can and cannot deliver. Importantly, one needs to understand, indeed to map, where equality and diversity *expertise* resides.

1. In practice, those responsible for generating diversity information are often somewhat removed from the line operation and strategic decision-making arenas where equality and diversity decisions and actions are taken on a day-to-day basis.

2. It is important that there *are* those that have 'lead edge' expertise, who spend time and effort in obtaining and disseminating the latest information on behalf of the organisation, much of which might be obtained from contacts outside it. However, one needs also to identify how such information would be communicated or indeed, if there are mechanisms that will allow such communications from these 'specialist' nodes readily into the organisation as a whole. This is crucially important where the equality and diversity specialist network is the *primary* mechanism for the spread of E&D information around the organisation.

3. *Organisations that rely primarily on building E&D expertise within these specialist nodes may end up actually reducing the spread of E&D information organisation-wide.* Although the symbolic and specialist role of the diversity and equality expert is important, it is not of itself sufficient for the development of *local* expertise, and importantly, that is managed and owned within the line operation and strategic arenas for decision making.

In other words, there may be a concentration of best practice knowledge amongst experts but not only may this *fail* to transmit beyond them, but also it becomes easier to see E&D issues as 'someone else's knowledge base' and ultimately 'somebody else's problem'. So, although specialists will be able to advise on practice, they are not necessarily experts in line management and the dynamics of equality and diversity management within this context, and alternative strategies for generating and developing *situated operational equality and diversity knowledge* is proscribed.

How do we justify these assertions? The more contemporary sociologically grounded literature on knowledge and learning suggests that important context-specific elements need to be in place in order for learning to be truly embedded.

So for example, Gherardi, Nicolini and Odella (1998) highlight the importance of *situating learning in ongoing practice*, and argue that organisational knowing is fundamentally a collective endeavour, 'in which tacit and explicit knowledge goes through a process of being re-defined and re-negotiated within the organising process through the interplay between action and reflexivity.' (1998: 329)

Further, their work suggests that the relative power between the specialist and the line manager may be important not only in terms of what knowledge is noticed, but also in terms of whether it is seen as worth having.

Moreover, the work of Sylvia Scribner (in Sternberg and Wagner, 1986) suggests the importance of *practical thinking* as a distinctive (though related) mode of thought that is different from theoretical thinking. She defines practical thinking as 'thinking that is embedded in the larger purposive activities of daily life and that functions to achieve the goals of those activities' (1986: 15). In other words, skilled practical thinking, which it could be argued is the primary domain of the line manager when interacting with subordinates, involves problem formation and well as problem solution, is marked by flexibility and involves tacit awareness of the task environment (1986: 21–25). Further, Scribner suggests that: 'Skilled practical thinking often seeks those modes of solution that are the most economical or that require the least effort'

(1986: 25) [and that] 'Practical thinking involves the acquisition and use of specific knowledge that is functionally important to the larger activities in which problem-solving is embedded' (1986: 26). The implication of Scribner's ideas is that the practicalities of dealing with equality and diversity may not be seen as practical if the ideas presented to the line by specialists without this practical managerial task knowledge may be seen as:

- too remote as it is not grounded in specific (tacit and explicit) managerial knowledge;
- heavy on detailed recommendations but light on practical efficiency;
- as a problem-generating process originating *outside* of the task environment and the locale rather than a process that facilitates skilled practical problem generating and problem solution located within the task environment, and within the community of practice (Lave and Wenger, 1991).

The kinds of questions that might be asked within this situated learning tradition are highlighted within the questions posed by Engestrom (2001) in his observation of what he terms *expansive learning*. Within his theory of expansive learning, Engestrom argues that 'People and organisations are all the time learning something that is not stable, not even defined or understood ahead of time (2001: 137). . . . The object of expansive learning activity is the entire activity system in which the learners are engaged. Expansive learning activity produces culturally new patterns of activity. Expansive learning at work produces new forms of work activity' (2001: 139). Engestrom's ideas originate from activity theory. He suggests that he is interested in the development of third-generation activity theory in order to conceptualise and understand the role of dialogue, multiple perspectives and networks of interacting activity systems.

From 'divided' to 'holistic' accounts of knowledge and learning

Knowledge, knowing and learning: organisational perspectives

An attempt to develop categories of knowledge and learning within the 'situated' tradition has been attempted by Frank Blackler (1995). Blackler suggests that knowledge can be thought of as an active process of knowing that is 'mediated, situated, provisional, pragmatic and contested' (1995: 1). He highlights the importance of the cultural location of knowledge 'through which people achieve their knowing', and that it is important to pay attention to the processes through which new knowledge may be generated.

Blackler identifies five key definitions of what he argues are intimately inter-related forms of knowledge.

1. *Embrained knowledge* depends on conceptual skills and cognitive abilities (e.g. double loop learning).

Box 3.5 Blackler's activity theory

Within Frank Blackler's activity theory, the emphasis shifts from knowledge to knowing, and the various ways in which individuals and groups can come to know. Underpinning this theory are five ways in which it is argued knowing can be thought of, as *mediated, situated, provisional, pragmatic* and *contested*. These views of knowing create specific demands for those wishing to understand more fully the dynamics of knowing.

- *Knowing as mediated* necessitates research into the *dynamics of activity systems* and how they are currently changing. Detailed ethnographic studies are needed to illuminate the ways in which people improvise, communicate and negotiate within expanded activity systems.
- *Knowing as situated* makes it important to develop the notion of **situated knowledge** to the knowledge work debate. Too little is known about the ways in which people's understanding of their activities are changing as a consequence of the developing complexity of the contexts within which they are working.
- *Knowing as provisional* sets demands on research concerning the idea that knowing is *provisional and developing*.
- *Knowing as pragmatic* suggests that further

research is needed into the influence that 'informated' and 'communication-intensive' environments have on the approaches people take to their work. In addition, work is needed on the possibilities for developing *communal narratives within expanded activity systems*.
- *Knowing as contested* refers to *the relationship between knowledge and power*. It is predicted that conflicts within and between the new generation of symbolic analysts and problem-solvers, and established professionals and managers.

Building on the work of Collins (1993), Blackler then goes on to attempt to understand organisations according to how they engage with knowledge.

- *Expert dependent organisations* depend heavily on *embodied knowledge*.
- *Knowledge-routinised organisations* depend heavily on *embedded knowledge*.
- *Symbolic-analyst dependent organisations* depend heavily on *embrained knowledge*.
- *Communication-intensive organisations* depend heavily on *encultured knowledge*.

Abridged from Arvela
(Http://lpt.fi/~anarvela/reviews/blackler/Blackler.html)

2. *Embodied knowledge* is action-oriented, and depends on physical presence, sentient and sensory information, physical cues and gestures.
3. *Encultured knowledge* is concerned with achieving shared understandings – these depend heavily on language, are socially constructed and open to negotiation.
4. *Embedded knowledge* lies in systematic routines, e.g. economic behaviour relates to social and institutional arrangements, and is concerned with the significance of relationships and material resources, such as between technologies, roles, formal procedures and emergent routines.
5. *Encoded knowledge* is encoded in books, manuals, codes of practice and e-communications.

Arvela (2001) has suggested that interest in knowledge has shifted from 'traditional' views that knowledge that is embodied and embedded towards knowledge that is embrained, encultured and encoded. However, according to Blackler, the nature of knowledge in organisations is hotly debated by scholars in the field. Blackler encapsulates the position into what he refers to as *activity theory*.

There are many implications of Blackler's work. The most obvious is that the models-in-use of knowledge and learning, both for researchers and practitioners, neglect the richness of the experience of learning and thus, by implication, the range of options in which work-based learning and *knowing* in general, and in relation to equality and diversity in particular, can be facilitated.

Knowledge, knowing and learning: personal and group perspectives

What changes when we learn?

Philosophically, the psychologist George Kelly (1955/1991) believed that capacity for change is found within all individuals and groups, but there were many reasons why change may be made more difficult.

Further, Kelly argues that our mechanism for 'sense-making' could be thought of as a connection of bi-polar constructs, and that these constructs are located within constructs systems, parts of which are uniquely held, parts of which are shared with others, and that there are linkages, in particular what we might think of as implicative links, between parts of the system. We can think of subordinate constructs as more behaviourally laden, superordinate as more value and basic assumptions laden, and core constructs as axiomatic with self and personality. Stability of the construct system is sought in order to be able to best anticipate events, although excessive stability, rigidity or impermeability can result, often leading in extremes to 'dysfunctional' sense making.

Importantly, Kelly does not make the assumption that the constructs are represented solely as of the head, but are a 'knowledgeable ensemble' of head, hands and heart.

First, some key definitions. Although Kelly dismisses the need for an elaborate definition of learning, he does embrace the idea of learning, but in a particular way. For Kelly, learning is not a special class of processes but a core process, as 'a person's construct system varies as he or she successively construes the anticipation of events' (1991: 53).

Re-examination and shaping of our constructs and the linkages is something that, for Kelly, is a continuous process, but when major change and learning are undertaken, *constructs of transition* become important. Kelly argues that these constructs of transition may come into play when the nature of the change is particularly challenging. We have identified three in particular, threat, hostility and anxiety, which, typical of Kelly, he defines with precision. Specifically,

- *threat* is the awareness of imminent comprehensive change in an individual's or group's core structures;
- *hostility* is the continued effort to exhort *validational evidence in favour of a type of social prediction* which has already proved itself a failure; and

- *anxiety* is the recognition that the events with which one is confronted lie outside the range of convenience of one's construct system.

Further, Kelly suggests that two cycles of construction occur when people are going through such transitions. The first is the *C-P-C cycle*, an acronym for processes of circumspection, pre-emption and control, which leads to choice and which helps the individual or group come to terms with and then encompass specific issues. The second he labelled the *creativity cycle*, the associated processes being loosening and tightening. Crucial to our discussion, he suggests that loose constructs are often pre-verbal, known but often a feeling, where 'feeling' is the manner in which Kelly addresses *emotion*.

So, the implications of Kelly's work are as follows:

- Learning can have an emotional component, and when personally challenging, will create different degrees of difficulty, discomfort and anguish.
- There are positive but also negative outcomes that are likely to result from learning that may be difficult to articulate but that will none the less be felt.

So in summary, there are a number of aspects of learning in organisations that create opportunities and challenges for equality and diversity learning, as a source of information and knowledge generation. Importantly, *we would suggest that the more embedded these are, the more likely that they can provide the basis for continuous, sustainable learning and development*. Further, there are important implications for creating *embeddedness*, as it demands attention be paid to *local learning processes*, and mechanisms for learning that are likely to be *meaningful*, owned and enhanced at this level also.

However, although more sophisticated approaches could be created from different configurations of the learning ideas and methods that are commonly in use, it could be argued that, as they largely originate from the dominant paradigms in use, new approaches, from different paradigms, are needed in order to ensure that things are moved on, and that the potential for paradigm challenge of the capabilities equality approach to materialise is enhanced.

Conclusions

Organisations have traditionally used formal measures of evaluation that draw very strongly from a labour economics tradition, in order to evaluate equality and diversity action. It is suggested that this is a very important aspect of gaining insights, but is proscribed in nature, and fails to capture some of the aspects of 'felt fair' equality that are perceived by employees. The work of Sen suggests strongly that a richer information base, that captures a wider array of information, would not only enhance our understanding of inequality, but better guide our action. Having drawn on an array of approaches to understanding measurement from which we have drawn analogies and important lessons, it is clear that there are some significant areas for improvement in the manner in which organisations develop their information and knowledge bases for understanding and addressing workplace equality.

At the heart of these suggestions is the view that an ensemble of measures, rather than many facets of a single kind of measure, would not only create a more representative account of workplace inequality, but also provide a more pluralistic, multi-actor and multi-domain view that draws upon micro-, meso- and macro-perspectives. Further, we suggest that benefit can be derived from drawing upon, at least broadly, the principles of both human and social capital, so that inequalities and freedom of opportunity that reside within the individual as well as those that reside within social relations and structures are both incorporated within the attempt to widen the envelope of measurement of formal and informal, and tangible and intangible aspects.

In addition, we have argued that an important source of information and knowledge, those generalised through learning processes, can be integrated into the enriching of the organisational equality and diversity information and knowledge base. Again, there are a range of traditions of representation of learning in organisations that enable us to pay attention to the individual, groups, the relationship between manager and subordinates, the structures that learning are situated within, and so on, in order to develop *knowing*, which is mediated, situated, provisional, pragmatic and contested. Further, it is suggested that more integrated models of knowing and learning, such as those developed by Blackler, provide a strong basis for distributed but integrative learning as an important engine of sustainable learning strategies from which equality and diversity knowledge can develop at the micro-, meso-, and macro-levels of an organisation.

There are many choices of what kind of information and knowledge, and what mechanisms for generating information and knowledge can be identified. There is no blueprint, but there are general design principles that organisations need to decide on. The key design choices for organisations are, first, to develop an information base that is meaningful to it, that balances formal and informal, tangible and intangible measures; second, that creates genuine 'act fair' and 'felt fair' equalities; and third, that affords the opportunity to develop insights and opportunities for the enhancement of capabilities and freedoms. Importantly, whatever is decided on as the appropriate configuration of information, knowledge and learning processes and structures needs to be manageable, reflect authentic employee voice and include 'felt fair' attributes. Finally, what should be sought is sufficiency and manageability: information overload is always a potential difficulty and of course, a credible array of information, knowledge and learning processes and structures can only deliver if subsumed within strong equality values and will.

Text-based questions

1. What role does monitoring play in ensuring that recruitment, selection and induction policies and practices are increasing the diversity of the organisation?
2. Why might flexible and family-friendly policies and practices promote diversity in the workplace?

3. What is the value of mentoring in supporting a new employee in an organisation or department?
4. What objectives can a manager agree with people in his or her team that will promote diversity?
5. What training and development programmes would support diversity?
6. Why do good grievance and discipline policies and practice support diversity in the organization?

Library and assignment-based questions

1. Select the Annual Reports of five leading organisations and critically evaluate the extent to which they include diversity in their mission, value statements and/or Annual Report. What do those statements tell you about the attitudes of those organisations to promoting diversity in their organisations?
2. Examine the graduate recruitment literature (either online or on paper) from three organisations and critically examine the extent to which the literature encourages applicants from diverse backgrounds. What changes might you make to the literature?
3. Design an induction programme that would support a new starter to understand the 'informal' aspects of an organisation. How might a mentor help with this process?
4. What training and development do managers need to enable them to support and promote diversity in their organisations?
5. To what extent do you believe that setting diversity objectives for managers promotes diversity within organisations?

Internet resources

Marks & Spencer http://www2.marksandspencer.com/the company/
The Runnymede Trust http://www.runnymedetrust.org/

Further reading

Anonymous (2001) Monitoring for equality. *IRS Employment Trends*, January, 4–13.
Lin, N (2001) *Social Capital: a theory of social structure and action*, Cambridge University Press, USA.

References

Anonymous (2001) Monitoring for equality. *IRS Employment Trends*, January, 4–13.
Argyris, C and Schon, D (1978) *Organizational learning*, Addison-Wesley, Reading.
Argyris, C (1994) *On organizational learning*, Blackwell, Oxford.

Baron, S, Field, J and Schuller, T (2000) *Social capital: critical perspectives*, Oxford University Press.

Barry, B and Bateman, TS (1996) A social trap analysis of the management of diversity. *Academy of Management Review*, **21** (3), 757–790.

Blackler, F (1995) Knowledge, work and organisations: an overview and interpretation. *Organisational Studies*, **16** (6), 1021–1046.

Cornelius, N, Gooch, L and Todd S (1999) Managers leading diversity for business excellence. *Journal of General Management*, **25** (3), 67–75.

Cornelius, N and Gagnon, S (2002) Still bearing the mark of Cain? Broadening the information base to build an ethics of equality in the workplace. *Business Ethics: a European review* (forthcoming).

Cummings, TG and Huse, EF (1980) *Organisational development and change*, West Publishing, USA.

Di Bella, AJ, Nevis, EC and Gould, JM (1996) Understanding Organizational Learning Capability. *Journal of Management Studies*, **33** (3), May, 361–379.

Easterby-Smith, M (1990) Creating a learning organisation. *Personnel Review*, **19** (5), 24–28.

Easterby-Smith, M (1997) Disciplines of organizational learning: contributions and critiques. *Human Relations*, **50** (9), 1085–1114.

Engestrom, Y (2001) Expansive learning at work: towards an activity theory re-conceptualisation. *Journal of Education and Work*, **14** (1), 133–161.

Fiol, CM and Lyles, MA (1985) Organizational learning. *Academy of Management Review*, **10** (4), 803–813.

Gagnon, S and Cornelius, N (2000) Re-examining workplace equality: the capabilities approach. *Human Resource Management Journal*, **10** (4), 68–87.

Garvin, DA (1993) Building a learning organization. *Harvard Business Review*, July–August, 78–91.

Gherardi, S, Nicolini, D and Odella, F (1998) Toward a social understanding of how people learn in organizations. *Management Learning*, **29** (3), 273–297.

Golembiewski, R (1995) *Managing diversity in organisations*, University of Alabama Press, Tuscaloosa.

Harris, L and Cornelius, N (2002) Organisational considerations for e-business, in P Jackson and L Harris (eds) *Introduction to E-Commerce*, Routledge, London.

Kelly, GA (1995/1991) *The Psychology of Personal Constructs*, Routledge, London.

Kirton, G and Greene, AM (2000) *The Dynamics of Managing Diversity*, Butterworth Heinemann, Oxford.

Lave, J and Wenger, W (1991) *Situated learning: legitimate peripheral participation*, Cambridge University Press, Cambridge.

Lebas, M (1993) Tableau de bord and performance measurement. Paper presented at the Management Accounting Research Group annual conference, London School of Economics, 22 April.

Liff, S and Cameron, I (1997) Changing equality cultures to move beyond women's problems. *Gender, Work and Organisation*, **4** (1) (January), 35-48.

Lin, N (2001) *Social capital: a theory of social structure and action*, Cambridge University Press, USA.

Macintosh, NB (1994) *Managing accounting and control systems: an organisational behavioral approach*, Wiley, Bath.

Marguiles, N and Raia, AP (1978) *Conceptual Foundations of Organisational Development*, McGraw Hill, New York.

Nahapiet, J and Ghoshal, S (1998) Social capital, intellectual capital and the organisational advantage. *Academy of Management Review*, **23** (2) 242–266.

Nussbaum, M (1999) Women and equality: The capabilities approach. *International Labour Review*, **138** (3), 227–245.

Nussbaum, M and Sen, A (1995) *The Quality of Life*, Oxford University Press, USA.

Otley, D (1999) Performance management: a framework for management control system research. *Management Accounting Research*, **10**, 363–382.

Pedler, M, Boydell, T and Burgoyne, J (1989) Towards the learning company. *Management Education and Development*, **20** (1), 1–8.

Pedler, M, Burgoyne, J and Boydell, T (1991) *The Learning Company: A Strategy for Sustainable Development*, McGraw Hill, USA.

Romme, G (1996) Making organizational learning work: consent and double linking between circles. *European Management Journal*, **14** (1), February, 69–75.

Sanglin-Grant, S and Schneider, R (2000) *Moving On Up? Racial equality and the corporate agenda*, Runnymede Trust, London.

Schultz, T (1961) Investment in human capital. *American Economic Review*, 51 (March): 1–17.

Scribner, S (1986) Thinking in action: some characteristics of practical thought, in RJ Sternberg and RK Wagner (eds) *Practical intelligence: nature and origins of competence in everyday life*, pp. 13–30, Cambridge University Press, New York.

Sen, A (1999) *Development as Freedom*, Oxford University Press, Oxford.

Simons, R (1995) *Levers of control*, Harvard Business Review Press, Boston, MA.

Snell, R and Chak, AMK (1998) The learning organisation: learning and empowerment for whom? *Management Learning*, **29** (3): 337–364.

Thomas, Jr, RR (1996) *Redefining Diversity*, Amacom, New York.

Thomas, DA and Ely, RJ (1996) Making differences matter: a new paradigm for managing diversity. *Harvard Business Review*, September–October, 79–80.

Thorman, C (1990) 'Shapers' Within the Stream of Consciousness: Some Conceptual Models and Analogies. Paper presented at the PCP Conference, York, UK.

Trapp, R (1994) The uses of diversity. *Human Resources*, Autumn, 10–16.

Part II
The implications of 'capabilities equality' for application

Managing people – equality, diversity and human resource management issues for line managers

4

Larraine Gooch and Alan Blackburn

Chapter overview

In Chapter 2 attention was drawn to the need for human resource policies and practice that recognise equality as a tenet for effective management in general and human resource management in particular. It was shown that some approaches are more conducive to supporting and promoting *combined capabilities* than others. The importance of the psychological contract and the critical role that perceptions of organisational justice play in reinforcing that contract were highlighted. It was argued that HRM subsystems create the essential hygiene factors that influence employee voice, motivation and exit.

In Chapter 2 it was also recognised that HR practice is increasingly delivered through line managers and that it is their behaviours that to a large extent shape employee perceptions of organisational justice. Indeed, Cornelius *et al.* (2000) argue that diversity management is likely to be most effective when there is proactive line management involvement.

In recent years there has been evidence that managers have been taking increasing responsibility for aspects of human resource management in their organisations (Guest 1987; Hutchinson and Wood, 1995; Bevan and Hayday, 1994; McGovern *et al.*, 1998; Hall and Torrington, 1998). The devolution of personnel/HRM to managers provides the potential to empower managers to take responsibility for managing people. However, research suggests that line managers are selective about the aspects of personnel/HR management that they would choose to be involved with (Brewster and Hegeswisch, 1994) or indeed are committed to (McGovern *et al.*, 1998). The main source of line manager motivation towards involvement in employment management issues is the setting of short-term people-centred business targets (Leach, 1995). Where managers are convinced by business cases for diversity, the role of the manager to integrate equality goals within broader business strategy becomes the lever to the necessary culture change.

Research conducted by Hutchinson and Wood (1995) for the Chartered Institute of Personnel and Development showed that the personnel/HR areas in which managers have the most involvement are recruitment, selection and induction, identification of training needs and handling grievance and disciplinary issues.

The focus of this chapter is 'good practice' in those HR areas in which line managers are primarily involved in creating an environment in which perceptions of organisational justice can flourish and commitment to a culture and climate of equality and diversity management can take root. In other words, an important role for the line manager is *the management of an organisation's social capital*: its interpersonal transactions, values, group climate, ethos, trust relationships, and so on. Strong social capital is an important foundation for creating a positive attitude towards workplace equality and diversity, and is equally important as an enabler of many other people-centred organisational activities. Therefore, it could be argued, it is another part of the 'business case' that can be built for diversity. Equally important is the role of the manager in providing *local leadership* in relation to equality and diversity: not only as a role model and manager of equality and diversity policy and practice, but also as a *moral agent*, part of whose remit is to uphold the dignity and respect of his or her colleagues and subordinates, in this context, in relation to equality and diversity action in particular. So from a capabilities equality perspective, it is the line manager that has a pivotal role in delivering combined capabilities on the ground, and it is the effective design of policies and procedures that can enable *instrumental freedoms* (see Chapter 1) to be more likely to be present and exercised.

Learning objectives

After studying this chapter you should:

- be aware of the ways in which human resource management policies and practices might support the promotion and management of equality and diversity in organisations;
- understand the human resource practices that in general managers are most frequently responsible for implementing in organisations (often with support from personnel/HR);
- understand how specific line-management-delivered areas of HRM identified in the research literature as the areas of human resource management for which managers play a key role – recruitment and selection, identification of training and development needs and handling of grievance and disciplinary procedures – need to be addressed in order that equality and diversity can seed at a 'grass roots' level;
- understand the impact of the above, in particular on organisational justice and transparency of action.

> **Key words**
> line-management-delivered human resource management ●
> organisational justice ●   transparency of action ●   procedural justice
> ●   social capital ●   harassment ●   bullying ●   training and
> development ●   grievance and disciplinary procedures ●   fairness
> ●   equal value

Introduction

There is increasing recognition that people differ in many ways – in age, gender, ethnicity, values, physical ability, mental capacity, experiences, culture and their attitudes and approaches towards work. We now operate in a global economy with many leading organisations operating internationally, recruiting, selecting and working with a diverse workforce not only locally, but also around the world to sell their services and products to a more diverse customer base.

Many successful organisations are seeking to secure this 'diversity advantage' by creating an organisational environment which is attractive to diverse labour markets and which is able to respond to changing social and demographic patterns. This can be achieved through effective strategies for managing people that enable organisations to attract, retain and develop a diverse workforce. Often in partnership with personnel/HR, the manager has a key role to play in creating an organisational environment that is attractive to people from diverse backgrounds and is supportive of their aspirations and ambitions, and importantly, promotes equality of opportunity which is 'felt' to be equally available to all employees, but particularly those from traditionally disadvantaged groups.

This chapter examines three key areas in which managers have major responsibilities for the management of people: recruitment, selection and induction, identification of training and development needs, and handling grievance and disciplinary issues. It looks at ways in which managers, often assisted by personnel/HR professionals, can make a difference by creating a working environment in which organisational justice can flourish and equality is more likely to be achieved and felt. The focus of the chapter is on highlighting what we believe to be the skills and knowledge that line managers need to take on the responsibilities for managing diversity and equality fairly. Many managers are selected for their ability to focus on the 'hard' skills of directing and achieving tasks (Carnevale and Stone, 1994) and need guidance and support to contribute to the creation of a diverse organisation.

The first area in which managers are concerned is recruitment, selection and induction.

Recruitment, selection and induction

The labour market

When we look at the external environment in which organisations operate it is clear that the pool of labour is diverse. This is the pool of labour from which managers need to recruit and retain the employees they need for their organisations. The diversity of this pool creates a need for 'fair and equitable' policies and practices that meet the needs of a diverse group of employees. An analysis of the labour market shows that:

- the number of women entering the labour market has been increasing and will continue to increase;
- ethnic minorities will make up a larger share of new entrants to the labour market;
- the workforce is ageing as the number of younger people entering the labour market will fall;
- as the population ages, so men and women at work will have increasing caring responsibilities for elderly dependants;
- increasing numbers of men and women will work part-time;
- a growing number of employees work flexibly; this includes the type of contract they have, the number of different employers they have and their place of work;
- childcare is a key issue for many, with the majority of two-parent families being dual earners; in particular, a high percentage of working women have dependent children under 16 years of age;
- a high percentage of disabled people are unemployed.

(Source: *Labour Market Trends*: February 1997; IPD Managing Diversity Position Paper (1997)

Note that the definition of ethnic minorities used in the Labour Force Survey is:

- Black (Black Caribbean, Black African, Black other);
- Indian;
- Pakistani/Bangladeshi;
- Other (Chinese, other non-mixed, other mixed, Black mixed);

and that disability is defined in the Disability Discrimination Act (1996) as physical or mental impairment, which has a substantial and long-term effect on the ability to carry out the duties of a job.

What we can see is that the workforce is diverse and as such has diverse demands and needs. Many people in the labour market need to be 'attracted' to work for the organisation and this means recognising and understanding that not only are they diverse in character, but they have *diverse needs* also. Part of this attraction is to be seen not only as a welcoming employer, but a fair one, given this diversity of need.

In Chapter 2 we saw the importance of HR strategies in creating an organisational environment in which equality and diversity flourished. Successful recruitment, selection and retention and organisational cultures that support procedural justice are clearly linked.

Creating an attractive culture means creating an environment in which diverse groups are comfortable. This does not just mean creating policies and practices that provide procedural justice, but also creating environments in which diverse options and freedom of opportunity are available for the different ways in which employees undertake and deliver their work.

Creating an attractive environment – family-friendly policies

Though it has a potentially negative and more exploitative side, it is recognised that flexible working strategies provide the opportunity to attract and improve retention of sections of the labour market that would not otherwise be available for work (IPD, 1994; Murray and Cornford, 1998).

A recent IRS survey found that employers continue to seek ways of making working time more flexible, in order to increase efficiency, meet customer demands and assist employees in balancing work and personal commitments (IRS Employment Trends 603 and 608).

Flexible working hours

Flexible working hours provide the opportunity for people with diverse needs to work flexibly; for this reason they are considered to be key to 'family-friendly policies' – policies which enable employees to balance the demands of home and work. The most popular flexible working hours policies identified by the IPD (1995) included:

- *part-time working* – usually defined as working less than 30 hours a week;
- *job sharing* – sharing the hours of a full-time job equally between two employees;
- *flexitime* – contracting employees to work for a weekly or monthly number of hours; a core time period is established (often 10am–12 noon and 2pm–4pm) when the employee must be at work, but hours worked outside of the core are flexible;
- *annual hours* – contracting employees for a number of annual hours; employees are guaranteed a fixed salary each week or month regardless of hours worked provided the total of annual hours is completed;
- *flexible daily hours* – different hours can be worked according to needs; normally a fixed number of contracted hours would be worked in an agreed period; unlike flexitime there is not necessarily a core time when the employee must be at work during each day;
- *term-time working* – working only during school term times to enable parents with school-age children to be at home during school holidays;
- *shift working* – working outside of the pattern of 9am–5pm; shift working

provides opportunities for employees who cannot work during those hours. Two-thirds of the American labour force now spend more than half their working life outside 9am–5pm.

Other ways of providing flexibility in hours include (Stredwick and Ellis, 1998):

- *maternity/paternity/adoption leave* – employees take breaks for agreed periods of time with the 'right to return to work'; giving employees the right to return to part-time working encourages retention and enables them to balance the demands of their childcaring role;
- *career breaks* – employees take breaks for agreed periods of time (typically a number of years) with a 'right to return to work' within a number of years;
- *sabbaticals* – employees with an agreed length of service have a period of time off and return to the same position at the end of the period.

In addition, proper provision for emergency leave can often limit the amount of time taken off to deal with genuine situations which cannot be planned for.

Flexibility in the place of work

An important part of a **flexible working** strategy is flexibility in the place of work. Organisations need to consider whether insisting that all employees come into a central place of work is really necessary. A UK County Council which led the way in introducing a 'flexiplace scheme' sees the benefits of such schemes as:

- reducing unnecessary travel and environmental damage;
- resulting in work being carried out more efficiently;
- helping employees to balance their work and family commitments more effectively;
- enabling employees with disabilities to enter or remain in employment where this would otherwise be difficult.

Such a scheme is successful because it is voluntary and recognises that insurance and health and safety issues must be in place to safeguard employees working from home.

The flexible working strategies identified above are also 'family-friendly' in that they create flexible working possibilities that enable employees to balance the needs of home and work. However, the 'best practice' organisations go beyond just providing flexible working arrangements by providing additional policies that attract those with family caring responsibilities. Stredwick and Ellis (1998) identify the following key provisions:

- *Childcare provision.* As increasing numbers of women and dual earners with dependent children under the age of 16 enter the workforce there is growing demand for workplace nurseries, crèches or nursery vouchers or a childcare allowance. Subsidies enable lower paid employees to afford to use these resources.

- *Out of school and holiday play schemes.* Employers can support these by taking places for employees' children. These can be particularly valuable to full-time employees and in school holidays.
- *Elder care.* This is as important as childcare support, with increasing numbers of employees caring for an ageing population. Support for places for dependants can help reduce absenteeism and stress and the cost of such help. A leading UK Hospital Trust provides a 'granny crèche' for those with elderly dependants.

If flexible working strategies and family-friendly policies are to attract and retain a diverse group of employees then it is important that employers create a climate of high commitment to their employees and do not simply use them to reduce costs (Purcell, 1997). Lewis (1997) is concerned that flexible working arrangements are introduced to meet organisational needs rather than to be 'family-friendly'. There is a danger, she states, that 'family-friendly' policies only apply to 'core' workers and that employees who are not reassured otherwise, believe that take-up of 'family-friendly' policies can be limited because of fear of the impact it would have on their career. Lewis (op. cit.) identifies that the following are the main barriers to the take-up of 'family-friendly' policies:

- They are often interpreted as 'perks' rather than basic needs.
- They are seen by the organisation as a cost which cannot be afforded in times of economic difficulties (they can create problems in such times with those who do not need them).
- Perceptions between hours spent at work, productivity and commitment; productivity and commitment are often seen in terms of hours spent in the office.
- There is a view that commitment outside of work reduces the level of commitment at work.
- Those who work long hours are valued.
- There is a dilemma over governmental responsibility and employer responsibility.

In addition, there is a view that employers, particularly small employers, will avoid recruiting those who are likely to have need for 'family-friendly' and flexible policies.

The links between flexible working and diversity are clear. McEnrue (1993; cited in Kandola and Fullerton, 1994) identified that the main reason for managing diversity was to attract and retain employees in the face of labour shortages and changes in the demographic composition of the workforce. Flexible working enables organisations to attract and retain employees with diverse needs provided that those employees are treated as fairly and equitably in respect of contract terms, conditions of service and training opportunities as 'core' employees. Lewis (1997) believes that a culture shift is needed here so that diverse and different patterns of work and careers are equally valued, and that this value will apply to the careers of both men and women.

So far in this chapter we have discussed the value of flexible policies and practices for providing an environment in which recruitment and selection practices that support diversity can take place. We now need to look at the practices that will enable managers to recruit and select a more diverse work-force.

The selection and induction process

Before any recruitment and selection practices can be put in place it is essential to clearly establish strategies and targets.

Setting targets for diversity

At a minimum, an organisation that seeks to be diverse should reflect within its workforce the diversity of the population in which it operates. This means setting recruitment targets for men, women, ethnic minorities, disabled and older people. This does not mean positive discrimination; this should not happen at the point of selection. What it does mean, however, is that progress towards achieving diversity can be monitored and policies and practices evaluated against achievement of targets.

Cornelius and Gooch (2001a) identified eight steps in a fair and effective recruitment and selection process (see Figure 4.1); at each step in the process it is important to be aware of legal requirements as well as 'good practice'.

Defining the selection criteria

Not all vacancies mean that there is a need to recruit an identical replacement. Consideration should be given to the needs of the organisation and the

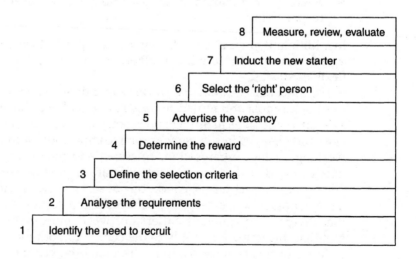

Figure 4.1   The eight steps in the recruitment and selection process

resources available in the organisation. In addition, consideration should be given to encouraging a more diverse group of people to apply by making the requirements of the job more flexible. Ways of introducing flexible working practices have been discussed earlier in this chapter.

In a fair and systematic selection process it is essential to define the **selection criteria** against which applicants are to be assessed and selected. Job or role descriptions describe the tasks, responsibilities or competencies that comprise the job or role. Bias can easily occur in the writing of the job or role description; it should not overstate or understate the duties, requirements and outputs of a job, nor should it be biased towards a particular group of the working population. Tasks, responsibilities or competencies should only be included where they can be shown to be a valid and necessary function of a particular job.

The person specification is the profile of the 'ideal' person who could fill the vacant job or role; this profile needs to state the 'essential' and the 'desirable' criteria for selection and is produced from material gathered for the job or role description. The profile provides the criteria against which applicants can be systematically and fairly assessed. Unnecessarily high requirements for the person specification can lead to 'indirect discrimination' – when any requirement or condition is imposed which can be complied with by a smaller proportion of one group than another and cannot be shown to be justifiable. This includes requiring a standard of English higher than needed for safe and effective performance on the job.

When establishing the criteria for selection it is important to ensure that applicants from diverse backgrounds who can bring 'different' and 'unique' approaches to the job or role should not be excluded by criteria which exclude them unnecessarily from selection. Such organisations will fail to gain competitive advantage from attracting and retaining diverse talent.

It is also important to ensure that any criteria that are not essential to a vacant position and might adversely affect disabled applicants should be avoided (e.g. good eyesight, driving licence, stamina). Kandola and Butterworth (1996) recommend that the interview process should be standardised and only focus on criteria established at the outset of the recruitment campaign. Interviewers should be briefed on disability etiquette in an effort to ensure the interview runs smoothly. Practical arrangements should also be made with respect to the disabled person's needs, e.g. parking, access to the building.

Determining the 'reward'

Having determined the criteria against which applicants are to be measured, the next step is to determine the **reward package** to be offered; this includes both pay and benefits.

The starting point is to look at the level of the job or role in the organisation. This should be determined by an analytical job evaluation scheme, which should value fairly the work of all the different groups of employees it is covering and not give additional weighting to features of the job which are unfair or discriminate unfairly between different groups of employees with different backgrounds. Paddison (1997) believes that there is evidence that job evaluation schemes may undervalue features of work traditionally undertaken by women (e.g. caring). Job factors with a time dimension, e.g. length of service and experience, have been shown to strongly favour male jobs, as do factors with physical activity dimensions, while factors with a caring dimension and for dexterity have been shown to strongly favour female jobs.

The level of reward package to recruit at depends not only on ability to pay but also on internal relativities and established reward policy and structure as well as perceptions of equity and fairness. The use of market surveys in isolation may be detrimental to morale and longer-term working relationships; it may also lead to the importing of discriminatory reward practices, particularly for those jobs or roles which have traditionally been held largely by women and attract a generally low market rate and benefits.

'Fair' pay means giving consideration to the market rate and also to the relationship between reward packages within the organisation; it is also important to work within the legal requirements of the equal pay legislation and to judge the 'fairness' of the reward being paid. If flexibility is a key link to diversity and more and more employees are to work on non-standard contracts then it is essential that they are treated on the same basis in respect of reward as employees on full-time contracts and paid fairly for their contribution to the organisation. A recruitment and selection policy which promotes and develops all members of the workforce equally plays a major part in preventing the 'ghettoisation' of women and minority groups.

Flexible benefits benefit many employees as they can choose from a 'cafeteria' menu, and this can have advantages for working with diversity. Individuals are motivated by different needs depending on their circumstances and age (Armstrong, 1999). A young mother might find crèche facilities particularly valuable while a new graduate might prefer an interest-free loan. An older person might want additional pension allowances. Flexible benefits that enable individuals to choose can help attract and retain diverse people with diverse needs.

Attracting applicants

The person specification or competence definition provides the information on which the recruitment advert wording is based. The image portrayed by the organisation's recruitment advertising can determine the image held by customers and applicants of the organisation.

Recruiters who wish to appeal to a diverse labour market need to be aware of their organisation's image. Lorraine Paddison (1990) identified particular areas for attention – advertising media that are associated with a particular section of the population can exclude others. Young male white images in adverts and brochures can exclude women, ethnic minorities, disabled and older people from applying to an organisation. Confining advertisements to areas or publications which would exclude or disproportionately reduce the number of applicants of a particular group can restrict the pool of talent that can apply for a particular job; this also applies to advertising by 'word of mouth' or by 'cards in the window'. Restricting advertisements to internal applicants can also exclude diverse groups from the organisation unless the 'pool of talent' from which the applicant is to be selected internally is diverse. It is important to avoid prescribing requirements which are not relevant, such as length of residence or experience in the UK, and to make it clear that comparable qualifications obtained overseas are as acceptable as UK qualifications (CRE, 1993).

Managers who complain that a diverse group of talent does not apply for their vacancies need to look at their human resource processes and practices. It can be important to develop links that encourage more members from the breadth of the community. These include working with local community groups and their leaders, attending community events, working with local charitable organisations and offering job placement and work experience opportunities. The CRE (1993) has shown that work placements and training on assessment procedures can improve selection possibilities for ethnic minorities. 'Open days' can give potential applicants the opportunity to familiarise themselves with the organisation and encourage applications.

Selecting for interview

Application forms

A number of organisations ask applicants to send in CVs; however, the application form has the advantage of asking the questions the organisation wants to be answered. The application form is also an important part of the 'image' an applicant gets of the organisation and questions should not be asked on application forms which would or might discriminate. For example, questions which deal with age, marital status, families, ages of children or intimate personal details can discriminate. Employers should not disqualify applicants because they are unable to complete an application form unassisted unless that is a valid test of the standard of English required for safe and effective performance on the job.

When scrutinising application forms, particularly of women, it is important to recognise that many women have breaks in their formal careers while they look after children or other dependants. In order to ensure that applicants have the opportunity to provide all relevant information, a section on the application form that enables individuals to detail voluntary or unpaid work can provide valuable information that might not otherwise have been provided.

Selection tests

Research shows that the traditional method of interviewing is not necessarily very reliable and that selection testing can improve the reliability of the recruitment and selection process. However selection tests results are used in the selection process, it is important that they should only be administered by trained testers and are valid predictors of performance. Saville and Holdsworth, a major UK testing agency, stress that if tests are being used they should be psychometrically sound; it is also important that they do not discriminate:

- The skills or attributes the test measures should be specified and should only be those necessary to do the job; the content of the test should be similar to that found on the job.
- The level of difficulty at which the skill is measured should be appropriate to the job. Care should be taken where there is a tendency for one particular group to reach the required standard.
- Test performance must be related to job performance and a validation study must be carried out to establish that the tests correlate with job performance or other relevant criteria. Test results should be monitored for any differences in scores by different groups of applicants (sex, ethnic group, age, disabled).
- Practice items at the beginning of tests enable those less familiar with them to cope better with the main test and allow time for questions.
- Only qualified people should administer the tests; results should be fed back to the applicant.
- Results should be evaluated in relation to the performance of a comparison 'norm' group. It is important that the 'norm' group is a diverse group; very often this is not the case.

When testing people with disabilities the above apply but in addition special arrangements need to be made in respect of allowing practice tests, access to rooms, use of equipment, specialist help and ensuring that instructions are understood clearly.

Assessment centres

Many organisations believe that interviews are poor predictors of performance as they tend to focus on current or previous job performance, and for this reason they use **assessment centres** to select the right person. The skills needed in a new job or role may be completely different, and by simulating those skills assessment centres give an insight into likely future performance (IDS, 1995). Assessment centres combine interviews with other exercises to provide a more 'complete' picture of the candidates. Usually before an assessment centre is designed, the job or role to be filled is broken down into competencies. It is important that those who are acting as assessors are fully trained to assess appropriately (IDS, 1995). This includes cultural awareness training. This training is essential if diverse groups are to be recruited into the organisation.

Work sampling

Work sampling has high **validity** (Levy-Leboyer, 1990; Wood, 1994) and can provide immediate evidence to match against criteria. Examples of work sampling might include:

- word processing a report;
- giving a presentation;
- negotiating a sale;
- watching a video and answering questions on it;
- making a simple object;
- taking a telephone call;
- dealing with a difficult customer.

Care should be taken to ensure that there is a direct link between the **work sample** and the selection criteria to ensure that the test is valid.

References

Employers have no obligation to give references, but if they do so they must ensure that any reference given to prospective future employers is accurate and truthful. It is important to remember that applicants who have not worked for some time may need to provide references from areas other than their working experiences.

Selecting the 'right' person?

The purpose of the selection interview is 'To obtain and assess information about a candidate which will enable a valid prediction to be made of his or her future performance in comparison with the predictions made for any other candidates' (Armstrong, 1996). Interviews have been shown to be unreliable predictors of future performance but when conducted by a trained interviewer in a systematic and fair way, their reliability improves. Panel interviews are often preferred to individual interviews in that the judgement of candidates can be shared, but they can be intimidating, particularly for applicants less familiar with the selection process. Sequential interviews one after another can be another way of sharing judgement but in a less threatening way.

In order to improve the reliability of the interview it is essential for the manager who is carrying out selection interviewing as part of their role to undertake training in selection interviewing. To ensure fairness in the selection process for ethnic minorities, the manager needs to have an understanding of cultural differences between the manager's own culture and the applicant's culture. To ensure fairness for disabled people, the manager needs to have an awareness of the needs of disabled people and to ensure that they are given every assistance to participate fully in the selection process. The learning outcomes of any training programme should enable the manager to understand the key issues of diversity, to conduct a systematic and fair recruitment and selection interview and to recognise the induction needs of the new recruit.

The purpose of the interview is to seek evidence that enables the applicant to be measured against the previously determined selection criteria. In addition, the interview provides an opportunity to clarify queries relating to information provided on the application form (e.g. gaps in career history) and to give information about the organisation.

Preparing for the interview is as important as the interview itself. Preparations will include inviting applicants to visit the location to familiarise themselves with it prior to the interview. This is particularly important for those with disabilities or those who have not been in a workplace for some time. Each person who is invited to attend the interview should know what will be expected of them during the interview and the Person Specification for the job or role they are being interviewed for.

Preparation also means preparing questions which enable you to clarify information provided by the application form and to measure the applicant against the requirements of the Person Specification.

It is important to check assumptions and expectations clearly at the introduction stage of the interview and to check for understanding throughout the interview. For those unfamiliar with an interview process it is important to explain what will happen in the interview and what is expected of the applicant.

In the interview the interviewer should use open and probing questions which seek to clarify information on the application form and look for evidence to enable the applicant to be matched against the previously identified Person Specification. **Behavioural questions** which seek for evidence to match the applicant against the selection criteria are particularly valuable in selection interviews as they are founded on the assumption that evidence of behaviour in past performance is the best predictor of future performance. Evidence need not only apply to the workplace, and applicants without a great deal of work experience should be encouraged to think of examples outside of the work environment.

Jargon and technical language should only be used if it relates to the selection criteria.

Body language can also often be misunderstood across cultures. In some cultures, to express one's opinion firmly in a team meeting is regarded as disrespectful, whereas in others it is taken as a sign of individual initiative and is rewarded. Assumptions about understanding should be checked during the interview as the implicit message is often misunderstood across cultures.

National, cultural and religious differences inevitably influence use of language, argument patterns and non-verbal behaviour, possibly leading to misunderstandings from applicants from visible minorities and assessors (Echiejile, 1992; Macdonald and Hakel, 1985).

Some of the possible sources of misunderstanding that assessors need to appreciate include the following:

- degree of reticence or openness of an applicant speaking about a colleague or superior;
- willingness or reticence to speak openly about personal or organisational strengths or weaknesses;
- the degree to which body language is used when communicating and differences in the types of body language used;
- willingness to make public personal aspirations;
- willingness to disagree or say 'no' to potential superiors.

At the close of the interview applicants should have the opportunity to ask questions and be told when they will hear the outcome of the interview and what the next stage in the selection process (if any) will be. Applicants should be informed how they can seek feedback if they are unsuccessful, as this can help their personal development.

Induction

Having selected the right person for the job from a diverse pool of talent, it is important that they are welcomed into the organisation. It can be particularly difficult for people from minorities joining an organisation; they often take longer to be inducted and socialised into organisations (Gordon *et al.*, 1991; Cox and Blake, 1991, cited in Kandola and Fullerton, 1994). Gordon showed that women and ethnic minorities in particular were unaware of expectations of new employees and what was needed in order to progress within the organisation. There can also be particular difficulties for disabled people.

The purpose of induction is to help new employees to adjust to their new jobs and organisational environment, to help them become fully integrated into their work teams or groups and to prevent a high incidence of early leavers (Fowler, 1990). An example of an induction process which helps new recruits adjust to their new working environment is at Daewoo Cars. New recruits are sent a video and a set of workbooks with exercises to complete before they join the organisation; these deal with company philosophy, product knowledge and the no-haggle retail process. More information is then provided in the first two days of starting in the organisation.

Research shows that many new employees face an 'induction crisis' in their first six weeks of joining a new organisation and that turnover rates of new starters are very high during these weeks. Causes of early leaving can arise from the gap between the 'official' and 'unofficial' expectations of the employer and the expectations of the employee. Gooch and Cornelius' model (2001) (see Figure 4.2) shows that the induction process involves 'expectations'. There are the new recruit's expectations and the organisation's expectations of the new recruit. Induction can play an important part in helping the new recruit to understand the 'formal' rules of the organisation and to shape behaviour in terms of standards of behaviour/dress, health and safety and, particularly important, diversity. Induction can also play a crucial part in helping recruits to understand personal development support available and promotional routes.

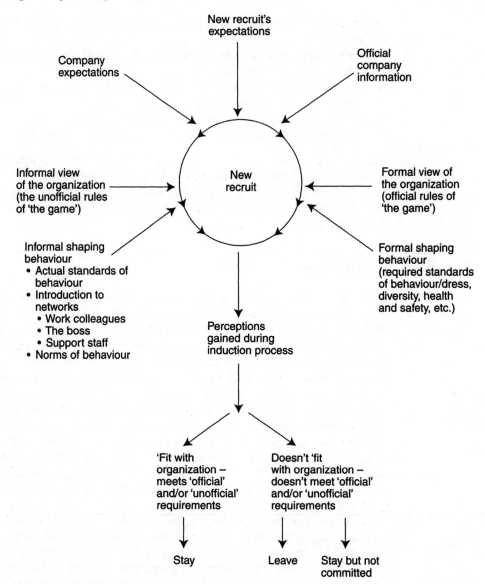

Figure 4.2 The induction dilemma

In addition to these 'formal' processes are the 'informal' processes that also shape behaviour. These are, if you like, under the surface. They are about actual standards of behaviour in the workplace, about the 'norms of behaviour' of work colleagues, about the behaviour of the manager and about the support and networks which are available to staff. It is these experiences which shape the 'informal' view of the organisation and lead to understanding of the unofficial rules which govern promotion or achievement or progression.

New recruits make a decision about the organisation on their perceptions gained during the induction process. They decide they 'fit' with the organisation – they meet the 'unofficial' or 'official' requirements and they stay, or they decide they don't 'fit' with the 'official' or unofficial' requirements of the organisation and they leave or stay because they have no where else to go but are not committed.

In order to ensure that the new employee feels comfortable in the organisation Kandola and Fullerton (1998) recommend:

- a mentoring process whereby a more experienced person can help and guide the new starter – this might be supplemented by networks which the individual can join (this is discussed more fully later in this chapter);
- managers are properly trained in induction techniques and recognise the problems of settling into organisations, particularly for individuals from minority backgrounds.

In addition, a support network can be very important indeed. These support networks can range from the Black Police Association, which has provided a support network in the UK for ethnic minority police, or they can be counsellors or mentors or buddies. Most support networks are run by volunteer employees who become knowledgeable in particular areas, e.g. **harassment** and **bullying**, and are able to provide confidential support and advice.

Monitoring

Carrying out a **monitoring** procedure as part of the recruitment and selection process is a valuable tool in evaluating recruitment processes. Monitoring involves collecting and analysing statistical data on existing employees, on applicants and on recruitment and selection processes. The CRE (1994) recommends that employers should regularly monitor the effects of selection decisions and personnel practices and procedures. This involves not only monitoring recruitment and selection campaigns but also regular audits of the workforce. This provides a clear, overall picture of what is actually happening in terms of the structure of employment in the organization.

Monitoring involves:

- obtaining information on the ethnic origins and disability of all employees and job applicants; many organisations have a separate tear-off sheet attached to the application form which is removed before the application is read;
- examining, by disability and ethnic origin, the distribution of employees across the organisation and the success rates of applicants/candidates for jobs, training and promotions according to the type of job or role, grade and department;
- measuring against targets set for diversity.

All methods of selection should be validated against results and constantly reviewed to ensure fairness and reliability. Selection decisions should be based on a range of selection methods, and specialist training and help may be needed in some of the methods. Particular care needs to be taken with selection methods to ensure that they are 'fair' and non-discriminatory; in the USA, under the Civil Rights Acts of 1964 and 1991 organisations can be found guilty of discrimination if it is established that methods used had an adverse impact on particular groups.

Monitoring and evaluating can help to refine plans, policies and procedures to reflect best practice and improve performance, to realign targets and resources and to be proactive instead of reactive to change within the organisation, within the community and with new legislation (Meto, 1999).

Exit interviews can also provide valuable sources of evidence and should always be conducted by the manager when someone plans to leave. Keeping a record of exit interviews provides valuable data for future action plans for recruitment, selection, development and induction.

If a diverse group of people are to be attracted, recruited and retained by the organisation, it is essential that support mechanisms are in place to support their role in the organisation and their development. Mentoring plays a significant role in supporting diverse policies and practices.

Mentoring

Kandola and Fullerton (1998) identified that **mentoring** played an important role in helping and guiding the new starter. If organisations are to be truly diverse then they have to provide those support mechanisms which provide the pathways through the 'informal' organisation.

Much has been written about mentoring, a mentor's role, who should mentor, mentoring relationships and effective mentoring skills (Clutterbuck 1991; Megginson et al., 1995). There is, however, no definitive answer to the question of what mentoring is (Taylor and Stephenson, 1996); it remains an area open to interpretation (Stidder and Hayes, 1996). For clarification, a useful definition of the term 'mentor' is suggested as an off-line person who helps other individuals to address the major transitions or thresholds that the individual is facing and to deal with them in a developmental way (Megginson, 1994). From this definition we can see that mentoring provides a crucial developmental tool at a critical time within the organisation for the new starter or the existing employee who is moving through the organisation and trying to find their way through its 'culture'.

Mentoring is best undertaken by a competent, more senior manager who is prepared to give up time on a regular basis to facilitate the learning of a more junior colleague – the learner. Mentees and potential mentors need to be briefed about the purpose of the mentoring scheme and overall aims whilst allowing individual learning preferences within each mentoring relationship. Where possible, mentors should be selected by mentees, in that the relationship is more likely to work if some rapport and trust has already been established and the learner admires the management practice of the mentor or where the mentor can offer support for certain developmental activities. For the new starter, selecting their own mentor is not really an option because of their lack of organisational knowledge. For this reason, selecting the mentor for the learner needs careful consideration. The choice of mentor is crucial as the mentor's accumulated knowledge underpins subsequent learning for the learner. Selecting a mentor who has cross-functional responsibility can offer wider organisational learning.

Mentor relationships should be facilitated by a third party, where *reflective learning concepts* should be embedded and encouraged, enabling an informal mentoring contract to be agreed. The narrowness or openness of issues within the contract is determined by the mentor and learner to encourage ownership of the process. Some mentoring schemes may wish to include 'shadowing' as part of mentoring, where the learner shadows the mentor undertaking particular aspects of work. Other mentoring schemes may be limited to regular meetings where mentoring is undertaken through formal and informal discussion through an exchange of views. The frequency and duration of mentoring meetings should be agreed, plus contingencies for less formal contact as particular issues arise. Moreover, the learning and support expected of the mentor should be agreed and linked to the aims of the mentoring scheme (Blackburn, 2000). Learning will differ from one mentoring relationship to another due to contextual and environmental differences; during the lifetime of the mentoring scheme, therefore, an evaluation of mentor-supported learning should be undertaken and disseminated.

Having created an environment in which recruitment, selection and induction is attractive to those from diverse backgrounds, the manager needs to retain that employee by identifying their training and development needs.

Identifying training and development needs

Identifying training and development needs is a key part of a manager's role. It plays a key part in attracting and retaining staff and helping them to identify clearly with organisational objectives. Research shows (Hutchinson and Wood, 1995; Bevan and Hayday, 1994; Brewster and Hegewisch, 1994) that line managers take responsibility for identifying training needs, often at performance management interviews. This section therefore looks firstly at performance management and then at the role of the manager in identifying training and development needs.

Performance management

Performance management consists of a systematic approach to the achievement of organisational objectives by providing an interconnected set of goals that link at organisational, departmental, work team and individual levels.

Performance management encourages regular informal and formal feedback to individuals, work teams and departments. Moreover, the resulting outcomes are an important source of management information as emerging

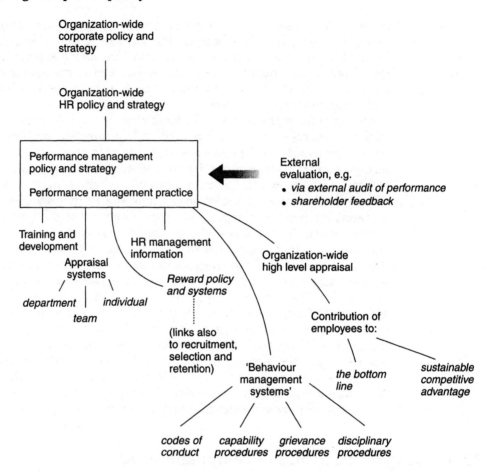

Figure 4.3   A strategic perspective on performance management

trends can be derived from across the organisation, enabling targeted managerial intervention. The process also enables managers at all levels to identify
the performance and behaviours of work groups and individuals for which
they have a direct responsibility. This in turn provides the potential for recognising achievement, whilst encouraging improved relations between managers and staff by increasing levels of clarity about what is expected of
groups, individuals and managers in relation to each other's role, duties and
responsibilities, that is an inherent part of the system. As a by-product of this,
communication and problem solving can also be improved, which can generate positive and constructive relationships across the organisation as people
become focused on performance and behavioural expectations.

Figure 4.3 shows how organisational objectives are linked through a hierarchy of objectives to strategic plans. The system operates as a loop with objectives and targets being distributed from corporate level to departments and
people. These objectives and targets are structured to enable everyone in the
organisation to contribute effectively towards the achievement of corporate

objectives. Information to monitor progress against plans is provided via monitoring arrangements and interim targets that are fed back up the organisation to enable any corrective decisions to be made. The accuracy of goals and monitoring arrangements is important to maintain the effectiveness of the system at all levels. The performance management process should not be a bolt-on system, but an integral part of managing employees and producing a more rounded management information system.

Performance management in action

The major element of performance management systems is the regular meeting between managers and their staff for a discussion of the job, job changes, successes, difficulties, aspirations, etc. The precise subject-matter must be established by both parties, not imposed by the manager.

Focus

A discussion then ensues which takes as its basic theme what they together can do to discover what has happened since the last meeting, why those things happened and what can be done to resolve difficulties or to build on strengths. The focus is on two people attempting to resolve problems, both contributing to the discussions and solutions. The aim is to make the person's job more efficient and more satisfactory and to allow both parties to air their views and their feelings.

Setting objectives

It is important for performance management systems that the employee should be clear as to the standards against which judgements will be made, or the expectations that exist of the level of performance required. Ideally, the employee should agree in advance to standards on which performance will be judged so that a greater commitment to achievement will be generated.

Standards of performance

Standards of performance need to be understood by all employees and to be discussed and agreed. High expectations, standards or criteria for judging success are needed because they lead to higher performance. Standards set at the level of a good performer will motivate others to perform better. Even if you cannot get absolute or measurable standards, you should aim for consistency in the expectations set so that everyone understands what they are and that, as far as possible, they are applied fairly. In these cases there is a need to keep monitoring the achievement of standards to maintain that consistency.

Objectives should always have a target date for completion. This does not necessarily have to be for the next interview, it can be sooner or later but the manager then needs to make sure of following it up at the right time to check its achievement. One way to see whether objectives contain all they need to be effective is to think of the initials SMART – *S*pecific, *M*easurable, *A*greed, *R*elevent, *T*imed.

Box 4.1 Performance criteria for measuring achievement of objectives linked to achieving cultural diversity in a police authority

Level 1. Lacks knowledge and understanding that may result in the outward display of prejudice, inappropriate behaviour and/or lack of respect for others' feelings and their rights to dignity.

Level 2. At times may be insensitive to the feelings of others and does not consistently demonstrate knowledge and understanding of the diverse make-up of the community. Aware of the need for good community relations but does not demonstrate a complete understanding of the issues and/or does not display full commitment to the principles of good community and race relations.

Level 3. Understands the role of the police in providing service to diverse communities within a multi-racial society. Aware of community and race relations issues. Presents a positive image by fostering and improving good community relations. Recognises how own attitudes, values and prejudices may affect judgements and dealings with others. Demonstrates, through dealings with others, consideration, understanding, fairness, integrity, and respect for the right to equal treatment under the law (irrespective of race, class, gender, age, disability and sexual orientation). Openly challenges any incidents of inappropriate language/behaviour displayed by colleagues without causing bitterness.

Level 4. Takes an active role in working in and with the community. Effectively establishes contacts with key community representatives and partnerships with the aim of furthering improvements in community relations. Identifies, promotes and supports the development of community and race relations initiatives. Possesses a good understanding of the cultural differences of the various minority groups present within the community and demonstrates empathy with these. Recognises when cross-cultural communication problems may occur and how these can be overcome. Able to provide diversity-focused training and raise the level of cultural awareness

for colleagues within the area/department. Demonstrates considerable sensitivity and understanding of the feelings and views of others and is able to provide support to people who feel victimised or subject to harassment or unfair treatment irrespective of race, class, gender, age and sexual orientation.

Level 5. As for level 3 plus: monitors and supervises an effective response to racial crime, incidents and reports of harassment and recognises the possible tensions/disputes that may exist in a multi-racial/cultural society and seeks to resolve them equitably. Establishes high standards in respect of community and race relations and acts as a role model to junior staff. Recognises and positively challenges any incident of inappropriate, unacceptable or improper behaviour/language and takes the appropriate action.

Level 6. As for level 3 plus: recognises and responds to the implications of different policing styles on the development of good race and community relations. Delivers workable solutions with the community of other agencies, recognising possible conflicts, and effectively reviews the policing of racial crime incidents and reports of harassment. Monitors quality of service and performance against agreed qualitative targets. Identifies and establishes appropriate mechanisms for local community consultation and consults opinion leaders within local communities to identify the policing needs of their different groups.

Level 7. As for level 3 plus: implements and drives through initiatives and programmes which significantly contribute to the development and improvement of community relations within the area. Effectively reviews and monitors these and influences area/department-wide standards and procedures on race relations and community relations. Ensures the delivery of the Policing Minority Communities and Race Relations Strategy.

Some performance management systems also set goals in terms of behaviours and practice, i.e. how the job should be done, or to encourage what are seen as key practices; setting goals in terms of behaviours and practice can set the standards on which diversity builds. The scales used to rate performance usually contain broad categories related to the achievement of objectives or the manager's view of the effectiveness of a member of staff. They may provide every member of staff with a list of the key practices and tell them that some of them will be discussed at each review session. By setting standards for diversity expected by all managers and employees, and embedding them in a performance management system, performance management becomes a powerful mechanism for managing diversity. Box 4.1 shows how a police constabulary set performance criteria for measuring achievement of objectives linked to achieving cultural diversity.

Personal development plans

If performance objectives are to be achieved, then it is essential to incorporate longer-term development plans into performance schemes in which skills and knowledge levels overall are improved. Many employees are now encouraged to develop self-development plans containing job-relevant but personal aims and objectives in order that they can develop their own knowledge and skills in a more generic way. These development plans can be used to strengthen diversity management in two ways: firstly by identifying knowledge and skills areas where diversity training and development would be valuable, e.g. learning more about disability or cross-cultural interviewing, and/or by developing knowledge and skills to help individuals achieve their potential and to continually develop and grow. The manager has a key role here to develop and sustain diversity initiatives through the performance management scheme and through the identification of personal development plans which are the outcome of performance management interviews.

Assessing individual and group performance

Team working and multi-skilling are common organisational features (Thompson, 1995a). Appraising team performance can encourage collaborative working that requires drawing all team members together to achieve team objectives. In turn, this creates a learning environment where team members learn to work productively, through which working arrangements are adjusted to develop team norms. Introducing a combination of individual and team goals will encourage appropriate behavioural modifications.

The essential educational unit in a learning organisation is the team (Cook, 1995). Setting team objectives related to diversity embeds diversity in the heart of the organisation and facilitates collective learning through sharing and building on existing knowledge and experiences.

Rewarding performance

There is a view that linking payment to appraisal corrupts the developmental aspect of performance appraisal systems (Bevan and Thompson, 1992; Kohn, 1993; Thompson, 1995b). Rewarding performance and behavioural modification, however, will reinforce the message that the organisation rewards particular aspects of employee behaviour and performance. Rewarding the achievement of diversity objectives does not need to negate the developmental aspects of performance management but can be seen as a complementary aspect of it. Marc Thompson (1995b) believes that in the end appraisal may be more important than paying for performance and that it is the process of setting goals that is the key to improving performance. In this light, setting goals for the achievement of diversity and monitoring their achievement would seem a critical way to managing diversity in organisations.

In this section we have highlighted how performance management systems can be used as part of an organisational approach to managing equality and diversity. This can be achieved by not only setting objectives that link to diversity, but also providing training and development opportunities that support equality and diversity. Fair and equitable systems that are transparent and clear provide systems of procedural justice in which capabilities equality can grow.

Handling grievance and disciplinary issues

Diversity management builds on good equal opportunities practice (Gooch and Cornelius, 2001; Ford, 1996). The management of diversity requires systematic management action and changes to working practices and organisational cultures. This means that all policies and practices have to be looked at and analysed and questions asked about whether they create barriers to diversity or promote diversity. Creating a climate in which diversity flourishes means having policies and practices that promote procedural justice throughout the organisation to stop discrimination, bullying and victimisation.

The purpose of a **disciplinary procedure** is to ensure that an employee who has broken company rules is treated fairly, that each situation is investigated thoroughly and that sanctions for punishments are imposed consistently. The purpose of a grievance procedure is to enable employees to have a formal procedure to follow where they are able to express and resolve their dissatisfaction.

Grievance procedures

Grievance procedures are often invoked because employees are complaining against harassment or bullying. Harassment takes many forms and is described (IPD, 1997; IRS, 1996b) as 'unwanted behaviour, which a person finds intimidating, upsetting, embarassing, humiliating or offensive'; it includes coercion for sexual favours. The IRS (1996b) states that the most effective procedure for channelling complaints is through a specially designated individual. This may be the personnel officer, the harassment officer, trained counsellors or a trade union representative. Organisations such as Littlewoods and Kent County Constabulary which have had success with diversity policies and practices have alternative channels of complaint through volunteer members of staff who are trained by the organisation and located throughout the organisation. Their contact details are available to all staff. These confidential counsellors can offer informal advice, give information on personal rights and advise victims on options to resolve problems.

Bullying is a particular form of harassment. Kent County Constabulary (1999) define bullying as:

> behaviour which intimidates an individual, making him/her feel demeaned and inadequate. It is a gradual wearing-down process that undermines self-confidence and self-respect. It can be difficult to detect, often taking place where there are no witnesses. It can be subtle, devious and difficult for those on the receiving end to confront the perpetrator. Bullying includes shouting and/or swearing; public humiliation; ignoring or excluding someone from a group, constant criticism, removing areas of responsibility, refusing to delegate, patronising or belittling behaviour, setting unrealistic targets, setting up to fail, making fun – inappropriate use of humour/nicknames; spreading malicious rumours; over-supervision and blocking training applications for no good reason.

It is important to have policies in place which make it clear that harassment and bullying are unacceptable in the workplace. It is managers who play a key role in managing these policies and having good practices in place. The IRS (1996b) recommends:

- Communicating the policy to the whole workforce in order to raise awareness of the issues and the organisation's procedures for tackling the problem. This should make it clear that all employees have a positive duty to establish and maintain a workplace free of harassment and bullying and that no employee will be victimised for bringing forward a complaint. It should also make clear the disciplinary penalties for such actions.
- Training staff and managers involved in upholding the policy.
- Any complaints procedure should suggest that, in the first instance, the complainant should ask the person responsible to stop the harassment and/or bullying. Where the victim is uncomfortable with this approach, they should seek the aid of a counsellor or friend to do so. The complainant should keep written notes of dates and details of incidents and the names of any witnesses.

Where an informal approach has failed, more formal procedures need to be pursued. The IPD (1997) recommends that:

- harassment and bullying be treated as a disciplinary offence;
- investigation procedures should be prompt;

- investigators should be independent;
- representation should be received from both parties;
- a time-scale should be established for resolving the problem;
- confidentiality should be established;
- records of complaints and investigations should be made;
- where a complaint is upheld it may be necessary to transfer one of the parties involved.

It is important to convey the organisation's policy on harassment and bullying at induction and through any training. Managers have a key role to play in ensuring that this training and development is completed. In addition, the personnel/HR department needs to ensure that the effectiveness of the organisation's policies and practices should be monitored and re-evaluated on a regular basis.

As mentioned above, where informal approaches fail, the manager has a responsibility to ensure that sound discipline and grievance practices are in place to support diversity in the organization.

Discipline and grievance policies

Good disciplinary and grievance policies (ACAS, 1987) should:

- be clearly communicated in writing and through induction and training to all employees so they are aware of the procedures; those administering the policies need to be specially trained for their role;
- specify to whom they apply;
- make it clear that all disciplinary offences and grievances will be fully investigated;
- state the types of sanction that may be applied in disciplinary cases; no employee should be dismissed for a first breach of discipline unless the offence is serious enough to be classed as gross misconduct, e.g. assaulting a colleague, drunk at work, etc;
- make clear the right to make representation at a hearing and to be supported by a friend, colleague or trade union representative at the hearing;
- specify levels of management who can make decisions;
- provide the opportunity for appeal.

The manager has a key role to play in ensuring that these procedures and practices are known to employees and are followed in situations where informal processes have failed. By following the ACAS guidelines, managers provide an environment in which individual rights are known and supported. Importantly, the potential for abuse of such procedures, in particular by line managers of disciplinary procedures, should be both understood and reflected in supporting training.

Case study – Littlewoods plc

Littlewoods is an organisation which has won awards for leading the way in innovative and advanced working practices in the workplace (EOR 1998). Littlewoods' winning package includes:

- The Leadership Challenge
  A board-level equal opportunities strategy committee has been established to ensure senior managers take responsibility for equal opportunities. Group directors are required to produce equality action plans linked to business plans.
- Equality Means Business
  Equality action groups for each business function making all managing directors responsible for the implementation of equal opportunities within their part of the business and getting them to set quantifiable equality objectives in their business plans with appropriate financial provision and within an agreed timetable. In addition, the organisation provides a full range of family friendly initiatives and targets for women in senior and middle management.
- Dignity at Work
  This policy aims to eradicate all forms of bullying and harassment and to ensure all employees are treated with dignity and respect. Supporters offer confidential information and support, investigators investigate allegations and managers have responsibility for promoting good practice and preventing victimisation.

Littlewoods Equal Opportunities Policy states that:

Littlewoods is committed to equality of opportunity and dignity at work for all, irrespective of race, colour, creed, ethnic or national origins, gender, marital status, sexuality, disability, class or age.

We aim to ensure that we:

- Recruit, retain and develop the best people
- Provide the best possible service to our customers
- Access the supply of goods and services from a diverse business community
- Show responsibility towards the community in which we live and work.

Surinder Sharma (2000), Equal Opportunities Director for Littlewoods plc, states that the payback for Littlewoods is:

- 62% of all employees work flexibly;
- 98% of women return from maternity leave;
- 160 different shift patterns at the Sunderland Customer Service Centre;
- 63.3% of the workforce are women;
- 20% of the main board members are women;
- 30% of women are in senior management positions;
- No employment tribunal cases.

Conclusions

This chapter has examined three key areas in which managers take responsibility for managing people at work. These three areas are recruitment, selection and induction; identifying training and development needs; and handling disciplinary and grievance issues. Cornelius *et al.* (2000) argue that diversity management is likely to be most effective when there is proactive management involvement. If organisations are to be diverse then they need to have effective policies and practices that underpin a culture of organisational justice. As managers have key responsibilities in these three critical HR areas, they can provide the environment in which diversity and capabilities equality can flourish.

As organisations increasingly operate in a diverse labour market, so the 'diversity' advantage comes by fully using and developing the talents of diverse groups of people. The policies and practices outlined in this chapter help to support the full utilisation and development of those groups. However, care needs to be taken that not only is there fair access to opportunity, but that employees from traditionally disadvantaged groups have freedom of opportunity when they become organisational members also.

To achieve this, executive responsibility and commitment are essential from the top of the organisation. This commitment, however, must be supported and underpinned by line management. The processes and practices mentioned in this chapter should all be managed by line managers (Cornelius *et al.*, 2000). In order for managers to achieve this, they need training, development and support from a range of professionals within the organisation or from outside consultants if they are in a smaller organisation. The benefits of achieving the 'diversity' advantage within an equitable environment outweighs the costs.

Text-based questions

1. What role does monitoring play in ensuring that recruitment, selection and induction policies and practices are increasing the diversity of the organisation?
2. Why might flexible and family friendly policies and practices promote diversity in the workplace?
3. What is the value of mentoring in supporting a new employee in an organisation or department?
4. What objectives can a manager agree with people in their team which will promote diversity?
5. What training and development programmes would support diversity?
6. Why do good grievance and discipline policies and practice support diversity in the organisation?

Library and assignment-based questions

1. Select the Annual Reports of five leading organisations and critically evaluate the extent to which they include diversity in their mission, value statements and/or Annual Report. What do those statements tell you about the attitudes of those organisations to promoting diversity in their organisations?
2. Examine the graduate recruitment literature (either online or on paper) from three organisations and critically examine the extent to which the literature encourages applicants from diverse backgrounds. What changes might you make to the literature?
3. Design an induction programme that would support a new starter in understanding the 'informal' aspects of an organization. How might a mentor help with this process?

4. What training and development do managers need to enable them to support and promote diversity in their organisations?
5. To what extent do you believe that setting diversity objectives for managers promotes diversity within organisations?

Internet resources

ACAS http://www.acas.org.uk/

Chartered Institute of Personnel and Development UK http://www.cipd.co.uk/

Commission for Racial Equality UK http://www.cre.gov.uk/

Daewoo Motor Company http://www.daewoomotor.com/

Kent County Constabulary http://www.kent.police.uk/services/sitemap.html

Littlewoods plc http://www.littlewoods.co.uk/corporate/index.htm

Saville and Holdsworth http://www.shlgroup.com/home.asp

The Runnymede Trust http://www.runnymedetrust.org/

Further reading

Kandola, R and Fullerton, J (1998) *Diversity in Action, Managing the Mosaic* (CIPD) and Kirton, G and Greene, A-M (2000) *The Dynamics of Managing Diversity*, Butterworth-Heinneman, Oxford, provide some good material on HR practices which promote diversity.

In addition, Gooch, L and Cornelius, N have a chapter 'Recruitment and selection in a diverse context' in N Cornelius (ed.) (2001) *HRM – A Managerial Perspective*, International Thompson Business Press, London.

Other useful books are Blakemore, K and Drake, R (1996) *Understanding Equal Opportunity Policies*, Prentice Hall, Hemel Hampstead, and ER Kossek and SA Lobel (eds) (1996) *Managing Diversity – Human Resource Strategies for Transforming the Workplace*, Oxford Brookes University, Oxford.

References

ACAS (1987) *Discipline at Work: the ACAS Advisory Handbook*, ACAS, London.

Anonymous (1995) IDS Study Assessment Centres, January: Study 569.

Anonymous (1995) *Flexibility at Work in Europe*, IPD, London.

Anonymous (1996) Sexual Harassment at Work 2: Developing Policies and Procedures, IRS, London, October, 7–12.

Anonymous (1996) Labour Market Trends – February, Office for National Statistics, London.

Anonymous (1993) *Towards Fair Selection*, Commission for Racial Equality, HMSO, London.

Armstrong, MJ (1999) *Reward Management*, IPD, London.

Armstrong, MJ (1996) *A Handbook of Personnel Management Practice*, Kogan Page, London.

Bevan, S and Hayday, S (1994) *Helping Managers to Manage People*, Report 254, Institute of Manpower Studies, Brighton.

Bevan, S and Thompson, M (1992) *Performance Management in the UK*, IMS, Brighton.

Brewster, C and Hegewisch, A (1994) *Policy and Practice in European Human Resource Management*, Routledge, London.

Blackburn, A (2000) Mentor Supported Learning. A Case Study of a Postgraduate Management Course, unpublished PhD research.

Carnevale, AP and Stone, SS (1994) Diversity: beyond the golden rule. *Training and Development*, October, 22–39.

Clutterbuck, D (1991) *Everyone Needs a Mentor, Fostering Talent at Work*, Institute of Personnel and Development, London.

Cook, P (1995) The learning organisation: rhetoric or reality? *Organisations and People*, **4** (1), 10–14.

Cornelius, N and Gooch, L (2001a) *Human Resource Management – A Managerial Perspective*, 2nd edition, Thomson Learning, London.

Cornelius, N and Gooch, L (2001b) Performance management: strategy systems and rewards, in N Cornelius (ed.) *Human Resource Management: a managerial perspective*, Thomson, Padstow.

Cornelius, N, Gooch, L and Todd, S (2000) Managers leading diversity for business excellence. *Journal of General Management*, **25** (3), Spring, 67–78.

Cox, TH and Blake, S (1991) Managing cultural diversity; implications for organizational competitiveness. *Academy of Management Executive*, **5**, 45–56.

Echiejile (1992) *Equal Opportunities Recruitment and Selection*, The Book Guild Ltd, London.

EOR (1998) Littlewoods increasing diversity, increasing profits. *EOR*, **81**, September/October.

Ford, V (1996) *People Management*, November, IPD, London.

Fowler, A (1990) How to plan an induction programme. *Personnel Plus*, September, pp. 27–32. IPD, London.

Gooch, L and Cornelius, N (2001) Recruitment, selection and induction in a diverse and competitive environment, in *Human Resource Management – A Managerial Perspective*, 2nd edition, Thomson Learning, London.

Gordon, G *et al.* (1991) Managing diversity in R&D groups. *Research Technology Management*, January–February, **34** (1), 18–23.

Guest, D (1987) Human resource management and industrial relations. *Journal of Management Studies*, **24** (5), 503–21.

Hall, L and Torrington, D (1998) Letting go or holding on – the devolution of operational personnel management activities. *Human Resource Management Journal*, **8** (1), 41–55.

Hutchinson, S and Wood, S (1995) *The UK Experience in Personnel and the Line: Developing the New Relationship*, Institute of Personnel and Development, London.

IPD (1997) *Managing Diversity, a Position Paper*. IPD, London.

Kandola, R and Butterworth, A (1996) The Disability Discrimination Act (1995) implications for recruiters. *British Psychological Society*, **12** (3), June.

Kandola, R and Fullerton, J (1994) *Managing the Mosaic*, 1st ed., IPD, London.

Kandola, R and Fullerton, J (1998) *Managing the Mosaic*, 2nd ed., IPD, London.

Kent County Constabulary (1999) *Bullying at Work, Fairness in Action*, Kent County Constabulary.

Kohn, A (1993) Why incentive plans cannot work. *HBR*, September–October.

Labour Market Trends, February 1997, National Statistics Office, London.

Leach, J (1995) cited in Torrington and Hall, Letting go or holding on: the devolution of operational personnel activities. *Human Resource Management Journal*, 1995, 41–55.

Lewis, S (1997) Family friendly employment policies: a route to changing organizational culture or playing about at the margins? *Gender, Work and Organization*, **4** (1), January.

Megginson, D (1994) What's happening in mentoring research, European Mentoring Centre Conference, Sheffield Business School.

Megginson, D *et al.* (1995) *Mentoring in Action, a practical guide for managers*, Kogan Page, London.

Meto (1999) *The Value of Diversity*, National Forum For Education and Development, London.

Macdonald, T and Hakel, M (1985) Effects of applicants, race, sex, suitability and answers on interviewers' questioning strategy and ratings. *Personnel Psychology*, **38**, 321–334.

McEnrue, MP (1993) Managing diversity; Los Angeles before and after the riots. *Organisational Dynamics*, Winter, **21** (3), 18–29.

McGovern, P, Gratton, L, Hope-Hailey, V, Stiles, P and Truss, C (1998) Human resource management on the line? *Human Resource Management Journal*, **7** (4), 12–29.

Murray, C and Cornford, D (1998) *Flexible Working survey*, Gee, London.

Paddison, L (1990) The targetted approach to recruitment. *Personnel Management*, November, IPD, London.

Paddison, L (1997) Reviewing pay systems for sex bias. *Equal Opportunities Review*, **74**, August, 30–34.

Purcell, J (1997) A good question. *People Management*, April, IPD, London.

Saville & Holdsworth Ltd (undated) *Best Test Practice in the Use of Personnel Selection Tests*, Saville & Holdsworth Ltd, London.

Sharma, S (2000, unpublished) *The Entrepreneur's Viewpoint – The Business Benefits*, Managing Diversity Conference, Law Society, March.

Stidder, G and Hayes, S (1996) Monitoring rhetoric and reality. *Mentoring and Tutoring*, **48** (5), November.

Stredwick, J and Ellis, S (1998) *Flexible Working Practices*, IPD, London.

Taylor, M and Stephenson, J (1996) What is mentoring? in M Mawer (ed.) *Physical Education: Issues and Insights*, Falmer Press, London.

Thompson, M (1995a) BBC Broadcast, unpublished.

Thompson, M (1995b) *Team Working and Pay*, IES Report 281.

Distinctive organisational characteristics and their influence on equality and diversity action: the illustration of 'professionalism'

5

Nelarine Cornelius

Chapter overview

It could be argued that all organisations have their own distinctive attributes and that the nature of their core service or product greatly influences these. In turn, the common characteristics of the occupational group that has responsibility for delivering the core service or product will influence the character of an organisation also. This has many implications for workplace equality and diversity action. In this chapter, rather than consider character in abstract terms, the illustration of organisations whose core activities and services are delivered by professional workers will be considered and, in particular, those where the key services are provided by employees from long-established professions with strong traditions and culture, such as medicine and legal practice.

Why have we have chosen to look at such organisations? There are a number of reasons. This group has been selected as they are amongst those for whom there are the strongest expectations of how they should conduct their work, both by the state and also by members of the communities they serve. Moreover, for most long-established professional groups, the manner in which work is conducted is powerfully shaped by the professional bodies and institutes of which they are members. Importantly, such groups often hold public and esteemed positions within society; and in turn, society expects such groups to work in its best interests. So, professionals are in this sense highly visible, are expected to act for the benefit of society, enable the well-being of members of the community, and overall, to 'do good'. In combination, these factors help to generate strong group characteristics.

From the perspective of equality and diversity action, in this chapter we will concentrate on the experience of those from traditionally disadvantaged groups, both as fellow professionals in particular, and as recipients of professional services. Therefore, the overarching questions are, first, in what ways might an organisation's character influence the way in which equality and diversity issues are perceived, second, how might character influence the choices made when addressing equality and diversity issues, and third, how might the illustration of organisations dominated by professional groups help us to better understand the importance of 'organisational character'?

Learning objectives

After studying this chapter you should:

- appreciate the power of strong organisational characteristics in shaping responses to equality and diversity action, and how dominant work groups are part of this shaping;
- understand the influence of culture on equality and diversity action;
- understand how the social structures that in part define 'the professions' provide insights into the difficulties in tackling workplace equality and diversity;
- have gained insights into the mechanisms that help to create institutionalised discrimination;
- have a clearer appreciation of how to identify the equality levers for change in professional organisations;
- overall, have a heightened understanding of the specific equality and diversity challenges facing such organisations.

Key words
culture ● marking ● professionals and professionalism ● social closure ● sameness ● sharedness ● institutionalised discrimination ● patriarchy ● duty of care ● emotional labour

---

Introduction

Understanding organisational characteristics

All organisations contain important attributes that we might think of loosely as *'organisational characteristics'* or *'organisational predisposition'*. These characteristics help to highlight important, perhaps defining attributes that are likely to be significant in relation to understanding equality and diversity action.

To pursue this further, we have chosen for consideration organisations whose key activities are undertaken and shaped by professionals and professionalism as an illustration of the usefulness of understanding organisational character.

Why this type of worker? Professional practice is at the heart of many key services – all of us have at some stage needed the services of a professional: nurses, doctors, lawyers, accountants, teachers, university lecturers, police officers, social workers, and so on.

What is the nature of the work that professionals do? We are not going to attempt to focus primarily on activities of particular types of professionals (although this is important), but for our purposes, we will concentrate on the aspects of their work that defines these groups broadly as professional workers. At one level, professionals can be thought of as knowledge workers, possessing special, applicable and employable knowledge and expertise. Much of the work that these groups undertake has the power to improve, and indeed at times to transform, the quality of our lives. We expect professionals to be well trained, competent and to act in our best interests.

However, these views are a general 'feel', an outsider's idealised view, of what professionals do and why they do what they do. Researchers have undertaken a more systematic approach to understanding the work of professional groups. There are elements of this view of professionals (both the positive and negative aspects) that are found in some of the research. However, it is a much more complex and detailed picture that emerges.

We are going to focus on primarily is that of *what the professions share*, rather than the ways in which they are different. This is for two reasons. First, it is to ensure that the equality and diversity interventionist or researcher, in whatever capacity, is able to gain a rapid insight into important aspects of a *range* of professions and their organisations, especially given the size and complexity of many of these organisations. Second, it will hopefully help the interventionist identify more rapidly the general characteristics of such work, and thus also help to pinpoint more readily the genuinely distinctive nature of a specific profession, and further, individual local organisations within which those professions are cited.

Influencing organisational structure and practice

Henry Mintzberg's (1979) seminal paper on the structuring of organisations is a useful starting point. Mintzberg suggests that many of the more familiar ways of thinking about organisational structure belie the reality of what the structure is in practice, and how it actually operates both formally and informally. So for example, many organisations will have compiled the familiar 'family tree' type of organisational chart, within which is often represented a hierarchy of organisational roles and status, with the most powerful roles at the top and the less powerful ones below, with descending authority from top to bottom. However, Mintzberg argues that this is a limited view of how organisational structure *really* operates in practice, and that 'structure in practice' differs greatly from 'structure on paper'.

He suggests that it is important to establish which group within the organisation is most powerful and influential, and why this is the case (as this indicates the source of this sustained power and influence), as the structuring that operates in practice reflects the values, aspirations, policy and strategic agendas of that group. So for example, he argues that if managers are the most powerful group, their tendency is to create fiefdoms; if it is technologists or engineers, it is to standardise around the dominant technology; and so on. For organisations within which professional thinking and action is the primary shaper, *the 'pull' is to professionalise*: to reproduce the values of autonomy, self-regulation, and to create across the organisation an environment within which these values are core, with all of the associated structures, rules, and formal and informal expectations. In other words, the organisation is driven by the desire to deliver a 'high status' professional practice.

Psychological contract within 'communities of practice'

Other researchers have highlighted what professionals value, what they expect from their psychological contract, and what they give willingly in return. For example, Etzioni (1964) has indicated the importance of freedom to make judgements, organise one's working day and 'light' control as what professionals want. In return, they are prepared to give more than they are often required to do without additional remuneration: part of the reward is worker autonomy. Academics such as Pollitt (1993) have also questioned what they argue is the 'managerialist' and inherently anti-professional project of increasingly centralised control and scrutiny that has characterised changing administrative practice in professionally dominated organisations, such as in the UK public sector, in for example NHS hospitals and local authorities in the past 20 years. Indeed, the work of scholars such as Etzioni would suggest that the 'give and take' of the 'professional' psychological contract gives way to more inflexible, rule-book-compliant working as bureaucratic controls over the work of professionals increase.

Certainly, professionals are knowledge workers, and researchers such as Lave and Wenger (1991) have highlighted the importance of the social aspect of how the knowledge of such workers is enhanced, in their work on *communities of practice*. These researchers highlight the importance of informal methods of knowledge exchange, shared experiences and learning as important sources of the enhancement of competence and expertise. However, for professional workers, it has been suggested that there are core values and ethical positions that are strong and shared and that play a significant role in shaping the character of professionalism, such that the morality of action resides in many professional codes of conduct, for example. The expectation is that these values must be held in order to secure membership of the community.

Individual virtue and moral agency

According to Aristotelian ethical thinking, it is through being virtuous that an individual flourishes and is happy. So, the focus is the character of the individual actor, not the universal correctness of acts or preferred outcomes. In other words, we are not born with such virtue, but become virtuous through training, experience and the acquisition of practical wisdom (Mackie, 1977, p. 186). Hence, the implicit perspective underlying many equality and diversity developmental change interventions is that individuals can be helped to learn about, and be developed into, virtuous people. Part of this process, however, includes a recognition that practices will not change overnight.

This notion of individual virtue highlights the importance of the *individual as moral agent*. In addition, it highlights how there needs to be clarity regarding how large or small the impact is, i.e. whether they change the character of individuals and groups and in turn, organisations. For example, Douglas (2000), gives an account of her work on changing attitudes towards race in the UK police service. The individual officer is seen very much as the important point of leverage for *demonstrable ethical action*. This can be understood in the context of the nature of police work, and reflects the powers that the state certainly invests in constabularies, but crucially, in individual officers. This includes powers to use reasonable force legitimately, to police 'by consent' with the cooperation of local communities, to uphold the law, maintain the peace and reduce fear.

It could be argued that *virtue* in this sense is central to most models of professional education and development, as witnessed implicitly through the professional codes of conduct and increasingly, more explicit ethical codes of conduct. One well-known example is the Hippocratic oath within the medical profession. But although these codes often reflect socially responsible actions and a general sense of public service, it is not necessarily the case historically that professional ethos has traditionally been developed around notions of equality. Indeed, it could be argued that implicitly, equality of opportunity and diversity of membership are *weakly* represented core constructs within professional mores.

Understanding professionals and professionalism

The shaping and character of professionals and professionalism

In his book *Class in Britain* (2000), David Cannadine puts into historical context the way in which classifications used in relation to social class have been thought about. To quote two of the many examples of classifications that he uses:

> There was Aristotle's 'virtuous middle', moderately placed between the two extremes, thereby holding society together; and there were the three

functionally distinct yet interdependent medieval estates, consisting of those who prayed, those who fought and those who worked. (2000: 29)

This 'divine' duty, in service to 'the gods', possessors of special knowledge although its origins lie in the ancient world, has echoes within more contemporary understanding of the professions. It is worth recalling that religious authorities often traditionally held some responsibility for law making, before much of the law became a more secular activity. Religion and the law, direct descendants of the 'virtuous middle', are still around today.

We all have our views of what is it to be a professional. Although the term is widely used, the meaning of what it is to be a 'true' 'profession' and 'professional' has been studied over the years. There are accounts of how the 'establishment' professions developed in the nineteenth century (Clarke, 1964; Waddington, 1984). In his book *The sociology of the professions* (1999), Keith MacDonald draws from the literature (and particularly from the work of Max Weber) some of the views that scholars have developed that, in his view, help us to understand what has shaped the professions. MacDonald outlines what he regards as important attributes for understanding their nature. What is particularly significant about MacDonald's work is that his interest goes beyond the representation of the structures and processes that result in professionalisation and professional power.

He is concerned also with the implication of these for professional decision making and action, particularly in relation to deciding who should or should not be afforded membership of the professions, as well as the resistance to scrutiny of much professional decision making. At the heart of MacDonald's work is that much clusters around *social exclusivity*, via *social stratification*, *patriarchy* and *rare and expert knowledge*. This social exclusivity is often powerfully reinforced through the institutions of the state (though the manner in which the state's role is exercised differs according to national culture and associated historical context).

What is a profession? Some definitions

MacDonald defines professions as 'occupations based on advanced, or complex, or esoteric, or arcane knowledge' (1995: 245) and significantly, he also quotes Durkheim's view of professionals as 'the corp-intermediaries between the individual and the state', the latter of which echoes Aristotle's 'virtuous middle'. In Figure 5.1, MacDonald outlines the main elements that, in his view, provide a credible conceptual framework or 'working theory' of the professions. The main inter-related elements include:

- The **professional project**, pursued through the *means* of establishing both (a) a favourable economic order and (b) a favourable social order. The latter is achieved through:

  - monopoly of knowledge;
  - establishing strong **trust relations** with an array of stakeholders;

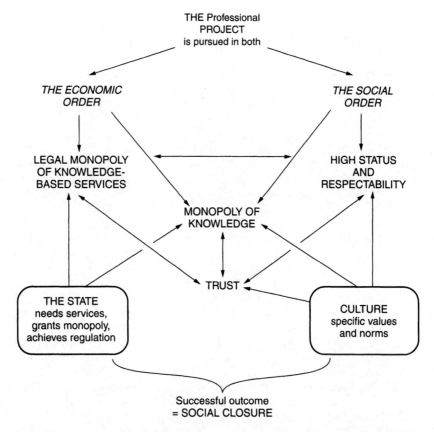

Figure 5.1 A working theory of the professions: a conceptual outline. *Source:* MacDonald, KM (1999) *The sociology of the professions.* Reprinted by permission of Sage Publications, Inc.

- strong culture, within which lies professional political culture developed within the national context of political power networks.
- The desired *outcome* is *social closure*, where legitimate membership and ineligibility is made clear and supported ideally with the weight of the state and its legislature (see Box 5.1)

The work of Larson on the 'professional project' (1977) is particular germane here. Like all work in this field, Larson's conceptualisations are contested, but none the less, her work remains highly influential. Larson refers to the 'professional project', which MacDonald develops further and illustrates with the example of accountancy in the UK. The professional project has specific characteristics, which include *main goals* and *sub-goals*.

The *main goals* of the professional project are:

- the *starting point*, with a specific occupational group that possesses skills and knowledge that provide an opportunity for income;
- the overall objective of *enhancing and then maintaining the position of the group*, maintained by the group's elite, who set objectives and criteria to this end;

Box 5.1 Important ideas within the 'professional project'

- *Organised autonomy* reflecting its licence and mandate to control its work, granted by society and the state by virtue of winning the support of a political, economic or social elite (MacDonald, 1999: 5).
- *Capital*: Monopolistic supply of services in the labour market, based on expertise. Here, MacDonald refers to the work of Bourdieu (1973) who refers to the nature of *capital* to professionals, where capital is 'the set of actually usable resources and powers . . . (that are) socially valued attributes and credentialled knowledge that characterise Weber's status order and the middle class respectively, (which) are brought together into a credible alternative (to a Marxist) basis for exploitation and social power' (MacDonald, 1999: 48). So that 'skills are not an axis of exploitation: rather they are a valued activity that is legitimated by a cultural field'. The monopolisation of professional knowledge and expertise, with the justification for monopoly even in anti-monopolistic markets, centres on status and moral authority

  Further, Macdonald refers to cultural capital, which is 'stored in people's heads and minds' and 'accrued to those who successfully impose their values on other groups and legitimate its culture'.
- *Producing the producers*: Within the professionals, there is limited delivery and accreditation of the education of professional members through elite institutions.
- *Middle class* status and values rather than petit bourgeois or *middling class* ones. The lawyer, the statesman and the priest were all part of the same class, the landed gentry. One implication of this is that, for example, in the UK, as many members of parliament were gentry also, they were probably reluctant to turn a regulatory eye on these professionals. So for example in the seventeenth century,

the legal profession was an example of a '*lesser government*', such that its members had control over their own affairs in every respect and their power over the functioning of the legal and judicial system was extensive (MacDonald, 1999: 76).
- *The role of the state*: The state can exercise an important role in legitimising the professions: 'professionalisation from above'. However, professionalisation has historically been strongest where the regulatory role of the state is relatively weak and specialist centres of knowledge distribution are established that are largely controlled by the professions themselves (e.g. in the UK) and weaker where middle class values were more strongly associated with the civil service and academia and state regulation of the professions is strong (e.g., France and Germany) (pp. 66–99).
- *Social closure*: Social closure is the principal method of professionalisation. Further, MacDonald argues that the longer established and more dominant professional occupations have traditionally emphasised their 'specialness' by insisting that their members were gentlemen, therefore establishing their superior status and exclusion based on *gender* (1999: 51), and have a strong *patrician* aspect to their character. Of particular importance is *exclusionary closure* (1999: 131): the exercise of power by an occupational association that is primarily concerned with the definition of membership in such a way as to exclude those whom the professional body and its elite regard as '*ineligibles*' or 'outsiders'. The manner of different kinds of closure in relation to gender has been fully elaborated by Witz (1992). Social mobility and respectability are often gendered also.

After MacDonald (1999)

- *the quest for monopoly* in the market for services based on their expertise, and for status in the social order;
- an underlying strategy of *social closure*, whereby '*ineligibles*' are excluded from the group and thus are denied access to its knowledge, its market and its status.

The *sub-goals* of the professional project are:

- to carve out a *jurisdiction* for itself;
- *producing the producers*: ensuring that all future entrants have passed through an appropriate system of selection, training and socialisation, and turned out in the 'standardised professional mould';
- *control of educational input* and *monopolisation of professional knowledge*;
- achievement of *respectability* within the society as a whole and, importantly, recognised by the state and ideally, internationally;
- *formal recognition and relations with the state*, with 'whom a regulatory bargain must be struck' (Cooper *et al.*, 1988: 8, cited in MacDonald, 1999) so that monopolistic practice (normally resisted in Western economies) is officially sanctioned, increasing market power, formally acknowledging status and affording moral authority;
- *cooperative and where necessary, competitive relations with other occupations* concerning their potential jurisdiction, including educational establishments;
- *presentation to the public* in a manner most likely to maximise business returns and social standing (as potential clientele);
- *context – social, political and cultural –* within which the professions aim to influence, e.g. social values and legislation.

So, to summarise, there are a number of elements that, it could be argued, characterise the professions:

- Professions occupy a number of key employment categories within society that enhance and potentially transform the quality of our lives.
- Professionals often operate within a psychological contract of 'give and take', where flexibility of working practice, personal autonomy, intrinsic motivation and operating beyond the formal employment contract and at times, beyond the call of duty, are taken for granted.
- They are cosmopolitan knowledge workers, who will often demonstrate great loyalty to their other professional colleagues, often across national boundaries, and to their profession in general and its institute: at times this will be at odds with what their host organisation may demand of them.
- The action of what defines professionals is in part knowledge-based but crucially, there is also a strong social network component.
- Some professional groups may wield significant power through their monopolistic supply of services that are grounded in high levels of hard to access skills and knowledge.
- The governing institutes and those who manage them have as a primary task the determination of 'ineligibles', the maintenance of the mechanisms of social closure and monopoly of supply of their service within the market.
- Regulation of professional workers is often primarily through 'internal governance' (lesser government) rather than via state regulation; there is also significant desire and power to maintain internal governance.
- Broadly speaking, there is an expectation that public and state scrutiny should be minimised and that professional judgement should only be

scrutinised by exception and where a strong professional expert authority determines what should or should not be open to scrutiny.

- Professional organisations are typically long-established, patrician cultures.
- Professional power is such that they are often able to exert organisation 'pull', so that its dominant paradigm and structures reflect their core values and preferred practices and also exert considerable political power in the broader environment.
- There is a strong internal sense and external validation of virtuous action and designated moral agency.
- Paradoxically and historically, the construct of **sameness** (what we hold in common) has been seen as highly desirable (as reflected in the predominance of patrician, gentlemanly culture, especially in the long-established male-dominated professions). However, **sharedness** (the values we hold around what we share) may be weakly elaborated (sharedness and sameness are discussed more fully later in the chapter – Clapp and Cornelius, 2002).

Perhaps one attribute of the professions that needs to be raised at this juncture is that of *'fair mindedness'*. Fair mindedness is often at the heart of public service professionals, where many professionals have as an integral part of their daily life decisions that need to be made about how to apportion or ration services, and seek to do this in an equitable way. However, how such decisions are made need not be, and indeed is unlikely to be, purely rational, and it is possible that unintentional biases may creep into decision making.

At times, it can be difficult to unpack the sources of what would appear to be the obvious statistical biases in, say, the disproportionate number of those from minority ethnic communities who are legally required to be in mental care hospitals, or in prison, or those from all minorities who appear in the senior echelons of specific professions. However, an overwhelming implication of the character of the professions is that even when the bias is clear and unequivocal, the mechanisms for change are less so, especially against the core characteristics of social closure, limited external scrutiny, and service expertise that is difficult to challenge.

Challenging professional decision making

In many ways, the Bristol Royal Infirmary case is driven by the issue of rationing and its impact on key stakeholders: hospital consultants, hospital management, the government, and not least, its impact on the kind of services that were and could be made available in Bristol. It is a complex case, and there was pressure for consultants and managers to increase throughput to meet targets. It could also be argued that the actions taken were an artefact of the criteria set for getting additional funding and establishing a specialist heart centre, during a period of public funding difficulties for the UK National Health Service.

Box 5.2 The Bristol Royal Infirmary Inquiry case

Background

The public inquiry, led by Professor Ian Kennedy, was set up by the Secretary of State for Health, Frank Dobson, to investigate the unusually high death rates among babies receiving complex heart surgery at the Bristol Royal Infirmary in the UK. It found that NHS managers were powerless to stop doctors performing operations at which they had poor success rates unless doctors first made them aware of the problems. Dr John Roylance, the hospital's former chief executive, and surgeon Mr James Wisheart were banned from practising medicine by the UK General Medical Council (GMC) for their part in the Bristol heart babies scandal. Between 1990 and 1994, Mr Wisheart carried out 15 atrio-ventricular septal defect operations. Nine of the young patients died.

Difficulties expressing concerns

The surgeons continued to conduct complex heart surgery when it became apparent that they had a poor success rate. Dr Roylance told the inquiry that 'health care was run by consultants . . . That was not something I imposed. It was my recognition of reality. I recognised it was impossible for managers to interfere.'

A nurse supporting specialist who realised that something was wrong with children's cardiac surgery at BRI told the inquiry why she did not blow the whistle. She found out by talking to colleagues at other hospitals that were centres of excellence in paediatric cardiac surgery that death rates were higher at Bristol. She discovered that babies were spending longer in the operating theatre, and subsequently in intensive care. However, the nurse told the public inquiry that she was a 'weak player' and that her views would not be listened to. Eventually, anaesthetist Dr Stephen Bolsin compiled his own audit of success rates which led to the biggest surgical scandal in the history of the National Health Service. The nurse discussed her fears with Dr Bolsin and concluded, she said, that he would be a better person to voice such concerns. 'I was a weak player at this time whereas he was a strong player' she said.

A few months after Dr Bolsin arrived at the BRI as a consultant anaesthetist, he became concerned at the amount of time that children who had undergone heart surgery were spending under general anaesthetic, and eventually, by the death rates also. He compiled his own statistics, and although other colleagues acknowledged there was a problem, they were extremely reluctant to voice their concerns in public. When Dr Bolsin did decide to raise the issue, he was put under enormous pressure by senior managers and consultants to desist. In 1990, he had written to the then head of the district health authority, later to be the BRI chief executive, to raise his concerns about what seemed to be a higher than average death rate for babies (which he was able to confirm was higher than the national average).

The key event

In an interview with a BBC journalist, he said that he had been quite distressed by the death of one child in January 1995. The night before the child's death, an extraordinary meeting of the cardiac team took place. Every doctor, except Dr Bolsin, agreed that surgery should go ahead. But concerns about the cardiac programme had spread outside the hospital because Dr Bolsin had contacted a key official from the government's Department of Health. That evening, Dr Roylance, by then the chief executive of the BRI, had a phone call from the official, Dr Peter Doyle. Dr Doyle expressed worries about the operation going ahead. Dr Roylance said that although he was a doctor, he could not intervene over the clinical judgement of the doctors directly involved. Meanwhile, the child's parents knew nothing about the debate. The child died the next day during the operation. This was the catalyst that made Dr Bolsin risk his career and talk to the media.

Supporters of the disgraced Bristol doctors and their opponents alike were frustrated by their attempts to question the president of the GMC (between 1983 and 1988), Sir Donald Irvine, at the inquiry. They were told that Sir Donald would not be allowed to discuss the GMC case for legal issues. Instead, he answered general questions about the GMC's role in regulating doctors' performance. The council had come in for criticism that it served only to protect doctors' interests. Sir Donald said this had arisen from a misunderstanding of its function – instead of monitoring standards, the council could only advise on medical education, qualifications and standards. It could act only after it had received a complaint, he said, but pointed to a huge increase since the 1995 Medical Performance Act as evidence that the system worked.

Abridged from BBC News Online Report (includes interview with Dr Stephen Bolsin):
http://news.bbc.co.uk/english/health/

None the less, the case in Box 5.2 is a powerful example of the methods with which it is possible to resist even the most legitimate of challenges. At times, the 'professional network' agenda – hospital consultants and management, the General Medical Council of the UK, the British Medical Association – appeared to be more about maintaining the integrity of individuals in the eyes of the public, resisting the challenge that was made by an individual lower in the status hierarchy than those being challenged, and avoiding a loss of public confidence.

Of course, closing ranks, burying bad news and a desire to maintain the status quo are not unique to the professional organisation. However, what is distinctive is the scale of the losses that were at stake for the accusers and the accused: being taken to court; struck off the General Medical Council of the UK's list of physicians on the grounds of being unfit to practise; a loss of faith by the community; loss of professional recognition by colleagues; and, ofcourse, the risk of legal action. However, the belief of the surgeons in the rightness of their action was such that in spite of assuring the Department of Health that no more operations of this kind would be undertaken pending discussion and review, they proceeded anyway, triggering the tragedy of the loss of another child's life and finally forcing the issue out into the open.

The enormous pressure put upon what was, until his initial complaints, a highly regarded colleague and a consultant in his own right over a period of many years was such that only when he had secured a post in Australia (he had accepted that he would never get a post again in the UK) did Bolsin feel sufficiently empowered to take matters much further. His systematic marginalisation from insider to outsider was sustained, intense and multidimensional, and the implicit threat of professional loss was real. The extreme nature of the number of child deaths in this tragic case meant that it was likely that somebody would be willing to make the ultimate professional sacrifice, and the bravery of Stephen Bolsin, given such overwhelming pressure, cannot be overestimated. However, his systematic marginalisation from the 'in-group' to 'outsider' could be swiftly enacted, with even those colleagues who felt his cause was just unwilling to support him.

Understanding the 'character' of organisations

Social psychological models of culture

The study and conceptualisation of organisational culture is a patchwork of perspectives, paradigms and practice. There is no one view on what culture is, or indeed, how it might be defined. In many ways, it is the slipperiness of the concept, given the number of potential attributes that it might be said to have, that makes it so difficult to pin down. Although there are many definitions and approaches, we have selected only a few as the basis for a defensible simplification that can assist the reader within the context of this chapter.

One of the most widely known, but also challenged, definitions of culture is that offered by Ed Schein (1992), which provides a starting point. Schein offers a social psychological definition of **culture** or sub-cultures in organisations; specifically, that culture is:

> a pattern of basic assumptions – invented, discovered or developed by a given group as it learns to cope with its problems of external adaptation and internal integration (see Table 5.1) – that has worked well enough to be considered valid and, therefore, to be taught to new members as the correct way to perceive, think and feel in relation to those problems. (1992: 12)

Further, Schein argues that there are levels of culture that interact, specifically

- *artefacts and creations*: things such as technology, art, visible and audible behaviour patterns – this level of culture is visible but often hard to decipher;
- *espoused values*: these are testable in (a) the physical environment and (b) by social consensus. These manifest themselves through strategies, goals and philosophies, or *espoused justifications*.

There is a greater level of awareness of these than what Schein argues is the fundamentals of culture, namely:

- *basic assumptions*: This level of culture is taken for granted beliefs, perceptions, thoughts and feelings that are invisible and unconscious, therefore it may be difficult to articulate but is nonetheless 'felt' and shared. These assumptions are concerned with the relationship of a group/organisation to the environment; the nature of reality, time and space; the nature of human nature; the nature of human activity; and the nature of human relationships. It is the ultimate source of values and actions. (1992: 17–23)

Within Schein's theory of culture, attention needs to be paid to *cultural paradigms* – interrelated sets of assumptions; linguistic and behavioural rules, inclusion, identity, control, power influence, intimacy, shared understanding, and emotional dynamics, the influence of leadership, and so on (Table 5.2). As stated before, Schein's theory is primarily social psychological theory – not a sociological, strategic, anthropological, national, cross-cultural or ethnographic one – and as such clearly operates within this particular range of convenience. However, this would be to miss important points. Schein's work highlights the complexity of culture, and the array of representations of it that reside within it, within the domains of emotion, action and thought, and also within the pre-conscious (and by implication, pre-verbal).

Within his key definition of culture, the key words and phrases – 'a pattern of basic assumptions'; 'external adaptation and internal integration'; validity; 'to be "taught" to newcomers as the correct way to perceive, think and feel in relation to problems' – are each substantial areas of theory in their own right. Put very simply, at the heart of Schein's understanding of culture is social 'cognition' (which includes emotion, action and thought), common values and assumptions, sense making and belonging. By implication, within this array, the more embedded these are, the stronger the intra-culture bonds and dynamics, and the stronger the culture.

Table 5.1   The problems of internal integration (Schein, 1985)

1. *Common Language and Conceptual Categories.* If members cannot communicate with and understand each other, a group is impossible by definition.
2. *Group Boundaries and Criteria for Inclusion and Exclusion.* One of the most important areas of culture is the shared consensus on who is in and who is out and by what criteria one determines membership.
3. *Power and Status.* Every organization must work out its pecking order, its criteria and rules for how one gets, maintains, and loses power; consensus in this area is crucial to help members manage feelings of aggression.
4. *Intimacy, Friendship, and Love.* Every organization must work out its rules of the game for peer relationships, for relationships between the sexes, and for the manner in which openness and intimacy are to be handled in the context of managing the organisation's tasks.
5. *Rewards and Punishments.* Every group must know what its heroic and sinful behaviors are; what gets rewarded with property, status, and power; and what gets punished in the form of withdrawal of the rewards and, ultimately, excommunication.
6. *Ideology and 'Religion'.* Every organization, like every society, faces unexplainable and inexplicable events, which must be given meaning so that members can respond to them and avoid the anxiety of dealing with the unexplainable and uncontrollable.

Table 5.2   Basic underlying assumptions around which cultural paradigms form (Schein, 1985)

1. *Humanity's Relationship to Nature.* At the organisational level, do the key members view the relationship of the organization to its environment as one of dominance, submission, harmonizing, finding an appropriate niche, or what?
2. *The Nature of Reality and Truth.* The linguistic and behavioral rules that define what is real and what is not, what is a 'fact', how truth is ultimately to be determined, and whether truth is 'revealed' or 'discovered'; basic concepts of time and space.
3. *The Nature of Human Nature.* What does it mean to be 'human' and what attributes are considered intrinsic or ultimate? Is human nature good, evil, or neutral? Are human beings perfectible or not?
4. *The Nature of Human Activity.* What is the 'right' thing for human beings to do, on the basis of the above assumptions about reality, the environment, and human nature: to be active, passive, self-developmental, fatalistic, or what? What is work and what is play?
5. *The Nature of Human Relationships.* What is considered to be the 'right' way for people to relate to each other, to distribute power and love? Is life cooperative or competitive; individualistic, group collaborative, or communal; based on traditional lineal authority, law, charisma, or what?

Formal and informal arenas for social learning

In relation to dealing with difference, although established formal processes such as induction and training, part of the formal acculturation of employees, may help a general understanding of what behaviour the organisation requires, informal arenas are where much *social learning* is likely to take place. Kelly identified the importance of the quality of such formal and informal learning environments, or *'the laboratory'*, as important for the facilitation of re-construal and change. Much of the common understanding of 'in-groups' and 'out-groups' is likely to reside in *informal laboratories* (for example, after-hours drinking, meals, the locker room) and questions such as 'how do these outsiders fit into our way of thinking, feeling and doing?' are likely to be tested in these.

What emerges from these accounts is the relative tightness of important aspects of professional culture, the high value placed upon autonomy, the resentment of managerialist practices, particularly those which demand more and closer scrutiny of professional behaviour, and the power that many professions wield as the major, often monopolistic, provider of many statutory services. It could be argued that the positive side of this is that such professions are able to resist what the public may see as unreasonable politically or managerially informed choices, such as hospital closures, or general reduction in service levels. However, such strong professional culture may also provide a difficult environment within which to challenge the actions taken by its members in relation to equality and diversity issues, especially in those professional organisations that regard themselves as 'fair-minded'. Inequalities and disadvantage may not have been subject to scrutiny or review for many years and indeed, may have been construed more positively as affording misplaced exclusivity and status. These are likely to have been subject to limited challenge, and factors such as 'specialist-intern' dependencies and limited external scrutiny embedded such thinking within the fabric of the custom, practice and core values (attributes) of the profession and its 'host' organisations, through the dominant discourses played out during training, education, advancement, and the most common theories 'in use' intrinsic to practice. This may make equality and diversity change difficult.

The importance of interpersonal understandings: sameness and sharedness

Drawing from another area of psychology, that of personal construct psychology, there are complementary insights into understanding culture. Within his personal construct psychology, George Kelly (1955/1991) argued that

> People belong to the same cultural group, not merely because they behave alike, nor because they expect the same things of others, but especially because they construe their experiences in the same way.

For Kelly, culture is associated with what he refers to as *commonality*, which he defines in this way:

> To the extent that one person construes the construction of experience of which is similar to that employed by another person, their processes are psychologically similar to that of the other person. (1991: 63)

For our purposes we can interpret this as **sharedness** (Clapp and Cornelius, 2002): in other words, an internal map or a construction of experience. Importantly for us, sharedness differs from **sameness**. Sameness is, in practice, the aggregate of individual differences for the development of common understandings. In contrast, sharedness requires making explicit the constructs of sharing and belonging that are ordinarily held.

Further, Kelly also makes the distinction between commonality (associated with shared construction of experience) and *sociality*. In sociality, the person who is to play a constructive role in the social process with another person need not construe things in the same way as the other person does, but should share the other person's *outlook*. Thus, from a Kellyan point of view, there is a need for *interpersonal understandings* (which connect to sociality), as well as *common* understandings (consistent with commonality).

This distinction between sameness and sharedness is a useful one. Much professional activity – education, training, professional social and networking activities and general modes of acculturation – is most likely to generate the attributes of commonality and sameness, through regulating the experience. For sharedness, there is the opportunity, driven by willingness, for individuals to play a role in the interpersonal processes of others in order to develop and establish interpersonal understandings.

Clearly, these are just two, albeit important, ways in which culture in organisations can be understood at the level of interpersonal transactions. As stated before, these draw upon psychological traditions. Within the field of sociology, there are alternative ways within which culture is understood. Once again, for the purposes of this chapter, we will take a particular viewpoint – that of the interaction between purpose, social structures and action – to understand the development of culture within the specific context of the professions.

'Us and them' thinking and differently valued social norms

In-group and out-group thinking does not need to arise out of conflict but can emerge from an array of social processes. MacDonald's work, outlined earlier, highlights that *in-group–out-group thinking* is a core attribute of the professional project. For example, *differently valued social norms* can be thought of as where the norms of one group (typically the dominant group) are regarded and treated more favourably than those of another. Indeed, some authors have argued that these norms are not only more favourably treated but in fact 'taken for granted', to the extent that they would be difficult for those from the majority group to articulate easily. There is a need to establish proactively how such differences are embedded or emerge, given the predisposition organisations have, as suggested by Annas (1995, in Sen and Nussbaum, 1995), to have a clearer understanding of *historical* sources of injustice and inequality than current ones. Most importantly, differential social norms are likely to be a powerful source of different treatment, and thus, **institutional discrimination**. In part this is because, unless sought proactively and systematically, the discrimination may not easily be discerned by those members of the organisation affected by it or indeed, creating it.

Thus, although maintenance of power and status is likely to be a component of leaving largely intact the systems and strategies that reinforce institutional discrimination, the less easily discernible character of different norms is also likely to play a key role. Evaluating norms can also help to highlight the degree of inclusion or exclusion of those from traditionally disadvantaged groups.

The establishment of in-groups and out-groups – defining 'us' through positive and negative construing of 'them'

Within George Kelly's personal construct theory (PCT) (introduced in Chapter 3) there are a number of key components, one postulate and a number of corollaries. The postulate, which Kelly named the *fundamental postulate*, contains the importance of *anticipation*, specifically that

> a person's processes are psychologically 'channelised' by the ways in which he anticipates events. (1991, Vol. 1: 32)

Within a tight, coherent group, PCT would also indicate that the channelisation will contain aspects that are strongly shared with others, both positively and negatively, in terms making personal sense of group membership and interpersonal transactions, as:

> the network is flexible and is frequently modified, but it is structured and it both facilitates and restricts a person's range of action. (1991: 34)

One could argue that for tightly knit groups, particularly those in which mutual care, support and protection and physical, intellectual or emotional threat are central for psychological well-being, that tightness may well characterise important areas of construing for the group, especially in relation to who is regarded as an *insider or outsider*, as, erroneously, it may be believed that anticipations of the nature of outsiders may be made more speedily. This describes the socio-psychological mechanism of what we would more commonly think of as *stereotyping*, which can be said to occur when members of a group are assumed to possess certain characteristics that prevent impartial assessment of an individual. Often, the effects of stereotyping are subtle: so for example, individuals from the stereotype groups will be viewed with reference to deviations from the stereotype. Stereotyping prevents balanced and fair assessment of an individual or group regarded strongly as 'other'. Often, the effect of stereotyping is subtle, with an individual or group viewed with reference to the stereotype.

Patriarchy and professional culture

MacDonald (1999) makes the distinction between 'personal' service professions, associated with what is sometimes referred to as human or caring professions such as nursing and social work, and 'impersonal' service professions, for example law and accountancy. He uses this contrast as one way of illustrating a distinction of, in general terms, the gendered perception of such work. However, he argues that a more powerful organising principle is *patriarchy*.

The caring professions are also mediative, that is, the state or another powerful third party (for example, the medical profession) mediates between these workers and their clients, and thus greatly reduces their autonomy. Non-mediative professions are typically patriarchal in character. Walby (1989, 1990) (in MacDonald, 1999) suggests that patriarchy, like class, is often intangible, but has specific structures that constitute a system of patriarchy that include:

- a patriarchal mode of production;
- patriarchal violence (physical or psychological);
- patriarchal relations within waged labour;
- a patriarchal state;
- patriarchal culture.

Further, MacDonald suggests that the collegiate egalitarianism is central to impersonal professional services, but in an intangible manner, and with, at their heart, a lesser role for women. Drawing on the parallel of the role of women in science, he cites the work of Reskin (1978) and Atkinson and Delamont (1990), to help clarify his assertion, and highlight 'its cultural pervasiveness that gives cultural practices their mark of legitimacy' (1999: 126). Specifically;

> because people learn sex-role behaviour long before they learn scientific collegiate ones, and the two systems of interpersonal relationships do not fit well together, problems arise when the two systems have to be merged into one. She [Larson, 1977] points out that male scientists can forget gender and relate to women as scientists only, or forget the science and relate only as men and women, but more frequently they choose an intermediate position where 'they adapt conventional gender roles to the scientific setting to create a hybrid of gender and collegial roles that systematically introduces sex-role differentiation into the scientific community. (Reskin, 1978: 10)

> (In Western society patterns of male–female role relationships) . . . include those based on kinship (father–daughter), on marriage, on romance (where the woman is reduced to the status of wife, girlfriend or mistress) or quasi-scientific roles (where the woman is seen as a lab technician or assistant). All these models impede the development of egalitarian colleague-ship for women – instead the woman is left in a position of structural dependence. (Atkinson and Delamount, 1990: 101)

These observations, made from the perspective of gender, might equally well apply to other forms of difference, such as ethnicity or disability. A number of important points emerge from an understanding of patriarchy. First, that notions of care may, in fact, be very necessary within what traditionally may be viewed as impersonal professional services such as medicine, but the gendering of the notion of care, within the context of reinforcing patriarchy, may downgrade its perceived importance and indeed, may be taken as a dilution of the profession's 'seriousness': it is not regarded as 'manly'. Second, its intangibility means that patriarchy is often seen wrongly as axiomatic with professionalism. Third, social closure may be defined according to patriarchal attributes, in terms of who is deemed legitimate or ineligible members of a profession. Significantly, it is often a core construct of many long-established professions, thus making it much more difficult either for commonality or sociality, sameness or sharedness, artifacts, espoused values or basic assumptions, to incorporate patriarchy-challenging attributes. Importantly, it will play a vital role in shaping how services, that are less likely to be accommodating of challenge, service recipient voice, or any other challenge to patriarchal authority are provided.

Institutionalisation of discrimination and inequality

Hidden realities: the danger of the 'retrospective' position: seeing inequalities in 'them' but not in 'us'

We would like to refer to Julia Annas' (1995, in Nussbaum and Glover, 1995) work again, but from a slightly different angle, in order to highlight one dangerous trap of dealing with equality and difference: we may see more easily where we have been. I am sure that we can all recount with horror the experience of entering an organisation which we thought of as 'being in the dark ages' with regard to dealing with diversity and equality. However, we are likely to be relatively unreflective or, more fairly, unknowing about the sources of those injustices when we have 'dealt' with the 'old and bad' ways of doing things. Annas' main interest is in the inequalities between women and men, and she summarises the difficulty of the dynamic nature of such a situation thus:

> we are often ... backward looking and confused or uncertain about our own society, but able to discern more clearly the wrongs in a society more traditional than our own ... If we can more clearly discern the injustice of practices that we no longer suffer from, will we not always be one stage behind, unable rationally to criticise the injustices of practices that we do still suffer from? Our grasp of the injustice of sex-divided norm (is largely based on something) that we no longer live with. (p. 295)

This suggests not only that it might be difficult to understand current inequality and diversity injustices in general, but, given the character of many professional organisations, that the nature of many professions and their associated institutions adds an additional dimension. It may be that in 'old', well-established and highly regarded professions, retrospection that results in the perpetuation of inequality and discrimination is likely to be particularly difficult to challenge. Further, it may be that this plays an important role in the institutionalisation of discrimination and inequality.

Individual and personal integrity, and institutionalised discrimination

Clearly, employees are more likely to behave with personal integrity within a system that has integrity as its core ethos and in turn reflects these in its systems and procedures. But it can be argued that dynamics of the public face, organisational culture, and community service provided by public sector professions are, in operational terms, delivered by individuals.

In other words, professionally dominated organisations, which are professional in their core attitudes and mores, are likely to be shaped primarily by the actions and attitudes of the professional members (Etzioni, 1964; Mintzberg, 1979). It is clear that one important aspect for changing these characteristics towards issues such as equality and diversity does depend on developing and implementing clear, strong and effective systems, structures and policies that reflect combined capabilities thinking, in part through creating clear and *ethically grounded equality and diversity systems integrity*.

However, the high autonomy of action typically employed by members of professional groups means that it becomes imperative to deal with the individual as moral agent also if sustainable ethical change is to be achieved and *personal equality and diversity integrity* is to be developed and secured. Further, the strong acculturation, professional strictures and codes, in combination with 'designated' authority to act ethically, may provide, in a more negative way, an environment in which institutionalised discrimination and inequality can take root.

To reiterate, we can think of *institutionalised discrimination and inequality* as the systemic presence of discrimination and inequality, which by permeating the organisation's formal and informal systems and structures undermines the capacity of an organisation to provide an equitable, 'felt fair' working environment and equality of work opportunities. This also limits the scope for equitable and 'felt-fair' delivery of service to clients and the community as a whole, but in particular, those from historically and newly traditionally disadvantaged groups. Further, such institutionalised discrimination and inequality undermines an organisation's 'moral integrity' and indeed, may be rooted in other, firmly rooted sources of inconsistencies of moral integrity, such as covert patronage or the tolerance of various forms of petty and major corruption. (Corruption here is being thought of in organisational and cultural terms, and more broadly in how certain values and inactions on the part of organisations allows unacceptable individual deviations from the required behaviour, in other words individual acts of corruption, to take root and flourish).

Moreover, if an organisation has such an institutionalised lack of *ethically grounded organisational equality and diversity integrity*, then it becomes more difficult for those with the will to enact equality and diversity change to create sustainable change. In addition therefore, it creates a potentially hostile environment for those who would wish to act with individual equality and diversity integrity so to do.

In other words, the potential for creating a virtuous environment within which individual members are empowered externally (e.g. by the state) to act and to develop their virtue, and here, specifically, ethically grounded *personal equality and diversity integrity*, is greatly compromised, as the organisation (or the profession) lacks organisational equality and diversity integrity.

Moreover, increasing demands by the public for greater accountability and access to information, reflecting the *transparency guarantees* of instrumental freedoms discussed previously, as many such professional groups are also in the public sector or, as in the case of lawyers, may be paid by the state to act on their behalf, are exerting real and tangible pressure on such organisations to justify their actions more openly.

'Us-and-them' equality

Without doubt, any approach will encounter real and sizeable difficulties, and not always in an overt and readily tangible manner. Central difficulties include the depressingly robust scope of those in positions of power and status to reinvent the rules of the game, in a manner that allows some progress in relation to equality and diversity management, but in a limited manner which leaves the substantive advantages of those within an organisation's elite intact. We might think of this as *'us-and-them' equality*, where transparency of action, decision making and opportunity is seen as valuable for those further down the organisation, particularly at the point of entry to an organisation. However, the more seniority is gained, the less transparent and, importantly, the less accountable actions become. Further, this obtuseness is jealously guarded and readily defended, for example in the guise of the levels of complexity of senior managerial and professional work, or the 'difficulty' of finding suitable candidates for senior posts.

So for example, the discriminations that were inherent in semi-skilled manufacturing work (where workers' educational, social and cultural experiences may be very different from those at the top) and reinforced through 'differentials' are obvious, and could more readily form a target for action for, say, ensuring that women and men received equal pay for work of equal value. However, it could be argued that a *superordinate level of differentials* operates, whereby greater value is placed on the skills and knowledge possessed by those higher up the status hierarchy, in ways which traditionally have been less open to the scrutiny of industrial relations machinery such as joint consultation committees.

Further, this 'us-and-them' equality is likely to extend beyond jobs and roles *per se*, and incorporate also the attributes of those occupying them. Gender segregation in internal and external labour markets is well documented and such segregation also applies to other traditionally disadvantaged groups (statistics that illustrate this are presented in Chapter 1). However, what we are saying is not just economically driven: what we are suggesting is that the status of more powerful groups and to some extent defining them is, in part, defined proactively, albeit informally and covertly, by limiting the opportunities, empowerment and development of others. Further, those who are in closer proximity to those who are from the tradi-

Box 5.3 Institutionalised discrimination

Institutionalised discrimination can take many forms. Fundamentally, it is concerned with the formal and informal systems, structures and culture that create inequalities for members who are not part of the established order, and also leads to inequalities in the services provided by an organisation, as a result of these characteristics, to those within the community who are not of the majority, often indigenous, group.

In the UK the issue of institutionalised discrimination was highlighted in particular by the murder of the black London teenager Stephen Lawrence. Stephen's parents were crucial in maintaining the issue in the public eye, and challenging the accounts of what had happened before and after Stephen's murder. The Public Inquiry into his murder, led by Sir William Macpherson, found the local constabulary to *be institutionally racist*, which Sir William defined in his report as:

> the collective failure of an organisation to provide an appropriate and professional service to people because of their colour, culture or ethnic origin.

There were major failures in the manner in which the investigation was conducted that, it was felt, contributed to the failure to secure a conviction. The police service as a whole was required to come under the Race Relations Act (from which it had been previously exempt) and also to take on board a list of recommendations, which now also apply to other public bodies, including the judicial system, the National Health Service and schools. The recommendations include:

- openness, accountability and the restoration of confidence;
- stronger family liaison;
- the adoption of new definitions of racist incidents ('a racist incident is any incident that is perceived to be racist by the victim or any other person');
- codes of conduct for the reporting and recording of racist incidents and crimes;
- review of police practice for the investigation of racist crime;
- proper support for victims and witnesses, with necessary training;
- new procedures for the prosecution of racist crimes;
- training for physical restraint of suspects;
- racism awareness and valuing cultural diversity training;

- policies and procedures for employment, discipline and complaints in relation to race;
- training in action and record keeping for 'stop and search';
- setting higher targets for the recruitment of minority ethnic staff;
- education in schools, mediated through the National Curriculum.

However, some have questioned whether the definition of institutional racism, and by implication the fit with the recommended actions, needs to be better defined. For example, Anthias (1999) has questioned the concept of 'unwitting racism' found in the Macpherson report. She argues that it is important to separate more clearly the unintentional effects of procedures from procedures that relate to the exercise of judgement and agency. Institutional power, the gendered nature of racism and, in particular, the role of masculinity are important ways of understanding what went wrong, and whether real progress can be made.

Unrest in the academy

Within the academy, there are different kinds of institutional discrimination that operate, though often of a more subtle kind. For example, the London School of Economics (the LSE) was found to have directly and indirectly discriminated against Dr Helen Mercer, who told an employment tribunal in London she was rejected for a job four months after having suffered a miscarriage.

She had joined the LSE in 1995 on a three-year contract after teaching at schools and universities, and writing a highly acclaimed book on business history. But despite a review of her performance which rated her a 'substantial asset' to her department, Dr Mercer's application for a permanent post saw her overlooked in favour of a younger and less qualified male applicant. The ruling in April 2000 followed a report that was produced earlier in April which accused universities of breaking equal pay laws, and unions said that Dr Mercer's case pointed to a wider problem of sex equality throughout higher education.

The college and the lecturer's union, Nafthe, have analysed statistics produced by the UK Higher Education Statistics Agency and found that even in traditionally 'women friendly' subjects with a high proportion of female academics, men are still paid more than women. Among their findings are that there are no women professors anywhere in the UK on the permanent staff in civil engineering, and fewer than five in the entire country in almost half the other subjects listed, including pharmacy, chemistry, physics and dentistry, and that they earn less (with the exceptions of nursing and paramedical studies, and architecture, the built environment and planning).

The explanation put forward by universities is that it used to be the case that fewer women than men became academics, so that there are more older men in senior, better-paid positions. But Nafthe says that analysis of the figures shows that this argument does not stand up. The Committee of Vice-Chancellors and Principals (CVCP) said: 'CVCP is serious and committed to taking action to tackle discrimination in higher education as an urgent priority. There are historical and structural reasons for the current situation, but this is no excuse, and institutional practices must be examined in a serious and committed effort to tackle discrimination.'

Abridged from: http://news.bbc.co.uk/hi/english/uk/
   ('Lawrence: Key recommendations')
http://news.bbc.co.uk/low/english/education
   ('Top college guilty of sex bias' and 'Universities break equal pay laws')

Reference

Web reference: Anthias, F (1999) Institutional racism, power and accountability. *Sociological research online*, 4(1) (12 pp) http://www.socresonline.org.uk

---

tionally disadvantaged groups, may wish to reinforce what perceived and actual advantages they enjoy. An analogy is the infamous nine-foot spiked 'Cutteslowe Wall' that was erected in North Oxford to separate working class council-owned houses from lower middle class private homes in the 1940s, the occupants of the latter often new to the middle classes, having earned sufficient job and economic advantages to just enable themselves to leave behind their working class roots. The division was not only physical but, it could be argued, psychological, in part sparked by the fear that there would be a loss in status for private house owners because of the proximity of the poorer occupants of the working class estate.

We can detect echoes of likely mechanisms for perpetuating difference and advantage through the language and practice of psychotherapy, in the form of in-group–out-group transactions, including infantilisation of other, the 'anxiety of success of "other"' (Bion, 1967) and parent–child transactions to maintain status, which becomes exaggerated when 'under threat' for high status 'privileged' groups and more child-adult (I'm being treated unfairly or victimised) when lower status 'privileged' groups are under threat (Berne, 1963).

Duty of care as an important 'benchmark' of equality and diversity management and change in professional practice

Views of duty of care: the private exercise of public duty

As stated earlier, many professionals are working for the public good, and often with those who are 'hidden' from public gaze, for example the physi-

Box 5.4 Culture of complacency pervades service.

CPS report
Investigation finds significant number of ethnic minority staff discriminated against, underpinned by management favouritism

Clare Dyer
Legal correspondent

Institutional racism 'has been and continues to be at work in the crown prosecution service', according to the findings of an 18-month independent investigation into race discrimination in the service, published yesterday.

Sylvia Denham, an academic lawyer and former chairwoman of Camden and Islington health authority, was asked to undertake the inquiry by the CPS in January 2000, when the service was threatened with a formal investigation by the Commission for Racial Equality after a series of bullying, harassment and discrimination cases were taken to tribunals by CPS staff.

After publication of the report David Calvert-Smith, the director of public prosecutions, admitted the service was 'institutionally racist'.

Ms Denham's 111-page report concludes there is unwarranted complacency within the CPS over the possibility of race discrimination in the prosecution process. Statistics suggest that the CPS ought, at the very least, to have serious concerns in this area. The policy directorate does not display the concern that might be expected.

A significant proportion of ethnic minority staff have experienced race discrimination within the CPS, the report says. Management favouritism has underpinned or permitted much of the discrimination.

White and black staff freely acknowledge that favouritism or cronyism have operated to a marked extent in the service over the years. In an organisation dominated by white managers, this tends to disadvantage minority staff, and falls squarely within the Macpherson definition of institutional racism.

Ms Denham says the CPS responded slowly to modern equal opportunity practices and legislation. Long-serving, largely white senior managers contributed to the unresponsive culture.

The report also found that most managers are not comfortable with the term 'institutional racism' or prefer to believe it is not relevant to the service, so its effects go unchallenged. This operates as a serious obstacle to a change of culture within the organisation.

A significant constituency within the CPS does not recognise any race equality problems, and the concept of 'institutional racism' is not generally understood.

At the heart of many of the problems lie poor management and inadequate management training. Senior staff feel more comfortable with 'lawyering' than managing.

Although ethnic minority staff are well represented in the CPS, they are seriously under-represented among the higher grades. Recruitment and promotion policies continue to be flouted by senior managers.

Vacancies are not always advertised when they should be. Ms Denham found that senior managers were good at paying lip service to the race equality agenda being set by their headquarters but had not started internalising it.

Ethnic minority staff have no confidence in the internal complaints procedure and most of those who believe they have suffered discrimination have not complained.

The CPS has set up a raft of equality committees and units within the past two years, but they lack strategic coherence and the impact of some has been limited. The report found there is also a growing backlash among white staff against equal opportunities initiatives, which they believe are leading to positive discrimination. Yet white staff are still faring better in terms of progression.

The employee relations unit, which is supposed to develop and coordinate equal opportunities policy, has been left seriously under-resourced. It has spent most of its time resisting the many employment tribunal claims brought by CPS staff, leaving it little time for its wider responsibilities and creating a perception that it is forever taking the side of management against staff alleging discrimination.

The report recommends a positive action programme to redress the under-representation of ethnic minority staff at the lower and middle management grades.

An existing proposal for equal opportunities complaints to be dealt with by external investigators should be implemented without delay, the report says. An external mediation service should be made available to facilitate the resolution of complaints through an independent third party. Ms Denham also recommends that all managers should understand that progression within the service depends on completing equality and diversity training.

Recruitment and progression should rely on objective techniques and should not substantially rely on the most subjective selection techniques such as interviews, she says, and there is a pressing need to clarify the respective roles and functions of the main equality structures in the CPS.

Finally, the white backlash by a significant minority of line managers against CPS equality initiatives must be acknowledged and addressed by senior managers but must not be used as an excuse for watering down race equality initiatives.

Source: The Guardian 27 July 2001.
Copyright © *The Guardian* 2001.

cally or mentally ill, prisoners, children and the elderly in care: in other words, community members who are particularly vulnerable or are made so by the situations they find themselves in. In such instances, professionals are tasked to exercise **duty of care**, in order to secure the best service from their care providers in a manner that ensures their physical, psychological and social safety. However, the private exercise of public duty is an important potential area of vulnerability for the service recipient and, within the context of this chapter, a potential source of discrimination.

Further, it could be argued that there is a pressing need for further elaboration of the concept: failure to exercise duty of care with care can result in real harm to both organisational members and the recipients of services.

In many public sector organisations, key decision-making systems are highly dependent upon the individual judgement of professionals, and it is taken on trust that those professionals will do what they see as right.

To restate, organisations like the legal and medical professions, which are less Tayloristic and more professional in their core mores, are likely to be shaped primarily by the actions and attitudes of the professional members (Etzioni, 1964; Mintzberg, 1979). Thus, changing the core ethos towards issues such as equality and diversity does depend on having clear, strong and effective systems, structures and policies in place. However, the freedom of action typically employed by professional groups means that it becomes imperative to deal with the individual as moral agent if sustainable ethical change is to be achieved.

Further, many such organisations are in the public sector, where employees have a specific remit as servants of the public. Importantly, *public service professionals* such as the police and medical professions have authority delegated by the state to do 'good works' to secure a safe and crime-free community and to take care of the nation's health, respectively.

Such relationships are highly dependent upon trust between the community and the profession (highlighted by the transparency guarantees at the heart of the capabilities approach) and importantly, a high degree of self-regulation by the mores and ethos of the profession itself. Hence, a further ethical consideration is that the perception of public servants may be further damaged if they are seen as compromising their 'delegated' authority to work for the common good, and thus, in turn, they are increasingly vulnerable, given a more demanding and less deferent public, to being seen as violating community expectations as moral agents for the collective good.

A real and present danger is that the context makes the evaluator jump to particular conclusions, as a consequence of the reputation that an organisation has. Failure to exercise adept duty of care increases the likelihood of shortfalls at best in the service offered and at worst, might have fatal consequences. Further, such failure may in part be due to individual shortcomings in the delivery of professional service, but may also be reinforced by a lack of sensitivity to 'cross-cultural' issues that may reside within individuals. But they are just as likely, if not more so, to be a reflection of structural and systemic, or institutional, causes of the service manifestation of poor duty of care.

Those who need to use emotion as an intrinsic aspect of getting their work done may be particularly vulnerable. As professionals, the assumption is that they are best placed to cope. But they require the necessary knowledge and skill to develop and make best use of *emotional competence*, and emotional competence can only be built effectively through an 'ensemble' approach, where the importance of emotion, action and thought in getting the job done is formally and proactively recognised.

So, duty of care issues become more fraught when issues of difference are not fully appreciated and understood, or are ignored through resentment, anger, 'blindness' or malice aforethought. However, poor duty of care is *not* inevitably the result of malice aforethought but may be an artefact of organisational structure and, in turn, accepted practice.

Emotional labour and equality and diversity change

What is emotional labour?

What police officers, prison officers, health professionals, etc., have in common with a number of other workers is that they are **emotional labourers** (e.g. Hochschild, 1979, 1983; Smith, 1999, 2001; Smith and Cornelius, 2001): that is, *changing the mood in others is a central and primary task within the context of paid work*. It may be that organisations within which emotional labourers predominate will need to consider how to address equality and diversity issues in ways which address explicitly this emotional aspect of the labour process also.

What we will be attempting to outline are defensible simplifications to illustrate the point: not only is emotional labour central to the work that many professionals do, but to do the job well, a great deal of emotional knowledge and skill is needed.

It will be suggested that *there is likely to be a link between the complexity of the emotional labour undertaking in such work and the difficulty in dealing with equality diversity*, but we would like to address other parts of the conceptual framework first.

The work of Arlie Hochschild

The work of Arlie Russell Hochschild is of particular importance. In her highly accessible book *The Managed Heart* (1979, 1983), Hochshild would beg to differ with the systematic devaluing of emotional labour, and has argued that traditionally, insufficient recognition has been given to the real skill and effort associated with much emotional labour. Further, she has argued that by failing to pay due attention to emotional labour, emotions are systematically being turned into commodities, to such an extent that some employees may become possessed or 'heart-captivated' by their work, so that they become unable to separate themselves from their job.

Arlie Russell Hochschild's work, as a piece of empirical research informed by the voice of a truly reflective practitioner, is remarkable. It opens our eyes to a group of workers whose core needs have been systematically neglected: the emotional labourer. A strong theme that runs through her work is a concern for the welfare, in particular the emotional and more broadly, the economic and psychological welfare, of the millions of workers for whom emotion is central to the primary task. We might see this as having implications for how organisations address 'duty of care', both morally and legally.

However, the mapping of the officer's emotional labouring suggested to me that perhaps it was a particular kind of emotional labourer that was of central interest to Hochschild's work (Box 5.5). Put crudely, disempowerment of the emotional labourer, and the role of organisations in that disempowerment – the latter to some degree, we might extrapolate, mediated through customer satisfaction and, in turn, empowerment through the rise of consumerism – is likely to increase the vulnerability and manipulation of the 'heart' in the interest of the corporation. Cynically, such manipulation values the commercial potential for exploitation of the heart (e.g. 'felt real' customer service) but at the same time, often violates its 'sacredness'.

However, as mentioned earlier, many professionals have relatively great power, often given by the state, which affords substantial controls over the manner in which their work is undertaken. We might think of these types of workers as *'empowered' emotional labourers*. Although many such workers will resent the increasing paperwork and public accountability that is seen as decreasing the core of what is valued in such work, such as professional autonomy and judgement, the latter remain high in such work. Indeed, this autonomy often limits the power that organisations have to reduce the power that such groups wield. Further, the power given through law and/or largely monopolistic delivery of services further empowers such workers and potentially affords the opportunity to increase the power distance between professional and clients and further disempower members of the community during citizen–professional transactions, be it on the streets, in the emergency room of a hospital, or in the law courts.

Emotion in labour processes

The 'knowledge' of the emotions

The observations by the philosophers David Hume that 'Reason is or ought to be, the slave of the passions' and Robert Solomon that 'Emotions are intelligent, cultivated, conceptually rich engagements with the world, not mere reactions or instincts' (1993) highlight the informative nature of emotions to thought and action, a position reflected in George Kelly's 'holistic' personal construct theory, within which emotion, action and thought are seen as equally informative.

Traditionally, in the study of business and management, there has been a mountain of research undertaken that has centred on the 'manual' (behavioural) and intellectual (cognitive) aspects of work. So for example, some of the 'big' ideas in the field include Fordism and Scientific Management, also referred to as Taylorism (and seen as approaches which de-skill by reducing mental engagement with work), human relations (concerned with the interpersonal aspects of work, seen as neglected in the heyday of Fordism and Scientific Management), knowledge management (concerned with the manner in which knowledge is represented, captured, used and valued) and organisational learning (concerned with the manner in which organisations adopt a more paradigm-challenging approach to changing the way that things are made sense of and acted upon).

To restate, emotional labour and emotional labour processes have received scant attention relative to the sizeable literature on behavioural and intellectual processes at work. Steve Smith (1999) has argued that this is because, in the West, there is a theological representation of emotion as adjacent to the 'heart', and therefore *de facto*, the soul. Therefore historically, the academic traditions and political ideologies of Western organisational scholars have implicitly regarded this as 'private territory' and not the stuff of base research (see also Smith and Cornelius, 2001).

The dimensions of emotional labour

Nurses are amongst those whom we might most readily regard as emotional labourers – those employees required to make full use of the heart as an integral part of their work, and in order to do their work effectively (Smith, 1992). The example of nurses highlights the dilemma for many emotional labourers: as their work is seen as 'driven by the heart' – a calling, or vocation – this 'sacred' domain is seen as difficult to place a value upon. Coupled with the gendering of such work (which may tend to exaggerate the perception of the significance of the emotional content, and locate it nearer to the 'emotional work' of nurture, which therefore should be freely given), emotional labour is often systematically undervalued. A further consequence of this is that the importance of emotion in the labour process may be 'downgraded', trivialised and seen as 'problematic', reinforced through the high value rightly placed on the intellectual and action-oriented processes, and the lower value placed on emotional labour processes.

It would be surprising if there were only one type of emotional labourer. Steve Smith (1998) has attempted to codify the dimensions of emotional labour. He has suggested the following dimensions:

1. Deep-acting (drawing upon real emotion from the inner self) and Surface-acting (the latter of which protects the health and safety of the inner self).
2. Hospitable and Hostile.
3. Relative Power and Powerlessness (status and gender differences colour the picture for this dimension also).
4. Sacred and Profane domains.
5. Public and Private Ownership.
6. Public and Private Spaces for encounters.
7. Authenticity and Inauthenticity.
8. Alienation and Involvement.

Obviously, not all the above dimensions impinge upon all emotional labourers; nor do all emotional labourers have to draw deeply on 'real' emotions. However, it is possible to locate interesting groupings of emotional labourers, albeit in broad brush.

Emotional literacy and ignorance

Specifically, we are suggesting, like Kelly and Hochschild, that there is much of the self in certain types of emotional labour. Doing things differently, changing the way that one conducts one's work, where emotion is central, across a range of dimensions, to the primary task, requires much loosening and some care. The 'pre-verbal' but felt quality of the emotional labourer's work demands attention to *emotional literacy and awareness* of how emotions are being used to change mood, avoid riots, comfort the distressed, and so on.

Further, the 'head' and 'hands' basis of which drives many interventions to manage difference are unlikely to be sufficient for this kind of worker: inevitably, such changes will have implications for the 'heart' and as such, care and protection of the heart need to be addressed proactively. Kelly suggests that a reason that much change is checked is because of a lack of the 'right laboratory', the right learning vehicles and environment within which the learning could take place. By implication, a subset of this is the right 'emotional laboratory', where there is permission for voice to be given to the emotions and their central role in enabling change to happen is legitimated. Changing social factors to value difference and equality is inevitably demanding, and a clearer understanding of the emotional labourer's landscape within which these issues sit is likely to increase our understanding of a key factor that lessens the likelihood of change. The cognitive sculpting methodology employed by the Royal College of Nursing in the UK as part of their Clinical Leadership programme is a good example of where such holistic approaches have proved successful (Cunningham *et al.*, 2001).

Box 5.5 Holistic learning for emotional labourers

Case example: 'Cognitive sculpting' at the Royal College of Nursing

In English usage, emotional experiences are often described as 'moving'. The Royal College of Nursing (RCN) Clinical Leadership Development Programme aims to develop clinical leadership by involving clinicians in moving, emotional experiences while acknowledging and containing their anxiety.

An emotional labour focus group (ELFG) was convened to consider emotional aspects at the invitation of the RCN. The membership included clinicians and academics, who were initially involved in a series of round table discussions about emotional labour. However, after a number of months, the clinicians became concerned

that no clear focus had been found. A very different dialogue was enabled by 'cognitive sculpting' which explicates knowledge through the discussants' use of an assortment of small objects to 'stand in' for their thinking. 'Talking through the hands', they select and place objects into a collective sculpture in a discussion about issues which may be complex, or emotionally charged – certainly difficult to talk about in any other way (Doyle and Sims, 1995). Different 'models in use' of the emotional labour dimensions of clinical leadership were elicited, drawn from the emotional and pre-verbal, could be described and discussed.

After Cunningham, Lister, Nash, Ashburton, Smith and Smith, 2001.

Issues of leadership in professional organisations

Managerial versus professional leadership

If, as we have argued in a previous chapter, *moral and managerial will* is important for creating a catalyst and subsequent momentum for change, this suggests that clear and demonstrable leadership is needed, not only from the top, but also in the line. This can certainly include the setting of *key equality and diversity leadership objectives as key 'business' objectives,* to ensure that not only is 'subordinate' employee action under scrutiny but managerial and senior professionals' action is as well.

The culture embedding mechanisms of leadership

Schein (1992) has suggested that the role of leadership in an organisation plays an important role in the shaping of culture. The founders of an organisation in particular exercise a powerful role in shaping culture, in that the emerging culture reflects the leaders' assumptions, and an organisation's style of operating and biases may reflect their biases and unconscious anxieties. He also argues that there are primary culture-embedding mechanisms (such as resource allocation) and secondary culture-embedding mechanisms (such as organisational rites and rituals) that influence first, the climate, then leadership culture, then organisational culture (Table 5.3).

Views on leadership and social learning

In this social domain sit social constructions and shared meanings, important for the facilitation of social learning. It has been suggested (Kelly, 1991) that a key role within social learning is that of the leader. Leadership within this context is, in part, a process of facilitation of shared meaning in order to generate a shared sense of direction. Therefore, leadership ceases to be an 'exclusive' label. We do not accept that agenda-shaping forms an adequate replacement for the concept of leadership, as it is possible to operate individualistically around person needs only; moreover, sharing is not essential to agenda-shaping either. Although it may operate as a subset of leadership, it is primarily a *political* construct.

George Kelly located the concept of leadership within his Sociality Corollary. He suggests an important relationship between the potential leader and the situation, but also 'followers', and in particular, nominators, the latter of whom make their selection of a leader on the basis of their understanding of what the situation demands. Kelly chose the example of a mobilising or rallying kind of leader, and suggests that:

> one does not have to be like certain people in order to understand them, but he does have to understand them in certain respects in order to rally them.

For Kelly, a leader was simply one who:

> performs a variety of jobs which are popularly recognised as leadership jobs. (1991: 70–71)

Table 5.3 Culture-embedding mechanisms (Schein, 1992)

Primary embedding mechanisms	Secondary articulation and reinforcement mechanisms
What leaders pay attention to, measure, and control on a regular basis	Organization design and structure
	Organizational systems and procedures
How leaders react to critical incidents and organizational crises	Organizational rites and rituals
Observed criteria by which leaders allocate scarce resources	Design of physical space, façades, and buildings
	Stories, legends, and myths about people and events
Deliberate role modeling, teaching, and coaching	Formal statements of organisational philosophy, values, and creed
Observed criteria by which leaders allocate rewards and status	
Observed criteria by which leaders recruit, select, promote, retire, and excommunicate organizational members	

Kelly goes on to suggest that people who select a leader are anticipating his or her likely contribution to the group and subsuming within their own constructions the part that he or she ought to play. Therefore, one implication of locating leadership within the Sociality Corollary is that an important characteristic of the leader is the extent, indeed the ability, to construe the construction processes of others, and the playing of a social role in the social process involving others.

Leadership, commitment and culture

Considering *culture* requires the appraiser to consider the core values and basic assumptions that operate formally and informally, and provide the social and psychological 'glue' of organisations. Second, any organisation is rarely a uniform culture, but is more likely to be *a web of sub-cultures*. One sub-culture may share some values and assumptions with others but will have characteristics that are unique to a particular group, section or cadre. From a diversity viewpoint, *organisational sub-cultures* (along with *organisational sub-climates*) can be thought of as the social, psychological and ethical environment that those from traditionally disadvantaged groups enter, and it is this environment that is often a major shaper of employee alienation, or acceptance of difference.

Leadership is a concept that is often conflated with that of management, but has been theorised as a distinctive concept (e.g. Zaleznik, 1977). We are not concerned only with leadership at the top of an organisation. Leadership at the top is clearly essential for setting the moral tone; role modelling and shaping the organisation's ethical processes and, more basically, affording access to the resources that may be necessary to develop the strategy, policy, practice and structures to enable diversity to be managed effectively. However, we are also concerned with the *character and distribution* of general leadership attributes and action *throughout* the organisation, which in turn reflect the *distribution of moral leadership* through the organisation. Such leadership helps to influence and shape the sub-cultures and sub-climates within an organisation. We are suggesting that the moral agency of leaders, irrespective of their formal designation, can have a profound effect on climate and culture through the *local role models of moral agency* and the resultant outcomes that it can provide.

Finally, we suggest that *equality* should be a sustainable approach. Typically in the current HRM literature, it could be argued that it is often conceptualised or represented in a normative or unitarist manner. We have conceptualised commitment in this context as a long agenda process of continuous improvement, for which commitment creates the momentum and motivation, even when difficulties arise. These elements highlight the importance of a focus on the transformation of 'soft' as well as 'hard' systems of employment management, as they incorporate social and core value development.

Professional 'character' and capabilities equality

Exploration of patriarchy in the professions

There are numerous insights that can be drawn from capabilities theory-based understanding of inequality. For example, recall from Chapter 1 that combined capabilities are internal capabilities operating in combination with suitable 'external conditions' (such as formal and informal organisational structures) that enable someone to function fully, as s/he would wish to do. So, for example, in spite of the excellent training that all professionals receive, in capabilities terms, 'good internal states of readiness to act', strong, patriarchal professional cultures will struggle to see such a requirement as legitimate, as a key attribute of patriarchy is to consolidate social closure. Coupled with disabling male–female relationships in such organisations, combined capabilities is likely to be seen as a frontal challenge to maintaining the status quo. Further, if individual and collective agency only flourish if an enabling environment – combined capabilities – is present, agency is unlikely to take root easily.

Moreover, part of the enabling environment of combined capabilities is instrumental freedoms. Many professions have made serious attempts to address inequality but Sen (1999) argues that freedoms should be subject to systematic evaluation, and *the effectiveness of any intervention should be assessed against the freedoms that it affords*. The instrumental freedoms – political freedoms, economic facilities, social opportunities, transparency guarantees and protective securities – are all likely to struggle to embed themselves in patrician organisations, where patriarchal action is seen as legitimate.

So for example, the opportunity of access to advancement (social opportunities) is compromised if the method of promotion is largely hidden and opaque to those from traditionally disadvantaged groups (as transparency guarantees are violated). And, as instrumental freedoms provide a basis for the development of individual and collective rights, the likelihood of establishing and extending the rights base is proscribed. Further, new kinds of 'us' and 'them' equality may emerge. So for example, in organisations where it is the senior tiers that are the professionals, and lower tiers are drawn more commonly from those of 'middling' or working class mores, different kinds of masculinity may operate, such that the 'middle class' values of the upper levels are preserved as intangible and taken for granted. In contrast, the actions of those further down the hierarchy are made newly visible, or 'marked' (Robinson, 2000), creating resentment in this group.

Final considerations – enhancing capabilities and freedoms in professional organisations

There are many options that could be pursued in order to develop capabilities equality in organisations. However, an organisation's character plays a vital role in determining which steps are likely to create the greatest movement. Albeit that they are not, and should never be regarded as, a blueprint, some of the kinds of reflections, changes and interventions that may be useful for creating 'felt fair' embedded equality and diversity action and change in professional organisations are as follows:

- *Developing leadership styles and practice* that create movement away from patriarchy. The intangible and hidden nature of patriarchy should be sought, not only in terms of how it is embedded in an organisation's social, economic, political and power structures, but also how it is embedded within the operational definitions of human and social capital. Bordieu's cultural capital is taken to extremes in the patrician organisation. The impetus for such movement is unlikely to take place unless there is political will within the machinery of the state.
- *Critical points and key nodes of influence and power* (such as career progression points and senior decision-making arenas), in particular, need to be scrutinised in order to make visible the 'real' formal and informal barriers to progess and repositories of the intangibles of patriarchy, and to avoid being sidelined into 'sweating the small stuff'.
- *The adoption of 'capabilities thinking'* – with its combined capabilities, instrumental freedoms, rights, agency and voice – makes it less likely that a 'pick and choose' sleight-of-hand approach to equality (for example, focusing on training but then ignoring career advancement) will be seen as acceptable.
- There are major issues around *measurement*: the information and knowledge base on which equality is measured needs to incorporate all of the attributes of a 'capabilities equality' information, knowledge and learning base, as outlined in Chapter 3. This is clearly likely to be a difficult issue, particularly against a background of concerns about creeping managerialism. A broadened information base, with greater transparency guarantees and attention to human and social capital and, in particular, belongingness and voice, is likely to be useful in this context, and should operate at all levels of the organisational hierarchy.
- The *'professional project'* has not been universally accepted as the benchmark of good professional practice. Social work in the UK is one example of a profession that has, in one way, 'deprofessionalised', through moving from an ethos of quasi-psychiatric-based 'case work' practice to more generic, practice based in social science. This was done partly in response to the Seebohm Report (1968) but also to move away from *indeterminancy*. Indeterminancy operates where the greater the element of judgement required in professional knowledge, the less likely the professional tasks will be open to routinisation and inspection. Further, the patrician heart of indeterminancy is reinforced through the use of qualities that are not explicitly taught but that are more likely to be understood informally within 'middle class' professional educational practice (MacDonald, 1999). A more egalitarian and inclusive approach, with reduced professional–client power distance, was sought, and the membership criteria democra-

tised. Approaches that seek to challenge established forms of profession-alism and seek newer ones are to be welcomed.

- *Initial and ongoing professional development* should have incorporated with-in it mechanisms for creating and embedding values that challenge patri-archy and 'ineligibles' thinking grounded in social and class types, rather than internal states of readiness. Such thinking should also be reinforced through psychological contracts. Thompson (1998) highlights a number of areas that can helpfully be incorporated into practice for human service professions, including legitimising reflection and discussion of reflection and naming processes (elegant challenging) of that which creates or re-inforces disadvantage, critically reflective practice, revitalisation of the theory of practice, and care with language in use.

- As stated before, rights emerge from instrumental freedoms. Sen (2000 and personal communication) has developed these ideas further, building the Kantian philosophical terms of *perfect obligations* (for example, murder is wrong, and often is reinforced in law) and *imperfect obligations or co-related duties* (which equate broadly with social duties, and in an organi-sational context, may be policy based or informal). Greater thought should be given to developing a framework of co-related duties that centre around capabilities equality-based values.

- The leverage of **duty of care** and highlighting of **emotional labour** processes help to make clear the impact of individual and institutional discrimination on practice.

- Within the environment, changes to organisational policy, of this degree, are more likely to be achieved against a background of *law* that reinforces these in employment law in general, and for professional practice in par-ticular.

- The *interventionist* faced with such challenges is unlikely to be successful unless given the *power and authority*, and real, powerful, high status sup-port, within the organisation. An interventionist that lacks political acu-men and dexterity at operating, given the power plays that are likely to result, and has limited membership of a supportive alliance, or no alliance at all, is unlikely to be successful.

Conclusions

When facing the challenge of trying to improve or change equality and diver-sity action in any organisation, an important question is 'what might work?'. In this chapter, a number of important considerations, centred around organi-sational character, have helped to highlight how difficult answering this question can be.

However, the intention is primarily to highlight the importance of making informed choices and how to think about what information may be important for informing these choices. An important test of whether an intervention is likely to work is 'is it credible with key stakeholders?', and credibility will, at times, manifest itself by generating resistance and antagonism. The resources needed for such changes, which are often root and branch, fundamental change, require intervention strategies and ongoing practice where there is a need to 'raise the game', and proceed on a number of related, critical fronts.

Although we have used the example of professionals and professionalism as an illustration, any organisation where equality and diversity action and change is being pursued should be evaluated using a similar rationale, if the resultant proposals and actions are to be viable, workable and credible.

Text-based questions

1. In what ways does patriarchy shape the character of 'professional culture'? What are the challenges that face equality and diversity action in traditional, patrician organisations?
2. What is the 'professional project' and what are its main characteristics? What are the representations of equality that reside at its heart?
3. What might considerations of 'duty of care' highlight, regarding (a) institutional discrimination and (b) inequalities in professional practice?

Library and assignment-based questions

1. (a) Find examples of professional codes of conduct on the Internet or in a library. What views on equality and inequality are implicit?
   (b) Find the corresponding equal opportunities or diversity management policy statement and if available, practice recommendations. Given the information you have obtained, evaluate the likely equality and diversity challenges that these organisations are likely to face.
2. Compare and contrast information collected on two professions, relating to the kind of information collected in question 1. What are the similarities and differences in practice that are likely to influence the effectiveness of equality and diversity interventions?

Internet resources

Cambridge University http://www.cam.ac.uk/
Metropolitan Police http://www.met.police.uk/

Further reading

Bourdieu, P (1973) Cultural reproduction and social reproduction, in R Brown (ed.) *Knowledge, education and cultural change*, Tavistock, London.
Hochschild, AR (1983) *The Managed Heart; the Commercialisation of Human Feeling*, University of California Press, California.

Larson, MS (1977) *The rise of professionalism: a sociological analysis*, University of California Press, USA.

MacDonald, KM (1999) *The sociology of the professions*, Sage, London.

References

Annas, J (1995) Women and the quality of life: two norms or one?, in M Nussbaum and A Sen (eds) *The Quality of Life*, Oxford University Press, USA.

Atkinson, P and Delamount, S (1990) Professions and powerlessness: female marginality in the learned professions. *Sociological Review*, **38** (1), 90–100.

Bion, WR (1967) *Second Thoughts*, Aronson, New York.

Berne, E (1963) *The Structure and Dynamics of Organisations in Groups*, Grove Press, New York.

Bourdieu, P (1973) Cultural reproduction and social reproduction, in R Brown (ed.) *Knowledge, education and cultural change*, Tavistock, London.

Cannadine, D (2000) *Class in Britain*, Penguin, London.

Clarke, G (1964) *A history of the Royal College of Physicians of London*, Clarendon Press, Oxford.

Clapp, R and Cornelius, N (2002) A PCP exploration of resistance to change in the professions. Paper presented at the European Personal Construct Association Conference, Florence, March.

Cooper, D, Lowe, A, Puxty, A, Robson, A and Willmott, H (1988) Regulation in the UK accounting profession: episodes in the relation between the profession and the state. Paper presented at the ESRC Conference 'Corporatism', December, London.

Cunningham, G, Lister, S, Nash, S, Ashburner, C, Smith, P and Smith, SL (2001) 'Cognitive sculpting' in the Royal College of Nursing Clinical Leadership Programme: emotion strategies in leadership development. Paper presented at the British Academy of Management Conference, September 2001, Cardiff.

Douglas, D (2000) Ethical Challenges of an Increasingly Diverse Workforce: The paradox of change. Paper presented at the Centre for Organisational and Professional Ethics Conference, Brunel University, UK, December.

Etzioni, A (1964) *Modern Organisations*, Prentice Hall, Englewood Cliffs, NJ.

Hochschild, AR (1979) Emotion work, feeling roles and social structure. *American Journal of Sociology*, **85**, 551–575.

Hochschild, AR (1983) *The Managed Heart; the Commercialisation of Human Feeling*, University of California Press, California.

Kelly, GA (1955/1991) *The Psychology of Personal Constructs*, Routledge, London.

Larson, MS (1977) *The rise of professionalism: a sociological analysis*, University of California Press, USA.

Lave, J and Wenger, W (1991) *Situated learning: legitimate peripheral participation*, Cambridge University Press, Cambridge.

MacDonald, KM (1999) *The sociology of the professions*, Sage, London.

Mackie, JL (1977) *Ethics: inventing right and wrong*, Penguin, London.

Mintzberg, H (1979) *The structuring of organisations*, Prentice Hall, USA.

Nussbaum, M and Glover, J (1995) *Women, culture and development: a study of human capabilities*, Oxford University Press, USA.

Pollitt, C (1993) *Managerialism and the public services: cuts or cultural change in the 1990s*, Blackwell, Oxford.

Reskin, BF (1978) Sex differentiation and the social organisation of science, in J Gaston (ed.) *The sociology of science*, Jossey Bass, San Francisco.

Robinson, S (2000) *Marked men: white masculinity in crisis*, Columbia University Press, USA.

Schein, EH (1985 first edition, 1992 second edition) *Organisational Culture and leadership*, Jossey Bass, San Francisco.

Seebohm Committee (1968) *Report of the Committee on local authority and allied social services*, HMSO, London.

Sen, A (1999) *Development as Freedom*, Oxford University Press, Oxford.

Sen (2000) Consequential evaluation and practical reason. *Journal of Philosophy*, XCIV (9) 477–502.

Sen, A (2001) Personal communication (interview conducted at Trinity College, Cambridge, July).

Sims, DPM and Doyle, JR (1995) Cognitive sculpting as a means of working with managers' metaphors. *Omega*, **23** (2): 117–124.

Smith, P (1992) *The emotional labour of nursing*, Macmillan, Basingstoke.

Smith, SL (1998) *Managing emotional labour*, in DS Sims, S Smith, M Somerville and P Jackson (eds) *Managing the future*, Brunel University distance learning MBA module, Uxbridge, Middlesex.

Smith, SL (1999) The theology of emotions. *Soundings: Journal of Politics and Culture*, (Spring), 152–158.

Smith, SL (2001) Emotion and labour in cultural comparison, in M Stroinska (ed.) *Relative points of view: linguistic representations of culture*, Berghahan Books, Oxford and New York.

Smith, SL and Cornelius, N (2000) Cognitive metaphors: broadening methods for changing front-line practice. Paper presented at the European Institute for Advanced Studies in Management Conference, Barcelona.

Smith, SL and Cornelius, N (2001) Implications of polychronicity of labour processes and sub-processes for 'duty of care', sense-making and learning for 'front-line' emotional labourers. Paper presented at The International Conference on Spacing and Timing, Palermo, Italy, 1–3 November.

Solomon, R (1993) *The Passions: Emotions and the meaning of life*. Hackett Publishing, Indianapolis/Cambridge.

Thompson, N (1998) *Promoting equality: challenging discrimination and oppression in the human services*, Macmillan, London and Basingstoke.

Waddington, I (1984) *The medical profession in the industrial revolution*, Humanities Press, London.

Walby, S (1989) Theorising patriarchy. *Sociology*, **23** (2), 213–44.

Walby, S (1990) *Theorising patriarchy*, Blackwell, Oxford.

Witz, A (1992) *Professions and patriarchy*, Routledge, London.

Zaleznik, A (1977) Managers and leaders: are they different? *Harvard Business Review*, May–June, 67–78.

Managing equality and diversity in a global context

6

Clive Wildish and Nelarine Cornelius

Chapter overview

This chapter focuses on the management of equality and diversity within an international business environment. First, it explores the role and responsibility of management across the organisation in creating an awareness of the contribution that effective cross-cultural relations can make to organisational performance and competitive advantage. This responsibility engages all levels of management throughout the organisation and is not perceived as the sole prerogative of the international HR manager.

The chapter then traces the evolution of the global corporation and reflects upon the development of the respective responsibilities of the global business manager and the HR practitioner in sustaining cross-cultural awareness, sensitivity to cultural variance and the core competence of the international manager. The chapter also provides an insight into some of the dilemmas that the global business manager faces in attempting to achieve cultural fit between his/her own cultural norms and those of the host countries in which he/she operates.

In particular, attention will be drawn to the challenge of different values and beliefs in relation to equality and difference, and the importance of transcendence as an important context for workforce diversity.

Learning objectives

After studying this chapter you should understand:

● the importance of diversity management in an international context, in particular the management of multinational teams;
● culture, multiculturalism and cross-culturalism;
● the historical context of **globalisation** and the development of the global corporation;
● the impact of internationalisation and globalisation on aspects of work organisation and HR processes;
● the notion of corporate HR and corporate values and the degree of fit or difference with local HR and values;
● how new inequalities can develop through 24-hour global operations;
● the importance of transcendence as an enabler of workforce diversity and its management.

Key words
cross-culturalism ● multiculturalism ● teams ● transcendence
● globalisation

Introduction

The related phenomena of multiculturalism and cross-culturalism have become, in recent years, increasingly significant for both societal and organisational life. The distinction between these two phenomena can perhaps be seen in terms of the degree of diversity that exists within the organisation. An organisation or social grouping that contains more than one culture within defined borders might loosely be referred to as 'multicultural', whereas the concept of 'cross-culturalism' characterises a distinct breadth and depth of diversity within the grouping and across borders. The ultimate extension of this latter concept is 'global diversity' which might be made up of 'multiculturalism', 'dual cultures' and 'monocultures'.

According to Tayeb:

> In a broad sense, workforce diversity refers to the varied background of employees in terms of race, colour, gender, education, social class, mental and physical capabilities . . . This new trend in managerial thinking is in a way a challenge to the previously established assumption that the workforce has a largely homogeneous character. (1996: 174)

Today many companies both large and small operate in a global village without the need to physically cross national borders. Irrespective of their national or international orientation, the issue of *understanding cultural differences* is as relevant to the non-international firm operating in a culturally heterogeneous country as it is to the multinational corporation whose domains span national borders and who are often engaged in joint ventures and strategic alliances of one kind or another.

The concepts of diversity and multiculturalism can have a particular relevance for the organisation that might not have been readily assumed by either management or staff. This is particularly so where the organisation is located in an area or region whose society itself is multicultural. Tayeb also highlights the significance, for many countries, of the legacy of colonialism in shaping those who are present in developed world labour markets, and the positive and negative impact of the history of these ties.

Culture and society

Broadly, it can be argued that the culture of a society comprises the shared values, understandings, assumptions, and goals that are learned from earlier generations, imposed by present members of society, and are passed on to succeeding generations. This shared outlook results in common attitudes, codes of conduct, and expectations that subconsciously guide and control certain norms of behaviour. The cultural variables in turn determine basic attitudes towards work, time, materialism, individualism and change.

Lawrence and Lorsch (1967) introduced the dual notions of differentiation and integration as sociological phenomena when analysing behaviour within the context of organisational behaviour. These concepts have since been extended and elaborated to reference the management characteristics of global and transnational management styles (Bartlett and Ghoshal, 1989; Doz, 1976; Prahalad, 1976; Prahalad and Doz, 1987). Lawrence and Lorsch argued that in an ideal situation, optimal organisational performance was closely associated with the careful management and coordination of diversity, with an understanding and appreciation of the richness of differentiation at one level, matched against an injunction to work towards common goals at another.

Some definitions of culture

Writers in the field of cross-cultural management have tried to get to grips with what culture means in this context. For example, Fons Trompenaars argues that:

> A fish discovers its needs for water when it is no longer in it. Our own culture is like water to a fish. We live and breathe through it. What one culture may regard as essential, a certain level of material wealth for example, may not be so vital to another culture. (1993: 174)

Alternatively, Geert Hofstede has a more cognitive model of culture, suggesting that culture is:

> The collective programming of the mind which distinguishes the members of one organisation from another. (Hofstede, 1991)

Although the definitions and details of the theories developed by these and other authors may vary, the consensus is that managing different cultures is a challenge, albeit a worthwhile and necessary one.

Managing multicultural and cross-cultural working

In the international context the term culture refers to at least two different determinants, *organisational culture*, namely the traditions, beliefs, norms of behaviour and management style that characterise a particular organisation, and *national culture*, the language, codes of conduct, attitudes to human rights, ethical standards and historical influences that characterise behaviour in a particular country or region of the world. These two different cultural determinants will often overlap, for example when we look at the influence of German or Japanese national culture on the way in which German and Japanese organisations are structured and managed. The issue of cultural diversity arises where organisations from disparate cultural backgrounds, whose cultural make-up represents a blend of national and organisational cultural influences, engage in business relationships. The issue may also arise where within the international organisation itself there exists a blend of national cultural influences which must be managed within the context of project teams or matrix structures.

As Derek Torrington (1994) points out:

> Managers who deliberately or unwittingly work counter-culturally will constantly be frustrated by failing to get a response from colleagues, by being misunderstood or by being bypassed. Managers who try to work out the nature of the culture in which they are operating can at least begin the process of change and influence the direction of the cultural evolution. (p. 31)

A classic example, perhaps, of the mismanagement or misunderstanding of cultural diversity is the attitude of British companies conducting business within the international arena. For many it is a cruel accident of birth that English is used as an official language in over 60 countries (Crystal, 1987). Indeed, English is commonly regarded as the 'lingua franca' of the global business world. As a result, there appears to be no injunction for the English manager to learn other languages or become multilingual. The problem is that although British managers may be able to converse at the formal level with overseas business partners and competitors, they are often unable to converse at, perhaps, the more important informal level where the appreciation of cultural nuance may be critical to striking a deal or to negotiating terms.

Geert Hofstede (1994) contends that *there is no such thing as universality in management*. This provides further support for the view that global management in the 1990s had as much to do with the appreciation of difference as it did with a focus on similarity, often contextualised in terms of *standardisation* and *universalism*. He illustrates this by pointing to the origins of the word 'management' itself:

The linguistic origin of management is from Latin 'manus', via the Italian 'maneggiare' which is the training of horses in the 'menege' . . . the word also became associated with the French 'ménage' . . . the art of running a household. The theatre of present-day management contains elements of both 'menege' and 'ménage' and different managers and cultures may use different accents. (1993: 82)

Predominant views in the cross-cultural literature

The literature relating to understanding the role of national culture in the context of international operations is largely found in two literatures, the cross-cultural management literature and the international management development literature. The primary consideration of these literatures might be described as:

- enhancing the effectiveness of cross-cultural understanding and communication;
- reducing the likelihood of cross-cultural misunderstanding and conflict.

Although there is an effectiveness theme implicit in much of this literature, there is also the important dimension of *respect and dignity*. This sits well with the capabilities equality as built on the desire to secure personal dignity (as related fully in Chapter 1). There can, at times, be a tendency towards the 'business etiquette' end of promoting respect and dignity. This approach, though limited, does have the benefit of focusing on the importance of developing skill and expertise at the level of interpersonal transactions, and on promoting the understanding of cultural similarities and differences, in order to better handle the difficulties, but also the synergies, that might be secured when working in diverse teams. In the drive to secure 'business overseas', all of these are areas that have often been ignored.

Cultural values underlying organisational behaviour

One well-known framework for understanding how basic values underlie organisational behaviour is proposed by Hofstede (1991). Drawing on his research in over 50 countries on 116,000 IBM employees in the late 1960s, he proposes four *value dimensions*:

1. power distance;
2. uncertainty avoidance;
3. individualism; and
4. masculinity.

Power distance

This is the level of acceptance by a society of the unequal distribution of power in institutions. In the workplace, inequalities in power are normal, as evidenced in hierarchical boss–subordinate relationships. However, the extent to which subordinates accept unequal power is societally determined. In countries in which people display high power distance (such as Malaysia, the Philippines and Mexico), employees acknowledge the boss's authority simply by respecting that individual's formal position in the hierarchy, and they seldom bypass the chain of command. This respectful response results, predictably, in a centralised structure and autocratic leadership. In countries where people display low power distance, superiors and subordinates are apt to regard one another as equal in power, resulting in more harmony and cooperation. Clearly, an autocratic management style is not likely to be well received in low power distance countries.

Uncertainty avoidance

This concept refers to the extent to which people in a society feel threatened by ambiguous situations. Countries with a high level of uncertainty avoidance (such as Japan, Portugal and Greece) tend to have strict laws and procedures to which their people adhere closely, and there is a strong sense of nationalism. In a business context, this value results in formal rules and procedures designed to provide more security and greater career stability. Managers have a propensity for low-risk decisions, employees exhibit little aggressiveness, and lifetime employment is common. In countries with low-level uncertainty avoidance (such as Denmark, Great Britain, and to a lesser extent the United States), nationalism is less pronounced, protests are less structured and less formal, some managers take more risks, and there is high job mobility.

Individualism and collectivism

This concept refers to the tendency for people to look after themselves and their immediate family only to neglect the needs of society. In countries that value individualism (such as the United States, Great Britain and Australia), democracy, individual initiative, and achievement are highly valued; the relationship of the individual with organisations is one of independence on an emotional level, if not on an economic level.

In countries where low individualism prevails, such as Pakistan and Panama, collectivism is likely to predominate. Here, according to Hofstede (1991), one finds tight social frameworks, emotional dependence on belonging to the 'organisation', and a strong belief in group decisions. People from a collectivist country like Japan believe in the will of the group rather than that of the individual, and their pervasive collectivism exerts control over individual members through social pressure and fear of humiliation.

Hofstede's findings indicate that most countries scoring high on individualism have both a higher gross national product and a freer political system than those scoring low in individualism, wealth, and a political system with balanced power.

Masculinity

This dimension refers to what Hofstede saw as the degree of traditionally 'masculine' values, such as assertiveness, materialism, and a lack of concern for others. In comparison, femininity emphasises 'feminine' values, such as a concern for others, for relationships, and for the quality of life. In high masculine societies (such as Japan and Austria for example), women are generally expected to stay at home and raise a family. In organisations where there is high masculinity there may be job stress and organisational interests may be seen to encroach on employees' private lives. In countries with low masculinity (such as Switzerland and New Zealand), less conflict and job stress may be found. There may be more women in high-level jobs, and a reduced need for assertiveness. The United States lies somewhat in the middle, according to Hofstede's research.

Geert Hofstede's original research was conducted some thirty years ago, focusing on the values of IBM employees around the world. Although he has revisited and largely confirmed these findings, anxieties remain about how such a view of culture might limit what we believe its role to be in a very different and evolving international context.

Multiculturalism, cross-culturalism and different cultural profile of teams

The concept of **multiculturalism** is concerned with bringing together, within the wider society, a variety of cultures and their attributes, in addition to the indigenous one, that are embedded within non-indigenous communities. This becomes a significant issue for organisations when aiming to reflect the increasing multiculturalism in society, within itself, and has a particular relevance for human resource management policy and practice within those organisations. However, some companies might seek to ignore the significance of appreciating the nature and richness of the multicultural population of its workforce. They might treat their culturally diverse workforce as if it were entirely homogeneous. In yet other companies the rhetoric of the value of multiculturalism may fail to translate into reality.

There is also likely to be a link here between an appreciation of the critical importance of managing multiculturalism and indeed, cross-culturalism, and achieving competitive advantage whether it be at the local or indeed global level. **Cross-culturalism** is more concerned with the management of those who are normally resident in the country of their birth, but may, say, become part of a project team made up of those from different nationalities, or the parent company expatriate manager of one of its daughter operations overseas. Nancy Adler (1991) argues that it is important to appreciate the specific character of team diversity in relation to culture, as there will be different dynamics that may operate. Her work suggests that the distinction needs to be made between:

- culturally homogeneous teams;
- token teams (where all but one member is from the same cultural background);
- bi-cultural teams (where teams consist of two national cultures only);
- multicultural teams (made up of members from a diversity of national cultural backgrounds but all normally resident in the same country);
- cross-cultural teams (made up of members from a diversity of national cultural backgrounds but all normally resident in different countries).

Adler argues that multicultural diversity is particularly important to multidomestic, multinational and global firms. She suggests that, for example:

- *multi-domestic firms* need to be able to adapt their strategies and their products to that of the local culture in each of the countries in which they operate;
- *global companies* need to understand cultural dynamics for strategy formulation, locate production facilities and suppliers worldwide, and manage cross-cultural interactions throughout the workforce.

The implications of Adler's views are that there is a need for such companies to be able to engage sufficiently with the culture and socio-economic realities of the countries where they trade, and that local knowledge can provide a powerful source of useful information to this end.

However, the literature is riddled with accounts of the difficulties within cross-cultural teams or of expatriate managers unable to get the best from the companies or departments overseas for which they have responsibility.

Culture and group dynamics

According to Jackson (1993), the nature of group dynamics and the roles that people play may be influenced by cultural factors. Referring to Fiedler's work (1967) and the development of a contingency model, Jackson identifies two main types of behaviour in groups:

1. Task behaviour. This might be exemplified by the use of one-way communication, directing, explaining and information giving.
2. Maintenance or relationship behaviours. These might include placing stress on opening two-way communication and *encouraging and building trust*. These behaviours can be traced back to Hofstede's work, which was

considered above. For example, within a group situation a group member from a large power distance culture, perhaps France or Malaysia, may find it difficult to work in a group where there is little direction from a recognised authority. On the other hand, a group member from a low power distance culture, perhaps Austria or Denmark, may find it difficult to operate in a group where the leader is using a 'telling' style rather than a consultative, or participative, style. Again, a group member from a high uncertainty avoidance culture such as Japan or Belgium may find it difficult where the group has ill-defined terms of reference, objectives, or procedures.

Managing conflict in the multicultural workforce

Different approaches to the process and content of group decision making may give rise to tensions, and ultimately conflict. The way conflict is handled may also be perceived differently from one culture to another.

Schmidt and Kochan (1972) point to two main sources of conflict:

1. perceived goal incompatibility;
2. perceived opportunity for blocking or interfering.

Goal incompatibility occurs where two or more people have goals which are not compatible that may give rise to a win–lose situation. Leung and Wu (1990) make the distinction, when looking at cross-cultural analysis of disputes, between the subjective and objective dimensions of these two prerequisites. In cross-cultural encounters, what is seen in one culture as incompatible may be regarded as compatible in another. Similarly, blocking behaviour may be either objective or subjective. In an American or Western European business situation, a contract is seen as a sign of commitment. In Japanese business negotiations, a contract is seen as a sign of mistrust. They are seen as a block to negotiations, particularly in the early stages, when the insistence on the signing is seen as lack of commitment to collaboration. Another factor which may increase the intensity of conflict between cultures is the value placed on a goal. The more highly valued a goal, the more intense the conflict, the more that goal is seen as incompatible with those of fellow group members.

Overcoming conflict between cultures

The challenge of cross-cultural encounters

However, the authors are clear that many local differences around these clusters still remain. Further, beyond formal systems of control, issues can still regularly arise within teams. Process losses through slower and poor communications, dislike and mistrust and stereotyping can have the potential to bedevil such teams (Adler, 1991). Hofstede (1991) has also identified a number of positive and negative encounters of inter-cultural encounters, including:

● intended versus unintended inter-cultural conflict;
● culture shock and time taken to adjust to new cultures – acculturation lag;
● differences in language and humour.

However, Hofstede firmly believes that a number of these difficulties can be reduced through the development of the knowledge and skills needed for inter-cultural communication.

Understanding how different individuals participate in a group process may aid in the reduction of obstacles to communication. This focuses on the process itself. The content of communication within the group forum can be explored by discussing different approaches and outcomes (Jackson, 1993, p. 40)

Mead (1998) maintains that culturally diverse groups are more likely to succeed when members:

● value the exchange of alternative points of view;
● cooperate to build group decisions;
● respect each other's experiences and share their own;
● value the opportunity for cross-cultural learning;
● are tolerant of uncertainty and try to overcome the inefficiencies that can arise when members of different cultures work together.

HRM in an international context: convergence or divergence?

Schuler *et al.* (1994) define strategic international HRM as 'human resource management issues, functions, policies and practices that result from the strategic activities of multinational enterprises and that impact the international development and goals of those enterprises'. However, in spite of the suggestion that, for example, HRM practice is converging in such operations (e.g. Sparrow, Schuler and Jackson, 1994), local difficulties remain. Sparrow *et al.*'s research across twelve countries around the world suggests that there is *some* convergence, associated with 'internationalisation', with a greater emphasis on empowerment, diversity management, flexibility in job design, flatter organisational structures, customer-based measures of employee performance, greater flexibility in staffing, training and exiting decisions, and greater communication of company objectives and goals to staff. Indeed, Sorge's work on cross-national difference in personnel and organisations (in Harzing and van Ruysseveldt, 1996) would suggest that when analysing such differences, it is important to understand:

● the construction of actors (and their values and preferences);
● the formal and informal design of organisational systems;
● the social, political and psychological architecture of the organisations and the society within which they reside: in other words, personnel practice is the sum total of a number of such reference points.

Box 6.1 HRM menu; cultural determinants (Schneider and Barsoux, 1997)

HRM ISSUES	CULTURAL DETERMINANTS

Selection

Who to hire? How to hire?
- Desired behaviours – focus on skills/personality?
- Specialists versus generalists?
- Necessary qualifications?
  Level, discipline, or preferred institutions?
- How important is 'what you know' versus 'who you know'?

Doing versus being
Uncertainty avoidance
Power/hierarchy
Individual versus collective
Task versus relationship

Socialization

- What kind of 'initiation rites' are acceptable? Team building?
- What are the messages being sent? Competition versus cooperation? Individual versus team effort?
- To what extent will people engage in/reject social events?
- To what extent should efforts be made to ensure 'corporate culture' is shared?
- To what extent should the corporate culture be made explicit (pins, posters, slogans, etc.)?

Task versus relationship
Individual versus collective
Private versus professional life
High versus low context

Training

For what purpose?
- Develop generalist versus specialist perspective?
- Acquire company versus skill specific (technical) knowledge?
- Extent of job rotation?
- Role of mentorship?
- Competences versus networking?

Uncertainty avoidance
Individual versus collective
Hierarchy
Task versus relationship

How are training needs determined?
- By company? By individual?
- Who is sent for training? 'High-flyers' versus 'rank and file'?

What training methods are most effective?
- Case approach?
- Reading and lecture?
- Experiential exercise?
- Professor versus student driven?
- Groupwork?

Performance appraisal

- To what extent is individual versus team effort evaluated?

Individual versus collective

● To what extent is goal setting (MBO) useful?	Hierarchy
● To what extent do people expect feedback?	Being versus doing
And from whom?	Time monochronic versus polychronic
● To what extent will criticism be accepted?	High versus low context

Compensation and rewards

● Who gets what?	Equity versus equality
● To what extent should pay be linked to performance?	Doing versus being
● What degree of pay differential is acceptable?	Hierarchy
● To what extent are bonuses effective?	Control over nature
● To what extent should team versus individuals be rewarded?	Individual versus collective
● How much of salary should be fixed versus variable?	Uncertainty avoidance
● To what extent are financial versus non-financial rewards preferred?	Masculinity versus femininity

Career development

● Who gets promoted?	Being versus doing
● What determines career success?	Individual versus collective
● What type of career paths are desirable?	Task versus relationship
Internal versus external hiring?	Uncertainty avoidance
Within functions/across functions?	
Within company/industry?	
Across companies/industries?	
Between government and business?	
● To what extent are people mobile? Willing to move?	
● At what stage are 'high potentials' identified? At entry? After 5 years?	

Schneider and Barsoux (1997) also highlight some common cultural determinants of HRM issues and choices (Box 6.1). Further, they cite the work of Evans, Doz and Laurent on national patterns for career development. The authors use the illustrations of the 'Germanic' model, Anglo-Dutch model, Japanese model and Latin model in order to indicate that there are very different expectations regarding what kind of person, with what kind of background, is likely to be suitable management material (Figure 6.1).

The role of the HR manager in managing diversity in an international context

The role of the HR manager from a purely domestic let alone an international perspective can be crucial in identifying the potential benefits of an effectively managed, culturally diverse workforce. The somewhat overused maxim encouraging the imperative to 'think globally and act locally', if nothing else, illustrates the importance of looking at the management of the global organisation at two, sometimes distinct, levels.

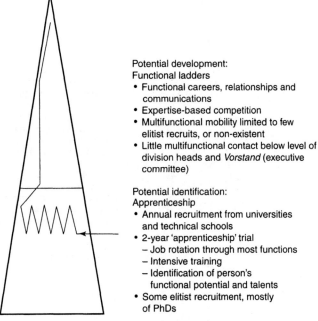

Potential development:
Functional ladders
- Functional careers, relationships and communications
- Expertise-based competition
- Multifunctional mobility limited to few elitist recruits, or non-existent
- Little multifunctional contact below level of division heads and *Vorstand* (executive committee)

Potential identification:
Apprenticeship
- Annual recruitment from universities and technical schools
- 2-year 'apprenticeship' trial
  - Job rotation through most functions
  - Intensive training
  - Identification of person's functional potential and talents
- Some elitist recruitment, mostly of PhDs

Functional approach to management development: the 'Germanic' model

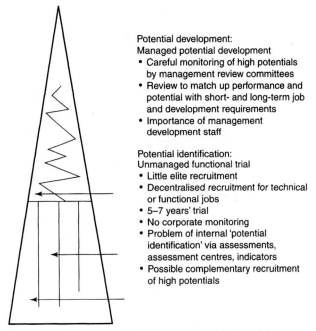

Potential development:
Managed potential development
- Careful monitoring of high potentials by management review committees
- Review to match up performance and potential with short- and long-term job and development requirements
- Importance of management development staff

Potential identification:
Unmanaged functional trial
- Little elite recruitment
- Decentralised recruitment for technical or functional jobs
- 5–7 years' trial
- No corporate monitoring
- Problem of internal 'potential identification' via assessments, assessment centres, indicators
- Possible complementary recruitment of high potentials

Managed development approach to management development:
'Anglo-Dutch' model

Figure 6.1a   Country patterns for career development. *Source:* Evans, Doz and Laurent, 1989.

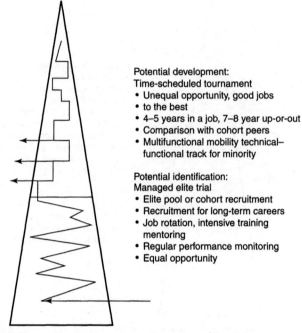

Potential development:
Time-scheduled tournament
• Unequal opportunity, good jobs
• to the best
• 4–5 years in a job, 7–8 year up-or-out
• Comparison with cohort peers
• Multifunctional mobility technical–
  functional track for minority

Potential identification:
Managed elite trial
• Elite pool or cohort recruitment
• Recruitment for long-term careers
• Job rotation, intensive training
  mentoring
• Regular performance monitoring
• Equal opportunity

Elite cohort approach to management development: the 'Japanese' model

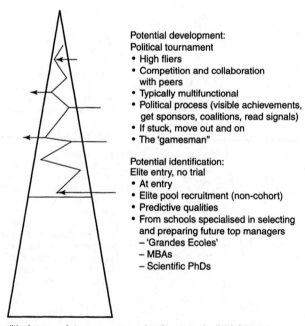

Potential development:
Political tournament
• High fliers
• Competition and collaboration
  with peers
• Typically multifunctional
• Political process (visible achievements,
  get sponsors, coalitions, read signals)
• If stuck, move out and on
• The 'gamesman"

Potential identification:
Elite entry, no trial
• At entry
• Elite pool recruitment (non-cohort)
• Predictive qualities
• From schools specialised in selecting
  and preparing future top managers
  – 'Grandes Ecoles'
  – MBAs
  – Scientific PhDs

Elite political approach to management development: the 'Latin' model

Figure 6.1b Country patterns for career development. *Source:* Evans, Doz and Laurent, 1989.

Commonly, the first of these may take the form of a management strategy based upon the concepts of *standardisation* and *universalism*. The principal focus is usually managers, and the principal aim is to create a management culture that is recognisable to a specific organisation wherever it operates around the globe. This is particularly important for the global company. However, as we will suggest later in this section, international management development programmes, the development of which is often a key activity for international HR managers, are not sufficient, on their own, to instil this culture of sharing and networking. Organisational designs and systems should be there to ensure that the cultural norms fostered within the development process become a reality. The ultimate focus should not be solely on the development of individual competencies but also on the collective competence of the organisation, where a worldwide view of management resources is taken.

The second level of strategy may involve taking different approaches to management in different locations around the world. This second approach may be particularly important where there are significant cultural differences, brought about by national and organisational culture, between one location and another. The role of the international human resource manager is, therefore, that of setting the tone of management for the organisation as it conducts business across the globe, dependent upon cultural variation and variety and market needs from one region to another. The focus of HR managers in this context often centre around staffing, management development, performance appraisal and employee relations (see, for example, reviews in Mendenhall and Oddou, 2000; Harzig and van Ruysseveldt, 1996; Briscoe, 1995).

The role of HR within the organisation is, however, often misunderstood. Where this occurs, the essence of HR as a critical player in the identification of corporate goals and the development of corporate wide strategy is often lost. Instead HR becomes yet another area of the business that is surrounded by rigid systems, procedures and policies, and a culture of 'one system fits all' emerges. There are examples of this in the computer and motor industries where espoused organisational values fail to 'fit' the requirements of the local operation. At the local level there may indeed be internal contradictions that conflict with the global HR policy. The significance of these contradictions may remain obscured where the sharing of knowledge is limited and organisational learning ignored. Importantly, the value add of HRM to international business and management can be too easily lost. Indeed, Dowling and Schuler (1990: cited in Scullion, 1995) have suggested that the human and financial costs of failure in international business are frequently more severe than in the domestic business.

However, it could be argued that in order to develop and sustain a culture of sensitivity to diversity issues, the organisation needs to embrace policies and procedures that facilitate communication and learning across the organisation *as a whole*. It is important that this development is not seen as a peripheral or cosmetic phenomenon. Where this is likely to be the case, improvements in performance are either fortuitous or short-lived. One of any global company's key resources is *information and knowledge*. The willingness to share information and learn from the successes and failures of one's colleagues operating in different parts of the world with, perhaps, very different responsibilities is an organisational cultural norm that should be fostered and developed within the international management development process. What is required of the organisation, in a very practical sense, are details and clear processes that will enable effective communication that can facilitate more rapid and open exchange of ideas. There need to be clear guidelines for practice accompanied by operational advice.

Learning, knowledge and international and global companies

Nigel Holden (2002) has moved beyond the narrow focus of many accounts of cross-cultural management, and has made explicit what is often implicit within this literature: the importance of cross-cultural management for effective knowledge management. As will have become obvious in Chapter 3, developing knowledge bases is a demanding task, and identifying the micro, meso- and macro-level learning processes and structures that can enable this is equally demanding. Holden suggests that cross-cultural management can be 'redesigned' as a *knowledge domain*. He asserts that

> there is a need to have 'a broad formulation of cross-cultural management, as opposed to the traditional, narrow one, which focuses disproportionately on cultural differences – or rather the potential occurrence of cross-cultural clashes. This is inadequate for mediating the kinds of experiences mediated (in my case research) because it does not allow for the possibility of regarding culture as an organisational resource. (2002: 208)

He then goes on to define cross-cultural management, centred around the management of knowledge. Specifically:

> The core task of cross-cultural management is to facilitate and direct synergistic interaction and learning at interfaces, where knowledge, values and experience are transferred into multi-cultural domains of implementation. (2002: 208)

Holden then goes on to outline what he believes are three important domains of cultural knowledge:

1. general cultural knowledge: descriptive and artifactual in nature and not easy to decipher;
2. specific cultural knowledge: selective for relevance to a firm's operations and can be tacit or explicit;
3. cross-cultural know-how: practical knowledge applied in cross-cultural contexts and continually updated based on experience; this kind of knowledge is subjective, experiential – it facilitates interaction, informs participative competence and stimulates cross-cultural collaborative learning.

A key aim, Holden argues, of international firms is to increase their cross-cultural management expertise, as this is an important potential source of organisational core competence. Moreover, increasingly, the work of those in the field of international HRM is also suggesting that this might be the case, and that effective international HRM has an important role in the facilitation of this (e.g. Roberts, Kossek and Ozeki, 1998).

Further, these views are also consistent with the assertion that effective management across borders is a potential source of competitive advantage. However, all of these views on what is the appropriate way of managing the cultural difference issues within an international context are now facing a new and, in many ways, more controversial challenge, that of the globalised company.

It is likely that there are real personal and organisational benefits to be gained from a deeper and more rounded understanding of colleagues and the cultural influences on the work that they do and the explicit, implicit and tacit knowledge relating to that work. Indeed, it could be seen as an enriching of the concept of community of practice. However, a limit of the cross-cultural approach that Holden promotes is that it focuses in particular on relationships at a similar, peer level and may be less useful in informing management–subordinate relationships, especially where the power distance is great.

Managing the global workforce

Global management is seen by Bartlett and Ghoshal (1992) as the utilisation of a network of specialists that includes a business manager, a country manager, a functional manager and a corporate manager (see also Figure). They claim that today's international climate demands highly specialised, closely linked groups of global business managers. Transnationals integrate assets, resources

---

Case example: Managing the global enterprise – the top-down approach. IBM's personal business commitment and becoming one voice

IBM's Personal Business Commitment (PBC), where managers and peers give their input on the achievement of the corporate objectives cascaded down and throughout the organisation, or their Business Conduct Guidelines (BCG) which are based upon a corporate moral or ethical dimension worldwide, or, indeed, the introduction of corporate iconography such as Becoming One Voice (BOV).

The essence of competitive advantage here is about giving culturally diverse groups the freedom to interpret these corporate codes within the context of their own culture and being alert to the fact that the interpretation that senior management wish to attach to the code may be entirely different from the meaning that culturally diverse management and staff, in other parts of the organisation, may naturally attach to the iconography.

Becoming One Voice might be interpreted as an expectation that all staff around the world operate to exactly the same systems and procedures. An alternative interpretation might be that Becoming One Voice is about creating harmonies between a variety of tones and keys.

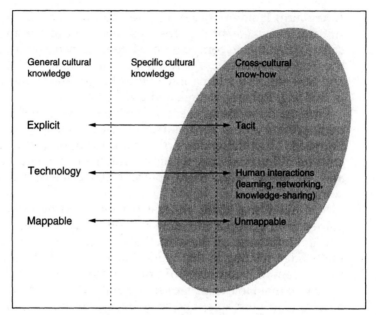

Figure 6.2   The domain of high cross-cultural management expertise (shaded). *Source*: Holden, 2000.

and diverse people in operating units around the world. Transnational companies build three strategic capabilities:

1.   global-scale efficiency and competitiveness;
2.   national-level responsiveness and flexibility; and
3.   cross-market capacity to leverage learning on a worldwide basis.

The challenge for many budding transnational organisations is a severe shortage of executives with the skills, knowledge and sophistication to operate in a more tightly linked, less traditional hierarchical network.

Examples of developing transnationals given by Bartlett and Ghoshal include Electrolux, NEC and Procter & Gamble.

The roles of global business, country, functional and corporate managers

Bartlett and Ghoshal claim that the building blocks for most worldwide companies are their national subsidiaries. If the *global business manager's* main objective is to achieve global-scale efficiency and competitiveness, the *national subsidiary manager's* role is to be sensitive and responsive to the local market. *Country managers* play the pivotal role not only in meeting local customer needs but also in satisfying the host government's requirements and defending their company's market position against local and external competitors. The need for local flexibility may put the country manager in conflict with the global business manager.

Box 6.2 The development of the global corporation

The history of managing business on an international scale has evolved from the colonial-style mentality of the last century, when only executives of the 'home country' could be trusted to hold important posts. In such an environment, international expansion tended to be limited to colonies or at best spheres of influence of the parent company. Interestingly, the Japanese still hold to this philosophy in business, and decision making is very tightly controlled by head office. The next stage in this historical process was a recognition, most apparent in the developed world, that each national operation was best run by a national of that country. Control in this phase tended to be largely financial (as long as the company was making a profit, you didn't replace the local manager!). As a result of this movement in the larger multinationals, there followed a period of regional integration. For example, US companies began to regionalise their overseas operations. Today, concepts such as the 'global village' and the 'global marketplace' are common currency within the international business environment, although they are not always fully exploited in any formal integrated way. The trend towards regionalisation and the increasing movement in mergers and acquisitions as the most common means of international expansion contributed to a growing tendency to appoint the best manager in the company to top-level positions, irrespective of nationality. Multinational companies with headquarters in small countries realised this even earlier. Nestlé is a good example: the last four CEOs of Nestlé have been German, Swiss, French and Italian.

At the same time, with the gradual lowering of trade barriers and the revolution in international transport and communications over the past fifteen to twenty years, companies have been able to treat the world in a much more integrated manner. The early triggers of globalisation were reinforced by a new wave of competitors, particularly from Asia, who capitalised on falling tariffs and efficient global distribution to leverage their country-specific comparative advantages. Global market segments were recognised or created, technology was initiated rapidly and diffused worldwide almost instantaneously, and scale economies were captured to exploit the benefits of the multiple market segments and free trade access. Progressively, the key management requirement was for global integration and cross-market coordination.

The modern multinational corporation has outgrown the stage in which managers at the centre coordinate a set of peripheral subsidiaries, largely independent of one another. The utilisation of the multinational network as an integrated and interdependent whole is presented as the basis for successful global business. The key words here appear to be integration and interdependence. Indeed, in some sectors there is evidence of a shift towards the geographical diffusion of core strategic activities and coordinating roles and a break with the notion of uniform hierarchy of decisions as well as organisational positions. This is certainly the view of writers such as Hedlund and Rolander (1990), who take the view that the genuine global MNC can be better thought of as what they term 'heterarchy' rather than a classic 'hierarchy'.

Kogut (1990) reinforces this point when he maintains that it is the management of a company's global network that eventually becomes the source of advantage, allowing it to achieve economies of scale and scope, to learn about foreign conditions, and to achieve the operating flexibility inherent in such a network. Gradually, lateral processes with widely distributed and shared responsibilities replace groupings of sets of functional activities under strict hierarchies with unity of command. In a sense this represents a shift away from command and control mechanisms, with the home country headquarters at the centre of operations, to a culture of worldwide empowerment.

The concept of 'transnationality'

Before we embark upon an analysis of the nature, role and function of the 'transnational' company it might be helpful to distinguish between multinational, global and international companies.

The term 'multinational' refers to companies that have developed a strategic posture and organisational capability that allows them to be very sensitive and responsive to differences in national environments around the world. In effect these corporations manage a portfolio of multiple national entities.

The word 'global', when used as a prefix to the word company, according to Bartlett and Ghoshal (1989), refers to organisations that have developed international operations that are much more driven by the need for global efficiency, and much more centralised in their strategic and operational decisions. These companies treat the world as an operational whole to whom the global operating environment and worldwide consumer demands are the dominant units of analysis, not the nation-state or local market.

'International' companies, however, adopt a strategy that is based primarily on transferring and adapting the parent company's knowledge or expertise to foreign markets. The parent retains considerable influence and control, but less than in a classic global company; national units can adapt products and ideas coming from the centre, but have less independence and autonomy than multinational subsidiaries.

The transnational solution

Bartlett and Ghoshal argue that environmental forces have dramatically changed the nature of the strategic demands in a wide range of businesses, and the traditional approaches of multinational, global and international companies can no longer yield an adequate response. This has given rise to the development of the thesis which Bartlett and Ghoshal refer to as the 'transnational solution'.

They describe the 'transnational company' as possessing the following characteristics:

- it has many centres;
- it makes extensive use of networks;
- it has an organic structure;
- it is process oriented;
- it regards information as a key resource; and
- it thinks globally and acts locally.

The concept of 'transnationality' has also been developed by Barham et al. at Ashridge (1991), who define 'globalisation' as 'the art of being local worldwide'.

Research undertaken by Kevin Barham at Ashridge was concerned with integration of the following areas:

- strategy and culture;
- culture (an international spirit);
- international management development.

The international business scene in the 1990s was described by Barham et al. as follows:

- an increase in the integration of the world economy;
- new economic alignments and sources of competition;
- the globalisation of communications and capital;
- speed, rapid change, interdependence (between different parts of the company within different parts of the world);
- the opportunity to both 'globalise' and 'customise' products;
- changes in service and know-how;
- opportunities for competition and collaboration;
- environmental concern (real competitive edge = ability to achieve organisational learning in terms of adaptability/flexibility).

The multinational company was described thus:

- one centre;
- hierarchical;
- rigid;
- boss–subordinate relationships;
- clear chain of command.

Organisations possessing the above characteristics were seen to be suffering from 'power hug', i.e. strategy was developed at the centre but information was held at the operating units.

Cracking the 'power hug' was seen by Barham as the key to developing the international manager within a globalised industry.

The essence of the transnational company is perhaps best understood by looking at the way in which it is managed. Indeed, understanding globalisation and the success, measured in terms of effective working practices linked to an overarching 'global' strategy, that corporations have achieved as a result of implementing the process may be largely attributed to the way in which it is managed.

As a sensor, the country manager must be good at gathering and sifting information, interpreting implications, and predicting a range of feasible outcomes. Consumer trends in one country often spread to another and technologies developed in a leading-edge environment can have global significance.

Relegated to support-staff roles, and often excluded from important meetings, functional managers are often given little chance to participate in the corporate mainstream activities. An organisation can, however, gain huge benefits by linking its technical, manufacturing, marketing, human resources, and financial experts worldwide.

In the transnational organisation, senior managers have a significant facilitator role connecting areas of specialisation throughout the organisation. This can be achieved by the use of informal networks and by creating channels for communicating specialised information and building a resource base of specialist knowledge that is available to those who wish to access it. Here, knowledge is treated as an important resource and not as something associated with power.

The role of the international manager, as indicated in previous paragraphs, is largely dependent upon the task that he or she has to perform, the culture of the local national and business environment and the period that the manager is expected to remain in that locality. It could be argued that what international organisations require is a high degree of specialisation in selecting and developing staff for overseas assignments. The role of line management in association with the international human resource specialist is to facilitate that process.

Bartlett and Ghoshal's work outlines the many options and difficulties for managers at the centre of the global enterprise. However, a shortcoming of their work, in common with much of the international management literature, is that it conceptualises globalisation as inherently a process where the emphasis is on *the manager* and their ability or not to 'control' what happens within their area of responsibility. It also is largely elaborated around the international manager, a cosmopolitan who is able to partake fully in the global labour market, and is far less well elaborated around the voice and needs of those who are interacting with global organisations but at a purely local level. Indeed, Schneider and Barsoux (1997) suggest that there is a shift away from the 'jet-setting elite' image around those who are concerned with managing across cultures. Schneider and Barsoux also suggest that there is a need to pay more attention to the issues of business ethics and social responsibility.

However, there is an alternative view. Certainly, there are voices of concern regarding the impact of globalisation on the developing world, and the potential gains by the developed world at the developing world's expense. Moreover, there is a similar story of winners and losers within these companies themselves, which brings back into the frame what is largely missing from most of the literature on cross-cultural and international management: *fairness and equality*. Although there may be some attention paid to how best to cope with different labour laws in relation to equality (e.g. Mendenhall and Oddou, 2000) this, again, often only deals with 'hiring and firing' legal contractual obligations.

International business, management and ethics

More recently, there has been some indication of a growing interest in how business ethics and social responsibility should be exercised in an international context. Schneider and Barsoux (1997) highlight the need to make 'moral sense' of commercial actions. In common with many of the international business ethics issues, they focus in particular on ethical dilemmas. There are many areas of concern that are increasingly becoming integrated into ethical business action, such as health and safety, child labour, inequalities and pay exploitation, employee collective representation and ethical investment.

A particularly controversial example that they give related to US Fortune 500 companies that operated in South Africa during the apartheid era. Some went the route of civil disobedience (e.g. Polaroid and General Motors), pursued corporate 'civil disobedience' and broke the apartheid laws. One hundred and twenty-five Fortune companies signed up to the 'Sullivan Principles' (1978). These principles were:

- non-segregation of the races in all eating, comfort, locker room and work facilities;
- equal pay and fair employment practice for all employees;
- equal pay for all employees doing equal or comparable work for the same period of time;
- initiation and development of training programmes that will prepare blacks, coloureds and Asians in substantial numbers for supervisory, administrative and technical jobs;
- increasing the numbers of blacks, coloureds and Asians in management and supervisory positions;
- improving the quality of employees' lives outside the work environment in such areas as housing, recreation, schooling and health facilities.

Others operated within the apartheid laws (e.g. Citybank). Changes in legislation in the USA, specifically the US Comprehensive Anti-Apartheid Act (1986), forced many of these companies to withdraw. No such law applied to European companies, however, although some, such as Barclays, withdrew after pressure.

As Schneider and Barsoux put it: 'Different countries and different companies adopt different decisions when faced with (similar) ethical dilemmas'.

The 'reach' of morality in economic matters

For many, their first introduction to business ethics is some version of Kohlberg's stages of moral development. An assumption underpinning this model is that organisations are likely to start at an 'amoral' stage and can grow towards the most 'advanced' phase of ethical development (Table 6.1). However, a limitation of this view is that there is a gradual growth from a narrow start point in ethical awareness and maturity and that it is unlikely that

Table 6.1   A traditional view of corporate moral development

Stage in moral development	Management attitude and approach	Ethical aspects of corporate culture	Corporate ethics artifacts	Defining corporate behavior
Stage I – the amoral organisation	Get away with all you can; it's ethical as long as we're not caught; ethical violations, when caught, are a cost of doing business	Outlaw culture; live hard and fast; damn the risks; get what you can and get out	No meaningful code of ethics or other documentation; no set of values other than greed	Film Recovery System Numerous penny stock companies
Stage II – the legalistic organisation	Play within the legal rules; fight changes that affect your economic outcome; use damage control through public relations when social problems occur; a reactive concern for damage to organisations from social problems	If it's legal, it's OK; work the gray areas; protect loopholes and don't give ground without a fight; economic performance dominates evaluations and rewards	The code of ethics, if it exists, is an internal document; 'Don't do anything to harm the organisation'; 'Be a good corporate citizen'	Ford Pinto Firestone 500 Nestlé Infant Formula R. J. Reynolds Philip Morris
Stage III – the responsive organisation	Management understands the value of not acting solely on a legal basis, even though they believe they could win; management still has a reactive mentality; a growing balance between profits and ethics, although a basic premise still may be a cynical 'ethics pays'; management begins to test and learn from more responsive actions	There is a growing concern for other corporate stakeholders other than owners; culture begins to embrace a more 'responsible citizen' attitude	Codes are more externally oriented and reflect a concern for other publics; other ethics vehicles are undeveloped	Procter & Gamble (Rely Tampons) Abbott Labs Borden
Stage IV – the emerging ethical organisation	First stage to exhibit an active concern for ethical outcomes; 'We want to do the "right" thing'; top management values become organizational values; ethical perception has focus but lacks organisation and long-term planning; ethics management is characterised by successes and failures	Ethical values become part of culture; these core values provide guidance in some situations but questions exist in others; a culture that is less reactive and more proactive to social problems when they occur	Codes of ethics become action documents; code items reflect the core values of the organisation; handbooks, policy statements, committees, ombudsmen are sometimes used	Boeing General Mills Johnson & Johnson (Tylenol) General Dynamics Caterpillar Levi Strauss
Stage V – the ethical organisation	A balanced concern for ethical and economic outcomes; ethical analysis is a fully integrated partner in developing both the mission and strategic plan; SWOT (Strengths, Weaknesses, Opportunities, Threats) analysis is used to *anticipate* problems and analyse alternative outcomes	A total ethical profile, with carefully selected core values which reflect that profile, directs the culture; corporate culture is planned and managed to be ethical; hiring, training, firing, and rewarding all reflect the ethical profile	Documents focus on the ethical profile and core values; all phases of organizational documents reflect them	????????

Source: R.E. Reidenbach and D.P. Robin (1991) 'A conceptual model of corporate model development', *Journal of Business Ethics*, 10, p. 282. Reprinted with kind permission from Kluwer Academic Publishers. Copyright © 1991 Kluwer Academic Publishers.

corporations would choose to 'front end' their development with a more sophisticated approach to ethical issues.

Amartya Sen (in Enderle, 1999) challenges this view. He puts it simply:

> There is an interesting asymmetry between the treatment of business principles and moral sentiments in standard economic analysis. Business principles are taken to be very rudimentary (essentially restricted, directly or indirectly, to profit maximisation) but with a very wide reach in economic matters (covering effectively all economic transactions). In contrast, moral sentiments are seen to be quite complex (involving different kinds of ethical systems), but it is assumed, that at least in economic matters, they have a very narrow reach (indeed it is often presumed that such sentiments have no real influence on economic behaviour). .... Business principles cannot escape being influenced by conceptions of 'good business behaviour' and thus involve the standard complexities connected with multiple goals. (1999: 15–16)

In addition, he suggests that caution should be expressed in making sweeping generalisations such as 'Asian values versus Western values' and 'Confucian ethics versus Protestant ethics', given the diversity that resides under each of these.

> Asia is where about 60 per cent of the total world population live. There are no quintessential values that apply to this immensely large and heterogeneous population, which separate them out as a group from people in the rest of the world . . . The analysis of values has to be much finer than that. (1999: 23)

Perhaps, however, the most crucial statement that he makes in his work is the following:

> The need to displace profit maximisation as a sole business principle does not call for the placing of another simple and uniform rule as an alternative general system, with the same level of universality. Rather, there is a strong case for analysing more complex structures, involving diverse concerns, and varying over time, space, and culture. A promising – and very versatile – framework of is that of *multiple objectives*, which can plausibly include the search for profits as one important objective among others. The other objectives can compete with other business behaviour, and can sometimes work as constraints influencing business behaviour, and can sometimes work as constraints reflecting established moral codes and social conventions. The force of profit maximisation may have to work subject to these constraints. (1999: 27).

So, the challenge that Sen has set for organisations is how to develop a framework of multiple objectives, within the context of a richness of cultural awareness. Some of the elements that Sen suggests could be incorporated into such a framework include:

1. the significance of cultural variations;

2. the need to avoid cultural stereotypes and sweeping generalisations;
3. the importance of taking a dynamic rather than a static view of culture;
4. the necessity of recognising heterogeneity within given communities.

Emergent inequalities?

Although, as already stated, fairness and equality issues are weakly elaborated in the cross-cultural and international management literatures, a particular kind of transactional dignity and respect does appear within it. Given this, the low presence of equality issues is strange. It might be possible to argue about neocolonial strategies or managerialism in order to secure 'profit maximisation,' though both positions are likely to play some part in this absence. In theory, and potentially in practice, the work of academics such as Amartya Sen sets out a strong challenge for *embedded moral agency* on the part of international organisations.

There is a substantial business ethics literature on the dangers of 'home and away' morality, and the inconsistencies in moral action that companies and their employees may enact or be pressurised to comply with (see for example,) and that organisations need to offer guidance on. The 'rule book' approach is likely to be able to address important but obviously, not every, moral dilemma that those working in an international context will face, not least because of the dynamic nature of communities and societies. However, clarity around the core values that employees will need to hold can help to guide moral choices, and is more likely to lead to informed choice at the level of both corporate social responsibility and individual action, and the potential to *display moral courage* when presented with complex or difficult ethical decisions (see Mahoney, in Enderle, 1999).

Embedded moral agency and multiple objectives and capabilities equality

Capabilities equality demands that attention needs to be paid to whether an organisation's members are able to have freedom of opportunity. To recall from Chapter 1, Sen argues that freedom consists in ensuring people's capabilities, defined as their 'ability to pursue what they have reason to value'.

If an organisation is going to work to achieve equality of all of its members, it needs to ensure that people's capabilities are enabled, and to ensure that this is done equally for *all* organisational members. Already, there are concerns that globalisation may be resulting in differential benefits and opportunities for different categories of employees (echoing the concerns expressed in Chapter 3 on the potential for structural inequalities and deficits in social capital).

Globalised operations often mean that the key activities for the delivery of goods or services are sited around the globe, so that information is available

24 hours a day, 7 days a week. So for example, you may have had the experience of asking for flight information and, according to the time of day, your call will be routed to a call centre in a different country, maybe London, New York, Dublin or Bombay. However, there is no guarantee that all employees will enjoy comparable terms and conditions of employment, and indeed, they may be experiencing different inequalities. Further, it may be that the nature of the work itself is creating new inequalities, with different treatment for different kinds of workers. For example, Goodhall and Roberts (2001) describe the art of *presencing*, in which the main concern is the difficulty of making one's present felt when 'away' from the main centre of parent company action because of organisational structural barriers. Other writers such as Kunda (2001) have argued that work and family time become very distorted when employees are expected to be available on a 24-hour global clock basis, which is obviously likely to be very demanding and potentially disadvantage those with family commitments in particular. In both instances, time and space are creating potentially new forms of different treatment and inequalities.

Transcendence and ethical choices

Perhaps one of the key questions that needs to be addressed in the cross-cultural and international management literature is 'whose values?'. The example given earlier of IBM's attempt to try to generate a range of cultural perspectives falls short of the substantial challenges that international organisations will face.

In his paper 'Other People', Amartya Sen (2000) has turned his attention to the issue of multiculturalism. He makes an number of important observations that help to put the question of 'whose values' into context. First, Sen suggests that in many multicultural societies, plural identity is a reality, and that inevitably, some of these identities will be competing, and others not, and all will be competing for our attention and priorities. So for example, he makes the illustration that:

> A person can be a Nigerian, an Ibo, a British citizen, a US resident, a woman, a philosopher, a Christian, a painter – each of these groups gives the person a particular identity which may be evoked in different contexts. (2000: 3)

Sen is not undermining the importance of the traditional categories of identity that predominate within the discussions of inequality and multiculturalism. He is clear about the importance of social identity also, but questions whether we need to have our identity linked solely to one group. Indeed, he argues that this can be used as a means of not seeing ourselves as whole, and further, by implication, may be how the traditionally disadvantaged are narrowly scoped: it is the dominant, majority groups that would end up with greater freedom to choose to foreground specific identities within their plural identity. He also argues that the sole identity might, at times, become a source of *new tyrannies of identity*, where traditionally disadvantaged groups choose to elaborate a narrowly scoped, single identity to the exclusion of all others, and expect members of their community to comply, whether they wish to or not.

He then goes on to describe the state of what he calls 'beyond identity'. This is his transcendent state, which transcends the domain of identity, and relates to *moral and political inclusion*. Importantly, transcendence provides a strong arena within which plural identity and identity choice may be more freely exercised than by dealing solely with the management of inter-cultural interfaces and transactions.

This notion of transcendence is important in the context of international management. First, it would require the elaboration of the democratic rights and good governance of those, in particular, who are the less privileged within the organisation. Second, when faced with the challenge 'whose values?', consideration would need to be given to whether the demand to exercise identity lies within identity choice and plural identity, or is intended to limit identity choice. So for example, if it is argued that it would be unacceptable for women to work in a corporation, not only would this be a violation of women's rights – and should lie outside of an international organisation's acceptable code of ethics, but also it may be *unrepresentative* of the wider choice in that society that group members, female and male, may *wish* to have, and would be inconsistent with the issue of voice and agency as the universal at the heart of transcendence.

So, capabilities equality automatically places ethical action towards employees at the heart of the agenda of managing in an international context. Moreover, the ability of the organisation to demand higher ethical standards within its walls than may operate outside of it also places the organisation in the context of corporate moral agency (see also the case studies: 'Building on a vision: "inclusive meritocracy" in a major multinational energy company' pp. 297–305 and 'Wearing warm clothes in winter: a pragmatic process approach to promoting cultural diversity in global succession planning', pp. 305–24.)

Conclusions

The principal aim of this chapter was to engender debate around a number of topical issues that are currently impacting on the management of diversity within the global corporation. In much of the literature, emphasis has been placed on the roles and responsibilities of management across the organisation with reference to the integrative function of International Human Resources.

Effective management of diversity and sensitivity to multicultural and cross-cultural dimensions can have a very positive impact upon individual and organisational performance. Taken a step further, this can lead to a very distinct competitive advantage. The chapter refers to a number of the key issues of concern, such as the management of conflict and the dilemmas that arise where the individual and the organisation are faced with conflicting values at the global and the local level.

However, there are areas that are weakly elaborated within the cross-cultural and international literature. Although its emphasis on the management of 'soft' cultural factors in order to enhance communications and reduce unnecessary conflicts is to be commended, there is a tendency within the literature to foreground the 'international manager', the cosmopolitan who is able to access the global labour market. Far less attention is paid to the equality and fairness issues that may affect those within organisations who are not part of this 'elite'.

Capabilities equality demands that more attention is paid to whether the freedoms and capabilities of all employees are being addressed. We would suggest that a fuller account of the opportunities for international moral agency that organisations can (and indeed, some are) exercise should play a much more central role in defining the effective and competent international corporation. Embedded moral agency, multiple objectives, in conjunction with transcendent values centred around moral and political inclusion, appreciative but not naïve towards cultural differences, may help to create a more sustainable and culturally aware ethical action that can provide a solid foundation for equality and diversity in an international context.

Finally, consistent with what we and our colleagues have discussed elsewhere (Cornelius and Spence, 2000), we believe that there is a need for a much more systematic application of ethical theory as an *analytical lens* on organisational practice than has hitherto been the case. When making decisions about how, for example, to implement a new strategy, change organisational structures or drive through a refocus on core activities, the actions taken should include an explicit understanding of right, in terms of justifiable ethical behaviour. However, rarely, if ever, is the ethically implicit made explicit. Only if underlying ethical drivers are clearly understood can consistency and integrity be a part of the practical realisation of decisions to change.

Text-based questions

What are the ways in which cross-cultural and international management have been conceptualised? What are the strengths and limitations of these from an equality and diversity perspective?

In what ways might the management of knowledge help to shape 'new' ways of understanding cross-cultural management?

Library and assignment-based questions

1. Identify three international organisations within the same industry or sector. Research the ways in which international managers are developed within them. In what ways are their approaches similar or different? In your view, how well does this development enable managers to address (a) cross-cultural issues and (b) workplace equality issues?
2. Compare and contrast the HRM policy and practice in two global compa-

nies. What are the strategies that they employ? How strongly or weakly are equality issues addressed?

3. Identify in a company report an organisation that intends to set up a new operation in a country within which it has not operated before. What are the challenges and opportunities that it is likely to face when addressing (a) cross-cultural and (b) equality issues? How might these issued be addressed?

Internet resources

ABB http://www.abb.com/
Coca-Cola http://www.coca-cola.com/
Du Pont http://www.dupont.com/
Electrolux http://www.electrolux.com/
General Electric http://www.ge.com/
General Motors http://www.gm.com/
Heinz http://www.heinz.com/
IBM http://www.ibm.com/
ICI http://www.ici.com/
McDonalds http://www.mcdonalds.com/
NEC http://www.nec.com/
Nestlé http://www.nestle.com/
Procter & Gamble http://www.pg.com/
Shell Oil http://www.countonshell.com/

Further reading

Enderle, G (1999) *International business ethics: challenges and approaches*, University of Notre Dame Press, USA. Contains a diverse collection of contributions, including comparative religious perspectives on ethics in business; business ethics in an Islamic context and emergent business ethics in east Asia and Japan, Africa and Latin America

Also:

Schuler, SC and Barsoux, J-L (1997) *Managing across cultures*, Financial Times/Prentice Hall, Hampshire.
Joynt, P and Warner, M (1996) *Managing across cultures: issues and perspectives*, International Thomson Publishing, London.
Sen, A (2000) 'Other People', Keynote Lecture presented to the British Academy. http://www.britac.ac.uk/pubs/src/pbamdex/britacad00.html

Europe

Brewster, C and Harris, H (1999) *International HRM: Contemporary issues in Europe*, Routledge, London.
Chris Brewster and Ariane Hegewisch (eds) (1994) *Policy and Practice in European Human Resource Management: The Price Waterhouse Cranfied survey*, Routledge.

Ariane Hegewisch and Chris Brewster (eds) (1993) *European Developments in Human Resource Management*, Kogan Page, London.

Paul Kirkbride (ed.) (1994) *Human Resource Management in Europe: perspectives for the 1990s*, Routledge.

IPD European Management Guides (various), Institute of Personnel and Development.

International

Hollingshead, G and Leat, M (1995) *Human Resource Management: an international and comparative perspective*, Pitman, London.

Leat, M (1995) *Human Resource Issues of the European Union*, Financial Times/Pitman, London.

Storey, J (ed.) (2001) *Human Resource Management: a critical text*, Second edition, Thomson Learning, London.

Brewster, C and Tyson, S (eds) (1991) *International Comparisons of Human Resource Management*, FT Prentice Hall.

References

Adler, N (1991) *International dimensions of organisational behaviour*, Kent Publishing, Boston, MA.

Bartlett, CA and Ghoshal, S (1992) What is a Global Manager? *Harvard Business Review*, September–October.

Barham, K and Devine, M (1991) The Quest for the International Manager, *Ashridge Management Research Group, Special Report No 2098*, Economist Intelligence Unit, London.

Briscoe, DR (1995) *International human resource management*, Prentice Hall, Englewood Cliffs, NJ.

Crystal, D (ed.) (1987) *The Cambridge Encyclopaedia of Language*, Cambridge University Press.

Cornelius, N and Spence, L (2000) Ethics and organisational change, making the ethically implicit, explicit. Paper presented at the Centre for Organisational and Professional Ethics Conference, Brunel University, December.

Dowling, PJ and Schuler, RS (1990) cited in H Scullion (1995) International Human Resource Management, in J Storey (ed.) (2001) *Human Resource Management: a critical text*, second edition, Thomson Learning, London.

Evans, P, Doz, Y and Laurent, A (1989) *Human Resource Management in International Firms*, Macmillan, London.

Enderle, G (1999) *International business ethics: challenges and approaches*, University of Notre Dame Press, USA.

Fiedler, F (1967) *A Theory of Leadership Effectiveness*, McGraw-Hill: New York.

Goodall, K and Roberts, J (2001) The art of presencing. Paper presented at the International Conference on Spacing and Timing, '*Rethinking globalisation and standardisation*', Palermo, Italy, 1–3 November.

Harzing, A-W and J Ruysseveldt (eds) (1996) *International human resource management*, Sage, Thousand Oaks, CA.

Hedlund, G and Rolander, D (1990) Action in heterarchies – new approaches to managing the multinational corporation, in CA Bartlett, Y Doz and G Hedlund (eds) *Managing the Global Firm*, Routledge, London and New York.

Hofstede, G (1991) *Cultures and Organisations – Intercultural cooperation and its importance for survival – software of the mind*, HarperCollins Business, London.

Hofstede, G (1994) *Culture and Organisations*. HarperCollins, London.

Holden, N (2000) *Cross-cultural management: a knowledge management perspective*, Financial Times/Prentice Hall, Dorchester.

Jackson, T (ed.) (1993) *Organizational Behaviour in International Management*, Butterworth Heinemann, Oxford.

Kogut, B (1990) International sequential advantages and network flexibility, in CA Bartlett, Y Doz and G Hedlund (eds) *Managing the Global Firm*, Routledge, London and New York.

Kunda, G (2001) Scenes from a marriage: work, family and time in corporate drama. Paper presented at the International Conference on Spacing and Timing, '*Rethinking globalisation and standardisation*', Palermo, Italy, 1–3 November.

Lawrence, P and Lorsch, J (1967) *Organisations and Environment*, Harvard University Press, Cambridge, MA.

Leung, K and Wu, P-G (1990) Dispute processes: a cross-cultural analysis, in RW Brislin (ed.) *Applied Cross-Cultural Psychology*, Sage, Newbury Park.

Malone, J (1999) Cultivating moral courage in business, in G Enderle (ed.) (1999) *International business ethics: challenges and approaches*, University of Notre Dame Press, USA.

Mead, R (1998) *International Management*, Blackwell Business, Oxford.

Mendenhall, M and Oddou, G (eds) (2000) *Readings and Cases in International Human Resource Management* (3rd edition), International Thomson Publishing, Canada.

Prahalad, CK (1976) Strategic Choices in Diversified MNCs. *Harvard Business Review*, July–August, pp. 67–78.

Prahalad, CK and Doz, YL (1987) *The Multinational Mission: Balancing Global Demands and Global Vision*, Free Press, New York.

Reidenbach, RE and Robin, DP (1991) A conceptual model of corporate model development. *Journal of Business Ethics*, **10**, 282.

Roberts, K, Kossek, EE and Ozeki, C (1998) Managing the global workforce: challenges and strategies. *Academy of Management Executive*, **12** (4). Reproduced in M Mendenhall and G Oddou (eds) (2000) *Readings and Cases in International Human Resource Management*, 3rd edition, International Thomson Publishing, Canada.

Schmidt, SM and Kochan, TA (1972) Conflict: towards conceptual clarity. *Administrative Science Quarterly*, **17**, 359–70.

Schuler SC, and Barsoux, J-L (1997) *Managing across cultures*, Financial Times/Prentice Hall, Hampshire.

Scullion, H (1995) International human resource management, in J Strong (ed.) *Human Resource Management: a critical text*, Routledge, Padstow.

Sen, A (1999) Economics, business principles, and moral sentiments, in G Enderle (ed.) *International business ethics: challenges and approaches*, University of Notre Dame Press, USA.

Sparrow, P, Schuler, P and Jackson, SE (1994) Convergence or divergence? Human resource practices and policies for competitive advantage worldwide. *International Journal of Human Resource Management*, April, 6–9.

Tayeb, MH (1996) *The Management of a Multicultural Workforce*, John Wiley & Sons, Chichester.

Torrington, D (1994) *International Human Resource Management*, Prentice Hall, Hemel Hempstead.

Trompenaars, F (1993) *Riding the Waves of Culture*, Nicholas Brealey, London.

Part III
Practitioners and practice

Whole organisation equality and diversity intervention strategies in practice

7

Ade Ajadi

Chapter overview

There are many lenses through which the complementary subjects of equal opportunities and diversity management can be viewed. In this chapter the perspective is on equality and diversity as an embodiment of change, especially the challenge for organisations to use these issues to create a dynamic for the pursuit of excellence. This chapter identifies one practitioner's stories about what the journey to successful change of **organisational habits** in this area has thrown up. It is very important to sound a note of caution: the challenge posed by the subject of this book is not a technical one that can be cured or addressed by a prescriptive profile of activities, but is the unwieldy and unpredictable reality of facilitating **human adaptation** in thinking, judgement and behaviour.

It is a truly humbling challenge where a large degree of '**conscious incompetence**' is needed and where the wider wisdom of all stakeholders is essential. The expressions in this chapter might sometimes challenge the wider view or different sections of this book, and this should be embraced and explored because the different lenses reach out to give meaning from the different perspectives in line with the subject. Ultimately the challenge of both equality and diversity is how organisations include and use the complexity and differences of the human family for productive goals whilst ensuring the proper nourishment and growth of the individual. The stories here review what has guided successful interventions in support of equality and diversity management. The chapter looks at the issues from the view of the organisation as a holistic living system rather than exclusively at the human resource function. My belief is that it will help to lay the foundations for understanding some of the practical challenges of pursuing the 'metasystemic' challenge of capabilities equality.

Learning objectives

After studying this chapter you should:

- understand the parameters from which organisations seek intervention;
- be able to match the relevant types of intervention to the appropriate circumstances;
- understand how to make your efforts in supporting diversity more sustainable;
- understand how others have managed to continuously improve diversity management as a habitual part of the pursuit of excellence.

Overall, this chapter should help the reader to develop an understanding of a range of interventions that have been effective in addressing different aspects of diversity challenges.

Key words
organisational access ● social capital ● learning and effectiveness paradigm ● starting organisation ● initiative organisation ● strategic organisation ● Equal Opportunities Quality Foundation (EOQF)

Introduction

In any discussion of equality and diversity management there is a primary need to review definition issues and the scope of our exploration of the subject. This will be set within the context of the approach to this chapter, which is primarily from the experience and observation of a practitioner. The convention of the chapter will not be academic referencing but a mixture of observations and storytelling which are grounded in over 10 years of consultancy with a variety of organisations on the national and international levels. Amongst other issues, we will explore the rationale for organisations to pursue diversity management as an imperative for sustainable success. This will be within the context of the rapid changes in the operating environment and relationships. Furthermore, we will set out the different paradigms from which organisations pursue diversity improvements and interventions. In each paradigm we will explore the following:

- identify the equality and diversity issues that arise within each paradigm, especially around commitment, processes, standards/outputs and results;
- describe different kinds of interventions used to address the issues and how they worked;
- expand on the effects of the intervention with examples of different organisations that have gone through the experience.

In conclusion, we will expand on the pursuit of excellence in equality and diversity and its twists, turns and effects.

Setting the context

Diversity as a 'fundamental principle' of the human condition

The simplest way to describe the challenge of diversity is by posing the question 'How do we harness people's creative energy to achieve individual fulfilment whilst delivering sustainable abundance and prosperity for the organisation?'

Diversity itself is not new but as ancient as life itself. In nature the existence of diversity always represents vitality, balance and success. When we talk of bio-diversity, what we mean is the balance of the spectrum of life necessary to maintain a successful habitat or environment for the long term. In the context of organisations, the dialogue or pursuit of diversity is no different since the focus is on how to engage the unique blend of social, biological and economic identity of each individual to leverage collective success and prosperity. In management, diversity is one of the challenges that will determine those who achieve real long-term value and those who are blips on the screen of excellence.

Rationale

The reasons for the above conclusion are many and varied but all are related to the nature, depth and speed of the changes that all organisations confront. These are illustrated by:

- demographic changes: the age of the average worker (ageing population), more women in work than men, ethnic minorities increasing in the pool of first-time entrants into the labour market;
- the information and technological revolution means that if information is power then everyone can get it in real time;
- the economic links of globalisation and a shift to a knowledge or service economy;
- the increasing benchmarking of organisations on the intangible values of ethics, stakeholder relations and reputation.

The fundamental result of all of these is that formerly marginalised people are becoming actors in both consumption and employment, armed with information to challenge and expect respect or otherwise exercise their choices and rights against institutions and organisations that deny them. In this overall climate the critical asset for management is the 1.3 kilograms of the human brain. It cannot be unlocked by directive or hierarchy management but by managing relationships and engaging individual choice and motivation. Essentially the art of diversity management is that of managing the intangibles. The old way of focusing on outputs and resources or measurable things to the near exclusion of all else is woefully inadequate in a knowledge or service economy. The manufacturing model that has typified the Human

Resource paradigm is increasingly becoming a thing of the past. As Prof. John Kay observed in a recent RSA lecture, 'Today competitive advantage lies in brands and reputation, patents and standards, relations with employees, suppliers and customers.'

Important principles for the practice of equality and diversity management

Diversity-based equality management should work on fundamental values of healthy human relations. Primarily all human beings are ends unto themselves, not resources or means. It also includes the fact that people should be treated the way they want to be treated, not the way we want to be treated. It means, more explicitly, that social capital such as trust and empowerment is woven into the fabric of management; that leadership is no longer a product of position and authority but an attitude that everyone should be able to display; that the pursuit of win–win solutions and achievement of balance are essential goals of management in our service or knowledge paradigm. For the employees it means responsibility and accountability. It means that managers and HR specialists are no longer expected to know all and have all the solutions. For all, the ability to identify who the organisation's customers and employees are, what is important to them, what their requirements are, and what condition produces the desired results for and from them, are questions critical to the achievement of sustained organisation success. Presumptions about 'the normal' or 'average' employee that underpin current marketing and human resource thinking are becoming ineffective. Differences in employee and customer requirements have always been there, but are increasingly coming into prominence in economic life and leading to profound consequences in productivity, innovation and overall effectiveness. The kind of diversity that drives these issues can be reflected in four general spheres:

1. *Individuals.* Every individual is unique. This is reflected in the different goals and work styles of each person, and can be the source of different motivations or, in the case of consumers, different buying requirements and patterns.
2. *Social and biological groups.* This dimension reflects the importance of different group identities, such as gender differences, ethnic differences and general cultural differences. These differences do not depict superiority or inferiority but essentially survival and prosperity strategies developed in different environments.
3. *Professional and vocational backgrounds.* This dimension covers professional and vocational orientations, including differences in technical language, competencies and general approach to problem solving. Professions such as lawyers, accountants and doctors, amongst others, foster their own cultures and perspectives that shape individual members, their choices and behaviour.

4. *Organisations.* Sector, functions and values that define the culture of organisations and have substantial impact on the individuals that work within them shape this dimension. These different dimensions are mixed in different proportions and dynamics in every individual and in each transaction. In essence, the challenge of diversity management is to create a climate that optimises the contribution of everyone for the collective prosperity of the organisation.

These four dimensions in different combinations shape and condition every person's goals and the approach they take to achieving them. It is therefore important that organisations engage the diversity of people constructively at all four levels. Doing this successfully will result in a positive impact on the following three areas:

1. *Reputation.* An acceptance that the organisation is perceived to be passionate, ethical and committed to the respectful and inclusive treatment of people, both inside and outside the organisation, helps to update the brand in terms of awareness and affinity. It also makes the organisation an employer of choice.
2. *Relationships.* An understanding and inclusive approach to people creates healthy and sustainable relationships with all stakeholders, mainly employees, management, customers, suppliers and the wider community. This increases productivity, innovation and problem solving. It reduces staff turnover and conflict and retains the loyalty of all stakeholders.
3. *Results.* These show the effect of the diversity process on the bottom-line performance indicators of the organisation, and how diversity initiatives are effective in achieving the overall financial or non-financial results for the organisation.

Paradigms and interventions in equality and diversity management

There are three well-observed paradigms that most organisations determined to address challenges in diversity go through:

1. The first is the starting level, which focuses on compliance and a reactive response to diversity issues. It is usually driven by moral and legal imperatives and the main focus of the paradigm is anti-discrimination.
2. The *initiative level* or **access and legitimacy paradigm** is the positive action level of diversity interventions. It is usually driven by the business case, but is limited by focusing on initiatives to improve access for marginalised groups and individuals. It generally means that the initiatives can ultimately provide access to niche markets.
3. The *strategic* or **learning and effectiveness paradigm** focuses on diversity as part of the organisation's journey of learning and continuous improvement. It is usually driven by the recognition that leveraging internal and external diversity is an essential competence for a healthy organisation that pursues excellence as part of its overall culture.

At each level, attempts will be made to identify the key issues to be addressed, supported with illustrations and examples of what other organisations do.

The starting organisation

The starting organisation would typically approach the subject of equality and diversity from a reactive standpoint. This standpoint would be based on legislative developments and would, therefore, be compliance-driven. Changes in equal opportunities legislation can be targeted at specific industries and sectors. For example, in the UK, due to recent changes to the Race Relations Act, it is the public sector that is required to respond and change policy prior to changes in the commercial sector. Any change would be in response to meeting minimum requirements. A key characteristic of the compliance-driven approach is that changes and developments external to the organisation generally drive intervention, as opposed to an internally identified need as part of a review of relationships. These external forces would probably be translated into an apprehension about non-compliance and its consequences for the organisation.

The key challenges

There are usually three key challenges for the starting organisation:

1. gaining the interest and commitment of leaders to the need for equality and diversity interventions;
2. engaging wider ownership of equality and diversity improvements in the organisation;
3. increasing employees' competence to interact and deal with equality and diversity in their everyday transactions.

These three areas, covering commitment, ownership and competence, are essential for organisations at any stage of development. Commitment from a senior level is extremely important, as any change will only be effective or sustainable with input or acceptance from those at senior level. The wider ownership of equality and diversity should be sought in order to ensure the practical implementation of change strategies or initiatives. The next step is to increase the competence of those within the organisation to have a positive and sustainable impact on planned developments.

Addressing the challenges

To address the challenge of commitment, it is useful to be able to identify different types of influences and who holds them. It can be helpful to use the following analysis of those who are influential or likely to be affected by the introduction of a diversity agenda. Essentially these are people whose support can be critical to your agenda. They will generally fall into the following four categories:

1. *Those who want to succeed, but will do nothing to aid you.* These are generally people who support the principles of diversity but are unable or unwilling to actively engage either because they are too busy, they are risk averse or it does not fit within their priorities.
2. *Those who want to succeed and will aid you.* These are often individuals who are risk takers, share the same priorities or are dissatisfied with the status quo for either personal or professional reasons.
3. *Those who want you to fail but will not actively block you.* These are often sceptical about the relevance or utility of diversity and might even perceive it as a distant threat or unwanted distraction from 'real issues'. They are not, however, sufficiently concerned to become active barriers.
4. *Those who want you to fail and will actively challenge/go against your efforts.*

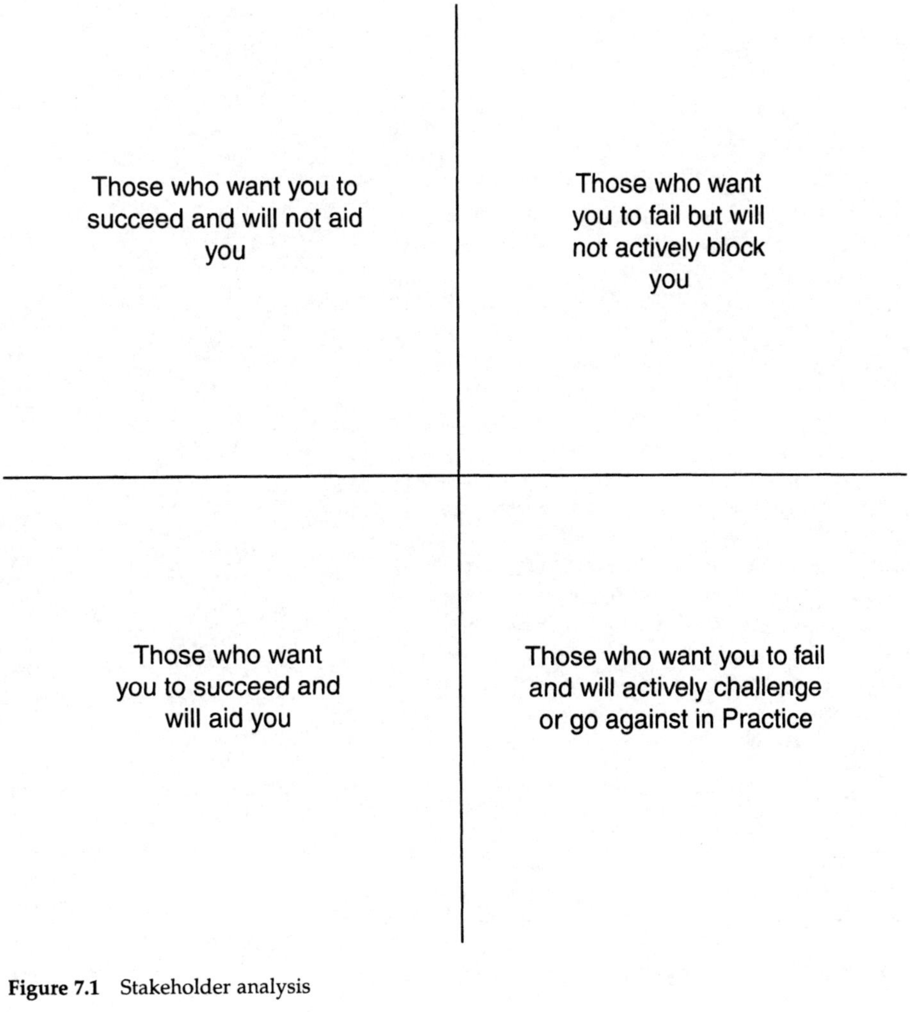

Those who want you to succeed and will not aid you	Those who want you to fail but will not actively block you
Those who want you to succeed and will aid you	Those who want you to fail and will actively challenge or go against in Practice

Figure 7.1 Stakeholder analysis

These are likely to be those who are about to benefit from the status quo and are directly challenged by what they perceive to be unwarranted change. Sometimes it is because of a perception that diversity is about positive discrimination. It is likely that they perceive diversity as a direct personal or professional threat.

All these descriptions are illustrative of different mindsets which are fluid and can change relative to the information that is available. It is important to understand that commitment is a never-ending journey of improvement and what you are trying to establish is a current snapshot of key individuals that you want to influence.

Case study illustration: the challenge of the industrial tribunal

The HR director of a multinational manufacturing company recently took on the challenge of diversity after a particularly bruising employment tribunal loss. Her goal as laid down by the Board subcommittee on employee relations was to do everything necessary to make the organisation 'bullet-proof' from future litigation. In taking on the challenge she was keen to bring in the diversity ideas from her recent Masters programme. Her first concern was around her conversation with the Managing Director, whose assumption was that all that was required was that their personnel procedures and practices should treat every employee in the same way and there would be no problems in future. She had recently spoken at a staff meeting and was surprised at the aggressive reaction she received from colleagues on the executive board against the idea of dealing in a more conscious way with the issue of diversity management. She had been asked by the Board of Directors to submit a plan of action that would address the issues raised from the tribunal case. However, the tribunal case occurred because the financial director, like most other senior managers, treated personnel procedures as nuisances which stood in the way of efficient management. She knew that this time their active support would be essential to the success of any plan of action. Using the tool set out above, she tried to develop a plan to win commitment from her colleagues.

Her first step was an **ideastorm** with interested members of her team of key stakeholders, followed by analysis of where in the four quadrants she thought they were at that moment. She then used her personal knowledge and the wider interest of committed members of her team to identify the drivers and barriers of each group of stakeholders. They covered the following:

1. They analysed the interest and concerns of the key players about equal opportunities/diversity.
2. They identified the best ways to address the concerns and communicate with the stakeholders.
3. They then tested out assumptions with a small group of stakeholders from each group.

The process led her to develop different campaigns for each of the four groups, which formed part of the first step in her action plan.

This analysis provided essential information in deciding who might take a positive approach to addressing developments in equality and diversity. A presentation of the envisaged benefits of adopting equality and diversity practices also helped in gaining wider interest. For example, she quantified the cost of the tribunal case and the unit cost of lost trained staff, which showed that the company could make substantial savings from keeping its trained staff. On the other hand, she was also able to show that by adopting a more people- or relationship-centred management policy the company was more likely to adapt to the climate in which it needed more intelligent and cross-functional working on the shop-floor. This interested key members of the executive team and she was able to get agreement for a training programme for all managers.

Traditionally, when training is agreed by the executive board it is mandated that employees attend; however, this needed to be approached differently. This was because any effective equality and diversity training will ask questions about participants' values and socialisation which are in effect very personal. In this particular case the agenda was set by the Board of Directors who essentially wanted a sea-change in the way the organisation responded to the overall subject. In fact they were willing to pilot the first training themselves.

The training project raised old and new questions for the HR Director and her team of staff. They had to engage a higher level of interest and commitment. To request people to set aside time and participate in training events is difficult at the best of times and in this case more so because even where employees wanted the commitment to diversity and equality to be improved they baulked at dedicating their direct time or efforts. There was also the issue of designing a training programme that balanced what the organisation wanted with the things that would engage individual interest. There was also the problem of delivering an event that would address rights and obligations under the law and company policy without opening the floodgates to complaints and allegations, and the ever-present challenge of training 5000 employees on a limited budget especially when there was very limited in-house expertise to carry out training in the subject.

The first thing was to address the issue of interest and involvement. The Managing Director agreed to introduce the idea of the project in his monthly letter to employees and invite volunteers from every department to be part of a steering group for the project. The members of this group were to work with HR on the successful development, implementation and review of the training. The request contained details such as the time commitment and qualities needed for effective participation. In the event that a full complement of eight volunteers was not achieved, their colleagues would nominate individuals. The required number of nominations was achieved and in fact oversubscribed.

The first activity was to have a planning meeting where efforts were made to identify the goals that such a training project should attempt to achieve. The group agreed with the HR representatives that there was a need to review the training needs of the employees and to use this opportunity to collect information about general expectations and concerns to build up indicators that would be used to measure the success of the project. They agreed to use focus group meetings facilitated by members of the group to get more information about the training to other employees and to collect information that would help tailor the programme. The focus groups were very successful in generating interest and wider involvement and in fact they built up an expectation of partnership through the life of the project. One of the products from the group was a detailed specification, which was used to recruit training consultants who

helped develop a programme, trained the board and cascaded the programme by training internal trainers from within the organisation. In the next six months every member of staff was encouraged and prepared to join a programme that covered the basic rights and obligations of diversity and equality, its relevance to the company's business goals and the processes for translating the principles into reality. Part of the work of the steering group was to use information gathered through focus groups to develop the indicators of measuring success. These indicators included post-course questionnaires, on-the-job review through the appraisal system and a full six-month assessment of all the information collected by the steering group, with a report to be presented by the managing director to the board.

Effects and lessons

The overall effects of the intervention were to set out clearly the level of commitment the organisation had to the challenge of equality and diversity and, more importantly, to address the issue of vicarious liability in a qualitative and sustainable manner. The training especially helped to introduce the knowledge, skills and attitudes required to translate the commitment into daily action. However the most critical aspect was the process of intervention, combining leadership, particularly from the HR director and the board of directors, with the partnership developed to embrace the wider organisation in responding to this challenge. There were key tactics that helped to move things forward:

- analysing the motivation of key stakeholders for supporting or rejecting diversity, especially where all four dimensions are reviewed for different strands of drivers or barriers;
- engaging the managing director's support in promoting the training;
- setting up a steering group of different departments and sections of the organisation;
- involving the wider organisation in setting the agenda through the use of focus groups;
- using the board to pilot the training as a way of showing leadership;
- reviewing through the existing and accepted appraisal system.

Overall, the organisation like any other starting one, has just begun a journey and both commitment and the intervention to implement it are a never-ending cycle.

The initiative organisation

The initiative organisation is one that moves beyond compliance with the law towards recognising the benefits to both the individual and the organisation of improving and increasing access to a wider diversity of employees or customers. This often means that there are targeted initiatives, which are taken in conjunction with legislation to address any imbalances in workforce make-up or access to a segment of the marketplace. The organisation signs up to many initiatives from both the moral and organisational perspectives. These initiatives may be used as ways to achieve fast results for the organisation or as ways in which the organisation can be recognised as demonstrating its commitment to diversity. The initiative organisation does not have a cohesive and strategic direction that focuses and harnesses the initiatives to other processes in the organisation. There is often little linkage of equality and diversity to the organisation's vision, mission or strategic objectives and therefore, no definition of how equality and diversity activities can directly impact on the goals of the organisation. The Human Resources and corporate promotion functions mainly drive the equality and diversity developments.

The key challenges

There are four key challenges for the initiative organisation:

1. the role of leadership in extending diversity beyond the Human Resources function;
2. making existing initiatives widely accepted and understood within the organisation;
3. making current and new initiatives contribute to the goals of the organisation;
4. coordinating activities in a manner that integrates them into other improvement activities within the organisation.

Addressing the challenges

The key intervention has to be about translating individual initiatives into those that have relevance to the wider goals of the organisation. The key areas are in the setting of criteria for the choice of initiative, the setting of discernible indicators of success, regular and timely review of progress, the collection of information on impact and the integration of the learning into mainstream processes. The ever-present issue of commitment is also relevant in a different guise, especially around the integration of lessons and goals of diversity and equality into mainstream processes.

Case study illustration: diversity and equality management integrity during difficult economic times

A national bank had recently recruited a new CEO to improve the profitability of its core operation. He had shared his view that the primary focus of his tenure would be to reduce costs and gain competitive advantage by delivering the best quality service at the lowest possible cost. He set clear cost reduction targets for all departments but he took a different approach with equality and diversity programmes because the bank had a widely known reputation as a key supporter of many national initiatives in this area. In fact it had a senior executive responsible for diversity who was already an established legend within the organisation. In addition, he was aware of the success of recent initiatives to target Asian businesses which had increased market share in many inner city branches. He was also very concerned to maintain the wider influence that the commitment to equality and diversity appeared to give the organisation. His overall cost-cutting goals being paramount, he could not be seen to cut jobs and not cut initiatives, as there could not be any sacred cows. The planned reduction to the workforce had already led to a letter from the minority ethnic network of the bank raising concerns that if the current criterion of the last employee recruited being the first out were applied, all the gains in numbers of minority staff recruited would be lost. For these and many other reasons he decided to review the current range of diversity initiatives with the goal of reducing the numbers and thereby the overall cost.

His challenges were to do the following:

- Win support in the executive board for a different approach to cutting diversity expenditure.
- Retain and sharpen existing commitments.
- Make the diversity initiatives work better for the organisation.

His first step was to reassure the head of diversity management by discussing with her the way to proceed in order to maintain the integrity of the bank's commitment whilst reducing cost. She understood that he had to be seen not to favour any department and was grateful for the sensitivity being shown to her area. They were agreed on a review of initiatives and also concurred about the need for such a review to be perceived as transparent and independent. The next step was to work with the executive team who by and large had invested time and energy over several years to support the diver-

sity initiatives. Their discussion was most productive and led to a set of criteria to be used to identify initiatives to keep and those to cut. They also agreed that it was worthwhile to get an independent consultant to conduct this review and to advise on the alternative ways of keeping staff diversity in spite of the job reductions.

The criteria suggested were:

- initiatives should be compatible with the strategic goals of the bank;
- they should be in furtherance of existing diversity policy;
- they should explicitly add value to the direct targets of that year's business plan;
- the outputs from such initiatives should be both cost effective and in line with expectation;
- there must be an exit strategy for translating such initiatives into wider use.

A panel with representation from the five diversity networks and an executive team member recruited the consultant, who set out a process whereby the rationale, process, measures and implementation of each initiative was to be reviewed against evidence submitted by each programme's champion. This was followed by interviewing of the customers of the initiative. The final analysis was done against the criteria set out by the executive committee and interim and final reports were produced. On staff reduction, discussions and consultations were held with trades unions and the networks.

Effects and lessons

The review was completed and the accompanying report led to a widely agreed 50 per cent cost cutting and a reduction in the number of initiatives from 18 to 7. The seven initiatives remaining were fitted into the existing strategic objectives within the bank's business plan. In the area of job reduction, criteria were set to focus on jobs where the fit with core business was not established and the tactic was to pursue voluntary redundancy and natural wastage before looking for compulsory cuts. In effect, the organisation had transformed what appeared to be a looming end for its equality and diversity agenda into a way to refocus efforts and renew commitment. The key elements that led to the success of the intervention were:

- the new CEO's leadership and commitment to leveraging the current benefits of diversity;
- the willingness to look for creative solutions;
- the effort to find business justification for retaining diversity initiatives;
- the use of an evidence-based and transparent review to decide what survived;

- partnership with stakeholders.

For the first time, the organisation now had indicators to judge diversity outcomes in the same way as any other business commitment and this took their agenda to another level.

The strategic organisation

The strategic organisation has surpassed the starting and initiative levels. There is a clear vision of where the organisation wants to be and how equality and diversity activities contribute to these goals. Throughout the organisation, there is collective ownership of equality and diversity, where every individual is accountable for progressing and developing activities. The role of equality and diversity is regularly reviewed and directly and explicitly linked to business results (both financial and non-financial) and accomplishments achieved as a result of activities undertaken. Equality and diversity is recognised as a major contributor to business success and is integrated into the planning process, management thinking at all levels and working practices throughout the organisation.

The key challenges

There are three key challenges for the strategic organisation:

1. sustaining diversity development through continuous improvement;
2. showing that the diversity agenda contributes to the business goals of the organisation;
3. diversity is part of the habitual behaviour or culture of the organisation.

Addressing the challenge

The main method of diversity intervention on the strategic level that I use is the Equal Opportunities Quality Framework (EOQF). The Framework is a non-prescriptive system that I was instrumental in developing and testing to support organisations in reviewing and developing a strategic approach to the challenge of equality and diversity as part of their overall journey to excellence.

It provides a structure for identifying key priorities and issues, a process for reviewing progress and identifying gaps, and sets standards for recognising achievements. The EOQF is an internationally recognised benchmarking system for diversity and equality. It is based on the EFQM Excellence Model, providing a structure for reviewing and improving equality and diversity performance in order that it is sustainable and integrated within the overall dialogue of excellence in organisations. It rigorously examines the commitment, planning, resourcing and delivery practices. It seeks to identify the

Box 7.1 EOQF criteria

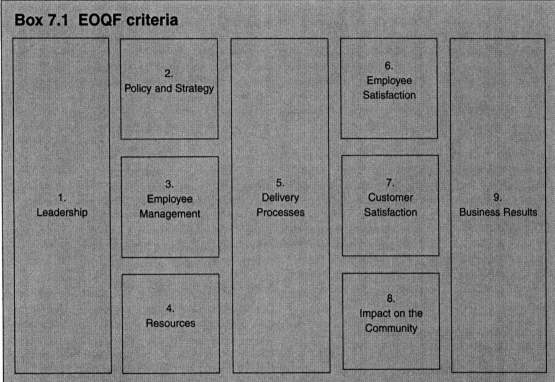

1. **Leadership:** How managers and all employees in team leadership roles inspire and drive continuous improvement in equality.
2. **Policy and strategy:** How senior management incorporates the values and concepts of equality in the determination, communication, review and improvement of the policy and strategy of the organisation.
3. **Employee management:** How the full potential of people is released.
4. **Resources:** How the organisation improves its management, utilisation and preservation of its resources, including financial information, materials and technological resources, in an equitable way.
5. **Delivery processes:** How the organisation identifies, reviews and if necessary, revises all key and support processes to ensure continuous improvement in equality.
6. **Employee satisfaction:** The perception and feelings of its people within the organisation. What are the successes in satisfying all their respective needs and expectations and using their diversity?
7. **Customer satisfaction:** The perception of customers of the organisation and its services. What are the successes in satisfying the needs and expectations of all customers and gaining new ones that reflect the diversity of the marketplace?
8. **Impact on the community:** How senior management incorporates the values and concepts of equality in the determination, communication, review and improvement of the impact on society of the organisation.
9. **Business results:** The organisation's achievements in relation to its planned performance and the results of all key internal processes. This is especially true with regard to the contribution of equality.

Case study illustration: using the EOQF in a government agency

As a government agency charged with the placement of the long-term unemployed into jobs and post-16 vocational education, the agenda for diversity as part of its daily operation was one to which this organisation was committed. The board had made considerable investment in the training of its staff and had been active in key national initiatives in the area of equality and diversity. The organisation had a diversity strategy as part of its overall HR plan and had done for over five years. A new government agenda on diversity had recently been set out, requiring targets to be met on the achievement of recruitment and retention of diverse staff. Whilst the board was quietly confident that it could achieve these targets, evidence from the annual staff survey suggested that staff were becoming sceptical of the organisation's effort in this area. The board vision to be exemplary in the field of diversity was beginning to be perceived as just warm words. A committee was set up to review ways in which the achievements of the many years' effort on diversity could be captured and benchmarked against other organisations. They were especially keen to review how inclusive their culture was and establish what could be done to improve future performance.

The committee received a presentation on the EOQF methodology and were persuaded as to its relevance to their needs for the following reasons:

- The organisation was already using the Excellence model to drive business improvement.
- The EOQF process enabled their staff to conduct the assessment of the organisation whilst acquiring new skills.
- The selected assessors from within the organisation would retain the capacity to continue improvements in the future.
- The organisation could benchmark, using the information from its assessment, against national and international contemporaries.
- Their review of other users showed they were able to link their efforts to improvement in processes and sometime results.

The organisation decided to proceed with an EOQF assessment and each region selected a couple of people who were duly trained as assessors. On completion of their training they laid out a plan to capture available evidence for each of the criteria. They chose to use a mixture of document review, interviews, focus groups and surveys to establish the current methods and practices of the organisation. This analysis was not done in isolation but with the active support of their colleagues in their respective regions. A comprehensive and impressive array of evidence was then analysed to fit the different factors of the Framework. This analysis was used to conduct the scoring and assessment detailing the strengths and the areas for improvement. At the end of the scoring workshop the current level of development of diversity in the organisation was evaluated against the different band descriptions of the EOQF. The overall results of this process were then written up as a factual report of the findings and submitted to the board to accept or reject as a true reflection of the current systems and practices. This was duly approved and copies were sent to every region for them to use in integrating future diversity activities into their business plans. The report was used by the board to inform its five-year strategic plan.

Effects and lessons

The assessment process developed a network of change agents in the organisation who were now armed with objective evidence about the organisation's systems and practices and the effect they were having. Fundamentally, the organisation for the first time had information about the inclusiveness of its culture from the perspective of all its stakeholders and an analysis of its processes. This information was critical to its benchmarking efforts since it provided a baseline for its dialogue with others and improvement action within the organisation.

The board now used the information gathered to set a clear set of strategic priorities (four) which covered the following:

- developing diversity competencies for management;
- integrating diversity objectives into every level of planning from personal to national;
- leveraging the lessons of effective diversity improvements into mainstream processes;
- timely, transparent and relevant reviews of the activities in diversity.

The fact that considerable financial and human

resources were allocated to these priorities sent out a signal of clarity and commitment. The fact that the process of management competence development and individual objective setting would affect nearly everyone in all local offices also shaped the response in a positive context. Most importantly, this was integrated into existing processes for everyday management. In effect, the organisation tackled the scepticism emerging from its staff whilst positioning itself to take on the diversity challenges from an intelligence-driven and strategic viewpoint which allows diversity to be a crucial aspect of its journey towards excellence.

The EOQF report also identified that quite a few regions had already exceeded the targets set by the government and it was possible to connect these achievements to specific local initiatives. This led to an internal benchmarking network to share processes with regions currently underachieving. Perhaps more importantly, the information resulting from the assessment led to the development of the first set of performance indicators informed by intelligence and based on realistic analysis or expectation of developments over the action planning period.

Overall, the organisation had developed a process to merge its diversity commitments into its business priorities efficiently whilst renewing partnership with its employees and other stakeholders in order that it could fulfil its performance objectives with integrity.

quality of the diversity and equality content of these management processes, which are titled the enabling factors. Furthermore, it reviews the consequences on all the potential bottom lines of the organisation, which are consequences to employees, customers, the wider community and business results to establish the quality and depth of progress made.

Conclusions

Within these conclusions it is also important to address the issue of the capabilities model and the dialogue on differences between equality and diversity.

Sen's capabilities theory is a very clear and improved way of showing the effect or dynamic of exclusion and its nuances. It has a greater explanatory capacity than a lot of the preceding positions on social exclusion. For a start, it is flexible enough to accommodate the variety of exclusionary experience in different countries and sophisticated enough to make allowances for individual choice. It has an excellent explanatory capacity in how it is possible for those living in a materially better off context can still experience the injustice of the limitation of opportunities in a way that still reduces dignity in a profound manner. However, in its essence of focusing on the exclusionary context of the diversity and equality experience it appears to fall into the trap of focusing on the limitation of freedom rather than celebrating its presence. This in effect means that there is a presumption that there are universal standards for the level of capability that is ideal. If this premise were accepted then whose standard would be used to judge? It might be argued by some that the UN Human Development Index is too Western in orientation. Furthermore, the capability theory can appear on first viewing to be rather linear and therefore its explanatory value for a complex phenomenon with a multi-layered dynamic such as diversity bears more detailed scrutiny. Finally, its focus on apparent choices and limitation does not reflect fully the capacity for individuals to make seemingly illogical sacrifices for no obvious reason.

In the context of effective interventions within organisations the capability theory will be an exceptionally useful framework to use in reviewing the quality of stakeholder experience before, during and after intervention. It can also be an integral aspect of a continuous improvement system. It raises the prospect that in a framework such as the EOQF, capability can be used to review employee and customer satisfaction criteria. In a smaller pattern such as the culture of an organisation it provides very useful intelligence regarding relationships and customs, especially the effect on people's opportunities.

It is worthwhile adding to earlier stated challenges to the presumed dichotomy between equal opportunities and diversity management. In a recent workshop that I held, the CEO of a company remarked on his reluctance or hesitation in wholehearted commitment to diversity rather than what he called anti-discrimination. He raised two very relevant issues (amongst many others): (1) diversity is a watering down of clear commitment to anti-discrimination and the uncomfortable questions it raises; (2) it spreads the intervention to remedy things too widely for any measurable or discernible change. Whilst I understand and sympathise with the concern, I feel that emphasising the dichotomy between equality and diversity is misguided for the following reasons:

- Diversity management is not a new technique or fad but an essential and ever-present part of healthy and sustainable relationships.
- Equal opportunities and diversity management are interdependent and can barely function one without the other since the ridicule of treating everyone the same will make equal opportunities a caricature of unrealistic clichés, and diversity management without recognition of the ethics and transparency demanded in equal opportunities will perpetuate existing injustices.
- Whilst diversity management is complex and intangible, its current renaissance is due to the real needs of the knowledge and service economy to address the challenge of managing the complexity of many intangibles in today's workplace.
- The fixation on anti-discrimination exclusively becomes the equivalent of confusing auditing and fraud detection as the summary of a financial system, thereby ignoring processes such as budget setting or cash flow forecasting.
- The real effect of targeting so-called disadvantaged groups exclusively is to institutionalise victim status and generate an undercurrent of backlash and belligerence towards the subject.

Overall, whether you label the efforts as equal opportunities or diversity is not critical to effective intervention in this area, so long as the essence is owned and understood by those people who are likely to be affected by it.

Effective intervention is therefore about clarity of thought, vision and direction, complemented by dogged determination to progress and a willingness to learn from past and current efforts. Perhaps most importantly, it is about a committee of minds and a fellowship of purpose.

In the end, in order to intervene effectively in the furtherance of equality, certain principles appear to work well on all levels.

- Comfort with the subject and its complexity, especially the fact that all the paradoxes do not need to be resolved, nor should they be reconciled. This should be complemented with a conscious incompetence or acknowledging limitation of individual knowledge (contrasted with the vastness of the subject).
- Engaging stakeholders in a dialogue and ownership of the what, why and how of the equality and diversity journey.
- An open mind about the many possible viewpoints and answers that will emerge, especially embracing the deviant voices and restraining judgements.
- Leadership that creates an inclusive space for the exploration of the pain, conflict, contradictions and pleasures of the change that are embodied in diversity management.
- A credible authority figure that disturbs equilibrium and assumptions.
- A continuous process of learning and improvement.
- Clarity about what success would look like and a rigorous examination of distance travelled.

There are no guarantees in intervention efforts, but they often deepen insight, increase foresight and improve judgement.

Text-based questions

1. What role can diversity play in the efforts to achieve organisational goals?
2. What are the key drivers for successful intervention to improve diversity?
3. How can relationships with stakeholders help or hinder diversity intervention?
4. What are the key characteristics of the strategic-level paradigm ?
5. What are the keys to achieving wider ownership and commitment to diversity intervention?
6. How does adaptive challenge differ from technical challenge?

Library and assignment-based questions

1. You are a consultant to a multinational enterprise that spans the EU and the United States, with a mandate to develop a plan for creating a diversity policy through wider dialogue and eventual ownership of employees, union, management and shareholders. In developing this plan you are to highlight your approach to engaging each group of stakeholders and winning their interest. Furthermore, you are to review the legal obligations in two countries in the EU and their implication for such a plan.
2. Examine and review submissions by any three organisations for a quality award system such as the EFQM Excellence Award (EU), Baldrige Award

(USA), Investors in People (UK), SIQ (Sweden) or the Deming Award (Japan) to critically evaluate how it reflects the organisations' approach to diversity. How integrated is the diversity agenda within the quality efforts and what changes can you make to improve it?

3. Review and evaluate the diversity policies of three public sector organisations and critically assess what paradigm they reflect and how they are likely to work in helping each organisation achieve its overall performance goals. Recommend improvements, giving reasons for each one.

4. Using an organisation of your choice, develop a case for the added value of equality and diversity management in adapting to a frequently changing operating environment.

Further reading

What I have related is very much a 'reflective practitioner' perspective, in which I have attempted to describe, reflect on and evaluate different kinds of practice in relation to managing workplace equality and diversity in whole organisation interventions.

Readings that I have found personally useful and that have informed my understanding of practice include:

Heifetz, RA (1994) *Leadership Without Easy Answers*, Harvard University Press, Cambridge, MA.

Pascale, RT (1981) *The Art of Japanese Management*, Simon & Schuster, USA.

Pascale, R, Milleman M and Gioja, L (2000) *Surfing the Edge of Chaos: The Laws of Nature and the New Laws of Business*, Texere Publishing, New York.

The following are also particularly useful:

Johnston, WB and Packer, AH (1987) *Workforce 2000: Work and Workers for the 21st Century*, The Hudson Institute, Indianapolis.

Ross, R and Schneider, R (1992). *From Equality to Diversity: A Business Case for Equal Opportunities*, Pitman.

Thomas, DA and Ely, RJ (1996) Making differences matter: a new paradigm for managing diversity. *Harvard Business Review*, Sepember–October, 79–90.

Thomas, Jr RR (1996) *Redefining diversity*, Amacom, New York.

Thomas, Jr RR (1993) From affirmative action to affirming diversity, in M Gentile (ed.) *Differences at Work*, Harvard Business Books, MA.

Thomas, DA and Ely, RJ (1996) Making differences matter: a new paradigm for managing diversity. *Harvard Business Review*, September–October, 79–80.

Stakeholder perspectives: a personal account of an equality and diversity practitioner's intervention experiences

Shaun Todd

Introduction

Sharing experiences of practice

This personal case study is based on my experience as an equality and diversity specialist – and specifically, an equal opportunities-centred diversity specialist, manager and general human resource practitioner. As a case study, it is not a 'theory piece': though theory is important, I am a practitioner, not an academic, and it is experiences that I wish to reflect upon and relate. Towards the end of the case, I do make reference briefly to academic concepts that have helped me understand my experience more fully. The main purpose of the case is as a vehicle to capture and share some of my experiences in a number of areas, which, I hope, has the potential to be useful as an 'on the ground' account, to academics, practitioners and students.

My approach is that of a *reflective practitioner*[1] – reflecting on and making sense of my own practice, which I see as important in developing equality and diversity within organisations. I would be wrong to say that all of my interventions were clear successes or that all of the **stakeholders** were happy with the processes or outcomes. However, there have been successes, and reflecting on difficulties and 'what went wrong' is as important as 'what went well'.

Towards the end of this personal case study, I have made a limited number of links with concepts presented elsewhere in the text (which are cross-referenced for the reader's convenience) and I have introduced one or two others as well. Some of these, such as *force-field analysis*, will be well known to both practitioners and academics alike and will hopefully provide a ready hook on which to position the reader's understanding. Others, such as Terry

Horne's recent work on the constructs of *lust and fear in workgroups*, are less well known, but I think really useful.

Finally, as reflections on my work to date, I realise that the 'capabilities equality' dimension has not informed much beyond my most recent work, but I have been surprised at how much of my practice is consistent with it. However, I do genuinely believe that a capabilities approach both challenges and goes beyond what is often regarded as best practice and ongoing practice. Certainly, I realise that a capabilities approach has the potential to be a much more demanding basis for equality and diversity interventions. In the light of this, I have first developed my case study by building on the foundations of past experiences, and I was pleased at how capabilities thinking helped to shed new light on many of these. Second, I have reflected on past conversations, the 'voices' of the stakeholders who are involved in equality and diversity issues: an approach that sits well with the 'multi-voiced' position of capabilities equality. Finally, I have reflected on what are the likely implications for practitioners of capabilities equality, what is more likely to be highlighted and, importantly, what I believe practitioners will need to do differently.

Key themes

For the reader, key themes permeate this case study that are important and relate to other concepts in previous chapters:

- fears of stakeholders;
- authentic conversations;
- loss of advantage of opportunity;
- managers' people management competence that can hide diversity or bring ignorance into the spotlight;
- rationing of opportunity – accountability of opportunity given or not given to staff;
- fear and uncertainty of the unknown;
- how equality and diversity are likely to change the psychological contract;
- how managers feel people see them and the decisions they make;
- managers feeling ready to take on board diversity – personnel expecting it;
- the concerns of the majority group, which many are not willing to talk about, but which are very real – including equality etiquette and fear of loss of advantage;
- having 'bad' behaviour exposed (blame culture) – how you manage people's mistakes in an environment of learning rather than resorting to past negative experiences;
- the role of the interventionist in understanding fear of blame and managing it with care;
- no fear is too small to pay attention to, and past negative experience can sow seeds of fear in the present.

A variety of stakeholders and their conversations

I have highlighted my involvement with different stakeholders and in particular, my experience of, and perspectives on, their views, anxieties and achievements. I have drawn upon a range of issues to illustrate a number of the practical difficulties that I have encountered regularly, as well as those that were illuminating for myself as well as the stakeholders involved.

I have reflected on conversations I have had that have given me insight into the stakeholders' world and their common understanding (as opposed to the policy and practice rhetoric in relation to equality and diversity issues).

The stakeholders I have included in this case study are:

- senior managers;
- middle managers;
- line managers;
- 'majority' staff;
- 'minority' staff and their families;
- candidates;
- suppliers;
- communities;
- the personnel professional/specialist;
- employee representatives and trades unions.

I include the themes that occur in their conversation that I will relate to you and, as a practitioner, why these themes are important.

By sharing my experiences, I hope to help the reader gain a clearer understanding of the challenges facing those who want to get their ideas, policies and strategies into action.

Finally, at the end of the case study, I will share my reflections on my work to date, and how in the future my work and those of other practitioners in the field may need to change, if a more 'capabilities centred' approach to addressing workforce equality and diversity is to be pursued.

The stakeholder conversations

Senior managers

Concerns and fears

In the past I have tried to get board commitment for equality and diversity programmes, but it can be a difficult and slow conversion! If I was fortunate, perhaps one member of the board would be a champion, but this was not always the case.

From my experience, I believe that senior managers' reluctance is not down to believing it should not be done, but rather through fear. Typical fears included the cost of introducing equality and diversity initiatives and the anxiety that shareholders may question how diversity initiatives are going to improve performance and bottom line benefits. They may also be concerned about how existing customers will react to new initiatives; also, the fear that equality and diversity will take effort and perhaps time and resources away from productivity or other functions. There may also have been the fear that the initiatives would not really have a positive impact on the bottom line.

Under the spotlight

While these fears may be valid, my experience suggests a different factor – senior managers championing the cause will be under the spotlight. They feel uncomfortable with this, particularly as they will be seen as a role model and it may be difficult to live up to expectations. This makes sense to me when I consider that your average senior manager is not an equality and diversity 'expert'. I also have experience of senior managers bowing to boardroom peer pressure and feeling uncomfortable in championing 'people' initiatives of any kind.

I gave various types of evidence to senior management teams on the business benefits and examples from other organisations' success. However, tackling the fear of individuals was not as easy.

Support or expertise?

As an 'expert' and champion of equality and diversity, I needed to help my senior colleagues realise that it was their support to the process and initiatives that was required and not necessarily their expertise in the subject (or lack of it). I could not expect all my senior managers to understand all the issues but I could help to 'educate' and develop them so they increased their expertise and therefore confidence in the subject.

Top team 'champions' – organisational symbolism

Often I found it was a senior manager's name on a project that benefited equality and diversity, because the manager sees the project as important rather than for what skills and experience s/he can bring to it. An example of this was seen in one of the organisations I worked for. The finance director was prepared to support some equality and diversity initiatives. Many were sceptical, as the individual concerned had not been known for his innovation in tackling equality and diversity issues. However, he was a powerful figure in the organisation. He attended my meetings and although he did not contribute from a theoretical or practical viewpoint, his presence and name on the minutes sent a very positive message to others; to staff – that the board was not just showing lip service, and to managers – that they should follow his example. I think I achieved his commitment by reassuring this particular director that he was not going to be expected to know all the answers, and that he was not going to be put on the spot and made to look foolish.

Equality and diversity as 'ethical conduit'

I found that one overlooked benefit of an equality and diversity initiative is often as an ethical conduit. Many organisations want to do more work on their ethical approaches. Equality and diversity can help facilitate ethical actions. A business manager I knew was charged with creating an ethical framework for the organisation. She found that the Equality Foundation's Equal Opportunities Quality Framework gave the key catalyst for her ethical framework, particularly those indicators looking at the community and suppliers.

Middle managers

I found these managers often had the hard task of taking initiatives from their managers as ideas only, and found it difficult to make it happen: line managers often needed a lot of convincing!

Priorities and avoidance

I have experienced many fears from middle managers about equality and diversity, and I have found them the hardest to convince of the benefits. I found a key difficulty is that the middle manager may have a hundred and one other initiatives to deal with and the equality and diversity one may be seen as low priority. The 'too busy' screen may also hide the fear that the managers are well aware there are problems and do not want initiatives that will highlight issues they feel would be best kept under wraps. Many managers I have had contact with feel the whole equality and diversity 'thing' is too difficult to tackle. This is often because it involves people, and middle managers see their subordinate line managers as those who do the 'people' things.

Pivotal role of the middle manager: gaining interest and commitment

I found that if middle managers can be got 'on board' they could be a very powerful influence to all in the organisation. This is illustrated by the case of a manager who rang me when I was working as an internal consultant on equality and diversity. He rang to tell me that the company harassment and EO policy was useless. This was after I had been in the job six weeks! I agreed there could be some improvement and asked if I could visit him to discuss it. He was taken aback, because, as a middle manager, he had never been asked for his opinion/input/evaluation of any of the equality and diversity initiatives.

I spent an interesting and challenging two hours with him, listening. Although he was frustrated about how he was expected to implement policy, he had some very genuine concerns on why some things were not working. He was surprised when I agreed with him on many points and said I would include his concerns in the policy review. From that point on, I had someone who was now interested and a champion.

Because I had listened to and involved him he then regularly sent me interesting articles and papers on the subject that he had started to read.

Line managers

Anxieties – being 'in the spotlight'

In most equality and diversity texts I have read, the line manager is cited as the key player in making equality and diversity work, or fail. I find that working with line managers is important, but also difficult. They seem to have various fears. The foremost is usually that it is more work and responsibility for them and also that, if things are not achieved, they will get the 'blame' from all sides. I have also heard managers tell me that they think equality and diversity initiatives will cause resentment with staff and that they do not think their managers have the commitment to make it work, seeing it as the 'flavour of the month'.

'Concrete' responsibilities

Frequently I discovered that line managers had not been explicitly told their responsibilities on equality and diversity. Wherever possible, I always include equality and diversity responsibilities in the manager's job description and ensure that it is an explicit area on the appraisal paperwork and performance review.

I find that communication and consultation are important so that line managers feel involved from the start and understand why the organisation is promoting equality and diversity and its benefits. Line managers needed to be able to express their concerns in an open and safe environment. This not only helped but also generated information for me so that I could tailor the project approach to ensure success. I felt everyone in the organisation needed to know their responsibility, so the line managers knew that things were not just resting on their shoulders. Line managers could often fail to commit to equality and diversity as they saw it as yet another one of the 'people' initiatives that had come and gone over the years. To help stop a 'flavour of the month' attitude, I encouraged middle and senior managers to ensure that their equality and diversity plans are seen as middle and long term and not just have a quick 'tick box' list before moving on to the next initiative.

Your fear is my fear: example of small-group facilitation of 'authentic' conversations

Unearthing concerns, ignorance, fear and prejudice

The issue of initiatives 'causing resentment' needed to be addressed. I found that when line managers expressed the fears of 'their' staff, they were, in fact, often talking about their own fears. This is why I give line managers a lot of attention so they can not only manage the processes effectively but also be clearer about what to tell to, and what to expect of, staff. Staff know the difference between a manager who is going through the motions and one who understands and accepts the concepts and reasons for the initiative, and then adapts them to their own team.

In one organisation where I was acting as a consultant, the senior team wanted all line managers developed in equality, diversity and equal opportunities. It would have been quicker and easier to come up with a standard workshop for delivery to all the managers. However, the personnel manager knew that the subject was regarded as 'delicate' by managers and together we agreed to have a pre-meeting to explore the issues and concerns of the managers and to see 'where they were at'. Although this meeting was a challenge to me as the facilitator, it provided an opportunity for managers to 'legitimately' voice their concerns.

Real concerns

These concerns included:

- recruiting male staff (issues around homophobia and stereotypes);
- 'encouraging' lesbian staff (issues around homophobia, the new EO policy and managing staff);
- not having 'time' to do EO (issues around seeing EO as separate from work);
- senior managers not 'trusting' them to do their job (issues around believing they knew all about EO and practised it already, and communication with head office);
- being made to feel different (issue around black manager being made 'an example' of).

The importance of the development of tailored programmes

We were able to address the vast majority of these concerns and devise a programme tailored to the managers. The programme we developed involved a slot for the senior managers to explain why equality and diversity were important and why the line managers were key to their success. Since the line managers felt that their needs had been addressed and they had been 'listened to', the actual training workshop was a success and the managers were confident to go to their teams with action points.

Majority staff

The 'majority staff', the indigenous population and, at senior management level in particular, usually male, always seemed to be the most powerful group in organisations that I have worked in – those whom the managers have to manage and those who set the culture and are the customer interface; those who are the colleagues of the 'minority' staff.

(Further, I say 'majority' staff as in those staff who often feel that they did not benefit from traditional EO.)

'Invalidating' past experiences and latent competitiveness

I found that these staff have fears (often understandably) at new initiatives, particularly if they have had experience of 'EO' in organisations ten to fifteen years ago. They may have seen colleagues disciplined for asking for a black coffee in the canteen, male colleagues being teased by female colleagues that they can't go to the Women in Management training 'because they are men', or been rebuked by managers for saying 'a person in a wheelchair' rather than 'a wheelchair user' (even though 'person in a wheelchair' was what they had learnt in their EO training four years ago). These are all real examples from my and my colleagues' experience.

Feel fair: the other side of the coin

Apart from the fears generated by previous experiences, other key fears appeared to be others taking jobs/promotion, 'it's unfair', not needed, others getting preferential treatment and 'political correctness at its worst'.

I always promoted, and genuinely believe, that equality and diversity management had the major benefit of involving everyone and benefiting everyone. As a practitioner though, it is often necessary to 'undo' any negative effects of previous initiatives, firstly by listening and finding out the negative impacts as well as the positive impacts.

Undoing past 'good' work: the 'Managing Fairly' project

In one case I was working in an organisation that had had major EO problems ten to fifteen years before and undertook a positive action programme for women coming into the industry. When I joined the organisation there was still a lot of resentment and 'hurt' from the male staff. They had obviously felt alienated and ignored. In fact, the positive action had worked very well, getting more women into the industry and women managers at the same ratio as total female staff. However, because of the way it was introduced 'EO' had a very bad name. The shutters went down as soon as it was mentioned. I needed to help relaunch the whole concept of equality and diversity and decided to call the programme 'Managing Fairly'. Although we were still going to address gender issues, the name was not as threatening, and an important key organisation value was captured in the title also.

Constructive conversations

I find it is vital in any programme that people realise 'what's in it for them'. The Managing Fairly workshops gave the staff an opportunity to express their fears of the programme and issues, using language that they were familiar with (we had a session on appropriateness of language later on).

Everyone can feel different

We asked the group to describe occasions when they had felt different. We got a blank look and I was told, 'Look Shaun, we are men in a man's world. We never feel different.' Pause. Then one engineer put up his hand and said, 'I was an Arsenal supporter in a train carriage full of Man U supporters – I felt different.' The conversation then flowed. I believe most people are capable of understanding the issues, if they are given the space and time to do so.

Where is the harm? Challenging offensive behaviour

Returning to the workshop situation – we were asked the question, 'Where is the harm in whistling at an attractive girl who walks through the depot?' Issues about policy, law, feelings, etc., were put across, but they could still not 'see the harm', until we asked the question, 'How would you feel if that was your daughter and your colleagues whistled?' 'I'd knock their . . . heads off!' The message clicked and whistling at women stopped.

These examples demonstrate that you have to know your audience and find out what makes them act in the way they do. Although the Managing Fairly course was about a specific problem, it had some surprising outcomes. One of these was the case of an engineer who said that he was not treated fairly as he was always asked to do extra jobs while his colleagues watched TV in the rest room. His manager was in the group and explained that it was because the engineer was the best and most productive staff member in the crew and he knew that he would do a quick and effective job. He had not known the resentment this had caused or that the man felt he was 'punishing his most effective team member for being so effective'! The other crew members were relieved that they were not being asked to do extra work, but realised that they were not going to develop their skill levels, unless they were.

Catalysts for new conversations

This conversation had never been had before. As a result of this workshop the management changed the work allocation system. Staff felt this was fairer and the manager said he had opened up a whole new communication channel.

Minority staff

Who's 'on the agenda'?

To illustrate some of my case examples I refer to minority staff as not just the 'traditional' minorities covered by EO and legislation, but any staff members who may feel 'different'. I think equality and diversity's strength is looking beyond the box, but we still seem to think in restricted ways in practice (for example, sexual orientation, religion and disability are less well understood and addressed than gender and ethnicity).

Under-representation forgotten

I find that organisations looking at equality and diversity, which are not EO-centred, start to forget about their responsibility to under-represented groups. My colleagues often say to me that they experience many companies who use equality and diversity as a means of not having to look at these groups specifically.

I am aware of stereotypes within equality and diversity. I find that most organisations I have worked with regarding practising equality and diversity will be aware of religious differences and be careful to address these. However, I have experience of organisations that will not bat an eyelid at a joke about Jehovah's Witnesses.

Do as I say: double standards

Double standards – my colleague and friend works with retailers who pride themselves on their approach to equality and diversity and 'women's issues' but who still sell 'girlie magazines' and think it is fine for their female assistants to serve them.

Anxieties, frustrations, and narrowly defined identities

From speaking to various people who considered themselves a minority in the organisation, I know that there are many fears, but here are some of the major ones highlighted to me over the years:

- being seen as a token employee and being always in the spotlight;
- resentment from peers for getting 'special' treatment;
- being expected to be an expert on every other minority group or sub-culture;
- that the organisation's policies are not updated or effective and culture change is a slow process.

I am sure we all have our 'cases' in this whole area. I am going to give an example outside of an organisational environment that demonstrates what happens when someone in the spotlight is seen as a token employee.

Becoming a 'universal' expert

A friend came out to her friends as gay. Her friends were delighted. She was invited to every dinner party, not as herself but as a gay woman. All the other guests, who had been told she was gay, not only questioned her about her lifestyle but also asked her opinion on everything from adoption to Section 28.

I have seen the same thing happen in organisations, whatever minority the particular staff member is identified with. The dinner party is replaced by meetings, workshops or conferences.

Without forgetting the individual, I do think it is very important to be aware and learn more about different minority staff as a group. For example, being aware of customs, religious observances and culture. With this information an organisation can ensure it is aware and can accommodate different needs.

Ignorance is not bliss

A real example of this was in a care environment. Unfortunately a patient died and staff followed the standard procedure for preparing the body. When relatives turned up they were distressed to discover this, which was totally against their religious observance. Had the staff been aware, they could have avoided this distressing situation.

The organisation wanted to learn from this negative experience and gave training on basic customs for different religions and cultures. They found that by getting staff together in discussion of the topics, there was an enormous amount of knowledge individuals could share.

I have also experienced that organisations may have very positive equality/diversity/EO policies and practice but there is little guidance for when minority staff are subjected to inappropriate behaviours from customers or visitors. Often the policies concentrate on issues with colleagues and not those outside the organisation.

The customer is not always right

This was highlighted in one workshop I ran where by the end of the session it was clear that many minority staff had been subjected to abuse from visitors and clients, but had not told management because, firstly, there was no guidance on a procedure to do this, and secondly, they felt management would take the view that the 'customer is always right'.

When minority staff had given their experience in the 'safe' environment of the workshop, other majority staff started to highlight times when they had been abused by visitors and clients, which made them feel very unhappy, and they too did not know what to do.

It is important that equality/diversity/EO policies address this issue and staff feel confident that management will take the matter seriously.

It is also important that organisations appreciate that discrimination is not a 'black and white' issue. If their workforce is diverse, there can be conflict between other groups. Organisations need to make sure that the policies apply to all staff.

Walking on egg shells

An example where this was important was an organisation that had large teams of shift workers who were mainly Asian and Afro-Caribbean. The supervisor had noticed blatant racial abuse between the two groups but did not want to address it as it was 'delicate' and he did not want to be accused of being racist for tackling it.

The supervisor was given support and the individuals were dealt with under the current policy, as it was clear that it applied to all staff.

The recruitment advantages of diversity

I have experienced that some minority staff will not be the only ones influenced by an organisation's actions. Their family and friends fear that the person is not being recruited to the organisation on the basis of their ability but to 'make up the numbers'. Once in the organisation, they fear poor promotion prospects for their friends/relatives and the worse-case scenario, harassment.

Parents know best?

I have found that if someone's family and friends feel and see that the organisation is a 'good employer' they will encourage them to apply. An example of peer influence comes from a contact who did some work in an organisation that was having harassment problems. She found the management and staff culture not willing to accommodate change or admit that there was any real problem. Her son (highly qualified and with marketable skills) was offered a job at this company. When she told him of her experience there he did not accept the offer.

Unnecessarily limiting customer/client base

I have experienced that marketing departments realise that they need to encourage new customers as well as existing ones. I worked in an organisation whose key customer group, according to the marketing department, was white middle-aged men. As a result, the majority of the budget and effort was spent on attracting this group. The marketing director told me, 'We know what our customers want, as they are regularly surveyed and I am not prepared to waste resources attracting other groups who do not use the service.' Fine, but after one equality and diversity audit it was discovered that they only ever surveyed existing customers and not potential customers in the community. When they did this (resulting from the joint action plan from the audit), they found that there were potential businesswomen who wanted to use the service but did not feel catered for!

External candidates

The recruitment advantage of diversity 2: culture and inclusion

Most organisations I have worked for needed to attract a wide range of candidates to get the benefits they want from their equality and diversity programmes. They ensured that they advertised in various media, had information that represented many groups and the equality and diversity policy statements were published. Although I found this commendable in one organisation – their drive to attract a wide range of the community or under-represented groups – they had not looked at the organisation's current internal environment and culture. They were attracting people, but if the people started and realised that the organisation was not always practising what it preached, they left (and probably told their family and friends). This is a key reason why I try to promote continuous implementation and evaluation in organisations I work with.

Breaking down the barriers

I found that candidates potentially applying for jobs may see a barrier to them gaining employment with the organisation or fear they will not fit in or be the 'exception'. They may believe, or have evidence, that the organisation is not a good employer or be uncertain what to expect if they join. I introduced many practical things to allay these fears. This included, in particular, trying to ensure that the organisation is presented in the best possible way, but also that the 'message' will only be believed and be sustainable if it reflects the true organisational culture, climate, environment and practice.

Making it happen

I think a good example of this is an organisation that wanted to attract candidates with hearing impairments. They did not just target the advertising but they installed Minicom, trained the receptionists and interviewers in deaf-awareness and retained the services of a lip-speaker for interviews and meetings.

In an organisation I worked for, we did have a diverse mix of staff and good practices but this was never shown in adverts or candidate information. I felt we should show that we were a good employer, so I arranged to have a candidate information pack designed outlining our benefits, equality and diversity policies and showing photographs of staff representatives of the company, including staff in non-traditional roles. For example, men doing 'traditional women's roles' and vice versa. I also wanted to show a wide age range of staff, in the various roles that we had to offer. As well as being good PR in the community we served, we hoped it would give candidates the confidence to apply. Although it was still early days when I left, we found an increase in returned application forms, including those from 'traditional' minorities, and our existing staff and managers were more aware of the positive aspects of the organisation.

Helping other professions to understand

Back to marketing on this one – I had battles trying to get the images I wanted. Marketing kept sending proofs back with photos from their advertising library. I wanted real photos from the staff magazine. Eventually we got there, but it was about educating the marketers and the design company on why I had these 'strange' requests. We cannot blame other professions for not understanding the issues. We need not to chastise, but to encourage them to understand the benefits. I thought I was just about there. All marketing had to do was add one more 'real' photo, including a member of staff with a slight facial disfigurement as this group are often forgotten and are included in the UK's Disability Discrimination Acts. My heart sank when the marketing manager brought me the final proof and was pleased to tell me that the design company had managed to airbrush out the disfigurement! (Needless to say, we did get the final product right in the end . . .)

Breadth of organisational impact on equality and diversity: the health and safety dimension

I have found that there is a key benefit to equality and diversity that is often overlooked. From my experience and reading I know that equality and diversity are cited as, for example, increasing morale, better productivity and increased bottom line, but I have worked for an organisation that felt equality and diversity was important for health and safety.

Duty of care

They believed it was part of duty of care – staff who are being harassed or distracted because of fears could be a risk to others and to their health and safety. Interestingly, the train companies recognised this many years ago. Health and safety is a huge concern and their harassment and EO policies came from a health and safety viewpoint. It was often implemented like health and safety. 'You may stand on a chair at home, but in this organisation you don't and if you do you'll be disciplined.' 'You may make sexist jokes down the pub but in this organisation you don't and if you do you'll be disciplined.'

Health and safety can sell

When I have difficulty 'selling equality and diversity' in any other ways, I try the health and safety route. In most organisations all staff and managers understand why health and safety is important. Care is needed: I have found that if you promote the health and safety angle too closely, it can run the risk of missing the point of equality and diversity – it should be achieved through awareness, understanding and the benefit it brings everyone, not because we have to and get into trouble if we do not.

I think there are many benefits for health and safety through promoting equality and diversity. If people feel valued and not discriminated against there will be less stress and more open communication channels, which will contribute to an increased duty of care. Health and safety training is important, and with equality and diversity principles organisations can ensure that access to such training is fair and that all individuals are given the opportunity of such training.

From my experience, health and safety training can often be 'old school' and it is important to ensure that the trainers used follow equality and diversity principles in their training, particularly if their participant base has been dominantly majority staff.

Can everyone understand?

Communication is vital for health and safety to be a success. In an organisation I worked for, all health and safety communication was written. After an equality and diversity audit, managers realised that many staff may not fully understand the written communication through education or language. They introduced a new procedure to establish whether any staff had an alternative communication need, e.g. verbal briefing. Without the equality and diversity initiative I do not think this aspect to health and safety would have been addressed.

Suppliers

'Supply chain' equality and diversity considerations

Some organisations I worked for ensured that equality and diversity should take into account its key suppliers. How embarrassing they thought it would be for a company, which is actively promoting equality and diversity, to find that their key suppliers are regarded as discriminatory employers in the community. The company felt it had a responsibility to open the dialogue and find out what their suppliers' policies and practices were. They found that suppliers were not usually going to volunteer this information. One procurement manager suggested to me that he felt suppliers might fear that they will lose business to the organisation, show their ignorance on issues or highlight poor practice. The organisation as customer needed to work in partnership with its suppliers on these issues. They needed to ensure that any fears of the suppliers do not interfere with the supply chain. However, they made it very clear that they expected cooperation and continual development from suppliers.

Communicate with suppliers

The company found it most productive to get key suppliers to a meeting to discuss the issues and share best practice. In the meeting, each supplier decided to audit itself on key themes, with help from the company, and then develop joint action plans. The company supported its suppliers with advice, encouragement and shared resources. I recently worked with a client who had lost a contract because part of the tender process was to supply their policies on equality and diversity and they did not match the standard expected. This provided enormous incentive for them to get things right for next time.

Communities

Community profile

Not surprisingly, in organisations I have worked with, it is the local community from which candidates and the workforce are mainly drawn. For me as an equality and diversity/recruitment practitioner, it was essential to find out what the composition of the community was, so that I could target limited resources effectively. Too often I have heard of colleagues who decide they need to target an under-represented group in their organisation with various meetings, adverts and open days, only to find it does not encourage more applications. On following this up, they discover, too late, that the targeted group are not living in the community. I too have been caught out, bringing in initiatives to obtain a 3 per cent registered disabled workforce (in the days before the Disability Discrimination Act) and consulting the local disability adviser on why we could only reach 1.5 per cent. With a smile she said, 'Well done! We only have 1 per cent registered disabled people in this area.'

The organisations I have worked with saw their community as vital to their success, not just for supplying the workforce but also for being the customer.

It was important that the community viewed them as a good potential employer and service/product supplier that met their needs.

What community are we in?

The organisation put a lot of effort into finding out who the community were and also what they required.

From this information they were able to prioritise initiatives to promote the organisation and its service/product to the community.

Much of this was about communicating in an understandable and appropriate way. This was not just about advertising, but speaking to the community via focus groups.

School/organisational links

The organisation also wanted to encourage future employees and customers, so it did a lot of work with young people and schools, so the young had a positive view of the organisation from an early age.

I believe work experience is an ideal way to promote an organisation to the community. It is of course important to market the opportunities widely and challenge job stereotypes by ensuring that equal numbers of boys and girls are involved in a range of positions. A positive experience for the child will influence how their families and friends view the organisation.

A 'true' view

When organising community focus groups, it is important to ensure that you are gaining a 'true' view of that community. For example, if you provide a venue that is not accessible you will restrict the opportunities for those in the community with mobility difficulties.

To illustrate this, an organisation prided itself on its links with ethnic community 'elders'. However, the young in that community did not feel that the elders represented their views, and therefore the organisation had to look at ways in which they got a balanced view.

The personnel/HR professional and specialist role

The personnel/HR specialist as 'record keeper' but not champion

Traditionally, as a personnel/HR professional, my department had responsibility and expertise for equal opportunities and later equality and diversity (which is meant to be the responsibility of everyone). My background is in personnel/HR and I still work as a part-time HR manager. I have been consistently disappointed by my colleagues' attitudes and actions on EO and equality and diversity. I have found that many personnel/HR professionals are not interested in the subject and will do the bare minimum. There are more 'exciting' topics to choose from – compensation and benefits, law, job design and evaluation, organisation design, employee relations – to name but a few. This always surprises me as I work on the fact that equality and diversity impact on all these areas and more. It is not just for recruitment, which in my experience is where any initiative or knowledge on equality and diversity stops. Of course, I know many committed and skilled personnel/HR practitioners and specialists championing equality and diversity. However, we only have to look at our publications and professional meeting topics to see that equality and diversity are given very little coverage in relation to all other HR things.

More work

I often have discussions with my colleagues and associates on why they seem to have a fear of promoting equality and diversity in their organisation. They have included the fear of more work, of not being supported, of showing their ignorance and being blamed if things go wrong. Also that their departments have got away from the old personnel images and they feel they could be seen as personnel 'police' in equality and diversity, or seen as too PC by staff managers and the board.

For me in my work, an equality and diversity approach has allowed the responsibility out of the personnel department to everyone.

Over-confidence

I also have experience of equality and diversity specialists being seen as experts in everything by their organisations. Organisations can be over-confident of our abilities and experience in all areas and this can lead to us as professionals trying to meet these expectations. From my experience, no individual has all the experience and knowledge in all areas of equality and diversity and certainly not all the various groups in the community. I always try to acknowledge this and look to others for help and advice, be they staff, managers or specialist organisations. This way I can ensure that we are contributing to providing the best service. It is important when working with clients to ensure that they understand I am not an expert in every area of equality and diversity, but I can find expertise from other sources, without compromising the project.

In my experience, successful organisations use their equality and diversity specialists (not necessarily in HR) as project manager, catalyst and change agent, rather than relying totally on their specific expertise.

Monitoring

Often when I audit organisations they cite their commitment to equality and diversity as the fact they monitor. However, this is rarely done in a holistic way. Some elements of recruitment may be monitored, but not training, promotion or profiles of management.

If monitoring is to be successful it needs to be complete and look at the whole picture. Also, ask many practitioners why they monitor and they will not be able to say.

Who uses the data?

I started in one organisation and was presented with very complete monitoring statistics. It took my colleague three days a month to compile. When I asked who used them, she confessed they stayed in her drawer and nobody else saw them. This is often the case. Unless the figures are used, they may as well not be compiled.

It is also important to analyse the figures and use them to prioritise and then plan action. I find it useful if the figures are published widely, e.g. on notice boards and in newsletters, so that there is an understanding across the whole workplace and added impetus to do something as staff will be asking questions!

Employee representatives

Getting to know the detail, not just the 'big picture'

Often a pressure group, organisation or charity represents the interests of a group of people. I have made use of their knowledge and expertise, but remember that they may have knowledge of one group or area but do not represent the whole, as of course those identifying with the group are still individuals.

A disability adviser illustrated this by telling me about her local deaf community. She was trying to organise local groups to come up with plans that local employers could use to help their deaf-awareness. She said, 'All they did was argue, especially those who signed and those who lip-read.' She told them, 'If you can't agree on the right way forward between you, what chance is there for the poor employer?' If the equality and diversity professional had spoken to just one of those groups they would have got an incomplete picture of the whole deaf community.

Trades unions: real benefits but more 'proactivity' needed?

I have found trades unions a useful source of information and discussion, and try to include them in the whole equality and diversity process. However, I have experienced many who do not promote equality, diversity and equal opportunities as rigorously as they could. I believe this is why many union reps do not actively push their organisations to do more on equality and diversity (apart from obvious legal and harassment issues).

I was fortunate to work with excellent union reps when in an organisation working on an equality and diversity project. They said to me that they were embarrassed by their own union's lack of equality, diversity and equal opportunity success. Their union senior staff did not demonstrate equality and diversity and they felt that their union was doing little to encourage equality and diversity from within. They gave an example to illustrate their points by explaining at their annual conference that the location had no wheelchair access or signers, even though a number of delegates were deaf and signed and individuals used wheelchairs.

I asked a trades unionist colleague what he thought the key fears of unions were. He said, 'One fear is showing ignorance, as many organisations' HR professionals have more knowledge of the issues and, secondly, traditional unions first and foremost want to protect their existing members who, due to the history of the industry, are not a diverse group.'

Changing for the better

I have experienced that this is changing and feel that unions can be of enormous help in promoting equality and diversity, especially in communicating with their members on why the organisation is taking action on equality and diversity.

Other benefits of having good trades union involvement include:

- Initiatives being accepted by the workforce and not seen as 'management' initiatives.
- Trades unions see another side and are useful to include in equality and diversity audits because of this.
- Union officials will often know of feelings and issues of members that they would not share with management. These 'hidden' feelings are important not to ignore.
- If there is a good working relationship with trades unions officials on

equality and diversity, it will help maintain the relationship for areas of less agreement.

- Trades unions often have equality and diversity specialists and advice at their HQ, which can be used on projects where there is union involvement. Useful statistics may also be available that the organisation cannot gain in other ways.

If union representatives are proactive and work with management they can get the best deal on equality and diversity.

A key role is for them to 'listen' to informal conversation, which enables them to identify and action institutional unfairness and 'feel fair'. This role of informal conversation 'hearer' can tap into line management who may not be able to get the authentic conversation of their staff.

This gives great potential for the union representative to fulfil an important role in equality and diversity and is a key reason why unions are of value and should be involved.

Concepts that help to make sense of these reflections

From reading my colleagues' chapters, there are certain concepts discussed more fully in these that have helped me to make sense, first, of what has underpinned my practice and which may help others also make firmer links between practice and theory. In addition to these, there are a few other ideas that I will mention briefly as being potentially helpful in making sense of my past practitioner experiences. I have cross-referenced ideas presented in earlier chapters as notes. These ideas include:

1. Relationship building and healthy relationships[2]
2. Lust, fear and marking[3]
3. Authentic conversation[4]
4. 'Force field' analysis[5]
5. Employee voice[6]
6. HR policy[7]
7. Accountability[8]
8. Fear of change of the psychological contract[9]
9. Fear of poor human relationships being made visible[10]
10. Wrongly placing problems at the door of one stakeholder group[11]
11. The interventionist's role set.

Why these ideas in particular? Let's start with *relationship building* (1). In my view, relationship building is important as it is key to ensuring that managers have access to authentic conversation to help them plan equality and diversity initiatives.

Lust, fear and marking matter as these concepts, developed by Terry Horne and based on his analysis of the transcripts of interviews in which thousands of managers and employees were interviewed, highlight the fear of loss of advantage for the majority and fear of 'being in the spotlight' for managers.

In particular, marking makes the unspoken spoken and the invisible visible for those normally out of the spotlight, the target of which is typically the 'soldiers' rather than the officers. This can be used constructively to build relationships and ensure that people feel 'safe' in this section of the organisation to voice their fears. Real dangers will emerge, however, only if the officers are subject to real scrutiny and reprimand, while officer action is masked and not readily brought to account.

Authentic conversation highlights the need to capture real conversation on a one-to-one basis and informally. It is often difficult for line managers to have authentic conversations, and other ways of tapping it are required, including the key role of unions.

The authentic conversation is a more reliable source of information when designing policy and practice: and although it is important to sell the benefits of policies, it is equally important not to ignore the feelings of those who are unsure.

Force-field analysis, developed as part of Kurt Lewin's field theory, is a way of representing graphically how to assess change. Lewin argued that it is necessary to identify those factors that are likely to drive change (driving forces) and those that are more likely to impede change (restraining forces) with a view to establishing the 'equilibrium point': i.e. is the change likely to happen (because driving forces predominate) or not (because restraining forces do)? The equality and diversity practitioner needs to understand which stakeholders and aspects of the stakeholder environment will make policies happen and which ones will stop progression. It is the authentic conversation and relationship building that helps demonstrate 'who the players are'.

Employee voice is key in designing and implementing diversity policy and practice. The saying that 'trust is earned' is true in equality and diversity management, and opinion and views on what does or does not 'feel fair' to stakeholders are critical. Trades unions can provide one mechanism for capturing employee voice. Focus groups or well-designed attitude and climate surveys, if they capture 'authentic voice' in the questions contained therein, are fair alternatives.

HR policy needs to be consistent to gain trust and deliver 'the promise'. It is important that all stakeholders are involved in formulation so that there is 'buy in'.

Accountability matters because it is important to manage managers' fears (at all managerial levels) in order that they are not marginalised and at worst, fail to be accountable.

For me, *healthy relationships* are the key to workplace equality and diversity but it is an area that is often lacking. Managers need to be developed in the importance of nurturing relationships and given the skills and support to do it. Finally, I think that *interventionists* are too often out of the spotlight in relation to equality and diversity interventions. I think that this is a crucial oversight for a number of reasons. First, it is for the interventionist to make sure that they are not part of the problem (e.g. become part of the blame culture)! Second, it is important that interventionists understand the limitations of our experiences. Finally, there are different levels of sophistication of understanding of organizations: some of us understand group dynamics and the inter-personal better than we understand how HR policies and systems will influence practice. Many organisations will produce a good enough specification to weed out those practitioners most likely to satisfy their needs. However, there are many that bring in the interventionist as a knee-jerk reaction to a lost court case, bad publicity or no real knowledge of what the symptoms of the problem are, let alone the causes. Real damage can be done by having the wrong interventionist in the wrong place at the wrong time.

My *modus operandi* to date

This case study has illustrated a selection of my experience and how I operate. The following will summarise personal reflections on my *modus operandi*.

1. I know *what* I know and where my skills and knowledge are and get development for those areas I need to improve, and make contact with groups and people who have the expertise to share with me. *I also know what I don't know!*
2. I ensure I have support, as it can be an isolated and lonely job at times. I try to find key champions in the organisation and develop a support network outside.
3. I listen. This is my key skill and helps me understand where people are coming from and the best way to implement initiatives.
4. I encourage people to 'celebrate success'. Too often we get bogged down with what we still have to do, rather than what we have achieved or do well.
5. I open up dialogue – communication in equality and diversity terms can be like shouting. Things are communicated but not heard over the exchange. Equality and diversity dialogue is about hearing the messages, understanding others' viewpoints and communicating in a reassuring and non-threatening way.
6. My 'customers, colleagues and clients' want to know what will be in it for them. I sell the meaningful and practical benefits, not the theory.
7. Everything cannot be tackled at once. I find out what are the relevant issues in the organisation and tackle those first. It would be nice to get 'everything' perfect but realistically my organisations need to concentrate on the areas that need the most action and give the biggest returns.
8. I acknowledge that different areas in the organisation may be at different levels. I ensure that initiatives are relevant to each area and tailored to their needs and level. For example, the issues in engineering may be different from those of customer service. Geography of sites will also give different needs and community make-up.
9. I encourage people to give me their ideas and views in informal ways without always resorting to formal meetings and communications.
10. I acknowledge that every group and person does not want to show their ignorance (or yet know what they don't know)! I try to ensure that any

workshops or meetings do not make people feel stupid and that everyone can put their views across in a supportive atmosphere. As a consultant I ensure I am fully briefed so I know the approach I am expecting for the group.

11. I acknowledge that there are negative aspects to any issue or group. I try to ensure that there is discussion of these and that particular groups are not put on a pedestal or seen through rose-coloured glasses, just because they are in a minority in the organisation.

12. I am prepared to take risks and encourage leaders to do the same in their policies and programmes. I have found 'women's' issues are now viewed with little risk, disability moderate risk, race high risk and homophobia – off the scale! I see part of my role as educating people and pushing boundaries.

13. I remember that there can be multiple disadvantages in any programme I devise.

14. I try to determine what is acceptable for the organisation. Although it is useful to benchmark other organisations, I make sure I am doing what is right for the current one, particularly its environment and culture.

15. I work where people 'are at' and work from this to what is expected.

16. When starting a project I use my 'innocence' to ask questions that allow me to gain a picture of what is really happening in the organisation. This window of opportunity is important because as time progresses staff may feel you are more 'management' and not give their opinion of where things are.

17. Where possible, I try to build partnerships with a few organisations over a period of time, rather than short projects with many. This involvement helps gain the trust and understanding to make programmes work.

My *modus operandi* – the implications of a 'capabilities' approach

The capabilities framework that has been outlined in the other sections of this book has allowed me to understand the strengths and limitations of my dominant *modus operandi*.

- The key *strengths* are that because I see communication as vital with all levels and stakeholders of an organisation, I am able to establish if there is a 'feel fair' culture in the organisation.
- Using consultants and outside agencies could ensure that the capability issues are audited.
- It may also highlight that when assessing the organisation I should be asking more challenging questions of senior management to ensure that they understand the importance of the capability issue.

Looking at the new approach, I can see that practice may have to be undertaken in a modified/different way. It will be important to ensure that the benefits and subtleties of equality and diversity are not lost, as this will still be a key driver for organisations. We may have to sell the 'business' benefits of ensuring capability opportunities for all, for example in light of recruitment and skill shortages.

More emphasis will need to be placed on *development* and using potential in a structured and open way. Many managers are aware of development best practice, e.g. Investors in People (IIP), and may relate this knowledge to equality and diversity.

The new approach has helped in some way to think about key practice problems differently. It is going to be more important to focus on the *environment*, as this gives access to capability and facilitates equality of opportunity. HR procedures are going to be used effectively to ensure that decisions that give people opportunity to gain and use capability are transparent, e.g. performance management and promotion interviews.

I think the broad implication for internal practitioners is the need for *new tools* and *processes to bring about change*. Any they develop will need to show value for money and how they are going to make a difference.

The existing skills and knowledge of internal practitioners may be challenged and I see them having to use more outside agencies to ensure that all groups are represented.

Communication skills for practitioners are going to be essential so that any new approach does not undermine past programmes and efforts.

The broad implication for external practitioners is going to be to ensure that they have the networks to bring a wide variety of skill and knowledge into the organisation. Also, auditing techniques to see where the organisation is in terms of environment and 'feel fair'. The consultants with HR experience are going to be in demand to provide a *complete service* as 'feel fair' and creating the right environment are going to demand innovative processes and policies with regard to recruitment and selection, performance management and training and development.

Practitioners will also have to build longer-term relations with clients and ask those probing questions!

Thinking more about capabilities

Capabilities vary considerably across all stakeholders. For me, the practitioner has to help prepare people for dealing with issues. These may be past issues, current issues or possible/definite future requirements. Although different people will have different needs, depending on their role, internal capability for all will empower all to get the best from any situation.

I think encouraging and listening to authentic conversations helps create fairness and sensitivity, and helps build credibility for the organisation and its employees.

Capabilities equality demands an ongoing development process, not a one-off quick fix. They say you can't turn straw into gold, and solutions will not become apparent overnight. It is best for the practitioner to help move the organisation towards a preferable position and to improve consistently to attain that. Equality and diversity success can be a measure of HR strategy and helps build the psychological contract block by block. Equality and diversity works best if people are grown-up about it and are able to share their fears and express reservation and limitation. Having discussed my current *modus operandi*, in the following table I comment on what other things I will have to think about when dealing with stakeholders to maximise my promotion of capabilities thinking and the implications for other practitioners.

Stakeholder	Implications for myself re: capabilities approach	Implications for practitioners in general re: capabilities approach
Senior managers	Ensuring/promoting that equal opportunities, training and development, communication, personal development reviews and recruitment and selection are on the agenda as well as diversity.	Ensuring a broad understanding of these areas and where other expertise is available if necessary.
Middle managers	Help them understand what typical barriers there are to capability and what lead they can take to ensure they are not creating or supporting them.	Gaining a broad range of organisational experience to be able to advise on what are invisible barriers.
Line managers	Help them to be aware of their staff potential and give opportunities to develop/use it. Also to ensure they are aware of other areas of expertise their staff may have that they are not using in their current position.	Ensure knowledge of personal development reviews, as a way of helping managers understand the aspirations of staff for the future and to help give them opportunities to develop capabilities in other areas.
'Majority' staff	When working with them, e.g. in discussion groups or training workshops, ask them to see if they feel the organisation is 'fair' and what barriers they see or feel.	Ensure when working with management that staff are involved in the work and take every opportunity to communicate with them.
'Minority' staff and their families	When working on projects, at every opportunity question to see if they think the organisation is 'fair' and what barriers they see or feel.	Learn as much as possible about minority issues and cultures in order to identify possible barriers in organisations.
Candidates	Encourage the organisation to show evidence of progression within when recruiting and demonstrate through recruitment material that it values diversity *and* will develop capabilities.	Encourage organisations to audit recruitment and selection systems for barriers and whether the organisation 'environment' would enable new staff to use their capabilities to the full and be comfortable in doing so.
Suppliers	Encourage the organisation to look at the capabilities of its suppliers.	Encourage the organisation to determine who are suppliers to work with their customers on the capabilities issues, i.e. make the first move!

Continued on next page

Continued

The community	Obtain more community contacts and, when networking with them, ask specifically about capabilities issues.	Research which groups would be able to provide advice and networking opportunities
The personnel professional/specialist	Help them understand their great role in promoting systems that will help capabilities, e.g. personal development reviews.	When in organisations with personnel functions, involve them and help develop them in capabilities concepts.
Representative groups	Help their understanding of capability issues when working with them.	Make contact with them and be aware that they do not represent everyone in that 'group'.
Trades unions	Help their understanding of capabilities when working with them. Involve them wherever possible.	Use their experiences of members.

Final thoughts

As a former manager I think managers have to ask: what does our organisation do to maximise staff potential and is it fair? But before trying to answer that question, I would need to ask: do I know what my staff's aspirations are? If I am honest with myself I would like to think I knew what they were in their current roles but probably not in their future roles. I think personal development reviews are an important opportunity to find out this information and to *encourage* staff to talk about their aspirations. It is only then that we can help develop them and inform the organisation of what staff's aspirations are. I will also make a point of encouraging managers to ask their staff if they think the organisation utilises their capabilities.

We also need to ensure that our staff are aware of what opportunities are available. I worked for one organisation that only showed the internal vacancy list to certain grades of staff! We as managers have a responsibility to ensure our staff are aware.

When we recruit new staff, we should ask about their outside activities – this will help inform us of other skills they have that may not be required for the current job, but could be for others in the organisation. When we have staff in our teams who we did not personally recruit, we should take the time to find out what other skills they have – we may be surprised. We need to be honest about our own abilities and get feedback on our own performance. We need to tailor any intervention or policy according to the local need. True information on 'feel fair' will only be available through informal communication channels. Therefore relationships have to be built around trust.

Development of capabilities needs to be looked at in the context of the existing policies and procedures and development of new ones. We need to ask ourselves how development can happen and what environment is required to help this approach. Development is for all stakeholders and, as discussed, the importance of stakeholder voice is paramount in understanding what the capability issues are.

Trades unions are a potential ally in channelling authentic employee voice to management ears. They are also important in helping to identify any issues of institutional discrimination. Organisations must not forget traditional equal opportunities if they are to create the informal arenas for informal conversations to replace more traditional areas that have benefited the majority, e.g. the golf course, after-work drinks, that have excluded traditional minority groups. Blame and the blame culture stops informal conversation and the opportunity for stakeholders to experiment. Therefore, organisations and practitioners need to help develop confidence and capabilities to stop blame. Language and political correctness can kill informal discussion, as people's conversations are stilted by the fear of saying the wrong thing. If relationship building is going to flourish, we as practitioners must be sensible and realistic about expectations of encouraging appropriateness of language but not turning it into the PC 'I'm an expert' façade.

If we can manage well, we will:

● get authentic conversations;
● not create additional problems, e.g. blame;
● know how to address people who have got things wrong in the past, so as not to kill their future open, authentic voice;
● enable people to have authentic conversation by avoiding PC language but being aware of derogatory language.

We must be willing to get it wrong on occasion, in order to get it right more often.

Notes

1. Within the social sciences, authors such as Schon (1983) are noted for the use of 'reflective practice' as the basis for the development of 'think pieces' which link theory and practice: in the equality and diversity field Thomas Jr (1996) is one of the best known examples of this approach. The gap between the rhetoric and reality of management practice is explored in a very accessible way by John Chicken (2001) – a 'warts and all' account of the experience of management.
2. Chapter 7 – human relations issues.
3. Chapter 3 – learning and change issues.
4. Chapter 1 – employee voice issues.
5. Kurt Lewin's force-field analysis.
6. Chapter 1 – employee voice; trades unions (three-pronged approach); Chapter 4 – partnership issues.
7. Chapter 2 – HR strategic archetypes and associated policy preferences; Chapter 4 on HR policy as facilitator of procedural justice.
8. Chapter 1 – discussion of combined capabilities, role of environment and designated responsibilities therein; Chapter 5 on 'professional' organizations, issues of perceptions of responsibility.

9. Chapter 2 – section on different types of psychological contract; Chapter 4 – issues of HR policy and psychological contract.
10. See in particular sections in Chapters 1 and 4 on line versus specialist responsibility for equality and diversity; plus Chapter 5 on professionals and selective perception of responsibilities.
11. See Chapter 7 on pros and cons of who to target for whole organizational interventions; see Chapter 6 on international for the dilemmas of company versus national values in relation to addressing equality and diversity issues.

References

Chicken, J (2001) *Real Management*, Thomson Learning, London.
Schein, E (1985) *Organisational Culture and Leadership*, Jossey Bass, San Francisco.
Schon, DA (1983) *The Reflective Practitioner*, Basic Books, New York.

Case study 2

Building on a vision: 'inclusive meritocracy' in a major multinational energy company

Suzanne Gagnon and Nelarine Cornelius

Background

Formed through the merger in 1998 of British Petroleum with American oil firm Amoco, BP Amoco is one of the world's leading providers of energy and petrochemicals. It operates in some 100 countries around the world, and employs 85,000 people working in 140 business units, its 'primary units of accountability'. The company has well-established operations in Europe, North and South America, Australasia and parts of Africa. Its products and services are wide-ranging and include gas and power, petrochemicals for plastics, fibres and fabrics, and solar power, in addition to fuel for transport. Its recent acquisition of American Richfield, or Arco, will expand this range of products and geography even further.

Following the merger, BP Amoco headquarters decided to take a fresh look at how the company promotes diversity and equality within the organisation. This ran in parallel with the company's development of its commitment to 'social performance', which it labels the third element of its 'triple bottom line'. The idea is that the business must be judged not by its financial performance alone, but also its environmental performance and social performance. BP Amoco includes within the latter its *behaviour* as an organisation – whether it lives up to its values, its *impact on people*, and its *overall contribution to society*. Thus within social performance the company judges itself against three stated business policies: commitment to ethical conduct, to employees, and to relationships with the wider community.

The vision for workforce diversity and inclusion

In line with this commitment to social performance, the company developed in mid-1999 a new statement of principles, intent and measures on the topic of diversity and inclusion. This started with a *vision* which reads as follows:

> BP Amoco works for mutual advantage as part of the diverse societies and communities where we operate. The diverse people who are BP Amoco will increasingly make our company distinctive by continually challenging how we think, what we do, and how we do it to achieve exceptional business performance.
>
> Our measures of success are the extent to which we create competitive advantage through:
>
> - seeking out, including, respecting and utilising the variety of thoughts and ideas of employees, customers, suppliers and partners, and
> - in so doing, causing visible changes to the composition and behaviours of BP.
>
> Amoco employees:
> We passionately believe that success means we will have a culture in which people from all over the world want to belong and contribute.

The drafters of the new statement were careful to define the key terms within this vision. 'Diversity' was defined as including 'differences that are visible and invisible and exist at the individual, team and organisational levels'. 'Inclusion' was defined as referring to 'intentionally broadening and being willing to accept the varieties of ideas, knowledge, perspectives, approaches and styles of people who participate and contribute'. This includes a recognition that 'every individual, team or part of the organisation has something to contribute but that no individual, team or part of the organisation has all the answers – therefore, openness to changing one's opinions, mindset, and behaviours is necessary for *progress and growth*'. Also included within this definition is the 'elimination of intentional and unintentional exclusionary behaviours' – 'there is no place for favouritism or disrespectful behaviours and zero tolerance for harassment, unlawful discrimination or hate'.

BP Amoco has asked itself the tough questions: 'Why are there relatively few women and members of minorities leading our organisation? Why do between one-fourth and one-third of our employees consistently report that equal opportunity is not available for all? Why is the gender gap in opportunity apparently widening during the course of 1999?' Chief Executive Sir John Browne asked perhaps the toughest question: could this be due to what he called a 'quiet, polite, corrosive litany of prejudice and discrimination'?

The business imperative

BP Amoco sees its policy on workforce diversity and inclusion as a way to meet both internal and external challenges. Internally, a determination to address the questions above, and to meet employees' legitimate expectations that they be treated with dignity and respect and that they will succeed on their own merits, is viewed as the 'key driver' of employee engagement and commitment. Externally, the need to deliver excellent performance in a context where customers, suppliers and strategic partners are increasingly global and multicultural means that the company must retain talent and capitalise on the potential of all of its employees. For example, the business is expected to grow in developing regions such as Asia and Latin America. Creating a culture that embraces difference is seen as acting as a catalyst for this growth.

The company sees addressing diversity and inclusion as central to the achievement of workplace equality, and as such, has developed a diversity-centred approach to equality management that it refers to as 'diversity'. Further, it sees diversity and inclusion as directly contributing to meeting both the internal and external challenges, and thus enhancing competitive advantage, through the following expected results of the policy:

- greater success in attracting and retaining employees, customers and suppliers, and strategic partners;
- being more responsive to opportunities, developing better relationships, and generating creative new business options;
- higher levels of employee engagement, motivation, commitment and creativity, giving the organisation new levels of capability;
- reduced costs of wasted human capital and lost knowledge.

The strategy

So how is BP Amoco bringing this vision about? It is doing so in the first instance through setting six strategic principles designed to underpin the commitment to diversity and inclusion in a *planned, integrated and long-term* fashion. These strategic elements are:

1. Commitment – recognising diversity and inclusion as important business issues, allocating the necessary time and resources, and undertaking personal engagement that challenge 'us' (BP Amoco staff) to go deeper with our learning about diversity and inclusion.
2. Communication – ensuring communication of policy and weaving consistent messages on this into public and internal communications.
3. Accountability – integrating diversity and inclusion into performance contracts at all levels and reporting annually the results in specific measurement areas:
   - employee monitoring statistics;
   - internal perceptions;
   - external perceptions;
   - group-wide strategic priorities.
4. Alignment – demonstrating leadership with diversity and inclusion by agreeing on plans and strategic actions to support business needs, including:
   - communicating a business case;
   - planning and implementing education;

- reviewing policies and procedures, both informal and formal, for their impact on diversity and inclusion;
- determining contributions to group measures and priorities;
- developing meaningful ways for engaging employee involvement.

5. Integration – embedding diversity and inclusion vision and goals into group HR policies and general business processes.
6. Recognition – providing recognition throughout the group for accomplishments and learning with diversity and inclusion.

Implementation: visible changes to workforce composition *and* behaviours of employees are needed

The company's position is that progress both in workforce composition and changes in employee behaviour are required to bring the results it desires, as shown by evidence across industries. 'Neither of these can be relied upon to cause the other', says its implementation plan.

While the vision and strategy were set at group level by expert headquarters staff in this area, the delivery and implementation of the diversity and inclusion commitment is the responsibility of each business unit, and business unit leader (BUL). This is consistent with the structure of the company where these are the 'primary units of accountability'. At this level, goals are set for employee statistics relating to workforce composition, internal perceptions (e.g. as assessed through employee attitude surveys), and external perceptions (e.g. as measured by customer and supplier opinion surveys). For employee statistics, the goals set measure progress in recruitment, development, deployment and retention of employees. Continuous improvement, leading to a genuine meritocracy, is the aim.

Target groups include women, non-UK/US nationals, and other under-represented groups. Each country defines 'under-represented groups' in addition to women and non-UK/US nationals according to the local environment and circumstances. Business units, operating companies, countries and departments set their contribution to group goals and also additional aspirations based on their own situation and business imperatives.

In order to operationalise the commitment to building diversity and inclusion throughout business units, five specific decisions were made by the group executives (GCEs):

1. The statement of principles, intent and measures was approved and its communication throughout the group was agreed.
2. A proposed framework for measurement incorporating employee statistics, internal and external perceptions and group-wide priorities was agreed.
3. A commitment was made to include diversity and inclusion in the group performance contract, through appropriate targets and standards applicable to all business unit leaders.

4. Learning opportunities were agreed to be undertaken for the top 35 executives in the company, based on acknowledgement that 'sensitive and passionate leadership' was vital to success.
5. Diversity and inclusions awards were established based on year-end accomplishments and learnings, in order to recognise and foster progress across the company.

In addition, senior-level diversity and inclusion champions were appointed for each of the company's streams or main businesses, comprising upstream, downstream, solar, and chemicals.

Actions to carry forward the building of an 'inclusive meritocracy'

To build upon the five decisions set out above, specific actions were identified by a think-tank of people from across BP Amoco, and reviewed with over 100 individuals and groups in 10 different countries. These actions include:

- At group level, a focus on the composition of group leadership – the aim over the next ten years is to build a visibly different group leadership across four dimensions of diversity – leadership competencies, nationality, gender and race-ethnicity. This will be done on merit, building an *inclusive meritocracy*.
- Given that changing the profile of the employee base needs to go hand-in-hand with changing the working culture of the organisation, and that many barriers to an inclusive meritocracy are cultural in nature, all group leaders set a specific individual objective to improve the awareness and implementation of diversity and inclusion principles.
- Appropriate selection and development processes for building an inclusive meritocracy. An example here is graduate recruitment and selection processes – internal audits would assess and potentially design (a) which are the targeted universities, (b) who are giving presentation to the potential candidates, and (c) who are interviewing and selecting applicants.
- Given that sustained progress takes place principally at business unit level, each business unit is to develop at least one goal that will significantly improve its implementation of diversity and inclusion principles. Business unit leaders are thus asked to take actions that are most meaningful for their own units. This avoids prescription and builds commitment and understanding, as well as preventing the dangers of 'tokenism' and artificial quotas.

Supporting actions include:

- Recognising that geography has a significant bearing on the social and political environment for work on diversity and inclusion, in addition to the work within business units, each region or major country is to develop a coordinated effort to bring progress in these areas.
- Communications and award.
- Learning for the top 35 operatives.

Local illustrations of actions to build an inclusive meritocracy

At the business unit level, different actions have been initiated to give local expression to the company's diversity and inclusion commitment. In one unit, for example, a series of measures has been put in place to embed the commitment into practice and behaviour throughout the workforce. These include the following:

- Personal performance contracts:
  - Each employee identifies five individual measures that will improve their personal satisfaction at work.
  - The employee signs the contract with spouse, friend or significant other.
  - All employee measures are rolled up into one business unit contract and if 80 per cent of the measures are achieved then a 1.5 per cent 'Teamshare' bonus is paid.
- Web-based system to promote and channel innovation; this includes a 'vent space' where employees can 'off-load' what's bothering them, and an online chat room with the HR director available for at least part of the week to participate and respond.
- Team leaders examine responses to survey questions on diversity and write a narrative to be submitted to the HR director, on how they are inclusive.
- Guiding saying: 'the business unit will show employees are valued as individuals, and your families will know it'.

A second example of local measures makes the link between diversity, inclusion and innovation, through:

- an innovation fund of US$6 million established to foster creativity and innovation to realize untapped, latent capacity in their people;
- a diverse innovation board consisting of group, business unit and an external representative to manage the process above;
- a measure to mature at least two of the resulting ideas with 'material implications' during the year which the business units will utilize;
- a 'representation' objective to 'proactively manage the composition of the management and teams';
- an 'awareness' objective calling for the management team to attend diversity training as a team;
- guiding saying: 'this region is about creating an environment of invitation'.

A preview of 2010 BP Amoco group leadership
The company says that a visibly different group leadership which 'drives distinctive performance through collective innovation based on their diversity' would have roughly the following profile. This is based on a desire to improve representation among the top 500 managers in the company, broadly equivalent to the company's future earnings base:

Nationality
230 North Americans (vs. 266 currently)
125 Europeans (vs. 224 currently)
60 Asians (vs. 2 currently)
30 Latin Americans (vs. 3 currently)
70 individuals from Africa, the Middle East, Russia and the rest of the world
(vs. 19 currently)

Gender
180 women (vs. 37 currently)

Race/ethnicity
Within each nationality, the composition of incumbents would reflect the racial/ethnic mix of that region/country's workforce.

Text-based questions

1. How might the question of ethics raised in the BP case study be considered in relation to the effective management of a multicultural workforce?
2. Illustrate how the six key elements of the BP vision might be brought together to form an integrated, globally acceptable strategy. What role might the 'inclusion champions' play in ensuring that such integration takes place?
3. Look at the website of any international organisation. What does it tell you about its approach to (a) managing managers in an international context, (b) managing more junior employees in an international context?

Internet resources

BP http://www.bp.com/

Case study 3

Wearing warm clothes in winter: a pragmatic process approach to promoting cultural diversity in global succession planning

James H. Ward and Diana Winstanley

Introduction

Diversity management and fair treatment of employees in order to maximise everyone's contribution to the business continues to be of great concern to today's organisations; in a recent survey by the Industrial Society, 67 per cent of UK organisations said that diversity was a high priority, with 77 per cent expecting diversity to become even more important over the next couple of years (Equal Opportunities Review, 2001). However, despite this apparent commitment to the issue, 41 per cent reported that their organisations had been involved in employment tribunal cases regarding diversity and equality issues.

So, despite organisations seeing the value of diversity, why are they still getting it wrong? One further statistic from the same survey might give us a clue. Even though great attention is paid to the recruitment process, other key stages in the individual's career tend not to be monitored; in the same survey, 77 per cent of organisational respondents monitored their recruitment processes for race and gender bias, with 72 per cent monitoring for disability, but post-recruitment processes were not monitored at all, suggesting that they may be open to discriminatory practices (Equal Opportunities Review, 2001). One of these areas, which is particularly vulnerable to prejudice and unfair practice, is promotion and succession planning. Indeed, many researchers have identified this area as one that is open to influence (Hall, 1986; Schneider, 1987; Woodall and Winstanley, 1998).

Indeed, according to a recent survey of FTSE 100 companies surveyed by the Runnymede Trust, ethnic minority groups remain under-represented at a senior management level in private sector organisations. And even if companies believe their policies do not discriminate, there is still a 'yawning gap' between companies' beliefs about their equality policies and how individuals perceive employers' treatment of them (Gagnon and Cornelius, 2000).

The situation is further complicated when the organisation operates in more than one country. Indeed, in a more global corporate environment, the likelihood is that the organisation will see the need to transfer their staff from one country to another. These international moves may be driven by the need to give managers international experience to enable them to become part of a senior team of a multi-national organisation at a later date, or simply be the result of an organisation requirement to fill a post. For whatever reason, there is more need for the global organisation to carry out its succession planning with greater care.

This case study argues that competencies have the potential benefit of supporting a diverse workforce by facilitating the succession planning process, making it clearer, more objective and fair. We report on research into the introduction of competencies for succession planning in a global environment and the potential impact on diversity, drawing on case study material from one international organisation, Rio Tinto. It argues that the introduction of competencies can make succession planning fairer through the application of more objective processes, concentrating on the skills and capabilities of the individual, rather than irrelevant factors such as race, gender, age, disability or sexual orientation.

Equality and diversity issues in traditional succession planning

It is worth beginning by defining what we mean by the terms diversity and succession planning. During the 1980s, political change in favour of the new conservative agenda on both sides of the Atlantic led to a rejection of the egalitarian welfare state (Webb, 1997), and the dominant mobilising vocabulary moved from the need for social justice and morality to the business case for equality (Dickens, 1997). The conservative, right-wing agenda of the early 1980s and 1990s in the UK and USA provided the political environment in which a deregulated, voluntarist, diversity approach could flourish (Noon and Ogbonna, 2001). Indeed, the 1970s and early 1980s agenda for equal opportunities, emphasising the achievement of equal rights by means of bureaucratic control and constraint, has been denigrated as a form of special pleading (Webb, 1997). Operating within this new paradigm, diversity management is about valuing difference, and although the concept of diversity management overlaps with equal opportunities, it places different emphases in its motivation, approach and methods for tackling this issue. It is more concerned with individual contribution than under-represented groups in the workforce, and whereas equal opportunities initiatives have focused on the ethics of rights and justice, and have used corporate policies backed up by regulation and a legislative framework (for example, in the United Kingdom, the use of the Sex Discrimination Acts 1975 and 1986, the Race Relations Act 1976 and the Disability Discrimination Act 1995) to promote fairness and equal opportunity, diversity management has concerned itself with building the business case for valuing difference, using organisational initiatives to emphasise the performance benefits of having a diverse workforce. As such, diversity management weds the ethical agenda for fair treatment to the business agenda for high-performing organisations. Like equal opportunities, it aims at achieving a diverse workforce and removing obstacles which prevent that, but the focus is less narrow than equal opportunities; previously race/ethnicity and gender were the most recognised forms of difference (Kossek and Lobel, 1996: p. 2) whereas the diversity paradigm is also constituted from recognising and valuing differences in sexual orientation, nationality, language, religion, lifestyle, ability and disability, family structure and age, amongst other aspects. However, there is little reason to assume similarity in either the experiences of disadvantage or the potential needs of the various (disadvantaged) groups (Noon and Ogbonna, 2001), and so it is nevertheless necessary to define the area of research focus.

For this case study, the prime concern is cross-cultural diversity, that is to say diversity with relation to ethnicity, race and national culture, although issues of gender, family and lifestyle are also relevant. One of the key ways in which cultural diversity in a multinational differs from diversity in the national context is of course that the protection of embattled 'minorities' starts to take on slightly ironic overtones, when those to be protected outnumber their protectors (Herriot and Pemberton, 1995).

Vital to the issues of diversity is the exploration of how decisions are made over senior management succession, particularly in international organisations. Senior management succession is a key area where decisions impacting on diversity become enacted. Indeed, while great attention is paid to the recruitment process (as shown in the figures at the outset of this case study), other key stages in the individual's career, such as promotion and succession planning, tend not to be monitored, leaving post-recruitment processes open to discriminatory practices (Equal Opportunities Review, 2001) .

The move away from the traditional equal opportunities paradigm to the diversity paradigm for equality management has developed the need to shift the emphasis away from introducing measures to help members of disadvantaged groups to changing organisations themselves (Dickens, 2000), and therefore looking at, for example, the processes that contribute to the way that the organisation works.

One of those processes, *succession planning*, is one of the most neglected areas of human resources, but is nevertheless a crucial one. The activity focuses on the future needs of the business, the career paths of individuals, and the links into training and development, as well as focusing on the skills and competencies which businesses require of individuals. It is broadened out in the concept of succession management to cover the analysis of organisational needs, the auditing of the supply of future managers, as well as assessment processes and development. Succession planning and management are carried out in the majority of large companies, yet traditional methods are the focus of much criticism, not least of which is concern in relation to secrecy, cronyism, narcissism, conservatism and conformism, all of which have ramifications for diversity (Hall, 1986; Kanter, 1977). In many organisations, succession planning has come to mean a secret meeting between senior executives and their peers where they pick successors without the individuals concerned knowing until the very last minute (Mabey and Iles, 1993).

Indeed, traditional succession planning, it might be argued, positively acts against diversity in the organisation. In succession planning, senior influential managers may wish to exercise their own preferences in managerial appointments (Woodall and Winstanley, 1998) and senior executives generally want to promote in their own image, selecting the 'right' kind of person (Hall, 1986; Schneider, 1987), a process referred to by Kanter (1977) as 'homosocial reproduction' (Kossek and Lobel, 1996: p. 3). This would suggest that traditional succession planning may actively prevent people from diverse cultures from reaching the top of the organisation (Ferris, Fink and Galang, 1994; Jackson, 1992). Exercising preferences is one area where discrimination may occur; the others relate to negative attitudes to and discomfort around people who are different, as well as stereotyping and prejudice (Wentling and Palma-Rivas, 1998). People are more comfortable around people who are like themselves, and so by implication are likely to be uncomfortable around people who are different (Wentling and Palma-Rivas, 1998). Discomfort may stem from lack of familiarity or from the belief that other people are inferior. Discrimination may stem from the fact that some people may view ethnic and gender differences as weaknesses, even liabilities. Stereotyping means that gay men and lesbians, women, people of colour, and people living with disabilities are not as successful as they could be; people belonging to these groups are seen as less intelligent, less hardworking and less committed; as a result, less is expected of them (Wentling and Palma-Rivas, 1998). Sometimes minorities will refuse to put themselves forward because they do not want to deal with issues concerning their non-traditional status (Reynolds, Nicholls and Alferoff, 2001). This is particularly true in a multinational context, where national minorities may feel that preference is given to home-country nationals. 'Fitting in' can also present difficulties for national minorities in a multinational organisation, adapting to the organisational culture and knowing whom to approach for support. According to Reynolds *et al.* (2001), perceived lack of support from line managers is a major barrier to career progression.

Homosocial reproduction is clearly extremely harmful for objectivity and fair treatment of employees. It can also breach legal rights and requirements. However, traditional approaches to promoting equal opportunities through legal compliance have had limited impact in this area. Moreover, the environment in a multinational reduces the impact of individual legal rights still further, because the legal framework extends mainly to the development of local managers in their national context, and not to the development of, for example, local managers into international managers by multinationals. Compliance is also more difficult to enforce in a multinational context. This leads to the promotion of other arguments for diversity and fair treatment based on the 'business case' (Liff & Dickens, 2000). Business case arguments focus around three main areas (Cox, 1993): (1) that the demographic profile of the workforce is changing; (2) a culturally diverse workforce will outperform more homogenous ones; (3) diversity actually provides the organisation with competitive advantage, bringing greater awareness of different consumption habits.

Following these arguments, then, homosocial reproduction is bad for business. Nevertheless, we should not ignore the argument for ethical treatment, since there are many organisations for which the economic argument is not paramount. We would argue, along with others (Liff and Dickens, 2000), that the motives for promoting diversity are not necessarily either/or (it is not always useful to explore diversity from one facet only), but it is an and/or issue – a focus on diversity can be justified for both ethical and business case reasons.

It therefore seems important to examine succession planning processes from the ethical standpoint as well as their functionality and their impact on diversity.

The role of competencies in succession management: solving the problem of diversity?

The literature on competencies does not discuss in detail the cultural issues of applying competencies. However, the work on the impact of national culture on multinational organisations (Hofstede, 1991; Trompenaars, 1993) has long pointed out that cultural characteristics in different subsidiaries vary enormously, even in a fairly homogenous company such as IBM. Managerial competencies can be defined as

> The skills, knowledge and understanding, qualities and attributes, sets of values, beliefs and attitudes, which lead to effective managerial performance in a given context, situation or role. (Winstanley in Woodall and Winstanley, 1998: p. 75)

Competencies are therefore concerned with behaviours which lead to effectiveness within a context. Rather than being 'traits' or 'dispositions' which pervaded much earlier work on management and leadership, and tended to have more genetic and immutable qualities of personality, they are viewed as being more focused on observable behaviour and outputs. Where leadership traits were viewed as being qualities people were born with, and possessed in a generalised way, competencies have been seen as more amenable to learning and development, and have focused on situation-based behaviours in certain work contexts.

On the face of it, competencies can be seen as a way of addressing the traditional problems of succession, by applying a non-discriminatory framework to the area of international succession planning. The identification of a clearly presented set of competencies, which can be demonstrated as being linked to capability and performance for senior roles in the organisation, and which are applied in the selection of candidates for future development at the higher level, seems to be one way of ensuring that the subjective, non-justifiable and performance-related criteria be eliminated. Being more open to observation and assessment, they are likely to contribute to more open and transparent succession decisions, based around evidence of performance, thus clearing the way for fairer and more ethical treatment, not subjected to racial and gender bias.

Another way of stating this is that competencies provide a common language as a basis on which managers from around the world can discuss succession decisions more objectively. One employee development manager interviewed put it like this:

> No one has any problem talking about football and why footballers are good; they talk about their skills and ability in a language that everyone can understand. Unfortunately, it is generally the case that when managers are asked to describe their employees, the description often centres around what the employee currently does, or worse, the manager will say that they are not sure why the employee is good, but they do have a gut feel. Competencies address this issue by giving every manager a common language which facilitates succession planning discussions, and enables them to talk about employees with the same ease that they talk about football.

However, the competencies are achieved not from their nature and content alone; success in this area is as much about the *process* through which the benefits are generated. Whether competencies can be seen as more objective and fair templates against which people are assessed for succession decisions is crucially reliant on the methods by which the competencies are generated. Valid and appropriate methods are needed to identify competencies and then to apply the competencies. However, assuming that this can be done, then the benefits for equal and fair treatment seem immense.

In addition, the will has to be present in the organisation to develop people regardless of demographic background; otherwise the competency framework will just mask the subjectivity on which the succession planning system is based. In the next section, the use of competencies in succession planning and the advantages that this can bring will be considered.

The relation of competencies to the capabilities approach

In this book, an important theme has been the expansion of diversity management to incorporate approaches based on capabilities. This leads to the question: 'how does an approach to promoting diversity in the area of succession planning, based on the use of competencies, relate to capabilities?' Or more specifically, 'are competence and capabilities one and the same thing, related or distinct?'

In essence, 'competence' is one necessary component of 'capabilities'. It has been suggested in earlier chapters (and elaborated in Gagnon and Cornelius 2000, p. 73, drawing on the work of Nussbaum, 1999), that capabilities is the freedom for individuals to lead the kind of life they value and make choices based on this. This equality freedom derives from three main forms of capabilities: basic capabilities, which relate to innate abilities; internal capabilities, which are to do with the readiness to act due to the development of competence; and combined capabilities, which enables readiness to translate into action should the actor so wish, due to the existence of a supportive operating environment. Competence therefore relates to the second of these capabilities – the internal state of readiness developed through education and training to equip individuals for decisions, jobs and roles. On its own it is a vital aspect of capabilities, but it does require the third point, the sympathetic environment to enable the translation of competences into practice. Take, for example, a competence or internal capabilities in team building; this may have developed through the support of a management development programme and some experience, and may even be based on innate talents, but it also requires appropriate structures, such as a team-based organisational structure to enable that person to translate that internal capabilities or competences into practice (combined capability). Competence therefore is one vital ingredient of capabilities.

Looking specifically at succession planning, the development and elaboration of competencies, supported by a policy which uses open systems for promotion based around these competencies, make it more likely that internal capability and combined capability will be present, and that an individual's freedom to choose (or not choose) to follow a path leading to promotion to higher levels will be enhanced. As capabilities equality is about freedom and choice, the individual can choose whether or not to exercise this capability freedom.

From the perspective of taking a capabilities approach to diversity, the development of competence, and systems to support succession planning based on competence, are crucial. This case study, however, does not concentrate on the role of agency and the managers themselves in this process, but on the development of conditions under which capability might flourish.

The case of Rio Tinto

Rio Tinto is one of the world's leading international mining groups, with an annual turnover of approximately $9.9 billion and a market capitalisation of $17 billion. It is listed on the London, Australian and New York stock exchanges, and was formed by the merger in December 1995 between the former RTZ in the United Kingdom and CRA in Australia, in a dual-listed companies structure. One of the objectives of the change was to create a seamless identity to better reflect the unified organisation. Rio Tinto's substantial interests in mining include copper, gold, iron ore, coal, aluminium, borates and titanium feedstock. It is a truly global operation with operating companies on every continent. The group's headquarters are in London, whilst its interests are predominantly located in North America and Australia, as well as in South America, Asia, Europe and Southern Africa. Products are sold worldwide, but particularly in North America, Europe and Asia. The group employs directly 28,000 people, with approximately a further 6,000 proportionate to the group's equity interests in part-owned associates and joint ventures.

There were several key decision points in identifying the competencies framework that embody implications for diversity. These key choices are identified below, with a discussion of their possible impact on diversity, and the decisions made by the case study company. In this discussion, there is no attempt to identify the company as portraying good or poor practice in this area, instead the reflections are intended to tease out some of the vital points of choice which require sensitivity, but where there may be no one clear 'right' way.

Defining the problem and identifying motivation

Before embarking on the issues of developing competencies it is vital to consider the purpose of the exercise (Woodall and Winstanley, 1998: p. 86). This includes making how far diversity issues are to be addressed an explicit aim of the programme, if they are included. When seen as contributory factors in business success, then it seems more likely that the impact will be positive in this area.

Rio Tinto's objectives in developing the competencies for succession planning were to deliver a more internationally flexible workforce for the organisation, for business as well as ethical reasons. There was the will to develop managers from diverse geographic, cultural and linguistic backgrounds amongst the managers interviewed, but this was wedded to the business case for diversity. The business case seemed to managers in Rio Tinto an essential underpinning, and this view came particularly to the fore over discussions of positive action through target setting and other measures. One senior manager stated:

> I will not compromise on the capabilities of candidates for the sake of meeting some arbitrary quota or other predetermined level of minorities.

Similarly another manager said:

> What we don't want to do is to create cultural diversity for the sake of it. What we want are culturally diverse, successful managers.

The rights- and justice-based case made for equal opportunities seems to be viewed as important only in so far as it contributes to the more utilitarian and performance-based arguments of diversity management.

Another motivation was wanting to help at the individual level in preparing managers for overseas assignments. Their experience had been that personal factors often make or break an overseas posting. Thus, they wanted to explore the possibility of competencies to meet the needs of both the company itself and its strategic requirement (getting the best people in the top posts) and also the career needs of the individual executives from diverse cultural backgrounds. Achieving a senior management team drawn from a more diverse range of backgrounds and cultures was seen as both desirable and likely to improve their business performance. For example, one senior manager argued strongly in favour of developing people from different cultures:

> First, Borax (a subsidiary of Rio Tinto) does business in nearly 100 countries around the world. It is important for us to understand our customers

and the business and social environments in which they operate. Second, people from different cultures bring different and fresh perspectives into Borax.

Thus, there is evidence in Rio Tinto of commitment to a diversified workforce. Also, Rio Tinto is a fairly decentralised company and a very international one. Most of Rio Tinto's 28,000 employees are based outside the United Kingdom, and the proportion of home-country nationals is extremely small compared to, for example, IBM. Thus some managers already feel that there is cultural diversity in the workforce at higher levels. As one senior manager concluded:

> I am lucky in that I do have culturally diverse managers reporting to me. They are a living testament to equal opportunity.

Finding the best people for a company like Rio Tinto means looking for essential competencies in any nationality. Indeed, Rio Tinto managers expressed this view in interviews with comments such as,

> In selecting candidates, we must not become an Anglo-Australian clique.

And

> We must appoint the best available candidate for the job, irrespective of origin.

It seems that there was some evidence that the current succession process in Rio Tinto was not working, and that competencies could help improve this process. One typical problem mentioned was the difficulties raised by the distance involved. One manager, based outside the United Kingdom said,

> I have a real problem putting people forward: it's much easier for someone (in the head office) to get their person into the job.

One manager interviewed even asked,

> Is there a career path for me? No one ever told me!

Another disparity, which emphasises the need for more active diversity management is the difference in promoting managers in their own countries, compared with movement internationally. As with many companies, Rio Tinto finds it easier to support host-country managers in their own context, than to develop them through assignments in other countries, unless they are part of the dominant cultures: as one manager said,

> We do develop managers locally; what we do not do enough of is to bring local managers into international managers.

Therefore, there is an identified need for action to be taken in this area, and motivation to support that, with competencies being one potential method for improvement.

Stand-alone competencies in succession planning, versus integrated with HRM

Many earlier approaches to competencies assumed that succession planning was one aspect of an integrated HRM system, where the competencies approach would cover not only succession planning, but also recruitment, selection, management development, and remuneration and reward (Boyatzis, 1982). Clearly there are advantages in so doing because the different aspects of HRM are closely linked. For example, management development might be seen as a logical extension of succession planning; once a manager has been identified for a particular job, the company can then develop the manager so that adequately skilled and trained individuals are promoted into key positions. In addition, competencies show what it means to be successful in the organisation, which is not only relevant for those inside the organisation, but also those looking to join it, thus supporting recruitment and selection. In performance appraisals, competencies make it possible to assess behavioural and attitudinal aspects of managers' performance, not just their skills.

For developing diversity, an integrated system has the potential to promote transparency and fairness across the organisation and its practices in a more comprehensive way, and where diversity is seen as one of the objectives, this could raise the profile of this issue, and embed its value in the culture.

However, there are practical reasons why succession planning may need to be treated differently, and which suggest problems in achieving a fully integrated approach. For example, succession management focuses on the skill requirements of the business rather than detailed knowledge of each individual post, and is, in effect, concerned with future management competencies rather than current jobs. In addition, it is important that succession plans define a profile of leadership (McElwain, 1991) so that the executive ranks gain new capabilities over time. It is important to identify the areas of knowledge, style and personal characteristics that are required so that the business can develop its best people based on this profile.

Likewise in promoting diversity, the particular problems for diversity faced by international succession planning and management means that a more generalised approach could lose the focus on tackling nepotism, cronyism and homosocial reproduction. It seems possible that diversity needs different actions in different areas to tackle the barriers. Logistics also suggest that it may be wise to use the Pareto principle, and tackle the area with greatest need first.

In the case study, the approach taken was to define a distinct set of succession planning competencies. This was done because there was no competency framework at the Rio Tinto level, even though some group companies may have developed systems of their own to underpin other areas of HR. In addition, most areas of Human Resource Management are devolved to the group companies, with the exception of succession planning, where the requirement to carry out succession planning is a policy driven from the centre.

Top down or bottom up?

Should the competencies be developed in a top-down or bottom-up way? A bottom-up approach would potentially have the benefit for diversity that each geographic locality would have the flexibility to generate competencies which reflected their own needs and culture. On the other hand, this would have the potential pitfall of creating cultural silos, preventing transfer across from one area to another. If bottom-up, the competencies would have been identified in different mining businesses and different cultures with varying individualist or collectivist characteristics. There were doubts about the capacity of the organisation, through this approach, to achieve a consensus across the organisation.

A top-down approach would have the potential benefit of a level playing-field for all – where whatever the cultural framework or area, people would be working towards the same competencies, perhaps preventing local subjectivity and more personalised decision making. The disadvantage for diversity here would be the likelihood that a 'top-down' system would create a template based on the dominant cultures in the organisation, further marginalising people from countries outside what were perceived to be the powerful cultures – British, North American and Australian.

The existing business structures and ways of working also need to be considered. In this regard, the degree of centralisation or decentralisation is important. A decentralised company would require greater flexibility in the application of competencies in different cultural contexts and operations than a centralised one.

In Rio Tinto, the top-down approach was taken because of the need to derive succession planning competencies from strategy. Also, there was some acceptance that when creating a framework to underpin global Human Resource practices such as succession planning, it was thought necessary to develop a global policy, and managers in different countries accepted that it is necessary to accept certain corporate standards. One Japanese manager from Rio Tinto said:

> If it's winter outside, everyone has to put on warm clothes!

However, because Rio Tinto is decentralised to a significant degree, it was decided that senior managers from different parts of the company would be included in the interviewing frame and that cultural flexibility would be key in order to allow local managers to adapt these to the needs of local cultures, a point returned to below.

How to generate the competencies – strategy or job-led?

It is difficult to know where to start in identifying the competencies – do you examine the strategy for indicators, or do you focus on identifying the requirements of the jobs conducted at this level? Methods that focus on developing competencies from focusing on jobs tend to focus on approaches such as questionnaires of job tasks and activities, observation of managers conducting their jobs, or activity diaries where managers themselves record their activities. However, for succession management, we are not concerned so much with basic-level competencies but more with high-performance competencies (Schroder, 1989). High-performance competencies are more appropriate for succession planning because succession planning is about high potential and high performance, as well as more transferable personal effectiveness skills. As stated above, succession planning is also about future strategic needs of the business and not just about the needs of one particular role or function. Indeed, effective companies match their succession strategies to their business strategies (Gratton and Syrett, 1990). Research into the succession management systems of 13 major UK companies supports the view that competencies in succession planning should be derived from the business strategy, rather than current jobs (Wallum, 1993).

This is a double-edged sword for diversity. The lack of clarity and tangibility of using future-orientated, strategic, high-performance competencies, contrasted to assessments based more on role and job analysis, takes away the standard approaches used for promoting equal opportunities. Much of the equal opportunities legislation in the UK and elsewhere relied on the premise that equal opportunities would be advanced by basing human resource practices around job-relevant criteria, and the basis for deciding on whether recruitment, selection and promotion decisions were both fair and seen to be fair derived from the existence of clear job-related criteria, often produced from detailed job analysis. Likewise, in equal pay cases, the standard advice meted out by the Commission for Racial Equality and the Equal Opportunities Commission in the United Kingdom was to conduct analytical job evaluation exercises.

An interesting aspect in the development of the diversity approach, contrasted with the more traditional equal opportunities approach, is that diversity approaches have moved away from standardisation and towards relying on business case and strategic approaches to support difference. Therefore, an approach to competencies based not so much around job and role analysis as strategic orientation and high performance may be more complementary in culture and practice with diversity management than older approaches to equal opportunities. Although the generation of competencies may differ from job analysis, there is still a large amount of standardisation in the competencies generated. The very idea of producing standardised templates of what constitutes high performance in itself is challenging for the notion of promoting diversity and difference. A danger here may be that the old homosocial reproduction based on nepotism and cronyism may just be replaced by a newer form of homosocial reproduction based on uniform transnational templates generated from dominant cultures. The points below identify those tempering mechanisms that need to be in place to enable some flexibility and cultural adaptation.

What method and how to involve?

Getting local managers to participate in the process of competency identification, communication, training and implementation is essential to the buy-in across cultures and national boundaries. This view is prevalent across different industry sectors, but especially in Rio Tinto where there is a culture of consultation. One developing country manager said:

> It is (always) desirable if the head office has solicited views of local management to formulate certain goals.

Language is, of course, an important issue; involvement from different English-speaking countries (USA, UK, Australia and South Africa) ensures acceptability of the English used, whereas early involvement by managers from a non-English-speaking environment will ensure appropriate translations.

Consultation is required with managers from diverse backgrounds, for the competences to be acceptable and appropriate, as well as the approach being sensitive to cultural issues. This is an ongoing process, and not one which stops with the initial generation of the competencies. From an exploration of the literature on the development of competencies, there were a variety of different methods that could be pursued, although some of these were ruled out because of being too job-focused as mentioned above – observation of managers, managers filling in time-activity diaries, job and role analysis questionnaires, for example. Having decided that it was important to include dialogue over the future strategy and direction of the company, as well as information from managers in a variety of cultural contexts, using structured interviews seemed to be the most practical approach. A total of 29 Rio Tinto senior managers were interviewed, of various nationalities (American, Australian, British, Italian, Japanese, Russian and Singaporean), based in different locations, working in different mining businesses and functions.

The importance of producing valid information meant that rather than just using the structured interviews, an additional process of triangulation was used. As well as discussion over the future direction of the company, the interviews with the cross-section of managers utilised a list of existing competencies used in Rio Tinto subsidiaries, as well as seeking out their views on important competencies not included in these lists, and ones which they felt reflected the strategic direction of the company. All the suggested competencies were summarised in one document, which was then passed back to the managers involved in the study for their comments and for them to prioritise. What came out of this process was a honed-down summary list of priority competencies presented in Figure C3.1.

Of particular interest for the focus here was that 'awareness of other cultures' came out as one of the potential competencies. Therefore competencies may not just aid diversity through the fairness in the process, but also through explicit recognition of this as something to be valued, by appearing as one of the competencies for succession planning itself. Of the 39 competencies listed in the original rating instrument where managers scored competencies on a

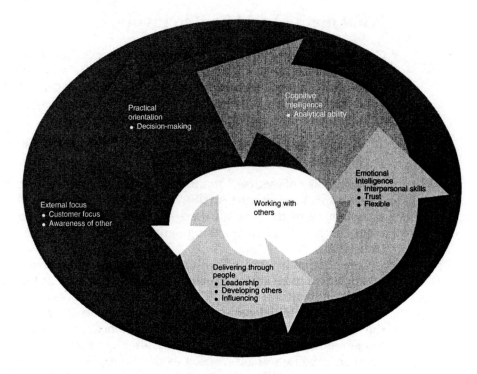

Figure C3.1   Summary of competencies, in clusters, chosen by Rio Tinto managers

rating of 1 (not relevant) to 5 (highly relevant), 'awareness of other cultures' came 17th with a mean score of 4.17. However, it had a high standard deviation score of 0.98, suggesting that there was some variation of opinion on its relevance. It is particularly interesting to note that out of those who answered, all those who gave high scores were from cultures other than the dominant cultures of British, American or Australian, whilst those from the dominant cultures gave low scores. This also shows the importance of the choice of respondents in a study of this type – 55 per cent of the respondents were British, and if more had been selected from non-Anglo-Saxon environments, it is likely that the score would have been higher for this competency. When a second questionnaire was administered with a honed-down list of 21 competencies (where only one manager refused to fill it in), with ratings being from 3 (essential) down to 0, this competence came 18th with a mean score of 1.91 and was kept in the final selection of 13 (divided into 6 areas – see Figure C3.1), due to its importance to non-Anglo-Saxon managers and its relevance given the objectives of the exercise.

A set of competencies to be used in succession planning across the whole organisation was established from this information. The interviews also explored managers' concerns surrounding their implementation in an international environment, full of people from diverse cultural backgrounds, and this generated a number of issues that may not otherwise have surfaced.

Flexibility in local implementation

The degree to which there is flexibility in implementation of competencies across national boundaries is an extremely important issue. For a company as culturally diverse and as decentralised as Rio Tinto, there was a dilemma arising from the development of succession planning systems and the identification of generic competencies. Given that they would be derived at the strategic level and introduced in a top-down fashion, there were concerns for cultural diversity and fears that this would not work in an organisation as decentralised as Rio Tinto.

Rejection of, or resistance to, a new system may be for different reasons in different countries. In the USA or Europe, for example, people may well be familiar with the concept of competencies, but unwilling to accept something which is imposed on them. In other countries, for example, they may be far more willing to adapt, but they may be unfamiliar with the concept. Both types of problem need to be surfaced at an early stage so that different, but appropriate, solutions can be applied locally.

Local buy-in to the competencies is more likely where local managers have freedom in implementation. Indeed, more than one manager made the point that those managers in operating companies know what works best for them locally:

> People on the ground can design pathways that achieve (successful implementation) using their own knowledge of cultural sensitivity.

As well as early involvement, another solution seemed to be to allow some customisation at the local level. This might mean, for example, slight differences in the definition of the competencies, or different prioritisation. Indeed, one manager said,

> Once you have identified behaviours and set targets, your first instinct is to say that they are all important. That is not always going to be the case; it is OK to have the same set of behaviours defined through the group, but we need to accept that they are not always going to have the same level of priority.

One example of this was the competency 'Decision making', where the definition differed in different cultures, the two main variables being decision quality and decision timeliness. Another example is the competency 'Awareness of other cultures' which has been discussed above, in its varying importance to UK, USA and Australian managers (the dominant cultures), contrasted to managers from other cultures.

An example of how the local implementation could work is furnished by Borax, a member of the Rio Tinto group. One of the recommendations of this study was that Borax should pilot implementation of the competencies. Since it is a global mining operation in its own right, it would gain the advantages of using an international competency framework. Borax's activities are the mining, refining and supply of borates.

Borax has its headquarters in Los Angeles; this office also manages the sales in North America. The principal mine, and source of 98 per cent of its products, is located 100 miles to the north of Los Angeles. The company employs about 1650 people in many different countries; the USA, Argentina, Brazil, most European countries, Singapore and Japan.

Borax began by holding a series of focus groups, one of the aims of which was to get cross-cultural support. The exercise involved 204 employees (about 12 per cent of the workforce) in the United States, Argentina, Spain, France and the United Kingdom (the latter focus group involving managers from different European countries). Borax illustrated the use of both consultation in the development and implementation of the competencies drawing on a culturally mixed sample of the workforce. It is too early to say how successful the programme has been, but preliminary findings suggest that the competencies have been well received. It is important that Borax continues to evaluate the programme's success, and to investigate its impact on the cultural mix at the senior level in the organisation.

Family-friendly practices

So far the discussion has focused on issues of cultural mix, and the use of competencies to improve this as a route to managing diversity. However, diversity management is not just about achieving a culturally mixed workforce at all levels of the organisation; it also involves drawing on other previously underrepresented groups and addressing other issues such as gender and family-friendly practices. With relation to employees with partners and families, international mobility can be difficult. It is now well documented that dual-income homes are an added complication to the issue of moving managers around internationally, and that the partner's career is more and more becoming the reasons for managers refusing a transfer. Although companies may no longer mark down employees who do not go where their company wants to send them, there is still the belief that it is not possible to lead a multinational without having worked in different cultures. This is one of the paradoxes of diversity management in international succession – to promote more of a culturally mixed workforce at the higher levels may require more international mobility and succession, yet paradoxically this may also be one reason why individuals in dual-career partnerships or with families may not get to the higher reaches of management; this has negative consequences for gender, as some women in particular feel unable to juggle this process when having reluctant partners and difficulties over childcare and rearing.

As well as investigating Rio Tinto's practices, other comparable companies' practices were sought in this area. One company (not Rio Tinto) was becoming more flexible on location, but as a senior manager with the organisation said:

> They are not doing it to help women; they are doing it to stop a brain drain.

Other organisations, in response to surveys of spouses, have set up job networks and information centres in other countries, and bursaries for training. Where an employee's spouse is located in another country where the partner cannot work, the company will pay for them to maintain and update their skills. Some companies put together information packs about countries so that managers can make informed choices about where to go. In one company, if both partners work for the company, they are asked to nominate one person as the 'lead career' and the other person will have to follow them as they are moved around the world.

This discussion, although limited, illustrates that competencies is just one of many routes to improving the management of diversity.

Do competencies help or hinder diversity management?

The interviews found that from the individual perspective a competency framework can provide a focus for the development of individuals and help underpin the link between succession planning and management development. In addition, this opening up of succession planning makes the process a lot more objective and addresses the criticisms of traditional succession planning in any company, its secrecy and subjectivity.

It would seem to be one step on the way to creating the environment for capability based on competence to thrive, and to open up more choices for those individual 'agents' from a range of backgrounds who had less capability freedom when the systems were less open and transparent. Of course other measures would be required to take this capability freedom further, such as putting in a system to develop the competences or internal capabilities of all staff, regardless of cultural background.

From the strategic and the diversity perspective, managers believed that an international competency framework could help to extend the organisational labour pool across national boundaries, making it easier to move employees into certain jobs, and more importantly, turning the searchlight on the corporate skill-base across the globe and making it easier to identify employees.

From talking to the 29 Rio Tinto managers, there were three guidelines which were thought to be crucial to allow for as much diversity as possible in the multinational organisation:

- global policy, local implementation;
- use competencies as a tool to develop all nationalities;
- local involvement as soon as possible.

However, it is important to be realistic about what competencies can and cannot achieve in promoting diversity in succession management. Some managers felt its impact would be small and, whilst competencies may help in this area, they will not bring about a dramatic change. One senior manager stated:

> Much of what we do is highly specialised and the pool of candidates from which we choose workers is very much self-selecting against diversity ... add to that the relatively low turnover of employees and the desire to

promote from within when possible, and you have a situation not likely to change very quickly.

There are also some reasons why a large multinational may not have a diversified top management which cannot be tackled by competencies alone. For example, one manager said that developing managers from developing countries was not easy, because there were going to be fewer and fewer managers to choose from. He described how globalisation brings with it the phenomenon of *disoccupation*, where operating companies in developing countries are encouraged by their foreign parent to restructure and reduce headcount; fewer jobs remain, creating a difficult background in which to develop people, with numbers always weighted in favour of the home-country nationals. This is a problem faced by many international companies and Rio Tinto has a smaller proportion of home-country employees than many. This returns us to the earlier point, that a range of human resource approaches need to be enacted; new procedures in succession planning on its own is not enough. Nevertheless, it should be recognised that Rio Tinto is a very international company and the proportion of home-country employees in Rio Tinto is extremely small.

Of course, amongst the existing population of managers the interviews suggested a range of attitudes towards cultural diversity, and different views on how to achieve it. From the above research for this organisation, positive action was not considered a fruitful route, and there was still some ambivalence over equal treatment. One factor, which also is challenging for diversity and requires action other than the use of competencies to address, is the notion of core and periphery workforces, or in other words a dual labour market. There is evidence in both attitude and practice that certain nationalities constitute the core recruitment base – for example, for the subsidiary Borax it is easy to assume that North America is used preferentially as a core recruitment base where two-thirds of its employees are in the United States. However, given that cultural diversity is important to the company, senior managers emphasis the need to 'develop South Americans, Asians and Europeans *along* with North Americans as the core'.

In conclusion then, this case study has reported on research into the establishment of competencies for succession management in a global multinational mining company, Rio Tinto. It has argued that using global companies can both support and cause problems for 'diversity', and that ethical sensitivity is needed to appreciate and respond to the issues raised.

This case study began with an outline of the issues in succession planning which undermine diversity and drive the requirement for a competency-base framework in this area. It identified important areas in the development and implementation of competencies in succession planning, where ethical and cultural sensitivity is required to maximise the beneficial impact of competencies and minimise harm in this area. It presented a range of views from managers in Rio Tinto on the implementation of competencies and their effect on diversity in this organisation. It has also shown that competencies is one of a number of ways of addressing diversity issues. It has been suggested that diversity management is one area where ethical concerns over fairness and openness can be wedded to the business case of improving performance. Moreover, competencies may be one way to achieve both ethical and business aims in the area of succession management, as long as some ethical sensitivity is applied in their development and application.

Text-based questions

1. Compare and contrast the different issues that are being addressed in case studies 2 and 3. Are there any apparent differences in the way in which BP and Rio Tinto are approaching the management of a diverse workforce?
2. In the case study, reference is made to the phenomenon known as 'homosocial reproduction'. How would you interpret this phenomenon?
3. Look at the website of any international organisation. What does it tell you about its approach to (a) managing managers in an international context, (b) managing more junior employees in an international context?

Internet resources

Rio Tinto Group http://www.riotinto.com/

References

Anonymous (2001) Most employers lack a diversity strategy. *Equal Opportunities Review*, **96**, 3.

Boyatzis, RE (1982) *The Competent Manager: a model for effective performance*, John Wiley & Sons, Chichester.

Cox, T (1993) *Cultural diversity in organisations: theory, research and practice*, Berrett-Koehler, San Francisco.

Dickens, L (1997) Gender, race and employment equality in Britain: inadequate strategies and the role of industrial relations actors. *Industrial Relations Journal*, **28** (4), 282–291.

Dickens, L (2000) Still wasting resources? Equality in employment, in S Bach and K Sisson (eds) *Personnel Management, a comprehensive guide to theory and practice*, pp. 137–169, Blackwell, Oxford.

Ferris, GR, Fink, DD and Galang, MC (1994) Diversity in the workplace: the human resources management challenges. *Human Resource Planning*, **16**, 41–51.

Gagnon, S and Cornelius, N (2000) Re-examining workplace equality: the capabilities approach. *Human Resource Management Journal*, **10** (4), 68–87.

Gratton, L and Syrett, M (1990) Heirs apparent: succession strategies for the future. *Personnel Management (IPM now IPD)*, **22** (1), 34–38.

Hall, DT (1986) Dilemmas in linking succession planning to individual executive learning. *Human Resource Management*, **25** (2), 235–265.

Herriot, P and Pemberton, C (1995) *Competitive advantage through diversity*, Sage, London.

Hofstede, G (1991) *Cultures and organizations*, McGraw Hill, Maidenhead.

Jackson, SE (1992) Stepping into the future: guidelines for action, in SE Jackson and Associates (eds) *Diversity in the workplace: human resource initiatives*, Guildford Press, New York.

Kanter, RM (1977) *Men and women of the corporation*, Basic Books, New York.

Kossek, EE and Lobel, SA (1996) *Managing diversity: human resource strategies for transforming the workplace*, Blackwell, Oxford.

Liff, S and Dickens, L (2000) Ethics and equality: reconciling false dilemmas, in D Winstanley and J Woodall (eds) *Ethical issues in contemporary human resource management*, pp. 85–101, Macmillan, Basingstoke.

Mabey, C and Iles, P (1993) The strategic integration of assessment and development practices: succession planning and new management development. *Human Resource Management Journal*, **3** (4), 16–34.

McElwain, JE (1991) Succession plans designed to manage change. *HR Magazine*, **36** (2), 67–71.

Noon, M and Ogbonna, E (2001) *Equality, diversity and disadvantage in employment*, Palgrave, Basingstoke.

Nussbuam, M (1999) Women and Equality: the capabilities approach. *International Labour Review*, **138** (3), 227–245.

Reynolds, G, Nicholls, P and Alferoff, C (2001) Disabled people, (re)training and employment: a qualitative exploration of exclusion, in M Noon and E Ogbonna (eds) *Equality, diversity and disadvantage in employment*, pp. 190–207, Palgrave, Basingstoke.

Schneider, B (1987) The people make the place. *Personnel Psychology*, **40**, 437–453.

Schroder, HM (1989) *Managerial competence: the key to excellence*, Kendall Hunt, Dubuque, Iowa.

Trompenaars, F (1993) *Riding the waves of cultural change – understanding cultural diversity in business*, Nicholas Brearley Publishing, London.

Wallum, P (1993) A broader view of succession planning. *Personnel Management (IPM now IPD)*, **25** (9), 42–45.

Webb, J (1997) The politics of equal opportunity. *Gender, Work and Organization*, **4** (3), 159–169.

Wentling, RM and Palma-Rivas, N (1998) Current status and future trends of diversity initiatives in the workplace: diversity experts' perspective. *Human Resource Development Quarterly*, **9** (3), 235–253.

Woodall, J and Winstanley, D (1998) *Management Development: strategy and practice*, Blackwell, Oxford

Final comments

Nelarine Cornelius and Nigel Bassett-Jones

Introduction

This book has developed two complementary thrusts. The first has focused on providing both an ethical and a 'new' business case foundation for addressing and building workplace equality and diversity. The second has addressed the same issues from the perspective of getting 'ideas into action' through informed and reflective intervention and good practice.

This final section of the book will draw these themes together by attempting to push our envelope of understanding further. To do this, we have chosen three issues that we think would benefit from further development. Methodological and practice limitations inform our view of what is possible. Emergent areas are becoming better established within 'HR' (as a general function, not just as a specialist support activity). New practices are accompanying these developments. Three areas in particular may be useful in this context.

The practical delivery of HR strategy

The first relates to the practical delivery of HR strategy. It will become increasingly important for organisations to enable their line managers to acquire the competencies necessary to manage and nurture human capital. Leadership ability (and demonstrable moral leadership) in these areas will become crucially important for local delivery of equality and diversity. This demands that more broadly based equality and diversity thinking be developed within the line that is founded upon a strong 'practical learning' orientation if it is to be seen as valid and relevant. There is a danger that if traditional EO is replicated within the new approaches to HRM then failure is likely to ensue, with consequences for both corporate longevity and social stability. Further, means will need to be developed to empower line managers to facilitate the creation of social capital within their areas of responsibility, as an important, primary mechanism for enabling capabilities equality, and in particular, inclusion and felt-fairness.

Measurement, support systems and structures

The second relates to more elaborate systems for the management and measurement of social capital, social and ethical criteria for sustainability, social accounting, change and transformational management, and so on. Each is developing a range of methodologies and approaches that go well beyond the administrative traditions of 'personnel practice' grounded in approaches to equal opportunities. In short, leading-edge HRM practices are shifting the skills and knowledge mix and a richer skills and knowledge base is becoming established.

Empowering employee voice and agency

Finally, the issue of employee voice will need to be addressed more extensively. A number of approaches throughout the text have been discussed but there is a need to establish how diversity management through the line can best be delivered in both the unionised and non-unionised firm. Some work has been done in this area (e.g. Mick Marchington's work cited in Storey, 2000), but more elaborate approaches will need to be developed. At this stage, we cannot assert what the specific approaches should be, but we can give some indications of the likely parameters that will be required to enable employees to seek and recognise authentic and purposeful conversations. Moreover, employee representatives working through their trades unions will need to address 'difference' in relation to equality with the same degree of concern they have historically shown for 'sameness'. Stakeholder partnerships that create structures for enhancing workplace democracy and have, at their core, strategies, mechanisms and rights for the expression of employee voice and exercise of agency are required. These will need to be developed through the incorporation of core values and basic assumptions into organisational culture. To succeed, employee participation, and an expectation of facilitation on the part of managers, will have to be championed by top teams and reinforced through regular assessment of each manager's ability and willingness to facilitate and support the necessary processes, probably within the context of a stronger legal framework.

Our objective, therefore, is to conclude by developing these suggestions and highlight particular courses of action that will support the process. In so doing, we aim to offer a hopeful view of both the challenges and the opportunities that confront organisations that are prepared to commit to a contemporary diversity agenda.

Environmental changes creating a more 'capabilities equality' friendly climate

The dynamics that are setting this agenda, as suggested in Chapter 2, are beyond the control of any organisation. They are to do with globalisation, changes in demography, changing societal expectations and accelerating rates of innovation and change. The issue confronting organisations is whether to embrace diversity as an opportunity or to ignore it. Embracing capabilities equality and diversity will demand changes of approach, ignoring it will exact costs.

Requisite variety and recursion

Ashby's Law, also known as the law of requisite variety, is a key concept within the tradition of soft systems methodologies rooted in cybernetics. According to the law of requisite variety, an organisation is a human activity system. In order to survive, it must adapt continuously to changes in its environment. Successful adaptation is a function of the effectiveness of its control system (management). To enable the organisation to survive, the speed and responsiveness of management must match the speed and complexity of the changes occurring in the environment. In other words, management must possess the necessary requisite variety. The principle of delegation, founded upon the idea that authority to act should be devolved to the lowest level competent to deal with a given situation effectively, is a recognition of Ashby's Law. It achieves two vital outcomes simultaneously: on the one hand it speeds up processes and responsiveness, and on the other, it prevents those tasked with being proactive becoming bogged down with the mundane.

One of the key axioms in cybernetics is that any viable system contains, and is contained within, a viable system. This phenomenon is known as *recursion*. Any living entity is composed of cells. Collectively the cells constitute organs that discharge different functions. When the organs function well, the viability of the larger system is assured. When there is a malfunction, the viability of the larger system is compromised. In soft systems modelling, this analogy is applied to human activity systems. Organisations that adopt and manage equality and diversity well are endowed with greater requisite variety at each level of recursion. The requisite variety is rooted in the array of individual lenses through which changes in the environment are monitored and interpreted. An organisation that is characterised by employee homogeneity, in contrast, will have a more simplified understanding of the same pattern of events. The creation of requisite variety demands that the practical delivery of HR strategy must be vested in the individual line manager in order to create agency. Only by so doing can the managers create agency in individuals and thereby deliver a genuinely empowered workforce.

The 'transformative capacity' of agency

Giddens (1990) described an agent as an individual with transformative capacity so that 'whatever happened would not have happened had that individual not intervened'.

This implies that agency does not refer to intentions, but rather to capabilities: 'action depends upon the capability of the individual to make a difference

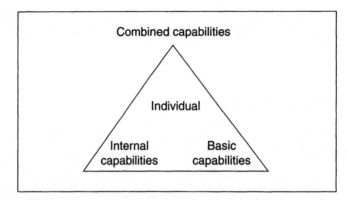

Figure 1   The individual in relation to capabilities

to a pre-existing state of affairs or events. An agent ceases to be such if he or she loses the capability to "make a difference", that is, to exercise some sort of power'.

In Chapter 1, Nussbaum's (1999) account of the ensemble of *capabilities* was explored. It was suggested that capabilities is a demanding concept that is founded on the goal of 'functioning'. Whilst it does not push people into functioning, it does present them with choice, with the potential for freedom of opportunity. *Managerial agency*, therefore, can either facilitate or inhibit the exercise of choice and with it, internal capabilities (internal state of readiness to act). This is illustrated at the first level of recursion in Figure 1.

Managerial agency can be thought of as being composed of three variables: emotions, thoughts and ideas, and actions that bring about changes that can be judged in terms of the individual manager's values and objectives. We also noted in Chapter 1 that agency can only flourish if all three types of capabilities are present, in an enabling environment. Such an environment must facilitate the exercise of the five instrumental freedoms by both individuals and managers. Whilst managers can create the enabling environment for individuals, it is the HR policies and systems that create communities of practice that afford an enabling environment for managers. If managers are to flourish and to grow to the point where they can exercise combined capabilities in the context of workforce diversity, they must be encouraged to develop *their own* internal capabilities.

This is depicted in Figure 2 at the second level of recursion. Managerial agency is highly influential in determining the extent to which individuals can exercise internal capabilities. Individual behaviours influence the behaviours of groups. When individuals believe that they have clear goals and a sense of purpose, and operate in an environment where the principles of both procedural and distributive justice are being observed, as we considered in Chapter 2, disengagement diminishes and group performance is enhanced, along with employee voice and the quality of the psychological contract.

In a climate such as this, there is a greater likelihood that diversity will enhance requisite variety and catalyse higher levels of creativity and innova-

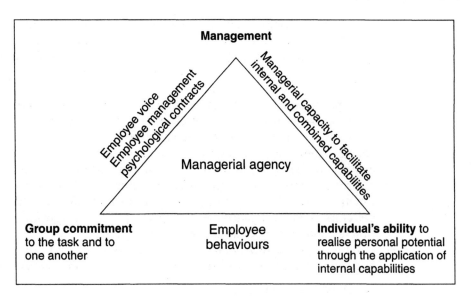

Figure 2   The role of managerial agency in creating combined capabilities

tion. This improves organisational fit with the environment and with it, prospects for long-term survival and growth. In short, effective equality and diversity management founded upon empowering HR systems that foster and promote effective managerial agency has the potential to become a distinctive core competence, and therefore, an integral component in an organisation's strategic architecture. The alternative is to ignore the emerging possibilities arising from greater employee diversity, constrain managerial agency through rigid or disempowering HR systems, reduce requisite variety and live with the consequences.

Measurement and models of HRM

Further, we believe that Ashby's Law can be linked to an important aspect of post-modernism, specifically the post-modern discourses argument as a mechanism for demanding a new look at the disempowering effects of traditional, professional mechanistic and 'guarded strategist' approaches to HRM (Brewster and Larson, 1992).

Generally, these approaches have supported equality policies based on *numbers* as the primary mechanism for measuring success in promoting equality and diversity. However, even when the numbers are right, if the principles of procedural and distributive justice are not being observed then the consequences can be demotivating and alienating as we saw in the Coca-Cola case cited in Chapters 1 and 2.

If more line management-centred delivery of HR and equality management is to be achieved, this also requires a change in many HRM and personnel departments' traditional responsibilities. There is a general trend to outsource or generate intranet-based systems for many of these traditional, more administrative and support functions in any case. One approach put forward by Brewster and Larson is towards a professional and business partner approach. However, we would support a somewhat different emphasis. The professional and business partner approach is certainly the bedrock, the demonstration of commercial know-how and real value-add expertise. But many of the suggestions made within the capabilities approach that we have outlined requires substantial expertise in the management of change. So for example, the change agent model suggested by Ulrich in his HR management style and activity model (1996), built on professional and business knowledge, is likely to prove an effective approach. The journey from traditional HR and equality practices to new ones can be greatly assisted by effective HR, but will be even better assisted if HR activities also develop into configurations and bundles of practice that enhance the impact of its support.

Within the critical management accounting tradition, three questions applied to the Coca-Cola case presented in Chapter 1 would be informative:

- What were they measuring?
- What standards were they using to set the measures?
- How useful was it for informing action?

A more holistic internal business perspective linked to some of the principles of innovation and internal service quality would provide an additional mechanism to link managerial agency and HR as change agent. HR could facilitate, enable and support managers as leaders, by crafting systems for providing painful feedback to facilitate double and triple loop managerial learning.

Strategic/long term

Business partner HR works closely alongside senior business managers (as a partner) to deliver that which is needed to achieve business strategy/does that which is necessary.	**Change agent** HR acts as a catalyst, a challenger at the overall organisational level. Is instrumental in changing what the organisation does and the way it does it.
Professional HR concentrates on the effective delivery to the organisation of a range of products and services that are professionally delivered, are examples of 'best practice' and are bench marked against others.	**Responsible employer** HR concentrates on the responsible employer aspects of HR, mainly those associated with individual employees, rather than the workforce as a whole, e.g. morale, welfare, employee commitment, counselling, etc.

Process (left side) — *People* (right side)

Operational/day to day

Figure 3   Facilitating employee voice: Ulrich's management style and activity model (1996)

Enabling the management and measurement of social capital

One critical area that will be needed to bolster *recursive empowerment* in operational and management teams involves the enhancement of social capital. We have mentioned this briefly in Chapter 3, but revisit it again from the perspective of measurement. Sen (2000a) has suggested that equality can be considered as *an additional feature of goodness in a society*. However, he argues that great conceptual clarity is required. What matters first to the individual is often intrinsic. Unfortunately, what can and should be measured in relation to capabilities is inherently ambiguous. Citing the work of Aristotle, Sen argues that for every science, the extent of the decision to measure with precision will vary. Trying to fine-tune measurement in an unthinking manner within the context of equality and diversity will result in a bad method if what gets measured is what can be measured, rather than what needs to be measured.

Thus, in addition to the issue of the inherent difficulties of the 'single measure' highlighted in Chapter 3, there needs to be an incorporation of the tolerance of ambiguity, and of the likelihood that some of what makes equality, inclusion and belongingness 'feel real' will be difficult, if not impossible, to 'measure' in the accepted sense. Hence the proposition that what is required is richer information, knowledge and a new base for learning. Capabilities equality represents such a foundation.

One important source of 'measurement' that might help with ambiguous evaluations is *values and constructions of what is shared*. The interpersonal understandings at the heart of sharedness provide a useful platform for authentic conversations, and the opportunity for day-to-day, rather than episodic, consideration and reflections. Indeed, the manager as reflective practitioner is also likely to heighten sense making by embracing more ambiguous, often informal, sometimes intangible, sources of information.

Facilitating employee voice

Individual and collective voice is central to capabilities equality. Some of the traditional mechanisms for facilitating employee voice, in particular trades union involvement, have always had the potential to address the equality agenda. As with other key stakeholder groups, capabilities equality will require a review of what approaches are most likely to be truly representative of the aspirations of a diversity of voice within union membership.

For trade unions, some of the actions that will need to be taken to enable them to take a stronger role in building workplace equality will need to begin 'at home', and are likely to mirror any organisation's attempt to reduce inequality in structure, strategy, policy and practice within itself. In addition to this, attention will also need to be paid to seeking new, more proactive mechanisms and channels for capturing employee voice, and with greater authenticity. In the non-unionised company, it is equally important to generate collective mechanisms for capturing authentic employee voice. Independent facilitation of focus groups, not only as an arena for dialogue, but also as the basis for generating employee-generated items for question-naires, may be helpful. In addition, clear channels to the top of the organisa-tion for those from the bottom up, which unions are able to achieve, also need to be incorporated. Partnership deals could provide an important mechanism for facilitating voice. Whatever the mechanisms involved, constructive and direct responses to issues raised as part of such processes of dialogue are cru-cial for the sustainability, viability and credibility of these mechanisms for ensuring that a diversity of voices can be heard, and that trust relationships can be nurtured.

Further, our discussion of Sen's most recent work on plural identity and transcendence (2000b), which was introduced in Chapter 6, is, in our view, one of the most significant areas where understanding workplace equality can be further elaborated. In the aftermath of the 11 September 2001 atrocities in New York and Washington, his concerns about some of the limitations of our current models of multiculturalism, and the need to elaborate transcendence as a vehicle for richer understandings and freedom of expression of plural identity, given in particular, the potential tyranny to the traditionally disad-vantaged of the single identity as defined by community leaders acting as gatekeepers to it, are particularly resonant, especially where the espoused core values are widely different (for example, liberal democratic traditions versus theocratic traditions). Equally, the opportunities for those from minority groups to be seen 'in the round', and having the right to celebrate their minority identity, but also to be seen in the fullness of plurality of iden-tity, many of which are in any case shared with the indigenous majority, are equally important. Both perspectives are necessary to meet the new emerging situations and challenges that multi cultural societies are now facing.

The challenge of inclusion

Finally, perhaps the greatest challenge to work organisations with regards to workplace equality is to find ways of defining and putting into practice inclu-sion. What we are referring to is the achievement of *full citizenship, membership and entitlements*, in terms of formal and informal groups, structures and processes, by those who have been traditionally disadvantaged in the labour market in particular. We suggest that inclusion will stand a greater chance of being achieved with a capabilities viewpoint, as the central requirement of being able to be or do what one has reason to value, also *demands* representa-tion, voice and freedoms. So, in one way, the capabilities equality position implicitly requires a focus on inclusion. In practice, this means that an impor-tant process is the continuous assessment of whether there is a dominant rhetoric of equal citizenship but a reality of differential citizenship.

Conclusions

To conclude, these thoughts are clearly, preliminary ideas. The capabilities equality approach is, at this stage, largely propositional. It forms the basis of an evolving and dynamic agenda for inquiry into ways of embedding dignity and respect as a core value in work organisations. What we hope has become clear is that the capabilities equality approach constitutes a real agenda that is founded upon both ethical priorities and sound business imperatives. The importance of 'the journey', an important metaphor in Chapter 7, is one that we would like to echo here. Vision and will are clearly important, but the journey towards building workplace equality should not be about 'arriving': understanding and building equality is ever-evolving and ever-changing, and development along the way, tolerance of error, risk-taking and learning, need to be an integral part of the journey.

Further reading

Sen, A (2000) Reason in East and West. *The New York Review of Books*, **XLVII** (12), 33–38.

Enderle, G (1999) *International business ethics: challenges and approaches*, University of Notre Dame Press, USA. Contains a diverse collection of contributions, including comparative religious perspectives on ethics in business; business ethics in an Islamic context, theocracy and emergent business ethics in east Asia and Japan, Africa and Latin America.

References

Brewster, C and Larson, H (1992) Human Resource Management in Europe: Evidence from ten countries. *The International Journal of Human Resource Management*, **3** (3), December, 409–434.

Giddens, A (1990) *The Consequences of Modernity*, Polity Press, London.

Marchington, M (1998) Partnerships in context: towards a European model, in P Sparrow and M Marchington (eds) *Human resource management: the new agenda*, Financial Times/Pitman, St Ives.

Marchington, M (2000) Involvement and participation, in J Storey (ed.) *Human Resource Management: a critical text*, International Thomson Publishing, Padstow.

Nussbaum, M (1999) Women and equality: The capabilities approach. *International Labour Review*, **138** (3), 227–245.

Sen, A (2000a) Consequential evaluation and practical reason. *Journal of Philosophy*, **XCVI** (9), 477–502.

Sen, A (2000b) *Beyond Identity*, British Academy, London.

Ulrich, D (1996) *Human Resource Champions*, Harvard Business School Press, Boston.

Glossary

Access-and-legitimacy paradigm

A level of diversity interventions that is usually driven by the business case, but is limited by focusing on initiatives to improve access for marginalised groups and individuals. It generally means that the initiatives can ultimately provide access to niche markets.

Agency, collective and individual

Agency is the freedom of opportunity of individuals or groups to have a say (see also 'voice') in defining and addressing the inequalities that they do or may face, and moreover, this influence is both a right and an expectation within a society. Greater freedom enhances the ability of people to help themselves and also to influence matters that are central to the process of development. Agency not only addresses inequality, but also the economic, structural and societal roots of social exclusion.

Assessment centres

Assessment centres are a way of providing a more 'complete' picture of the applicant through the use of a range of evaluation techniques. Typical assessment centre activities include psychometric testing, observation of group-based activities and interviewing applicants.

Behavioural questions

These are questions which seek evidence of past behaviour as a predictor of future performance, in particular the presence or absence of a skill or competence. An example of behavioural questions is as follows: 'Describe a time in any job you have held when you were faced with problems or pressures which tested your ability to cope. What did you do?'

Bounded commitment

An implicit understanding that the nature of the work and the employment contract is such that there is a limit to what the employer can expect of employees.

Business case

Within the context of workplace equality, traditionally, the business case refers to the operational, strategic or commercial argument for valuing difference, in particular regarding those from traditionally disadvantaged groups, in terms of widening recruitment to include these groups in the labour market as part of the 'war for talent', plus the expertise and knowledge that these groups have, in particular about their host groups, that can add to the know-how of an organisation. Increasingly, the business case also includes the view that social responsibility and broadening of its **social capital** are an integral part of corporate responsibility and sustainability, and these are also being integrated into the business case.

Bullying

Informal or formal physical, psychological or social aggression or intimidation against an individual or group, that persists in spite of requests by the bullied for it to stop.

Capabilities

Capabilities can be regarded at the most basic level as the gifts and talents that individuals possess in concert with factors such as education, training, legislation, policies and practices that allow these gifts and talents to be exercised. It is the *ensemble* of an enabling environment and individual and collective agency that allows the gifts and talents to flourish and therefore, individuals and groups to have the potential to function fully within a society.

Capabilities approach

The capabilities approach focuses on 'individuals' freedoms to achieve what they have reason to value'. Drawing from Sen's book, *Inequality Re-Examined* (1992), the basic question to ask when evaluating social arrangements using this approach is: what is the person's capability to achieve 'functionings' that he or she has reason to value? Does he or she have the freedom to do so? The focus on functionings differs from more traditional approaches to equality, involving concentration on such variables as income, wealth or happiness, and is closely related to the fact of human diversity. Methods centre on facilitation of 'internal readiness' combined with creating a political and social climate to enable full use of capabilities.

Capabilities equality

Capabilities equality is concerned with the things a person is substantially free to do, the real choices that he or she has. In the broadest sense, capabilities equality is a primary feature of individual well-being (physical, economic, social and self-actualising). Capability equality concerns the mechanisms that enable a person to 'function', and to achieve what a person can and wishes to do or be.

Conscious incompetence

A recognition that a person knows the limitation of their own knowledge

Continuous improvement

The journey of review and improvement as an habitual way to make sustainable progress.

Cost-reduction mass production

A method of organising work that relies on the learning curve and seeks to maximise output and minimise costs through the standardisation of processes and work methods.

Cross-culturalism

This refers to the interaction between those from different cultures, often amongst those who are working away from their place of birth and normal residence, with others who are also working abroad. In an organisational context, cross-culturalism is concerned with the interaction between people of different nationalities in the workplace.

Culture

Culture may be thought of broadly as the pattern of beliefs, values and assumptions that are held within a group, organisation or society. National culture is the culture of a society that comprises the shared values, understandings, assumptions, and goals that are learned from earlier generations, imposed by present members of a society, and are passed on to succeeding generations. This shared outlook results in common attitudes, codes of conduct, and expectations that subconsciously guide and control certain norms of behaviour. Organisational culture is the beliefs, values and basic assumptions that operate across the organisation, or that may have a distinctive flavour within sub-cultures within it. It is shaped by the founders and leadership, the nature of core operational activities, and the environmental issues that it has to address.

Cultural capital

The term was promoted by Bordieu and refers to the social and economic benefits that accrue to those who successfully impose their values on other groups and legitimate its culture. It is associated with high status and influential groups, and is shared and transmitted formally and informally through restricted social, educational and occupational elite channels. The acquisition of the dominant culture of skills and knowledge is transmitted to students who reproduce the values of the dominant culture. Bordieu's work highlights the maintenance of status and power through the use of cultural capital.

Disciplinary procedures

Formal disciplinary procedures centre on managerial discipline, and is the last resort when informal self and team discipline approaches have failed. Such action should be based on hard evidence, and seek to challenge poor performance and/or behaviour with a view to rectifying the matter. In the case of gross misconduct, instant dismissal usually follows.

Distributive justice

A theory of justice that posits that individuals will be deeply concerned if there are vast discrepancies in equality and income, or if they are confronted with circumstances in which they have no means of knowing what position they will occupy in a given social context. This can be understood as 'outcome fairness', and refers to the judgement that people make with respect to the outcomes received relative to the outcomes received by other people with whom they identify (referent others); a concept within organisational justice that emphasises equality of outcomes, or fairness in distribution of wealth or rewards.

Diversity

Diversity is concerned with understanding that there are differences among employees and that these differences, if properly managed, contribute to the achievement of organisational objectives and the quality of organisational life. Diversity factors include race, culture, ethnicity, gender, age, disability and work experience.

Diversity advantage

The diversity advantage is achieved by openly acknowledging, understanding and valuing differences and recognising that they provide a dimension which contributes to achievement of organisational objectives.

Duty of care

Professional workers in particular are tasked to exercise duty of care, that is, to secure the best service from those within their care in a manner that ensures their physical, psychological and social safety and well-being.

Emotional labour

Emotional labour is a term developed by the academic Arlie Hochschild, to define the kind of work for which changing the mood of others for pay is central to the primary task. Emotional labourers are those workers who undertake emotional labour, and include flight attendants, nurses, police officers, debt collectors, and so on.

Employment relations (*sometimes referred to as industrial relations*)

This is concerned with the employer–employee relationship. Traditionally, industrial relations (a termed used most commonly in the ascendancy of personnel management) is concerned with the balance of power within this relationship and how institutions such as trades unions, the law or government affect this balance. More recently, and within the context of HRM, there has been a shift towards the use of the term employee relations which has signalled a shift in emphasis towards participation and commitment strategies, which may or may not incorporate the role of the formal employee representative.

Equal opportunities

In its traditional form, equal opportunities is rights-based, liberal, rooted in legal compliance, based upon equality through 'sameness' and merit with a focus on non-discrimination, geared towards increasing the proportion of women and other under-represented groups in senior roles in organisations.

Exclusion

Exclusion in general terms refers to those who are on the margins of a society, who are often deprived economically, socially and educationally. The 'excluded' often feel that they have a limited, if any, stake in its goals and aspirations, and that opportunities for membership and participation are hard to come by and unlikely; indeed, it may be seen as undesirable. Within a work organisation context, exclusion comes about less through socio-economic deprivation (though it might) and more through barriers to entry that are largely created by organisations, though originating from what is seen as an 'inferior' or 'lower' socio-economic class may play a role. For minorities, exclusion is made up of tangible factors (lesser freedom and equality of opportunity) but also intangible factors (such as invalidation of non-indigenous cultures, exclusion from informal social processes and stereotyping).

Family-friendly policies

These are policies that create flexible working possibilities that enable employees to balance the needs of home and work. They include policies regarding childcare provision, flexible hours and provisions for care of dependants.

'Felt fairness'

'Felt fairness' refers to the perception of employee fairness, in particular by those at whom equality management is primarily targeted. Applying capabilities thinking, equality would clearly require that both procedural and distributive justice be present for 'felt fairness' to be present. A high degree of *distributive equality* would need 'equal outcomes' of organizational equality. The *procedures* used to determine outcomes would need to be viewed as fair. Demonstrable formal and informal access to the ends and means of equality, its outcomes *and* opportunities, plus agency *and* an enabling work environment, are essential to felt-fair equality.

Flexible working practices

Flexible working practices are working practices which are not covered by standard full-time work contracts, e.g. part-time working, job sharing and temporary and contract work.

Freedoms and instrumental freedoms

Freedoms of individuals are the basic building blocks of development. Therefore the expansion of freedoms of persons 'to lead the kind of lives they value, and have reason to value', is key. In capabilities theory, *justice* is seen in terms of individual freedoms and its social correlates: the social policies, processes and mechanisms that allow individuals to lead the lives they would choose to lead, and that allow them the opportunity to influence and shape the decisions and choices that in turn shape their lives. Thus, freedoms provide an alternative and fuller foundation for individual and social justice.

Specifically, Sen sets out five *instrumental freedoms* to explain what an enabling environment for development must contain. These freedoms should be subject to systematic evaluation within any particular social context, and the effectiveness of any intervention should be assessed against the freedoms that it affords. Universal in nature and sensitive to cross-cultural concerns, Sen's five instrumental freedoms have great resonance and potential application for work organisations. The fragmentation of these or concentration on one over the other undermines their meaningfulness. They are:

- political freedoms;
- economic facilities;
- social opportunities;
- transparency guarantees ;
- protective security.

Grievance

Within HRM, a grievance is a formal complaint, usually by an employee about his/her line manager or a colleague, where the employee believes that he or she has been in some way unfairly or unreasonably treated.

Globalisation

There are numerous definitions of the term globalisation. In a business and commercial context, it is concerned with the process of integration across national boundaries of the key processes for the production of goods or the delivery of services, facilitated in the main through the use of a range of technologies, with information technology being particularly important.

Harassment

Unwanted behaviour, which a person finds intimidating, upsetting, embarrassing, humiliating or offensive.

Human capital

This idea was developed in particular by Theodore Schultz (1961). Human capital is the value added to employees through the acquisition of knowledge, skills and other kinds of know-how: the *added value is embedded in employees themselves*, and adds to the value of their labour.

Human resource management (HRM)

Human resource management is an approach to employment management that is corporate strategy driven. The emphasis within HRM is the deployment of people or the 'human resource' to enable companies to achieve their strategic objectives. The mobilisation of long-range human resource decided on is determined by external conditions (e.g. the law and labour market dynamics) and internal organisational responses to it (such as pay strategies, training and development, performance management, and so on).

High commitment flexible production

A method of organising work that relies on high levels of skill and initiative within the workforce and on minimal supervision and high levels of trust and confidence on the part of managers. Empowered employees thus seek continuous improvement and deliver high levels of performance.

Human adaptation

The effort of any person to respond and be flexible to change.

Ideastorm

A word to replace brainstorm; a process for generating random ideas in quantity from a group of individuals.

Identity

Identity is concerned with the way in which we see ourselves, which has been formed by a range of social and cultural experiences. It is closely associated with the notion of self, and core construing and sense making. Plural identity is a way of thinking about identity that highlights the many identities that individuals hold, and that they may choose to exercise in different contexts. The different identities held within an individual's array of plural identity may be placed into conflict in certain circumstances.

Inclusion

In the context of workplace equality, this refers to the achievement of full membership, citizenship and entitlements of an organisation, in terms of its formal and informal groups, structures and processes, by those who have been traditionally disadvantaged in the labour market. Inclusion is primarily felt, not asserted as a fact, and it is as much psychological and social in nature as more tangible, in terms of freedom of opportunity to participate and to advance throughout the organisational hierarchy.

Information base

Within the context of workplace equality, it is the formal and informal sources of information that help to illustrate inequalities or improve equality within an organisation.

Institutional discrimination

Institutional discrimination is where formal and informal organisational and social structures result in different and inequitable treatment by an organisation by members from the majority and usually, indigenous population, or those members from minority and traditionally disadvantaged groups, as employees or as those who receive its services. If not sought proactively and systematically, such discrimination may not easily be discerned by those members of the organisation affected by it or indeed, creating it.

Interactional justice

This is a concept used to describe how individuals interpret and experience fairness in the way that they are treated. Research suggests that in settling disputes and grievances, people are sensitive to both structural and social factors. Structural determinants relate to the environmental context in which interactions occur and the extent to which reward allocations are delivered through mechanisms of procedural justice. Social determinants focus on the quality of interpersonal treatment that people experience when dealing with those in authority.

Learning and effectiveness paradigm

The *strategic* or **learning and effectiveness paradigm** focuses on diversity as part of the organisation's journey of learning and continuous improvement. It is usually driven by the recognition that leveraging internal and external diversity is an essential competence for a healthy organisation that pursues excellence as part of its overall culture.

Learning processes

The individual, social and organisational processes that facilitate learning, at all of these levels.

Liberal equal opportunities

Liberal equal opportunities is concerned with achieving a 'metaphorical level playing-field' for all, and individuals rights to universally applicable standards of justice and citizenship. This model of **equal opportunities** thus depends on an idea of equality as 'sameness': individuals should have access to and be assessed within the workplace as individuals, regardless of social group. The approach thus requires people to deny or minimise differences arising from social group membership and compete on the ground of individual merit.

Line-management delivery of human resource management

This refers to the delivery of human resource management as facilitated primarily by line managers rather than HRM specialists.

Managing diversity

Diversity management as an approach to workplace equality draws its distinctiveness largely from its focus on equality through 'difference' rather than 'sameness'. As it is most frequently theorised, it is distinct from equal opportunities although in theory and in practice both are intended to pursue and promote equality in the workplace. Diversity management depends upon organisational commitment, and it most frequently refers to a set of initiatives or interventions that are internally driven and proactive. It focuses on valuing difference ('equality through difference'), non-dominant or under-represented social groups, and respecting diversity at an individual level.

Managing intangibles

The focus of management on things that are not measurable in quantity but through assessment of quality.

Mentoring

A person who is not a line manager who helps other individuals to address the major transitions or thresholds that the individual is facing and to deal with them in a developmental way.

Monitoring

Monitoring equality involves collecting and analysing statistical data in terms of the percentage of employees from the majority population and those from minority or traditionally disadvantaged populations. It can be used, for example, to establish the representation of these groups and majority groups at different levels within an organisation. Within recruitment and selection, it is used to monitor the percentage of those from specific groups who apply and are selected for specific positions. Monitoring is primarily a density measure, derived from labour economics traditions.

Multiculturalism

The concept of **multiculturalism** is concerned with bringing together, within the wider society, a variety of cultures and their attributes, in addition to the indigenous one, that are embedded within non-indigenous communities. This becomes a significant issue for organisations when aiming to reflect the increasing multiculturalism in society, within itself, and has a particular relevance for human resource management policy and practice within those organisations.

Organisational climate

The climate of an organisation can be thought of as its motivational status. HR policy and strategy can help to create a more constructive and positive motivational climate, for example through reward strategies and management–staff relations.

Organisational habits

Customs, practices and procedures that guide organisational choices in any transactions.

Organisational learning

Organisational learning is concerned with the process of improving learning through better knowledge and understanding, as well as the process of detecting and correcting error (Argyris and Schon, 1978; Argyris, 1994). The underlying assumptions and values of the learning need not be questioned, but will need to be in order to question and change the criteria, procedures and values underpinning what is learned.

Organisational justice

A generic term that embraces distributive, procedural and interactional justice and addresses issues associated with the fair treatment of individuals and groups in an organisational context.

Output orientation

A managerial preoccupation with attaining stretch targets in contexts where processes are complex and employee skills are such that high levels of direct supervision are not required.

Performance management

Performance management may be viewed as a means of getting improved results from the whole organisation, by focusing at different levels (from the whole organization through to the work group and its members) through coordinated, holistic activities. It is a broad, systematic approach to the achievement of organisational objectives by providing an interconnected set of goals which are linked at the organisational, departmental, work team and individual levels.

Personnel management

Personnel management is a term that is sometimes used interchangeably with HRM. Traditionally, PM is concerned with the management of the administrative aspects of employment management. It is a more reactive, non-strategic approach to the formal process of managing people, and has a more day-to-day, short-term operational orientation.

Professionals

This is a category of knowledge worker who uses rare expert knowledge and skill, acquired through narrow and often state-regulated channels, whose work is often regarded as being done for the good of society, and may be empowered by the state to be the monopolistic supplier of specific services.

Professionalism

Professionalism refers broadly to the manner in which work is undertaken that has the characteristics of professional work. Codes of conduct and professional institutions reinforce these codes and the kinds of behaviours, attitudes and beliefs that are associated with professionalism.

Professional project

The **professional project** is pursued through the *means* of establishing both (a) a favourable economic order and (b) a favourable social order. The latter is achieved through monopoly of knowledge, establishing strong trust relations with an array of stakeholders, the development of a strong culture, within which lies professional political culture developed within the national context of political power networks. The desired *outcome* is social closure, where legitimate membership and ineligibility is made clear and supported ideally with the weight of the state and its legislature.

Power distance

A cultural dimension that measures the degree to which those who lack status and position power believe that their voice will be heard. High power distance implies a sense of powerlessness and distance from those who make decisions.

Procedural justice

In an organisational context, procedural justice is concerned with the processes through which grievances and disputes between individuals and groups are resolved. Whilst distributive justice is concerned with just and equitable outcomes, procedural justice is concerned with the machinery and processes through which justice is delivered. Just and fair procedures, besides being efficient, allow responsibility to be fixed on a particular officer or body at each stage of the administrative process. As such, it protects the rights of employees and protects management from criticism of having acted in an arbitrary manner. This is achieved by ensuring regularity and consistency in the treatment of individual cases.

Process orientation

A managerial preoccupation with monitoring and measuring process efficiency and productivity, normally involving high levels of supervision and control.

Psychological contract

A concept used in social and industrial psychology to describe the written and unwritten rules and implicit understandings that govern the conduct and behaviour of each of the parties to an employment relationship and their expectations of the other party.

Process knowledge

Detailed and in-depth knowledge of complex processes, procedures and practices that provide organisations with distinctive capabilities.

Radical equal opportunities

A 'radical' equal opportunities approach focuses on positive action to meet the goals of equal opportunities. This includes a focus on attempting to equalise outcomes, for example through hiring and promotion quotas.

Reliability

Reliability is the extent to which a psychometric test can be used repeatedly yet give the same or similar results. For example, if a group of managers was tested for numerical reasoning, their test scores should be similar if they were re-tested.

Reward package

The reward package includes all elements of pay, e.g. bonus, performance-related pay, shift payments and employee benefits such as holidays, sick pay, medical insurance and discounts.

Selection criteria

Criteria are standards against which judgements are made. In recruitment and selection, criteria are used to assess whether applicants are likely to be suitable for the positions available. The criteria can be developed from information gathered from a variety of sources, including job/role analysis.

Sameness

Sameness is, in practice, the aggregate of individual differences for the development of common understandings.

Sharedness

Sharedness involves making explicit the constructs of sharing and belonging that are ordinarily held through the development of interpersonal understandings.

Situated knowledge

Situated knowledge is concerned with the ways in which people's formal and informal understanding of their activities change as a consequence of the developing complexity of the contexts within which they are working.

Situated learning

Situated learning can be thought of as formal and informal learning through fundamentally a collective endeavour, in which tacit and explicit knowledge go through a process of being redefined and renegotiated within the organising process through the interplay between action and reflexivity, within the specific context of actors and social and organisational structures.

Social capital

The system of values and customs used in a transaction that are products of a culture mostly unwritten but understood and accepted as worthwhile in guiding the achievement of a desired result. Broadly, it relates to social networks, the reciprocities that arise from them, and the value of these for achieving mutual goals. The academic Lin argues that the premise behind social capital is that of investment in social relations with expected returns in the 'marketplace', where the market may be economic, political, labour or community.

Stakeholders

Those who are directly affected by, and hold an active interest in, the choices and changes in any process.

Strategic human resource management (SHRM)

Strategic HRM (SHRM) is concerned with the deployment of 'people systems' for the strategic ends of an organisation. HRM is essentially an approach grounded in strategic thinking. SHRM defines the nature of the strategy as fully integrated into an organisation's strategic decision-making processes.

Trust

Trust can be thought of as the manner in which relationships are enacted, and the degree and source of confidence exercised between individuals and/or groups.

Trust relations

Trust relations refer to particular kinds of relationships between organisational members. Specifically, trust can be thought of as the manner in which relationships are enacted, and the degree and source of confidence exercised between individuals and/or groups.

Validity

Validity is the extent to which a psychometric test measures what it is designed to measure. It is established by statistical analysis and is usually undertaken by a trained occupational psychologist.

Voice

Individual and collective voice refers to the opportunity for individuals and groups to express views in an authentic manner that accurately reflects hopes, fears, concerns and aspirations. This may take the form of freedom of individual and collective expression and association, and the 'right' to dialogue and critique in relation to formal and informal aspects of work organisation that affects all its members. The voices of the traditionally disadvantaged are traditionally less likely to be routinely heard or sought.

Win–win solution

Creative solution that achieves a result that is valuable to all parties.

Work sample

A work sample is a test in which one or more practical tasks that are part of the job itself are performed. For example, giving a presentation where the job involves giving presentations.

Author index

Subject index

Lightning Source UK Ltd.
Milton Keynes UK
UKOW020902181112

202302UK00003B/34/P